THE MIRROR OF HERODOTUS

The New Historicism: Studies in Cultural Poetics
Stephen Greenblatt, General Editor

THE MIRROR
OF HERODOTUS

*The Representation of the Other
in the Writing of History*

FRANÇOIS HARTOG

TRANSLATED BY JANET LLOYD

UNIVERSITY OF CALIFORNIA PRESS
BERKELEY   LOS ANGELES   LONDON

University of California Press
Berkeley and Los Angeles, California

University of California Press, Ltd.
London, England
© 1988 by
The Regents of the University of California

Library of Congress Cataloging-in-Publication Data

Hartog, François.
  The mirror of Herodotus.
  Translation of: Le miroir d'Hérodote.
  Includes index.
  1. Herodotus.   Historiea.   2. History, Ancient.
I. Title.
D58.H473H47   1988   930   86-30913
- ISBN 0-520-05487-3 (alk. paper)

Printed in the United States of America
1   2   3   4   5   6   7   8   9

This book is published with the support of a translation grant
from the French Ministry of Culture.

Originally published in French as *Le Miroir d'Hérodote: Essai
sur la représentation de l'autre*, Bibliothèque des Histoires,
NRF. Paris: Editions Gallimard, 1980.

For Dominique

Contents

List of Maps and Plates

Maps

Plates
(following page xxii)

xi

Translations of Texts

Taken or adapted from the Loeb Classical Library, W. Heinemann, Ltd., London, and Harvard University Press, Cambridge, Mass.

Aristotle, *Metaphysics*, trans. H. Tredennick, 1968; *Politics*, trans H. Rackham, 1972.

Arrian, *India*, trans. E. Iliff Robson, 1966.

Clement of Alexandria, *Exhortation to the Greeks*, trans. G. W. Butterworth, 1960.

Diodorus Siculus, trans. C. H. Oldfather, 1967.

Diogenes Laertius, trans. R. D. Hicks, 1980.

Herodotus, *Histories*, trans. A. D. Godley, 1966.

Hesiod, *Works and Days*, trans. H. G. Evelyn-White, 1970.

Hippocrates, *Airs, Waters, Places*, trans. W. H. S. Jones, 1948.

Lucian, trans. A. M. Harmon, 1962.

Pausanias, trans. W. H. S. Jones, 1965.

Pindar, trans. J. Sandys, 1968.

Plato, *Laches*, trans. W. R. M. Lamb, 1967; *Laws*, trans. R. G. Bury, 1967; *Protagoras*, trans. W. R. M. Lamb, 1967; *Republic*, trans. P. Shorey, 1946.

Plutarch, *Lives*, trans. B. Perrin, 1967; *Moralia*, trans. L. Pearson and F. H. Sandbach, 1965.

Strabo, *Geography*, trans. H. L. Jones, 1967.

Thucydides, trans. C. Forster Smith, 1969.

Xenophon, *Anabasis*, trans. Carleton L. Brownson, 1968; *Hellenica*, trans. E. C. Marchant, 1968; *Republic of the Lacedaemonians*, trans. E. C. Marchant, 1968.

Taken or adapted from University of Chicago Press, Chicago and London

Aeschylus, *Prometheus Bound*, trans. David Grene, 1956; *Seven against Thebes*, trans. David Grene, 1958; *The Suppliant Maidens*, trans. S. G. Benardete, 1956.

Euripides, *Andromache*, trans. J. C. Nims, 1958; *Bacchae*, trans. W. Arrowsmith, 1959; *Electra*, trans. E. T. Vermeule, 1959; *The Suppliant Women*, trans. F. W. Jones, 1958; *The Trojan Women*, trans. R. Lattimore, 1958.

Sophocles, *Oedipus the King* and *Oedipus at Colonus*, trans. David Grene, 1954.

Taken or adapted from Penguin Classics, Harmondsworth

Homer, *The Iliad*, trans. E. V. Rieu, 1950; *The Odyssey*, 1948, trans. E. V. Rieu.

Preface: The Name of Herodotus

*"It is a strange truth that Herodotus
has really become the father of history only in modern times."*

—A. Momigliano

The long procession of Herodotus's interpreters spans twenty-five
centuries, from his own day to modern times.[1] It includes translators, commentators, critics[2]—all those who at some point had
dealings with him and who, like others before them, insisted on
taking the witness stand in the interminable trial[3] that posterity
continues to hold on the Herodotus case. It is a judiciary process that
can never be concluded so long as Herodotus remains a distant figure

1. I should like to thank all those who in the course of this work have been so kind
as to lend me their eyes and ears: in particular, Michel de Certeau, Marcel
Detienne, Jean-Louis Durand, Pierre Lévêque, Eric Michaud, Jacques Revel, Jean-
Pierre Vernant, and Pierre Vidal-Naquet. I should also like to express my warmest
thanks to Janet Lloyd, who took on the heavy but also delicate task of translating
these pages into English.

2. The most up-to-date work on Herodotean studies is that of L. Bergson,
"Herodot 1937–1960," *Lustrum* 11 (1966): 71–138 (in which references for earlier
bibliographies may be found). See also G. T. Griffith, "The Greek Historians," *Fifty
Years (and Twelve) of Classical Scholarship* (Oxford, 1968), pp. 182–241. Apart from
the partial bibliographies in the books and articles that have appeared more recently
on Herodotus, see H. Verdin, "Hérodote historien? Quelques Interprétations
récentes," *L'Antiquité Classique* (1975): 668–85. Among recent publications, see
A. Corcella, *Erodoto e l'analogia* (Palermo, 1984); A. Momigliano, "La storia tra
medicina e retorica," *Tra storia e storicismo* (Pisa, 1985), pp. 11–24; and J. Redfield,
"Herodotus the Tourist," *Classical Philology* 80 (1985): 97–118.

3. *Translator's note: Procès* is the French word used. It means both "trial," as in
a court of law, and also "process." The use of "judiciary process" in the English
translation is an attempt to convey the word-play.

on the borderline of history, a trial in which no definitive judgment, indeed no judgment worthy of the name, is ever reached—since the latest judgment is forever recycled as evidence on which to base the next. Yet this endless trial is what ensures Herodotus's immortalization; it is the mark of his immortality. For Herodotus fascinates: he is the father who must ever be evoked or invoked, the phantom who must be exorcized, the ghost who must be banished.

For centuries, this trial aimed at convicting Herodotus by revealing all his lies. Then it took a new turn: the objective was now, for many years, to rediscover the real Herodotus, beyond all the interpretations, as if these could be bypassed or bracketed. To this end, all the resources of etymology, philology, and knowledge of the canon were tapped. Today, the meaning of that word *process* has itself changed; now it refers to no more than the trend in interpretation, the assumption being that the successive interpretations of his work are no less a part of the Herodotean oeuvre than the text of the *Histories* itself, for "the work gives us more and more to think about within the space opened up by the thought of others."[4] It is therefore impossible to write about the *Histories* of Herodotus without considering the history of how they have been interpreted. But a history of that kind leads to a history of at least the whole of ancient history—of history in general, if it is true that the name Herodotus designates the father of history.[5]

What little we know about Herodotus comes not from his own words but indirectly, from a few late sources of information whose fictitious nature a number of scholars have been at pains to demonstrate.[6] He is "Herodotus of Halicarnassus," the manuscripts claim, but "Herodotus of Thurii," according to the indirect tradition. Though he was a native of Halicarnassus, where he was born in about 480 B.C. it could also be claimed the he was from Thurii, in southern

---

4. C. Lefort, *Le Travail de l'oeuvre: Machiavel* (Paris, 1972), p. 24.

5. One way of sidestepping the problem is to split hairs over the matter of Herodotus's paternity. Thus, H.-I. Marrou: "Herodotus appears to us less as 'the father of history' than as an ancestor to some degree in his second childhood, and the veneration that we profess for his example is to some extent accompanied by a rather indulgent smile" (*De la connaissance historique* [Paris, 1975], p. 27).

6. For example, A. Bauer, *Herodotos Biographie* (Vienna, 1878). On his biography, see P.-E. Legrand, *Hérodote* (Paris, 1955), pp. 5–37.

Italy, for he became a citizen there.[7] For a while he lived in exile, in Samos. He traveled in the Middle East, particularly in Egypt; in the north, in the Black Sea region; in the west, in southern Italy; and also in mainland Greece.[8] For a while he lived in Athens, then moved to Thurii. He died, according to one tradition, around 420 B.C. in Thurii, where his tomb is said to be in the agora; according to another, he is buried in Athens, or perhaps in Pella, in Macedonia.[9] His life thus spanned the period between two major conflicts: the Persian Wars, which were more or less before his time, and the Peloponnesian War, whose initial stages, at least, he did live to see.

"What Herodotus . . . has learnt by enquiry [*historie*] is here set forth: in order that the memory of the past may not be blotted out from among men by time, and that great and marvellous things [*erga*] done by the Greeks and Barbarians and especially the reason why they warred against each other may not cease to be recounted." That is the opening passage of the work that we know as the *Histories* but that in fact bore no title, as was customary in those days. Those few lines in particular attracted the attention of commentators, to whom it seemed that by establishing the exact meaning of each word, and first and foremost of the most famous one, *historie*, they would be able to seize the purpose of Herodotus's enterprise.[10]

The *Histories* are divided into nine books, each of which bears the name of one of the nine Muses. Herodotus himself was not responsible for this arrangement, nor did he claim this patronage. Both are attested by Lucian (second century A.D.) but certainly do not antedate the Hellenistic period. They thus indicate not only the status enjoyed by the work but also the public's attitude toward it at that time: it was classed on the side of the Muses, that is, as poetry, pleasure, fiction. Herodotus himself speaks only of his *logos* or *logoi*,

7. Thurii was a Panhellenic colony founded in 444–443 B.C.; cf. E. Will, *Le Monde grec et l'orient* (Paris, 1972), pp. 276–82.

8. Herodotus's travels have also been questioned: We are told that he laid claim to journeys that he never or only partially made. The chief authority on this subject is A. H. Sayce, *The Ancient Empires of the East: Herodotus I–III* (London, 1883), pp. xxv–xxx.

9. *Suda*, s.v. *Herodotus;* Markellinos, *Life of Thucydides*, 17, even specifically states that the tombs of Herodotus and Thucydides lie next to one another.

10. Indeed, a grammarian of the time of Nero even went so far as to maintain that the prologue was not composed by Herodotus at all but by his friend Plesirrhoos, a poet (Photius *Biblioteca* 148b).

his narratives. To prevent what men have done from being blotted out and ceasing to be recounted, a number of different *logoi* follow one another, overlapping or even intersecting around the central project. The first four books are chiefly taken up with narratives concerning other peoples, non-Greeks (Lydians, Persians, Babylonians, Massagetae, Egyptians, Scythians, Libyans . . .); the last five are, in the main, devoted to the Persian Wars themselves.

What was the effect of the *Histories;* how were they received? It is not possible to provide a precise answer, since we have no means of reconstituting the "horizon of expectation" within which they took their place,[11] nor can we trace the history of their impact through the ages. However, it seems that the *Histories* very quickly became known, in Athens at least, and that they gained lasting recognition and renown throughout antiquity.[12] But they also appear to have incurred equally prompt and repeated criticism and attack: Herodotus was sometimes called a thief and, even more often, a liar. Antiquity thus fabricated a two-headed Herodotus and turned the name Herodotus, known to everyone, into a double name which designated both the father of history and also a liar—if not, indeed, the father of all liars.[13]

As late as 1768, Voltaire described the *Histories* as follows: "When he recounted the nine books of his history to the Greeks, they were enchanted by the novelty of his undertaking, the charm of his diction and, above all, by the fables."[14] Euclid explains the novelty of the undertaking to young Anacharsis, as he points to the history shelves in his library: "He brought the annals of the known world to the attention of the Greeks, presenting from a uniform point of view everything memorable that had happened within the space of about two hundred and forty years."[15] The "charm of his diction" is a

11. On the idea of a horizon of expectation, see H. R. Jauss, *Pour une esthétique de la réception* (trans. Paris, 1978), pp. 49, 257–62.

12. K. Riemann, "Das Herodoteische Geschichtswerk in der Antike," diss. Munich, 1967.

13. See A. Momigliano, "The Place of Herodotus in the History of Historiography," *Studies in Historiography* (London, 1969), pp. 127–42, where he gives a remarkable account of the fortunes of the name of Herodotus.

14. Voltaire, *Le Pyrrhonisme en histoire* . . . (1768), in *Oeuvres complètes* (Paris, 1879), vol. 6, p. 246.

15. Abbé Barthélemy, *Voyage du jeune Anacharsis en Grèce* (Paris, 1788), vol. 3, p. 458.

reference to all that had been written about Herodotus, the master of the Ionian language, from the fourth century down to the Roman Empire. As for "fables," that means Herodotus, the *muthos*-teller, the spellbinding mythologist whom Thucydides was the first to decry but whom Voltaire deemed it necessary to denouce all over again since an author as "distinguished" as Rollin was taken in by him and was "beguiling us with all Herodotus's tales."[16]

Voltaire's remark simply pinpoints the three traditional views of the author of the *Histories:* he was the first historian; he was a great artist; and he was a liar. But how can those propositions be sorted out? First and foremost, how should we distinguish between what is true—that is to say, history—and what is lies—that is to say, fable? Voltaire proposes one solution in his chapter entitled "On the History of Herodotus": "Almost all that he recounted on the strength of what strangers told him is fable, but all that he saw for himself is true." He chose the eye in preference to the ear, autopsy at the expense of listening (*akoe*); that is to say, *genomena*, facts, as opposed to *legomena*, words. In arguing for that method of discovering the truth, Voltaire was in fact following the recommendations of Thucydides: autopsy at all costs; without autopsy there can be no history. But Thucydides at least accepted the consequences of his methodological position: he condemned all his predecessors who had believed it possible to write the history of the past, even the recent past; all those who had believed (or promoted the belief) that they were writing a true history of, for example, the Persian Wars—and he was the first to condemn Herodotus.

Voltaire, on the other hand, while certainly adopting the Thucydidean criterion of truth, appears to forget to abide by its implications. Herodotus did not witness the Persian Wars; his narrative relies on *legomena*;[17] he should, therefore, be approached with caution. Yet, having rejected the storytelling Herodotus, Voltaire on the contrary retains the autopsy-practicing Herodotus, who, through some sleight-of-hand, turns out to be Herodotus the historian of the Persian Wars, that is to say, the "model of historians." Indeed, he goes further. Not only is a history of the Persian Wars possible, but

16. Voltaire, *Le Pyrrhonisme*, p. 236, referring to C. Rollin, author of an *Historie ancienne* (1730–1738).

17. Even if these words did not come from foreigners.

this history of the Persian Wars represents the true beginning of all history: "It must be admitted that for us history only begins with the Persians' operations against the Greeks. Before those great events one finds only a few vague narratives, cloaked in childish stories. Herodotus becomes the model of historians when he describes the amazing preparations made by Xerxes before setting out to dominate first Greece, then Europe."[18] Herodotus is the historian of the Persian Wars, and the Persian Wars are the beginning of history; therefore, Herodotus is the "model of historians." But the Persian Wars are only the beginning of history because Herodotus recounted them. Whether one passes from Herodotus to the wars or from the wars to Herodotus, the truth is that, either way, there is no getting beyond Herodotus.[19]

Voltaire's remarks rest on a distinction drawn between the historian of the Persian Wars and Herodotus the storyteller and traveler. Herodotus is known by not one but two names, a distinction Voltaire may have helped to establish but did not invent, as the engraved frontispiece for the 1715 Leiden edition by J. Gronovius testifies (see Plate I). A glowing nimbus divides the engraving down the middle. This cloud, which bears up the nine Muses (representing the nine books) stretches from the heavens down to the bust of a bearded and empty-eyed Herodotus. In the foreground on the right, four of the Muses have unrolled a huge parchment purporting to be a visual transcription of Herodotus's narrative, the narrative, that is, of the Persian Wars. One of the Muses stands beside the bust, resting her elbow on it and pointing to the parchment as an indication to the spectator-reader that what is displayed to his view here is the reason

18. Voltaire, *Le Pyrrhonisme*, p. 247.

19. Thucydides certainly attempted to minimize the importance of the Persian Wars in comparison to the Peloponnesian War (1.23), but on this point he was not followed by posterity, for which, to all intents and purposes, they symbolize the victory of liberty over the slavery of Asia. Thus, for Hegel, these battles "live immortal not in the historical records of Nations only, but also of Science and of Art—of the Noble and Moral generally. For these are World-Historical victories; they were the salvation of culture and spiritual vigour and they rendered the Asiatic principle powerless" (*Philosophy of History*, trans. J. Sibree [New York, 1956], p. 257). And for J. S. Mill: "The battle of Marathon, even as an event in English history, is more important than the battle of Hastings. If the issue of that day had been different, the Britons and the Saxons might still have been wandering in the woods" (*Discussions and Dissertations*, vol. 11, [London, 1859], p. 283).

for the historian's fame, the justification for his posthumous crowning. This Muse is recognizable as Clio, she who sings of the "fame of heroes" (*klea anthropon*), whose essential attribute, in figurative representations, is precisely the *volumen*:[20] here, standing between the bust and the great *volumen* of the Persian Wars, she is both the mediator of the narrative and the *histor*'s inspiration.

Then on either side of the cloud the background, the scenery, can be seen. In the upper lefthand corner, Babylon is easily recognizable with its walls, its great sanctuary tower, and the Euphrates flowing through the middle of the town. In the lower righthand corner, taking up rather more room, is Egypt, represented, inevitably, by the Nile and the Pyramids, but also by a group of "typical" objects: a squatting scribe, and hieroglyphics. The engraver's choice of these two themes is clearly not fortuitous, but what is most interesting about his treatment of them is that the theme of Herodotus the traveler appears as a background, and only a background, against which the great chronicle produced by the historian may be displayed. This all-in-all unexceptional engraving is thus constructed on the basis of a distinction which it is content simply to render visible: there are two Herodotuses, one the historian of the Persian Wars,[21] and another who is primarily the Herodotus of "others," of non-Greeks.

The distinction was given a new lease of life, in erudite fashion, within the field of classical studies itself. The long article by the greatest specialist on the Greek historians, which appeared in 1913 in that austere work of reference the *Real-Encyclopädie der klassischen Altertumswissenschaft*, was for many years considered to be authoritative[22]—as indeed it still is. Before becoming a historian, Herodotus was a geographer and ethnographer. So not only is there a distinction between the traveler and the historian of the Persian Wars, but also a progression from the traveler to the historian, and his work testifies to both stages. An evolution is combined with the distinction.

That being so, short of challenging this theory the only choice open to interpreters was to vary the line of demarcation between the

20. *Dictionnaire des antiquités grecques et romaines*, s.v. *Muses*.

21. *Hérodote, historien des guerres médiques* (Paris, 1894) is the title of a book by A. Hauvette, a work of importance in its own day.

22. F. Jacoby, *RE* Suppl. 2, 205–520.

historian and the other Herodotus, shifting it one way or the other depending on the breadth of their own definition of the word *history*.

Apart from one isolated study published in 1937,[23] this approach predominated until the 1950s.[24] Since then, particularly in the late 1960s, a number of works have appeared that modify it. Their authors set out to efface that dividing line by showing that it was not actually inscribed in the text itself; they aimed to prove that in reality the two names of Herodotus were one. Widely differing though these works were, they shared one feature: a distrust of presuppositions (such as a more or less explicit definition of history, for example) with, on the contrary, a desire to seek their answers in the text itself, treating it as a single whole. This was what Myres proposed doing when he set out to illuminate the composition of the *logoi* by means of a sculptural comparison. According to Myres, Herodotus's technique in describing a scene is like that of an artist who is at pains to create symmetry in sculpting the pediment of a temple or who observes a certain rhythm in the development of his frieze. Others— Immerwahr, for example—set out even more deliberately "to treat the work as an organic unit intelligible by itself."[25]

The division to which the frontispiece, Voltaire's text, and Jacoby's article each in its own way testifies made it possible to contain the thorny question of truth and falsehood and to introduce some order into that of paternity. But as soon as an analysis of the text concludes in favor of the work's unity, as soon as there are no longer two names but only one, then the question of history, which had for the moment been set aside, reappears. Now, though, it is contained by the text itself, where it explodes within the very name of Herodotus. In the last analysis, what are the *Histories*, what is *historie*, what is a *histor*, and even, is the father of history a historian?[26] Sooner or later the interpreter is bound to face these questions.

23. M. Pohlenz, *Herodot, der erste Geschichtschreiber des Abendlandes* (Leipzig, 1937).

24. J. L. Myres, *Herodotus: Father of History* (Oxford, 1953).

25. H. R. Immerwahr, *Form and Thought in Herodotus* (Cleveland, 1966), p. 10.

26. See, for example, S. Benardete, *Herodotean Inquiries* (The Hague, 1969), pp. 1.–6.

ΗΡΟΔΟΤΟϹ.

HERODOT
Halicarnaff.
LIBRI IX.
item
VITA
HOMERI
Gr: & Lat:

PROPONTIS

MARE ÆGÆUM

PELOPONNESUS

K. van der My inven.   F. Bleyswyk sculp.

LUGDUNI BATAVORUM.
Apud SAMUELEM LUCHTMANS. MDCCXVI.
Cum Privilegio Potentiſſ. D. D. Ordinum Hollandiæ & Weſtfriſiæ.

1. Herodotus, "historian of the Persian Wars," crowned by the Muses.
From the edition of J. Gronovius (Leiden, 1715).

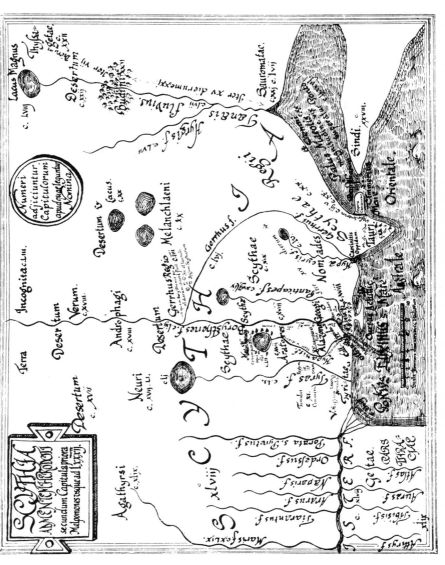

2. Scythia. From E. H. Minns, *Scythians and Greeks* (Cambridge, 1912).

Guerrier scythe.
British Museum, Londres.

3. Scythian warrior. British Museum, London.

4. Scythian wagon. After M. Gryaznov, *Sibérie du sud*, Archeologica Mundi Collection, Editions Nagel, Paris.

5. The "birth" of history: Herodotus and Thucydides, double bust. National Museum, Naples.

The starting point for the present book is indicated in its subtitle: "The Representation of 'the Other.'" Its initial aim was to discover how the Greeks of the classical period saw others—that is, non-Greeks; to reveal the way or ways in which the Greeks practiced ethnology; in short, to sketch a history of "otherness" with its own particular rhythms, emphases and discontinuities, always assuming these to be detectable. In such an inquiry it was clearly impossible to skirt around Herodotus, and it soon became apparent that he was, in fact, indissociable from it or, rather, that it was worth concentrating solely on him since it was in his text par excellence that a whole complex of questions took shape and were played out, subsequently to be reiterated, denied, transformed, or raised anew by his interpreters. They are questions which lead eventually to that of the practice of history itself. Thus this book finally came to be entitled *The Mirror of Herodotus.*

The *Histories* are a mirror into which the historian never ceased to peer as he pondered his own identity: he was the looker looked at, the questioner questioned, who always ended up by declaring his own status and credentials. Was he a historian, or a liar? Hence the importance, in the history of the interpretations of Herodotus, of drawing a clear line between the historian of the Persian Wars and the Herodotus of "the others," often treated as another Herodotus altogether. Where was he? In the service of a prince or of a city, in the capacity of a seeing eye and chronicler? Herein lies the importance of the debates surrounding the relations between Herodotus, Pericles, and Athens. Who was he addressing, and why? From this question follows those about Herodotus's public and about Herodotus as a lecturer and whether or not he was paid.

The *Histories* are a mirror in two other senses as well: if the "elsewhere" is a mirror image in the *logoi* devoted to non-Greeks, Herodotus's mirror is also held up to the Greeks themselves. Of all those *logoi*, I have concentrated on that devoted to the Scythians, for the Scythians never ceased to astonish the Greeks. It was they who routed the army of Darius, king of the Persians, and, oddest of all, they were nomads, without houses, towns, or ploughed fields.

The mirror of Herodotus is also the eye of the *histor* who, as he traveled the world and told of it, set it in order within the context of Greek knowledge, and, in so doing, constructed for the Greeks a representation of their own recent past; the *histor* became both rhapsode and surveyor. But beyond himself, he is also the mirror through which others, who came later, tended to see the world. Which brings us to the question of the effect or effects of the text, in particular, the text as history.

The various meanings taken on by the metaphor of the mirror reveal the links between the questions that lead in a continuous chain from Herodotus's Scythians to the case of Herodotus himself, from the reading of one *logos* to an investigation into the way to write history. In the course of some of the *logoi* devoted to "others," Herodotus treats his text as a traveler's tale, that is to say, as a narrative at pains to translate "others" into the terms of the knowledge shared by all Greeks, and which, in order to make credible these "others" whom it is constructing, elaborates a whole rhetoric of "otherness." The present study thus stems from the choice of a particular level of analysis. It is not intended to rule out other approaches or to suggest that other levels of analysis are less important. In focusing on the *contract* that binds the narrator to his addressee, it hopes to extract more from the text, not as a consequence of any kind of cult of the text itself but simply with the aim of sketching in a few proposals for a historical semantics.

The present exploration of Herodotus resembles its own primary subject, the nomad: it is neither closed upon itself nor a completed whole. Instead, it sets out to stimulate further investigation by posing once again the question of the effects produced by a historical text or, indeed, that of the historical genre as a whole, and by resuming the inquiry into the place and function of the historian in society. One approach might be to attempt a study of the historian's own vision and the eye of history itself: a kind of archaeology of the historian's vision, or at least a few fragments to put toward one.

In the case of Herodotus, the question of the function of the *histor* is inseparable from the history of his interpretations. If such a history, in turn, is to become more than just a history of ideas, it should include some reflection on the institution of history and the profession of the historian; in short, it should proceed from readings of Herodotus toward a general history of history, seen—to use M. I. Finley's expression—as a "practical subject."

However, to limit and focus such an inquiry one might concentrate in the first instance on the group that would consider itself to be on terms of the greatest familiarity with Herodotus: the ancient historians. The question of the *histor* then leads to an inquiry into the subject of ancient history considered as a discipline (what constitutes it, its position as an institution, how it functions, the rules governing the formation of new utterances or statements, the extent of its influence upon knowledge generally shared) and those who practice it. What, then, is a Hellenist? According to Father Labbe, he is first and foremost somebody who exploits Greek unfairly. That author's *Etymologies de plusiers mots français, contre les abus de la secte des hellénistes de Port-Royal*, published in 1661, attacks what Father Labbe took to be the Jansenist conspiracy against Latin and French.[27] And in a letter written in 1810, P.-L. Courier expresses himself on the subject of the name *Hellenist* as follows: "If I have correctly understood this word, which is, I confess, new to me, you can say Hellenist as one says dentist, druggist, or cabinet-maker [*ebéniste*] and, on that analogy, a Hellenist is supposedly a man who purveys Greek, who lives by it, selling it to the public, to booksellers, to the government."

27. Sainte-Beuve, *Port-Royal* (2nd ed. Paris, 1860), vol. 3, p. 454. For Sainte-Beuve, Father Labbe invented the name *Hellenist*.

Part One

The Imaginary Scythians: Space, Power, and Nomadism

*Is it you, Nomad, who will ferry
us to the shores of Reality, this
evening?*

—Saint-John Perse

The Scythians of Herodotus:
The Scythian Mirror

In the *Histories*, the Scythians are "others" with a special position: they are, after the Egyptians, those to whom Herodotus devoted the most space,[1] and yet, in contrast to Egypt, their country could offer scarcely any marvels or curiosities worth reporting.[2] Then what was it about them that prompted Herodotus to speak or write? Was it, perhaps, because he had traveled in the Black Sea region, or because Darius had fought against them?

Let us consider the Scythian *logos*. How should we read it? What questions should we ask? And who, in the first place, are Herodotus's Scythians? One way of answering might be to compare what the text *says* and what archaeology has *discovered*, the Scythians of Herodotus and the Scythians of archaeology, the Scythian *logos* and the "real" Scythians; on the one hand a discourse and a representation of the Scythians, on the other what they really were. On that basis, passing from the text to the archaeological remains and from the remains back to the text, it might be possible to seize upon the convergences and, above all, to ponder upon the divergences. This might lead to some conclusions regarding the accuracy of Herodotus's information: was his description good, or poor? His mistakes would probably be ascribed to misleading information, an insufficiently critical approach or naïveté. The "points of agreement," on

1. Herodotus 4.1–44.
2. Hdt. 2.35, 4.82.

the other hand, would be credited to his powers of observation and his freedom from preconceptions. If the debit side outweighed the credit side, he would be judged to have given a poor description; if, conversely, his credit was high, he would be deemed a truthful witness.

But, as a single example will suffice to show, the relationship between the text and the remains cannot be regarded in such a simple, positivist fashion, even assuming the archaeological evidence to be a reliable referent. Herodotus devotes several chapters to the strange funeral rites celebrated by the Scythians in honor of their kings. Now, it is generally agreed that he gives a good description of the princely *kourganes* and the daunting ceremonies that took place there. Rostovtzeff wrote: "Our knowledge of Scythian funerary ceremonial in the sixth and fifth centuries B.C., derived from the burrows excavated in the valley of the Kuban, corresponds pretty closely to Herodotus's account of the obsequies of Scythian kings and princes."[3] The text and the excavations thus tally.

But superposing the one upon the other leads one to overlook or pay scant attention to one detail in the text. According to Herodotus, the kings, and only the kings, were always buried in the same place, among the Gerrhi; that is to say, on the northern boundaries of Scythia, in *eschatia* or frontier regions.[4] But archaeology, on the contrary, shows the *kourganes* to have been scattered in valleys throughout the entire country.[5] If one superposes the archaeological evidence upon the text one literally does not notice this slight mismatch, and if one assesses the text against the archaeological evidence the discrepancy is explained away by being set down to, for example, the "inadequate information" at the traveler's disposal.

Instead of labeling this as a useless remnant of information, why not, rather, suppose that it may acquire a meaning within the text itself, that it is a detail stemming from and explained by the logic of the narrative, that it is the product of a particular representation of the Scythians which the *logos* is, precisely, in the process of constructing? More generally, by making a direct comparison of this

3. M. Rostovtzeff, *Iranians and Greeks in South Russia* (Oxford, 1922), p. 44; cited here as an example, not as evidence of the state of Scythian archaeology.

4. Cf. below, pp. 138.

5. See, for example, *Or des Scythes: Trésor des musées soviétiques*, catalogue of an exhibition at the Grand Palais (Paris, 1975), map on pp. 118–19.

kind between the text and the archaeological remains, one is in danger of not seeing the text as a narrative with its own peculiar organization (that is, the Scythian *logos* is not a monograph documenting the Scythians, but at a certain point forms part of the wider whole which we know as the *Histories*). I shall therefore not engage in an exercise in which the text would be supposed to validate the excavations, providing a kind of supplementary soul for them while, conversely, the excavations would validate the text, on which they would confer, if not reality, at least a kind of supplement to reality.

How, then, should the Scythian *logos* be read? Conceivably, by setting up a second type of comparison, not between the text and the archaeological evidence but between the chapters written by Herodotus and the Ossetian epic. For the past century and a half it has been known that the Ossetians, a people settled in the central Caucasus, are, through the Alains, the last descendants of the Scythians; they all belong to the vast group of Northern Iranians. Now, the Ossetians achieved

a double performance: the cultural content, a content which goes back to the last stages of the Scythian civilization, was preserved along with its linguistic vehicle, and, furthermore, was preserved down to our own times. In particular, a treasury of epic tales survives, full of archaisms, centered on heroes whose originality, despite the penetration of more or less universal folkloric themes, remains powerful and fresh. Better still: this literature was adopted to varying degrees by the neighboring peoples, who altered nothing in it except the features that were too specifically Ossetian or Scythian. [6]

Once this continuity is recognized, it becomes legitimate to compare Herodotus's narrative with the Ossetian epic, the *Legends of the Nartes*. To Dumézil there can be no doubt that "the tradition faithfully preserved by the Ossetians illuminates much of the Scythian information provided by Herodotus (and Lucian)."[7] Proceeding from there, by concentrating mainly on Herodotus rather than on the "Indo-European heritage" of the Scythians it may be possible to develop a line of thought upon his way of treating this Scythian-Ossetian material, noting the transformations and distortions he introduces and pondering how and why he did so.

6. G. Dumézil, *Romans de Scythie et d'alentour* (Paris, 1978), p. 9.
7. Ibid., p. 12.

But, leaving aside both my own incompetence in this area and also the fact that that particular approach has already been adopted and pursued by Dumézil, I shall not myself follow that path either. Why not? Because both these readings, the one based on a comparison with the archaeological evidence and the other appealing to the Ossetian texts, are, so to speak, *externally* oriented: both of them seek to step outside the text of the *Histories* in order to evaluate it, and both of them take the perspective of the Scythians themselves. Thus, the Scythian *logos* is read from the Scythian point of view and in relation to a Scythian referent. We have, on the one hand, what Herodotus says and, on the other, what is known from other sources. What is known is used to criticize what is said and what is said, once it has been criticized, adds to what is known. The whole text is evaluated from the point of view of the quantity and quality of the information it contains. That is, the question is asked, is Herodotus a trustworthy and full source of information about the Scythians?

But the first question that I myself would pose is not about the Scythians in general but simply about Herodotus's Scythians. It might be objected that if one starts by rejecting any comparison of the text with what is not the text itself, one runs the risk of becoming trapped within that text. The sole option would then be to develop, more or less skillfully, some mechanism for the production of periphrases and tautologies, eventually setting up a cult of the text— a cult which would not even admit to being such. In short, one would run the risk of evaluating the text for itself and the Scythians for themselves, thus indulging in what used to be called art for art's sake.

So what about Herodotus's Scythians? Although we are not concerned, in the present work, with comparing them with a *referent* (or what is set up as such, that is, the "real" Scythians), we should not reject comparison at all costs, particularly *within* the *Histories*, in which the Scythian *logos* occupies one particular place at one particular point. In other words, what we need to do is relate statements from this *logos* to other statements within the same context.[8] For example, Herodotus tells at length of the war waged by Darius against the Scythians.[9] This expedition has perplexed both commentators and historians: did it truly take place or what, if anything, is true about it, given that it cannot possibly *all* be true?

8. T. Todorov, *Symbolisme et interprétation* (Paris, 1978), p. 28 (syntagmatic indices).

9. Hdt. 4.83–144.

Now if, within the *Histories*, one compares segments of this account with certain elements in Xerxes' expedition against the Greeks, a number of convergences and echoes become apparent. In other words, Herodotus's Persian Wars (positioned later in the *Histories*) play the role of matrix to the narrative of Darius's war and provide a model of intelligibility for the reader, even if Darius's war cannot be reduced to this alone. The question of the more or less fictitious nature of Darius's expedition in Scythia immediately becomes, to say the least, inappropriate.

The way that some statements refer to others in the same context is an indication of what might be called the narrative constraints— constraints not external and imposed, but internal and produced by the narrative itself in the course of its elaboration. It follows that the Scythian *logos* does not represent immediate information about the Scythians, directly accessible to anyone reading this *logos* in isolation, nor is it, so to speak, evidence in the raw which may be compared directly to whatever it is not. A problem of classification inevitably arises here.

A second confrontation leads along, not "the way" of the "real" Scythians but "the way" of the Greeks. It involves setting these statements (or utterances) about the Scythians alongside the shared knowledge of the fifth-century Greeks. The possibility of such a comparison rests on the idea that a text is not something inert but is circumscribed by the relationship between the narrator and his addressee. Between the narrator and his addressee there exists, as a precondition for communication, a whole collection of semantic, encyclopedic, and symbolic knowledge common to both sides.[10] And it is precisely on the basis of this shared knowledge that the text can be developed and the addressee can decode the various utterances addressed to him. "The interpretation of an utterance by the one to whom it is addressed demands from the latter not so much a decoding as a 'calculation' which reconstructs the relationship between the utterance and a certain number of points of reference selected from the representations which the interlocutor shares, or thinks he shares, with the locutor."[11] The description of Scythia thus occupies a particular place within the general organization of the *Histories*, but that place is itself defined in relation to a Greek area of

10. D. Sperber, *Le Symbolisme en général* (Paris, 1974), and "Rudiments de rhétorique cognitive," *Poétique* 23 (1975): 390–415.

11. F. Flahaut, *La Parole intermédiaire* (Paris, 1978), p. 37.

knowledge, one governed in particular by the principle of symmetry: the north and the south of the *oikoumene* occupy symmetrical positions on either side of an "equator" which runs across the Mediterranean.

How should we set about this comparison between statement and shared knowledge? In the first place, the operation should not lead us outside the text. The addressee is in fact positioned inside the text, as a kind of "mold for a reader," an effigy of a reader to whom the narrator essentially addresses himself and upon whom he exerts his powers of persuasion. The difficulty stems not so much from the external nature of that knowledge as from its implicit, or largely implicit, character: it is on the basis of this knowledge both that the addressee calculates the meaning of a statement and that the narrator formulated it, precisely so that the addressee should be able to make that particular calculation. In view of all this, one might, as a working hypothesis, proceed as follows: treat the proper noun *Scythians*[12] as a simple signifier and track the range of this signifier within the space of the narrative, noting all the predicates[13] that collect around it so as eventually to construct an image of the Scythians. The sum of these predicates constitutes the Scythians of Herodotus.

As for those predicates themselves, they may be analyzed according to a complementary hypothesis, that of systematic differentiation. That is to say, we may read the text with the assumption that this or that Scythian practice may be interpreted in relation to its homologue in the Greek world. When Herodotus speaks of sacrifice among the Scythians, he sets up an implicit opposition with Greek sacrifice; and it is this that makes it possible for him to associate a range of diverse actions and gestures, regarding them as so many elements constituting a single practice which the Greeks call *thusia*. First, he identifies as a *sacrifice* an action which consists of strangling a trapped animal from behind; next, his description of the successive phases in the ceremony only takes on its full meaning in relation to the sequences in Greek sacrificial ritual.[14] Operating as an "absent model," Greek sacrifice provides at the same time a means of

12. On proper nouns, cf. below, p. 244, and, more generally, J. Lyons, *Semantics* (Cambridge, 1977), pp. 206ff.

13. *Predicates* in the widest sense: what the Scythians are and also what they do.

14. Cf. below, pp. 173ff.

apprehending this Scythian practice and of interpreting its otherness. If the addressee calculates correctly, he is provided with a
means of pinpointing the differences, should he wish to do so. We
thus proceed from the name to the predicates that constitute it, and
thence from the predicates to the codes that underpin them, in such
a way that the word *Scythian* is treated as a code name.

The purpose of comparing the statements in the text with the
shared knowledge of the Greeks is neither to evaluate Herodotus's
description nor to gauge the quality of the information but, rather, to
scrutinize the manner in which the description is purveyed and to
study how the information is treated. It is a question of *how* it is
done: how are the relationships between the statements in the text
and the shared knowledge of its recipients established? Ultimately
this poses another question, that of the conditions (one of them, at
least) under which such a narrative may be constructed. By speaking
of "others" as they relate to the shared knowledge of its addressees
and in terms of that knowledge, the text functions overall as a
translation. If that is so, we are bound to try to seize upon the
particular procedures and modalities it adopts.

One last question: how is it possible to distinguish and delimit a
shared knowledge which, by definition, we ourselves do not share?
How can we seize upon it when it is, by its very nature, largely
implicit? How can we give an account of it if, unlike the ethnographer, we have no means of questioning even an informant, let alone
of making a direct approach to those who do share this knowledge?
Take a simplified image of communication: the ethnographer, having
learned the relevant code or codes, is in a position to decode the
messages emitted by the locutors. But in the case of historians, the
more limited the documentary evidence at their disposal the finer
the dividing line between the code and the message becomes until,
at the limit, they reach a situation where, practically speaking, they
must interpret both code and message and also distinguish which is
which, all in one single operation. The Homeric poems provide a
good example of that extreme position, representing as they do a text
which is—for us, at any rate—closed upon itself.

How can we proceed in the case of the *Histories*? If it is true that
the text is circumscribed by the relationship between the narrator
and his addressee and if it is also true that the addressee is, in a
sense, established within the text itself, then mapping out the shared

knowledge does not imply "moving outside" the text. Furthermore, although this knowledge may itself remain largely implicit, that does not mean that it may not be indicated indirectly by pointers which themselves are made quite explicit. I am thinking of all the interventions on the part of the author or of secondary or delegated narrators, through which astonishment is expressed at something strange, underlining a difference or explaining an absence.[15] And in a more general sense, the narrator's very undertaking to name things is a way of referring to the knowledge that he shares with the addressee: he classifies the reality of others according to Greek categories.

All the same, is recognizing the action of strangling an animal from behind as *thusia* justification enough for setting up a precise comparison with a sacrificial model that was constructed by Greek scholars on the basis of evidence derived not only from texts but from figurative representations as well?[16] Assuming, as a working hypothesis, such an operation to be justifiable, I may set all the sacrifices of these "others" in perspective, interpreting their dispersion in terms of the distance separating them from the Greek model, and their incompleteness and heterogeneity in terms of their differences from that model. It also becomes apparent that none of these sacrifices actually contradicts the basic structure of the Greek model. Thus, once such a comparison is carried out, the hypothesis is legitimized and, conversely, the validity of the model itself is confirmed, even reinforced.

Such a reading, based on systematic differentiation, tends in this way to make sense of the text and, furthermore, justifies itself by reason of the sense that it confers. Aiming, as it does, to make explicit at least a part of the implicit knowledge to which the narrative refers or upon which it draws, it reconstructs a calculation which a fifth-century Greek listening to Herodotus did not need to make. Of course, it is not really possible to separate these two approaches, the one directed toward the context (the constraints of the narrative), the other involving the shared knowledge of the audience. Both draw modern historians not along the "way" leading to the Scythians but along the Greek "way," and they can thereby apprehend Herodotus's Scythians—that is to say, the Scythians as

15. Cf. below, pp. 292ff.

16. M. Detienne and J.-P. Vernant, *La Cuisine du sacrifice en pays grec* (Paris, 1979).

imagined by the Greeks, each group reflecting the other. In other words, they too construct the Scythian mirror. The point is, how did such people as the Greeks, who were forever declaring that city life was the only life worth living, imagine this figure of the Scythian, the essence of whose life was to keep constantly on the move? To put the question another way, how must the Athenians, who so insistently claimed to be of autochthonous birth,[17] have represented this alien figure whose whole being consisted in having no attachment to any place? It is not hard to foresee that the discourse of autochthony was bound to reflect on the representation of nomadism and that the Athenian, that imaginary autochthonous being, had need of an equally imaginary nomad. The Scythian conveniently fitted the bill.

17. N. Loraux, "L'Autochthonie: Une Topique athénienne," *Annales E.S.C.* 1 (1979): 3–26.

One

Where Is Scythia?

Scythia is a land of *eremia*, a zone of *eschatia*, a deserted place and a frontier: one of the ends of the earth. It was here that Power and Might brought Prometheus, to be chained up by order of Zeus: "Here we are on the soil of a distant land," declares Power, "journeying in the Scythian country, in a desert empty of human beings."[1] Aristophanes also uses the expression "Scythian wilderness" but applies it to a person: one of his characters is described as a "Scythian wilderness" (*Skuthon eremia*), as a way of saying that he is a savage, friendless brute.[2] Many years later, Quintus Curtius picked up the expression, putting it into the mouths of the Scythians themselves: in his expedition against the Scythians, a more successful repetition of that of Darius, Alexander, about to cross the Tanais, received a delegation of Scythians. Trying to persuade him not to attack them, they reminded him that the space of Scythia rendered them impossible to capture. They went on to say: "It seems that Greek proverbs

1. Aeschylus *Prometheus Bound* 1–2.
2. Aristophanes *Acharnians* 702–3: "How shocking that a man bowed with age like Thucydides should have perished, struggling in the clutches of that Scythian wilderness (*Euathlos*)." The context is a legal trial. The scholium to line 703 gives as an equivalent to the expression "Scythian wilderness" that of "wildness": *sumplakenta tei S. eremiai: sumplakenta agrioteti; touto gar deloi he S. eremia*. Taillardat (*Les Images d'Aristophane* [Lyons, 1962], para. 428), referring to Hesychius, who regards the expression as a way of denoting "abandoned people" (*epi ton eremoumenon hupo tinon*), understands Euathlos (who may be of Scythian origin) to be "nothing but a friendless brute."

even mock at the Scythian solitudes but we, for our part, seek out the deserts and an absence of civilization rather than opulent towns and countrysides."[3] There are indeed a number of proverbs on the theme of Scythian solitude. The expression meant "solitary and completely wild places," "people who, being in control of no land, constantly change the place where they live," "abandoned people."[4] The Hippocratic treatise *Airs, Waters, Places* cannot avoid it either but gives it a precise geographical definition: "What is called the Scythian desert is level grassland, without trees and fairly well watered."[5] Whether it applies to a place or, metaphorically, to a person, the formula was certainly a part of the shared knowledge of the Greeks, a ready-made expression denoting solitude, wildness, distant places.

Scythia really did belong to the ends of the earth; far away to the north, it extended to the margins of the inhabited world and even beyond. *Prometheus Bound* emphasizes the remoteness of Scythia. Zeus's representatives and their prisoner journey in "a distant land," and "the host of Scythia" (*homilos*) is described as "living on the edges of the world" (*gas eschaton topon*) by the stagnant Maeotis lake.[6] For a Greek city, *eschatia* meant the zone beyond the cultivated area; "it was the region 'at the end,' land with a poor yield, difficult to use and then only intermittently, out toward the mountains or in the mountains which always marked the boundaries of a territory; it bordered on the frontier and merged with it, the region of mountains and forests which separated two city-states, abandoned to the use of shepherds, woodcutters, and charcoal-burners."[7] To present Scythia as *eschatia* is thus to represent it as occupying, in relation to the *oikoumene*, a position analogous to that occupied by the frontier zone in relation to the city territory.

All that is formulary and implicit knowledge, purveyed at the very least from Aeschylus down to Quintus Curtius (that is, from the fifth century B.C. to the first century A.D.). But in Book IV of the

---

3. Quintus Curtius 7.1.23.
4. E. Leutsch and F. G. Schneidewin, *Corpus Paroemiographorum graecorum*, vol. 1, p. 453; vol. 2, pp. 208, 643. For another example of a proverbial use, see Demosth. Apol. in *CPG*, vol. 4, 284 R.
5. Hippocratic Corpus *Airs, Waters, Places* 18:*he de Skutheon heremie kaleumene pedias esti kai leimakodes kai psile kai enudros metrios.*
6. Aeschylus *Prometheus Bound* 416–47.
7. L. Robert, *Opera minora selecta* (Amsterdam, 1969), p. 305.

Histories, Herodotus brings it into question. For him it is not enough to repeat that Scythia is a land of *eremia*, a zone of *eschatia*, for the reality is much more complex. He goes on to show that this land of *eremia* contains its own deserts; this zone of *eschatia* has its own margins. Not only do the Scythians not represent a single, united group, since they are divided into a number of different peoples; furthermore, within their territory there are plenty of other peoples who are not of the Scythian "race" at all. Herodotus goes on to enumerate these various peoples, listing them and marking out the territory they occupy. Thus, within the historian's own discourse, a whole system of northern peoples is organized, a system in which it becomes clear that the "real" deserts—about which there is nothing to tell, for they lie at the limits both of space and of what is tellable— begin far to the north of Scythia, and that wildness increases the further north and northeastward one advances. That last proposition is only true if one adopts a global view; but the further one goes in that direction, the less evidence of the human race is to be found, until eventually one reaches those beings, known only by hearsay, who are men with the hooves of goats: Arimaspians or Griffons.[8] Clearly though, in this context the concept of the wildness of the Scythians changes: they become relatively less wild as others become more so.

Although the Scythians are probably the most important of the peoples of the north, for Herodotus they are still simply one of those peoples: he avoides the over-simplistic image of Scythia as a desolate land, situated almost beyond the most remote of men. Furthermore, Scythia is not simply one of the ends of the earth but occupies a place in Herodotus's global representation of the world. Myres has shown that when composing the *Histories*, Herodotus made use of a number of maps, in particular an Ionian one.[9] These maps rely heavily on the principle of symmetry: the world is organized symmetrically on either side of an equator which divides the Mediterranean, passing from the pillars of Heracles across to the Taurus Mountains, by way of Sicily and Delphi. To the north, it is cold; to the south, hot. In the north, things are explained by the cold; in the

8. Herodotus 4.25.
9. J. L. Myres, "An Attempt to Reconstruct the Maps Used by Herodotus," *Geographical Journal* 6 (Dec. 1896): 606–31.

south, by the heat.[10] Thus, the southern symmetrical counterpart to Scythia is Libya or, to be more precise, Egypt. When winter comes, the cranes leave the cold land of Scythia and fly to these regions.[11] But the symmetry operates above all in respect to those two remarkable rivers, the Ister (Danube) and the Nile: the Ister is to the north what the Nile is to the south. The fact that Herodotus adopts this symmetry is proved by a supposition that he makes at one point. Let us for a moment imagine an inversion of the seasons; that is to say, Boreas and winter on the one side, and Notos and the southern climate on the other, change places. In that case, "in his passage over all Europe, [the sun] would work the same effect on the Ister as he now does on the Nile;"[12] from this it follows that the Nile and the Ister are indeed equidistant from the equator and that, in their west/east course, they are the concrete marks of the extreme limits of the sun's movements—in other words, they represent the two "tropics" of the Ionian map.[13] Furthermore, the principle of symmetry is so evident that it has a certain heuristic value, for, knowing the course taken by the Ister, I can, by analogy, infer that taken by the Nile; by applying this principle I may thus propose a new solution to the thorny question of the sources of the Nile. Just as the Ister, which rises among the Celts, "cuts clean across Europe . . . thus I suppose the course of the Nile in its passage through Libya to be like the course of the Ister."[14] Finally, the Nile and the Ister are not only situated at the same latitude (which is remarkable enough), but also on the same meridian: the Ister debouches at Istria, and Istria is opposite (*antion*) Sinope. The Nile, for its part, debouches in Egypt, and Egypt is virtually opposite (*antion*) mountainous Cilicia; and from Cilicia to Sinope is only a five day's march in a straight line, so the delta of the Nile is opposite the mouth of the Ister (see Map 1).

This symmetry enables the narrator to envisage a relationship between Egypt and Scythia: one is the direct converse of the other. Thus, the heat and the cold, which respectively affect these two

10. Cf. below, p. 233; cf. also Hp. *Airs, Waters, Places.*
11. Hdt. 2.22.
12. Hdt. 2.26. According to Herodotus, the behavior of the Nile is governed by the sun; Boreas is the north wind, Notos the south wind.
13. W. A. Heidel, *Greek Maps: The Frame of the Ancient Greek Maps* (New York, 1937), p. 21.
14. Hdt. 2.33–34.

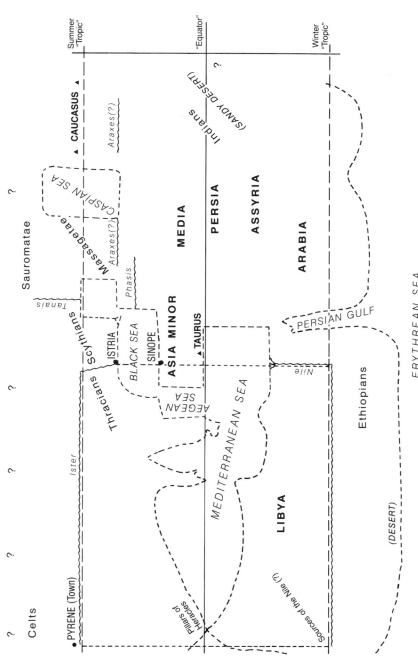

regions, produce opposite effects. The Egyptians, at least until the experiments of the pharaoh Psammeticus, considered themselves to be the most ancient of men,[15] while the Scythians, for their part, declared their nation to be "the youngest [*neotaton*] in all the world."[16] Generally speaking, the regions of the north are lands of ignorance, whereas the Egyptians are a people of very ancient wisdom.[17] The Greeks of the Black Sea refer to that contrast in the story of Salmoxis: his compatriots, the Getae, considered him as a deity, whereas the Greeks regarded him simply as a former slave of Pythagoras, and Pythagoras, like most of the "sages" of Greece, traveled to Egypt in his quest for knowledge.[18] From the point of view of knowledge, then, a chasm separated Salmoxis from the Egyptian priests. On the other hand, the Egyptians hold the same attitude as the Scythians regarding foreign *nomoi:* they reject them and, in particular, they reject the Greek *nomoi* utterly.[19] Herodotus's account also establishes a relationship between them with respect to warfare: in the course of his great wars of conquest, Sesostris reached Syria and "subjugated" the Scythians; he was to be the only one to do so, since Darius was to be unsuccessful.[20] In contrast, when the Scythians, for their part, overran and ravaged Asia, they were dissuaded from invading Egypt by the pharaoh's gifts and pleas.[21]

Another anology can be noted in the oppositions between Egypt and Scythia. If one accepts, as the Ionians did, that the frontier between Asia and Libya was marked by the Nile, then one has to

---

15. Hdt. 2.2. Psammeticus raised two newborn infants in isolation, and the first word they pronounced was *becos*, which means "bread" in Phrygian. He drew the conclusion that the Phrygians were the first men. Herodotus, for his part (2.15), considers that the Egyptians have always existed, at least ever since the race of man has (*aiei te einai ex hou anthropon genos egeneto*).

16. Hdt. 4.5.

17. "Generally speaking," for Herodotus excepts precisely the Scythians, especially Anacharsis, from this total ignorance (4.46). Cf. below, pp. 62ff.

18. Hdt. 4.94–95.

19. Hdt. 2.91 (on the Egyptians) and 4.76: "But as regards foreign usages, the Scythians (as others) [*kai outoi*] are extremely unwilling to practice those of any other country, and particularly of Greece." Legrand points out that "as others" appears to refer to the remarks on the attitude of the Egyptians toward foreign *nomoi*.

20. Hdt. 2.103.

21. Hdt. 1.105.

consider Egypt as a land between Asia and Libya.[22] Now, as we shall see, just so can Scythia be considered a territory between Asia and Europe.[23] Both can thus be considered as "in-between" countries.

If the Egyptian priests are to be believed, Sesostris was not only a conqueror but also the true creator of the space of Egypt. Before him, Egypt was "a land of horses and carts," a kind of nomad space, altogether comparable to Scythia, which was traversed by carts and over which horses grazed. But with the advent of Sesostris, the horses and carts disappeared, for he had many canals dug throughout the territory. "From this time, Egypt, albeit a level land, could use no horses or carts by reason of the canals being so many and going every way."[24] The canals were dug to bring water to towns distant from the river. Furthermore, Sesostris divided up the land, giving each man an equal allotment (*kleros*) and he fixed the dues to be paid for them. If the river carried away a portion of a *kleros*, the king sent his men to measure the loss and fix a proportionately lower tax; Herodotus regarded this as the origin of geometry.[25] In other words, the Egyptian space was a creation imposed by a power. It changed from being a space freely roamed over to being one divided, surveyed, distributed, and taxed.

To carry out these great works, Sesostris employed the prisoners he had taken in the course of his conquests.[26] He thus exploited the work force that they represented. The Scythians, also took prisoners, but they treated them very differently: they blinded them. In one strange chapter, Herodotus explains that they blinded their prisoners and then used them to milk their mares: "It is for this cause that the Scythians blind all prisoners whom they take, for they are not tillers of the soil but wandering graziers."[27] Curiously, then, it was their nomadism which in the last analysis, served to explain their behavior, even if the link between blindness and nomadism is not made explicit by the narrator. At all events, the difference between the two ways of treating prisoners is certainly an indication of the

---

22. Hdt. 2.16–17.
23. Cf. below, pp. 31ff.
24. Hdt. 2.108: *to prin eousan ippasimen kai amaxomenen pasan.*
25. Hdt. 2.109.
26. Hdt. 2.108.
27. Hdt. 4.2.

distance separating the Egypt of the pharaoh and the Scythia of the nomads.

Before Sesostris, the space of Egypt was an open range, as were the Scythian expanses, but after him Egypt came, quite astonishingly and artificially, to resemble what Scythia was naturally: "For their country is level and grassy and well-watered and rivers run through it not much less in number than the canals of Egypt."[28] But in the one case, the rivers are the "allies" (*summachoi*) of nomadism, whereas in the other the new canals put a stop to the circulation of carts and the movement of horses; the canals prevent what the rivers allow, and the canals impose a way of life controlled by the power of the pharaoh.

There thus appears to be, on the one hand, a power remodeling a new space in inescapable fashion; on the other, an "absence" of power adapted to a natural space. However, that description is simplistic. In fact, on two occasions Herodotus indicates that the Scythian territory is divided into nomes, each nome having a nomarch at its head; in other words, the Scythian space is now presented as a space inventoried and set under an administration.[29] Now, the word *nome* which Herodotus uses is the same one he uses to speak of the administrative units of Egypt and of the Persian satrapies. So the three countries where nomes exist are Persia, Egypt, and Scythia. It is a curious grouping: Persia and Egypt are ruled by a strong royal power, the Great King being, for a Greek, the epitome of royal—hence despotic, hence barbarian—power; but what is Scythia doing in such company, Scythia which appears to be ruled simply by an "absence" of power? We are alerted to a difficulty: the Scythians have kings, yet they are nomads. How can a Greek, with his images of royal power and of nomadism, conceive of a nomad power?

Who Are the Scythians?

The first question is that of their origins. How and when did they make their appearance? As often happens where origins are concerned, there is no single answer and Herodotus knows of (at least) four different versions, which he reports, one after the other. This

---

28. Hdt. 4.47. The description of the territory repeats virtually the same terms as the definition given in the Hippocratic treatise *Airs, Waters, Places.*

29. Hdt. 4.62, 66.

very accumulation of versions, clearly difficult or impossible to reconcile, cannot fail to make a definite impression on the narrator's addressee.[30]

The first version is that of the Scythians themselves. The Scythians say, *Skuthai legousi* (but the narrator gives no indication of how he came to hear of this *logos*):

There appeared in this country, being then a desert, a first man whose name was Targitaus. His parents, they say, were Zeus and a daughter of the river Borysthenes [the Dneiper]; and he had three sons, Lipoxais, Arpoxais and Colaxais, youngest of the three. In the time of their rule (so the story goes) there fell down from the sky into Scythia certain implements all of gold, namely, a plough, a yoke, an axe, and a flask. The eldest of them, seeing this, came near with intent to take them; but the gold began to burn as he came and he ceased from his attempt. Then the second approached and the gold did again as before. When these two had been driven away by the burning of the gold, last came the youngest brother and the burning was quenched at his approach; so he took the gold to his own house. At this, his brothers saw how matters stood and made over the whole royal house to the youngest. Lipoxais, it is said, was the father of the Scythian clan called Aukhatai; Arpoxais, the second brother, of those called Catiaroi and Traspies; the youngest, who was the king, of those called Paralatai. All these together bear the name of Skolotoi after their king. "Scythians" is the name given them by the Greeks. . . . Because of the great size of the country, the lordships established by Colaxais for his sons were three, one of which, where they kept the gold, was the greatest.[31]

Dumézil has shown that these four objects (which really only amount to three, since the yoke and the plough together constitute but one) symbolize the "three functions," "which constitute one of the principal frameworks for the thought of the Indo-Iranians who, in this respect, are the depositories of an Indo-European tradition: the bowl is the instrument of worship and festivals, the axe is a weapon of war, the plough and the yoke relate to agriculture."[32] The text raises a second question, that of the place of the two successive generations

30. Cf. below, 291ff.

31. Hdt. 4.5–7.

32. E. Benveniste, "Traditions indo-iraniennes sur les classes sociales," *Journal Asiatique* 230 (1938): 532–34. G. Dumézil, *Romans de Scythie et d'alentour* (Paris, 1977), p. 172, quotes a text of Quintus Curtius, confirming this interpretation. Scythian envoys try to persuade Alexander not to repeat Darius's disastrous experiment: "Understand that we have received as gifts an ox-yoke, a plough, a spear, an arrow, and a bowl. We use them with our friends and against our enemies. We give our

of brothers: Colaxais and his brothers, and the sons of Colaxais. In the opinion of Dumézil, these two triads are not duplications: the first expresses a functional division; only the second expresses a geographical division. "Aukhatai, Catiaroi and Traspies, and Paralatai are not ethnic names; they denote types of men performing different functions, wherever they may be. They are prototypes of the human beings who fulfill these three functions within any Scythian society. In contrast, the sons of Colaxais found dynasties destined to reign over distinct but adjoining lands."[33] Even if not "entirely verifiable," this hypothesis does account for the presence of the two triads, which it is pointless to try to reduce to one.

The crucial point is that in this version the Scythians present themselves as settled cultivators, not as nomadic herdsmen: from heaven fall a yoke and a plough, and the youngest brother carries these golden objects "home" (which indicates that even before the objects fall from the heavens, he lived a settled life; the arrival of the objects does not mark the end of an earlier phase of nomadism). Finally, "the ideology of the three functions" is not exactly typical of nomadic societies. Here, apparently, are people who describe themselves as settled but whom the Greeks regard, first and foremost, as nomads.

Furthermore, though this legend may be a version of the origin of the Scythians, it is even more a version of the origins of power among the Scythians: its primary concerns are royalty and the qualifications for exercising royal power. The youngest of the brothers, who is the only one able to approach the burning objects, seizes them *all* and is thereafter their sole possessor; these "functional talismans" which he keeps for himself are the mark of his election and qualify him to exercise *pasa basileia*, all the royalty, by himself.

An annual ritual is organized around the golden objects, a ritual which suggests a link between power and the territory. "The kings guard this sacred gold most jealously, and every year they offer solemn sacrifices of propitiation to it. Whoever at this festival falls asleep in the open air, having with him the sacred gold, is said by the Scythians not to live out the year; for which reason (they say) there is

---

friends the fruits of the earth which ploughing with our oxen affords; and with them we use the bowl to offer libations of wine to the gods; as for our enemies, we attack them from afar with the arrow and at close quarters with the spear."

33. Dumézil, *Romans*, pp. 178–92.

given him as much land as he can himself ride round in one day."[34]
This gold, never mentioned again by Herodotus either when he
speaks of sacrifices or when he tells of the Persian invasion, symbolizes royalty and represents its point of anchorage. By the same token,
whoever possesses the gold exerts his authority over the territory.
Now, curiously enough, should whichever of the Scythians who is
guarding the gold happen to fall asleep (which is interpreted as a sign
of his impending death), he receives "for that reason" (*dia touto*) a
parcel of land in the territory: an "ephemeral" property the size of
which is determined by the distance that his horse is able to cover in
a day. Thus a relationship between the king's gold and the division of
the land is marked at a second level, it having already been established at the start by the gesture of Colaxais, the first to take
possession of the gold, who divided the country into three kingdoms
for his sons.

However, not only does Herodotus not himself endorse this
version of the origins of the Scythians since, as he points out, it is
only the Scythians who "say" (*legousi*) it was so; he even discounts it.
Where the Scythians report that the parents of Targitaus, the first
Scythian, were Zeus and a daughter of the river Borysthenes, the
narrator adds: "to me that is not credible" (*emoi ou pista legontes*).[35]
And if the very beginning of the story is not true, how could the rest
of it be?

The second version is the one produced by neighbors of the
Scythians, the Greeks of the Black Sea (*hode legousi*). This was a
deserted land when Heracles arrived there, driving the herds of
Geryones before him. While Heracles was sleeping, his mares
disappeared. Having set off in search of them, he met a young snake-
girl who agreed to return his mares to him if he would have
intercourse with her, which he did. Three sons were later born from
this union. In answer to their future mother's questions about the
destinies of his children, Heracles replied:

When you see the boys grown to man's estate, act as I bid you and you will do
rightly. Whichever of them you see bending this bow thus and girding
himself in this fashion with this girdle, make him a dweller in this land; but
whoever fails to achieve these tasks which I command, send him away out of

34. Hdt. 4.7.
35. Hdt. 4.5.

the country. . . . She, when the sons born to her were grown men, gave them names, calling one of them Agathyrsus and the next Gelonus and the youngest Scythes; moreover, remembering the charge, she did as she was commanded. Two of her sons, Agathyrsus and Gelonus, not being able to achieve the appointed task, were cast out by their mother and left the country, but Scythes, the youngest, accomplished it and so abode in the land. From Scythes, son of Heracles, comes the whole line of the kings of Scythia.[36]

Like the first version, then, this one is an account both of the origin of the Scythians and at the same time also of that of the royal power.

It is also interesting from the point of view of its representation of distant lands. Heracles arrives in Scythia while traveling from the land of Geryones. Now, Geryones lives "beyond the Pontus . . . in the islands called by the Greeks Erythea, on the shore of the Ocean near Gadeira, outside the pillars of Heracles." According to Apollodorus,[37] to reach Scythia, Heracles had to cross Europe, land in Libya, pass through Tartessus (where he set up the famous pillars), and finally obtain the bowl of the Sun in order to cross the ocean. Situated on the very boundaries of the world, if not beyond them, the island of the monster Geryones furthermore belongs to mythical geography. Is not this establishment of a connection between Erythea and Scythia a way of suggesting that Scythia, too, belongs to that geography?

Traveling from Geryones' island, he arrives in Scythia (according to Apollodorus, he follows his oxen all the way to Thrace, but the version given by the Black Sea Greeks does not mention the various stages in his return journey), as if it were easy to pass from one to another of these marginal spaces. "After visiting every part of the country . . . , at last he came to the land called Woodland [Hylaia]; and there he found in a cave a creature of double form that was half damsel and half serpent [*mixoparthenon tina echidnan diphuea*]; above the hips she was a woman, below them a snake."[38] Such is the strange being that Heracles comes across in this region set slightly

36. Hdt. 4.8–10. When Herodotus mentions the Agathyrses and the Geloni, further on, he does not return to the subject of their ancestors; the Geloni are even called "erstwhile Greeks."

37. Apollodorus 2.5.10. In the *Theogony*, Erythea is situated "beyond the great Ocean" (1.294).

38. Hdt. 4.9.

apart from the rest of the Scythian territory; Hylaia is in fact the only wooded region in the whole of Scythia.[39] This version elaborated by the Greeks of the Black Sea refers back to the figure of Echidna as it appears in Hesiod.[40] It clearly does not cite the *Theogony* literally, but it adopts the same theme, not a common one, of the Mixoparthenos,[41] introducing a number of differences which themselves raise a number of questions. How is Echidna presented in Hesiod? The frightful Echidna (*lugre*),[42] born from Phorkys and Ceto, or from Peirar and Styx, resembles "neither mortal men nor the immortal gods" and lives "underneath," in a cave far from "both men and gods"; her dwelling-place is underground in the land of the Arimes.[43] Her body is "half that of a young woman with beautiful cheeks and sparkling eyes, half that of a huge snake, as terrible as it is large, spotted, cruel." Being herself a monster, she gives birth to a number of monsters. Among these are several that cross Heracles' path: Orthus, Geryones' dog; Hydra, the monster of Lerna; and the lion of Nemea, all three of whom Heracles slew.

A number of convergences between Hesiod's account and the version of the Black Sea Greeks thus become detectable: the physical appearance of Echidna is identical to that of the Mixoparthenos; however, Herodotus gives no indication regarding the origins of the young snake-girl, who, furthermore, is in no way presented as being fearsome or terrible. This figure, half woman, half snake, reappears in Diodorus Siculus: after being united with Zeus she gives birth to a son, Scythes; he is not the founder of the Scythian people, since they already exist, but he does become a famous king of this people to whom he gives his name. This time the text, which is presented as a story the Scythians tell of themselves, states that Echidna is "born from the earth" (*gegenes*).[44] Also noticeable is a certain proximity to Geryones: in Hesiod the family of Echidna is mentioned immediately after the figure of Geryones, and Echidna gives birth to Geryones' dog Orthus; in Herodotus the proximity is spatial, the

39. Cf. below, pp. 67f.
40. Hesiod *Theogony* 295–305.
41. Another figure described as Mixoparthenos is the Sphinx (Euripides *The Phoenician Women* 1023), who is the daughter of Echidna and Typhon.
42. Escher in *RE*, article "Echidna," pp. 1917–19.
43. The Arimean Mountains are also where Typhoeus "lies abed" (*Iliad* 2.783).
44. Diodorus 2.43.3.

connection being Heracles, since it is upon leaving Geryones that Heracles arrives in this hitherto deserted land which is to become Scythia.

What effect does the Echidnian context have on Herodotus's narrative? Why do the Black Sea Greeks make this Hesiodic "detour" in order to assign an origin to the Scythian people? In the first place, it is a way of indicating the "distantness" of the Scythians: they are distant spatially, as is, I believe, suggested by the reference to Geryones, and they are also distant culturally, for the Scythians are connected with a bygone age, an age of monsters. There is, then, to put it another way, a certain Scythian primitivism expressed here.

This reference to the genealogy of Echidna by the Black Sea Greeks also poses a number of questions with implications that extend beyond these four chapters of Herodotus. I can spot three. In Hesiod, Heracles intervenes by slaying three of Echidna's offspring: Orthus, Hydra, and the lion. For the Black Sea Greeks, in contrast, far from doing away with the children of the Mixoparthenos, Heracles himself gives her three sons. Why do the Greeks introduce this reversal, which turns the one who kills her offspring in the one case into the one who provides her with them in the other? Above all, what is the effect of this "patchwork" (*bricolage:* a term also used by Levi-Strauss) put together by the Black Sea Greeks?[45]

Echidna resembles neither mortal men nor the immortal gods, and the Mixoparthenos of Herodotus is half-human, half-animal. Endowed with this intermediary status, then, she is the mother of the Scythians. Now, the Scythians are, first and foremost, nomads. The question arises: what is the role of the hybrid? In other words, is the allocation to the Scythians of a mother who is neither truly human nor truly animal a way for the Black Sea Greeks to come to terms with nomadism? Is there a correlation between the status of a hybrid, and a nomadic life? To provide an answer to that question, one would have to undertake an inquiry into the question of what a hybrid meant to the Greeks.[46]

---

45. We might add that the Black Sea Greeks display something of a sense of humor: they have Heracles sleep with this snake-girl—Heracles who has had, ever since the cradle, a bone to pick with snakes . . .

46. Cf., in the Babylonian context, the analysis of the figure of Enkidu, the hybrid child, by E. Cassin, "Le Semblable et le différent: Babylone et Israël," *Hommes et bêtes* (Paris, 1975), pp. 115–27.

The third question is that posed by the intervention of Heracles. If the Scythians have a hybrid being for a mother, they have a hero for a father. Is not a kind of contradiction involved in giving a nomadic people a father who is, first and foremost, a civilizing hero? We are once again faced with the question of nomadism. For a whole section of the tradition,[47] Heracles is a traveler who "explores" and "marks out the limits of the earth,"[48] but he is also a defender of humanity. In particular, he is the founder of a large number of cities. Thus, within the space of no more than his expedition against Geryones, he could be credited with the founding of Hecatompylae in Libya; Seguntum in Spain; Alesia in Gaul; Bauli, Herculanum, and Croton in Italy; and Soli and Motye in Sicily.[49] He is, furthermore, the hero who purges the earth of its monsters, never hesitating to track them down to the very ends of the inhabited world, even to the underworld. He also tackles barely civilized peoples such as the Kylikranes and the Dryopes, who indulge in brigandage, and he crushes the Laestrygonians, who are notorious for their cruelty.[50] Tiresias had disclosed the destiny of Heracles to Amphitryon and told him "how many lawless monsters he would slay on the dry land and how many upon the sea; and how he would deal the most frightful death to many a man led by pride to leave the straight path."[51] As a founder of cities and dispenser of civilized life, he is thus diametrically opposed to nomadism, the chief characteristic of which is the absence of any life in a *polis*.

But the figure of Heracles also presents a degree of ambiguity. Constantly journeying over hill and dale, he is not always a civilizing hero, and sometimes not even a civilized one. Where food and sexuality are concerned, his behavior is marked by excess: in comedy he is represented as a glutton and a libertine.[52] Seen from

---

47. L. Lacroix, "Héraclès héros voyageur et civilisateur," *Bulletin de la Classe des Lettres de l'Académie Royale de Belgique* 60 (1974): 34–59.

48. Pindar *Nemean*, 1.26.

49. Lacroix, "Héracles," pp. 38–39; in the Black Sea region, Heracles appears as *ktistes* on the coins of Heraclea on the Black Sea and of Callatis. He even founded towns in India: Heracleia among the Sibae, Salibothra on the Ganges.

50. F. Jacoby, *Fragmente der griechischen Historiker*, 3 F 19, (Pherecydes), 662 f. (Lycophron).

51. Pindar *Nemean* 1.60–61.

52. Epicharmes, fr. 21 Kaibel (= Athenaeus, 10.411a); Aristophanes *Wasps* 60, *Peace* 741. Cf. E. des Essarts, *Du type d'Hercule dans la littérature grecque* (Paris, 1871), p. 109ff.

this point of view, Heracles is neither a "hero-god," as Pindar called him, nor a "divine man," as the Stoics considered him, but an "animal-hero."[53] Was it perhaps this ambiguity that made it possible for the Black Sea Greeks to consider him, without any contradiction, as the father of the Scythians? As for the Hellenocentricity which consisted in placing a Greek hero at the origin of non-Greek peoples, that is a constant feature of Greek anthropology.[54] In Herodotus, Heracles is credited with being at the origin of no fewer than three royal families: (1) the Scythian royal family (but in the case of the Scythians, he is also at the origin of the entire people); (2) Candaules, the king of Sardis, was descended from Alcaius, the son of Heracles;[55] and (3) the Spartan kings claimed Heracles as their ancestor.[56]

The last two versions, at least, have one feature in common: they both give an account not of the origin of the Scythians but of the arrival of the Scythians in the land now known as Scythia.[57] The first of the two is introduced by the following words: "there is also another *logos*"; the second is ascribed to the poet Aristeas of Proconnesus. In the first, the Scythians, who are nomads, suffering harassment from the Massagetae, cross the Araxes and invade the land formerly occupied by the Cimmerians, all of whom, except for the kings, have fled at the approach of the Scythians. In this version, the one which Herodotus is "the most inclined to accept," the Scythians are indeed nomads from Asia. In the other version, it is under pressure not from the Massagetae but from the Issedones, themselves ousted by the Arimaspians, that the Scythians trek southward and eject the Cimmerians: this makes them northern Europeans.

The Scythians have another distinctive feature: they call themselves "the youngest of all peoples."[58] According to their calculations, "neither more nor less than a thousand years in all passed from the time of their first king, Targitaus, and the crossing over of Darius into their country."[59] Now, one thousand years is, for example, the

53. C. Segal, "Mariage et sacrifice dans les *Trachiniennes*," L'Antiquité Classique 44 (1975): 31.

54. E. J. Bickermann, "Origines Gentium," *Classical Philology* 47 (1952): 65ff.

55. Hdt. 1.7.

56. The rest of the genealogy is described in connection with Leonidas: Hdt. 7.204.

57. Hdt. 4.11–13.

58. Hdt. 4.5: *neotaton apanton ethneon*. Justin 2.1 attributes the opposite opinion to them.

59. Hdt. 4.7.

time that has elapsed between the birth of Dionysus and the time of Herodotus. "Now, the Dionysus who was called the son of Semele, daughter of Cadmus, was about a thousand years before my time."[60] It also appears that in their society the principle of youth is highly prized: not only are they the youngest of all peoples, but it was also to the youngest of the three brothers that royalty fell. Does this suggest a kind of reversal in relation to societies that accommodate the privileges of age, as is the case in Greek communities?[61] A question begins to form: is there any connection between nomadism and the youthfulness of a people? At all events, in this text of Herodotus, the very noting of this youthfulness only becomes meaningful when it is set alongside what is said of the Egyptians, the most ancient, or almost the most ancient, of men.[62]

Another element enters into this question of the identity of the Scythians: the climate. In the *Histories* the climate is treated as an explanatory factor: there is a theory of climates, of a sort, at work here, according to which whatever is in the north happens because of the cold (*dia ta psuchea ginetai tauta*),[63] while whatever is in the south can be explained by the heat.

The climate of Scythia is unique.[64] The winter there is different from the winters in all other countries (*kechoristai*). The Greek term used clearly indicates a separation, a break in continuity.[65] Herodotus is not content simply to declare this difference, but proceeds to attempt to prove it, in order to convince his audience. The Scythians undergo a winter that is excessive by reason of both its intensity and its duration: for eight months it is "unbearably" cold.[66] It is imme-

---

60. Hdt. 2.145.

61. P. Roussel, "Essai sur le principe d'ancienneté dans le monde hellénique du Vᵉ siècle avant Jésus-Christ à l'époque romaine," *Mémoires de l'Académie des Inscriptions et Belles-Lettres* 42, 2 (1951): 123–65. The custom regarding sovereignty among the Scythians is similar to that among the gods: it is the youngest who exercises power. Cronos is the youngest of the Titans, Zeus the youngest of the Olympians.

62. Cf. above, p. 17.

63. Hdt. 4.30.

64. Hdt. 4.28–29.

65. The word is used, for example (Hdt. 1.4), to indicate what the Persians regard as the dividing line between Asia (their domain) and Europe (the domain of the Greeks); and then again at 3.20, in connection with the Ethiopians, who have *nomoi* that distinguish them from all other men.

66. Hdt. 4.28. Its excessive nature is indicated by the word *duscheimeros*.

diately clear that the gauge for measuring the Scythian winter is to be the Greek winter: in relation to what is it excessive, if not to the Greek winter? For the time being, however, that remains implicit. The first proof adduced by Herodotus is the following: "You shall not make mud by pouring out water but by lighting a fire." So in Scythia fire acts as water does elsewhere: instead of drying and cooking, it moistens and liquifies (instead of cooking the earth and forming some kind of gypsum, it produces mud).[67] And the liquid par excellence, water, solidifies whatever it touches and even itself becomes solid. Under the effect of the cold, the sea becomes a route over which carts can pass. There is thus a confusion between the categories of the dry and the wet, and equally between the liquid and the solid. Such is the weather pattern for eight months of the year and these are followed, not by four months of summer, as one might expect, but by four months of "ordinary winter" (*tous d'epiloipous tesseras psuchea autothi esti*). The Scythian climate is thus certainly exceptional and the difference tends, by reason of the demonstrative discourse used, to be expressed in terms of an opposition.

Herodotus then moves on to the rainfall pattern, and at this point the opposition definitely becomes a reversal: in Scythia it never (or virtually never) rains in the winter, which *everywhere else* is normally the season of rains; on the other hand, it never stops raining in the summer (*to de theros huon ouk aniei*). The rainfall pattern is thus reversed in relation to that experienced in Mediterranean regions generally. But the most important point, one that proves Herodotus is referring to a Greek model, is his use of the word *theros*, despite the fact that he has just stated that the Scythian year is divided into eight months of excessive winter (*duscheimeros*) followed by four months of ordinary winter (*psuchea*). In order to fit in with the Greek model and allow a system of oppositions to function, the four months of *psuchea* are obliged to become the equivalent of a "summer." It rains in the season when it should not rain and does not rain in the season when it should.

Once he has made this rule of intelligibility clear,[68] Herodotus proceeds to extend its use to apply far beyond the simple matter of climate. There are thunderstorms in Scythia when there are none

---

67. P. Ellinger, "Le Gypse et la boue, 1," *Quaderni Urbinati di Cultura Classica* 29 (1978): 32.
68. Cf. below, pp. 212–24

elsewhere, and if there is ever an exception to this rule, the Scythians "marvel at it for a portent" (*hos teras thaumazetai*). Similarly, an earthquake is considered by the Scythians to be a prodigious event (the implication being "in contrast to what happens in Greece"). Another field in which the reversal operates is that of the resistance of animals to the cold. In Scythia the horses, but not the donkeys and mules, can tolerate the cold, whereas elsewhere it is quite the reverse. Finally, Herodotus moves on to the respective effects of the heat and the cold upon the horns of animals: heat makes animals' horns grow rapidly, as can be seen from a line of Homer's on "Libya, where the lambs immediately carry horns"; conversely, the cold causes them to have hardly any horns at all, which explains why the Scythian oxen are without horns.

In the interests of persuasiveness, the narrator thus moves from drawing attention to a difference to setting up an opposition which is soon expressed as a reversal. The Scythians who endure this excess of winter are of course a northern people but, unlike the author of the Hippocratic treatise *Airs, Waters, Places*,[69] Herodotus does not draw any conclusions as to their physical constitution.

If the Scythians do not have a single origin, do they at least have a single place, a single country? Where is Scythia situated? Is it a European space or a part of Asia? To judge by Hecataeus of Miletus, there appear to be grounds for hesitation: "Scythian peoples" are mentioned in the book of the *Periegesis* devoted to Europe, but they also appear in the book concerned with Asia. For example, the "Black-cloaks" are described as an *ethnos Skuthikon* in Hecataeus's section on Europe, *Hekataios Europei*; and the same is true for the Murgetae. On the other hand, the Issedones, who are certainly an *ethnos Skuthikon*, appear in the Asiatic section, *Hekataios Asia*.[70] This uncertainty, which seems to make the Scythians a people midway between two different spaces, on the frontiers of Asia and Europe, in effect poses the question of the respective limits of the two continents.

In the treatise *Airs, Waters, Places*, the lake of Maeotis is given as

69. Obviously, the Hippocratic treatise *Airs, Waters, Places* is the text that carries this theory of climates the furthest.

70. Jacoby, *FGrHist*, I F 185, 190, 193.

the frontier between Europe and Asia,[71] and the Scythians indisputably belong to Europe, since even the Sauromatae, who live by the lake of Maeotis, are assumed to be Europeans.[72] Others (Herodotus does not specify who, but one was probably Hecataeus)[73] fix the frontier at the river Tanais or at the Cimmerian straits. Myres demonstrates convincingly that, moving from south to north, the Cimmerian straits, the lake of Maeotis, and the river Tanais were situated on the same meridian.[74] In the end, the essential point for a partisan of one of these three frontiers is to favor a north-south division between Europe and Asia. But Herodotus rejects that division, stating, on the contrary, that "Europe's length is known to be enough to stretch along both Asia and Libya."[75] It therefore follows that he favors a demarcation line running not north-south but east-west, and under these circumstances the Colchidian river Phasis suits very well.

The Phasis flows into the "northern sea" (*ten Boreien thalassan*) and marks the northern limit of the first Asiatic peninsula:[76] "On the north side, one of the peninsulas begins at the Phasis and stretches seaward along the Pontus and the Hellespont as far as Sigeum in the Troad; on the south side the same peninsula has a seacoast beginning at the Myriandric gulf that is near Phoenicia, and stretching seaward as far as the Triopian headland" (in Caria, near Cnidus). In Book 1 Herodotus reports that the king Cyaxares, when laying siege to Ninevah, was attacked by a Scythian army that had entered Media in pursuit of the Cimmerians, and he remarks that it was a thirty days' march from the lake of Maeotis to the Phasis.[77] Finally, when seeking revenge on Darius, the Scythians sent envoys to Sparta to suggest an alliance; they proposed a plan of action that would culminate in their attacking from the north "along the Phasis" and invading Media.[78] We may thus conclude that in the *Histories*, the frontier between Asia

71. Hp. *Airs, Waters, Places* 13.
72. Hp. *Airs, Waters, Places* 17.
73. Hdt. 4.45.
74. Myres, "An Attempt," pp. 606–31. Hdt. 4.57: "In its upper course, the Tanais begins by flowing out of a great lake and enters a yet greater lake called the Maeotian."
75. Hdt. 4.45.
76. Hdt. 4.37, 38.
77. Hdt. 1.103.
78. Hdt. 6.84.

and Europe is the Phasis; Scythia, then, is definitely situated in Europe.

So it is that when queen Atossa urges Darius to take action, he replies: "I am resolved to make a bridge from this to the other continent and so to lead an army against the Scythians."[79] Such an expedition was indeed a grave venture, for it was the first time a Great King had left his own domain, passing from Asia to Europe. As for the Tanais, it certainly marked a boundary. By crossing it, one in effect left Scythia:[80] when the Sauromatae (the young Scythians who went to marry the Amazons) were seeking a country in which to settle, they crossed the Tanais and marched northward for three days.[81]

But even if Scythia is in Europe, the Scythians are not necessarily Europeans. In fact, in the version of origins that Herodotus was inclined to favor, it was said that "the nomad Scythians lived in Asia" and that they moved to Cimmeria under pressure from the Massagetae, and so to Europe. Having entered Cimmeria (which then became Scythia), they set off in pursuit of the Cimmerians, lost their way and, leaving the Caucasus range to their right, invaded Media. There they conquered the Medes and for twenty-eight years dominated Asia, where "all the land was wasted by reason of their violence and their negligence [*hubris kai oligoria*] for, besides that they exacted from each the tribute which was laid upon him, they rode about the land carrying off all men's possessions."[82] But eventually the Medes recovered their supremacy, thanks to a ruse: they invited the Scythians to a banquet, made them drunk, and massacred most of them.

At the beginning of Book 4, however, Herodotus does not refer to this episode, but simply says that after twenty-eight years the Scythians returned "home" (*es ten spheteren*).[83] The Scythians are thus certainly characterized by their mobility: they move from one space to another. For them, the unquestionable division between Asia and Europe does not really exist; they pass from one continent to the other without even fully realizing what they are doing (in their

79. Hdt. 3.134: *Zeuxas gephuran ek tesde tes epeirou es ten heteren epeiron.*
80. Hdt. 4.21.
81. Hdt. 4.116.
82. Hdt. 1.106.
83. Hdt. 4.1.

pursuit of the Cimmerians, they take the wrong route). They fall between two spaces.[84] Nevertheless, in Herodotus's narrative it is clear that it is the war waged by Darius that is really to fix them in Europe, as the occupants of the continent which, without justification, the Great King invades.

84. However, certain difficulties remain in connection with the organization of these northeastern border territories, notably regarding the position of the Araxes. At 4.11, Herodotus says that the Scythians, "being hard-pressed in war by the Massagetae, fled away across the river Araxes to the Cimmerian country," as if by crossing the Araxes they passed over into Europe. The Araxes is a river one of whose arms flows into the Caspian Sea (1.204). The Massagetae live "beyond the Araxes" (*peren*), "opposite" (*antion*) the Issedones (1.201). "This sea called Caspian is hemmed in to the west by the Caucasus: toward the east and the sunrise there stretches from its shores a boundless plain as far as the sight can reach. The greater part of this wide plain is the country of the Massagetae" (1.204). The implication is that the Araxes is situated to the east of the Caspian Sea and flows from west to east. According to Diodorus (2.43), the Scythians at first lived along the banks of the Araxes; at that time they were few in number and little known; then they gradually expanded westward as far as the lake of Maeotis and the Tanais, and subsequently as far as Thrace to the south and to Egypt and the shores of the ocean to the east.

Two

The Hunter Hunted: Poros and Aporia

"The long expeditions which Herodotus attributes to Darius are not historical in character," writes Legrand on the subject of the expedition to Scythia led by Darius.[1] Like so many others both before and after him, Legrand thus attempts to draw a distinction between what is historical in this war and what is not, that is to say, between what is credible and what is not.

The details in the argument are of scant importance, for as Bury, even in his day, wrote: "It is useless to suggest that, though Darius certainly did not approach the Don, he advanced to the Dnieper, or that though he did not get to the Dnieper, he may have halted on the banks of the Bug, or that, if the Bug is out of the question, he at least reached the Dniester."[2]

While the boundary of credibility may shift more or less eastward, depending on the commentators, it is nevertheless agreed that Darius did reach the Ister (the Danube). What were the goals of this war? Some scholars think that the invasion of Scythia can only be understood in relation to the conquest of Thrace: for Momigliano,

1. P.-E. Legrand, *Hérodote*, book 4, p. 27. See also his "Hérodote, historien de la guerre scythique," *Revue des Etudes Anciennes* (1940): 219–26; A. Momigliano, "Dalla spedizione scitica di Filippo alla spedizione scitica di Dario, V," *Contributo 1* (1975): 500; also J. M. Balcer, "The Date of Herodotus' IV Darius' Scythian Expedition," *Harvard Studies in Classical Philology* 76 (1972): 99–132.

2. J. B. Bury, "The European Expedition of Darius," *Classical Review* 11 (1897): 227.

"the Scythian expedition can be explained as an ill-organized pro-
longation of the conquest of Thrace."³ Others believe that the gold
may account for it: Darius was after the gold of the Scythians or
Agathysae, "either as tribute, or booty, in order to continue to build
his Empire."⁴

But I shall move on from Darius, the gold-seeker; I shall not dwell
upon Darius, the forebear of Napolean, or upon Idanthyrsus, the
Scythian king and precursor to General Koutouzov. (The *Cambridge
Ancient History* suggests that this expedition was "Darius's 1812" and
that his crossing of the Ister resembled the crossing of the Be-
rezina.)⁵ I will set aside the rule of credibility and immediately tackle
the narrative given of the war, considering it from three points of
view: (1) that of the purely narrative constraints; (2) that of the hunter
hunted; and (3) that of the demands of Herodotus's ethnological
discourse.

The Narrative Constraints

By narrative constraints I mean everything in the Scythian War that
looks forward to, prefigures, or represents a preliminary sketch for
the Persian Wars. As has often been noted, the Scythian expedition
is a rehearsal for the drama soon to be played out in Greece itself. To
what extent can it be regarded as a prefiguration? First, in that it
marks a break in time, a disruption in the organization of space: when
Darius crossed the Bosphorus it was the first time that any Great
King had left Asia and set foot upon the soil of Europe. Now, as early.

3. Momigliano, "Dalla spedizione scitica," p. 505.
4. Balcer, "Darius' Scythian Expedition," p. 132. Bury had also reached this
conclusion.
5. G. Dumézil, *Romans de Scythie et d'alentour* (Paris, 1978), pp. 327–38, devotes
a chapter to this expedition, humorously entitling it "The Grand Army," after that of
Napoleon. "Since the account that Herodotus gives of this expedition is not 'history'
and since it is nevertheless made up of precise and colorful episodes, might it not
come from a 'native version' noted down by Herodotus at Olbia or some neighboring
town, a version formed over the years following the events, and incorporating
themes belonging to Scythian epic as it is still accessible to us through Ossetian
epic?" The fact is that the Ossetians do tell of a marvelous expedition led by Nasran
Aeldar, lord of the Nartes, against the lord of Egypt, which incorporates "themes
from the great combination which includes those of fantastical beings, the enigma or
triple *aporia* of 'sky-earth-sea' and the misleading fires in an empty camp."

as in the prologue to the *Histories*, it is stated that "the Persians claim Asia for their own, and the foreign nations that dwell in it; Europe and the Greek race they hold to be separate from them."[6] Of course, the narrator takes care to add that it was a prefiguration in miniature of Xerxes' invasion. The epic of the Persian Wars takes pride of place: "none were in any way comparable to it, neither the armament that Darius led against the Scythians, nor. . . ."[7] But there is more to it than that. The Scythian expedition is intelligible only seen through the model provided by the Persian Wars; giving an account of it therefore entails using schemata elaborated in Greece, chiefly by the Athenians, for the purpose of narrating the Persian Wars.[8]

In other words, in relation to the Persians, the Scythians resemble what the Athenians were in relation to those same Persians. This recurrent analogy, which serves as a model of intelligibility for the Scythian expedition, results in the Scythians, in this instance, being turned into Athenians of a kind. That being so, all we need to do is explicitly to establish the connections between the two expeditions, noting a number of references from one to the other that force one to read the first as a rehearsal for the second.

Darius had Mandrocles of Samos build a bridge over the Bosphorus;[9] Xerxes puts a yoke on the Hellespont. Before crossing over to Europe, Darius pauses for a moment to contemplate the Black Sea; in similar fashion, Xerxes contemplates the Hellespont and laments the brevity of human life. Likewise, at the end of these narratives, Darius's flight toward his threatened bridge prefigures Xerxes' flight to the Hellespont.[10] Just as the two armies are about to set off, two episodes take place which clearly occupy homologous positions, both with the function of introducing a propitiatory sacrifice. Oiobazus, a Persian, all three of whose children are in the army, begs Darius to leave him one of them. "No," said the King, "you are my friend and your desire is but reasonable: I will leave you all your

6. Herodotus 1.4; Asia is, as it were, their *oikos*, but *ten Europen kai to Hellenikon egentai kechoristhai.*

7. Hdt. 7.20.

8. P. Amandry, "Athènes au lendemain des guerres médiques," *Revue de l'Université de Bruxelles* (1961): 198–223; N. Loraux, "Marathon ou l'histoire idéologique," *Revue des Etudes Anciennes* (1973): 13–42.

9. Hdt. 4.87.

10. Hdt. 4.85; cf. 7.46, 4.142, 7.101.

sons," and he has all three slaughtered.[11] Similarly, the Lydian Pythius, with five sons in the army, asks Xerxes to exempt the eldest. Xerxes spares the lives of the rest of them but has the eldest killed and, having had his body cut in two, orders his army to file between the two halves.[12]

The continuity between the two expeditions is further underlined by the presence of the same person playing the same role of king's councillor in both accounts. Artabanus is Darius's brother and Xerxes' uncle. He has seen much and remembers it all. He is the king's memory, his *mnemon*.[13] Thus when Xerxes calls a meeting of the most important Persians, to propose attacking the Greeks, Artabanus is the only one to oppose the king's suggestion, and in doing so he specifically refers to the Scythian War: "I forbade Darius, your father and my brother, to lead his army against the Scythians who have no cities anywhere to dwell in. But he, in his hope to subdue the nomad Scythians, would not be guided by me. . . . You, O king, are purposing to lead your armies against men far better than the Scythians—men who are said to be most excellent warriors by sea and land."[14] He also points out that it is extremely risky to depend on a bridge. If Histiaeus of Miletus had not opposed destroying the bridge of ships across the Ister, Darius would have been overcome and the entire Persian Empire with him; similarly, if at the present time the Greeks should be successful in destroying the bridge across the Hellespont, what would become of Xerxes and his army? Artabanus, a living link between the two periods, thus emphasizes the way events repeat themselves: the Scythian war prefigures Xerxes' expedition, and the Persian War repeats Darius's expedition. It is as though the power of the Great Kings was a repetitive machine, always compelled to affirm its power and, by doing so, to destroy it.

Two other short sequences occupy homologous positions in the two episodes. Just as the Scythians and the Persian army are about to

11. Hdt. 4.84. Herodotus does not represent the scene as a sacrifice; he is content to underline its barbarity, in particular by his ironic use of the word *metrion*.

12. Hdt. 7.38–39; O. Masson, "A propos d'un rituel hittite pour la lustration d'une armée . . . ," *Revue de l'Histoire des Religions* 137 (1950): 5–25.

13. Hdt. 7.18: "Artabanus said, 'Remembering the end of Cyrus' expedition against the Massagetae and Cambyses' against the Ethiopians and having myself marched with Darius against the Scythians," listing all the extravagant wars undertaken by the Great Kings.

14. Hdt. 7.10.

come to grips in a pitched battle, a hare pops up between the two lines. The Scythians forthwith abandon all battle order and give chase. Totally bemused, Darius at last realizes the full extent of their scorn for him and decides to abandon the campaign.[15] In similar fashion, after the battles of Thermopylae and Artemisium, Herodotus recounts an episode that is reminiscent of the coursing of the hare. Some Arcadian turncoats are brought before the king. On being interrogated as to what the Greeks are doing, they reply that the latter are busy celebrating the Olympic festival; that is to say, they are watching a competition in which the victor's prize is an olive wreath. At these words, Tritantaechmes (who, as the son of Artabanus, has quite a reputation to keep up) bursts out: "Good heavens, Mardonius, what manner of men are these that you have brought us to fight against?"[16] Both episodes convey derision for an adversary regarded as of little account.

The alleged motive for undertaking both these wars is vengeance. Darius aims to take revenge upon the Scythians who, in their pursuit of the Cimmerians, invaded Asia and there imposed their disorganized rule;[17] Xerxes resuscitates the plans of his father and intends to punish the Athenians, for they had "set fire to Sardis and invaded Asia."[18] In both cases, then, the foe violated the Persian domain first. But faced with this danger, both the Scythians and the Athenians try to convince their neighbors that the expeditions are a threat to them too and that the alleged motive is simply a pretext. "The Persian is come to attack you no whit less than us, nor when he has subdued us will he be content to leave you alone,"[19] declare the Scythians. Their words are echoed by those of the Greek ambassadors to Syracuse: the Persian pretends to be marching against Athens but in truth intends "to subdue all Greece to his will."[20]

Sometimes it is all the mainland Greeks, or, rather, all the Greeks

15. Hdt. 4.134.

16. Hdt. 8.26.

17. Hdt. 4.1.

18. Note that Herodotus also makes Xerxes heir to the Trojan War: before crossing into Europe, "Xerxes ascended to the citadel of Priam, having a desire to view it; and having viewed it and enquired of all that was there, he sacrificed a thousand oxen to Athena of Ilium and the Magi offered libations to the heroes" (7.43). It is not known why *Phobos* spread through the camp on the night following these ceremonies.

19. Hdt. 4.118.

20. Hdt. 7.157: 7:138ff, gives Herodotus's guess as to Xerxes' true goals in this war.

"moved with the best of sentiments" toward Greece, who are said to be "like the Scythians." More often, though, the homology concerns the Scythians and the Athenians alone. If the kings of their neighbors refuse to ally themselves with the Scythians to repulse the Persians, the Scythians threaten to treat with the Great King or even to abandon the country;[21] similarly, the Athenians on several occasions threaten to come to terms with Xerxes or (through Themistocles, for instance) brandish the possibility of pulling out of Attica. Themistocles declares to the Spartan Eurybiades, the commander of the fleet: "Without more ado, we will take our households and voyage to Siris, in Italy."[22] Finally, the reasonable enough reply of some of the kings to the Scythian envoys, to justify their nonintervention—you were the first to contravene *dike*, by invading Asia, so now you have only yourselves to blame if the Persians pay you back in the same coin[23]— brings to mind the Spartans' reproach to the Athenians: "It was you who stirred up this war, against our will, and your territory was first the stake of that battle in which all Greece is now engaged."[24]

This conference of kings is a very strange one. It assembles the leaders of the peoples who live "above" (*to katuperthe*) the Scythians: the Geloni, the Budini, the Sauromatae (who are ready to conclude an alliance), the Agathyrsae, the Nemi, the Tauri, the Melanchlaeni (Black-cloaks), and the Androphagi (who, for their part, refuse to do so). Now, in Book 4, these peoples were represented to be mysterious, fabulous, primitive—even savages: the Androphagi, for instance, have neither *dike* nor *nomos* and are man-eaters.[25] But now, all of a sudden, all these peoples have kings (even if this is the only time they are mentioned), kings who, moreover, declare that they make their decisions according to *dike*. There is therefore reason to suppose that this meeting may be the homologue, in the Scythian *logos*, to the sending of ambassadors to Argos, Syracuse, Corcyra, and Crete by "the Greeks moved by the best of sentiments," in the account of the Persian Wars. The Greeks sought allies; the Scythians must have done likewise. Furthermore, this meeting has a part to play from a historical point of view: it provides a narratively plausible explanation of why the Scythians then refused to do battle with the

21. Hdt. 4.118.
22. Hdt. 7.139, 9.11, 8.62.
23. Hdt. 4.118.
24. Hdt. 8.142.
25. Hdt. 4.106.

Persians. Since they lacked the support of their neighbors, "they resolved not to meet their enemy in the open field."[26] This scene is thus doubly dictated by the purely narrative constraints: if the model of intelligibility is indeed that of the Persian Wars, it was necessary to introduce a sequence to occupy the same position as that of the Athenian ambassadors and to stand in its stead. Second, the Scythians did not engage in proper battle. Why was that? Because they lacked sufficient allies. As will be seen, as well as this narrative reason, there is also an ethnological one and, in a sense, there was never any call for the Scythians to engage in pitched battle.

The Athenians declared, proclaimed, and repeated ad infinitum that they had fought for the liberty of Greece, and Herodotus bears this out: "By choosing that Greece should remain free, they and none others roused all the rest of the Greeks who had not gone over to the Persians, and did, with the help of the gods, beat the King off."[27] The Great King is, on the other hand, the perfect figure of a *despotes* who enslaves everything that he encounters and who maintains that free men are worse fighters than a people led by a single ruler.[28] Now, the Scythians, to the extent that they oppose Darius, to the extent that they are Athenians of a kind, can only be fighters for freedom also. Thus, when Darius demands that they recognize him as *despotes*, they tell him to "go off and weep."[29] Herodotus goes on to note that "the Scythian kings were full of anger when they heard the name of slavery."[30] If the Scythians were not freedom fighters, they could not, mutatis mutandis play the role of Athenians. In contrast, when Darius conquers other peoples, we see no sign of this opposition between slavery and liberty,[31] and when Herodotus describes the Scythian *nomoi*, liberty does not appear to be a particularly important feature: in fact, the Scythian king is himself a perfect *despotes*.

The Hunter Hunted

The narrative constraints manage to render it narratively admissible that th̶ ͟   ween the Persians and the Scythians should be a war

nple, the Getae, but cf. below, pp. 91ff.

without a single pitched battle, a war in which the adversaries barely set eyes upon each other but in which, beyond any doubt, one side emerges as victor, the other as vanquished. How does fifth-century discourse on warfare present such a war, in which engagement and confrontation in pitched battle are continually shunned? The Scythians are in constant flight before the Persians, yet they constantly retain the initiative. They appear to proceed randomly, yet all the time they are implementing a strategy determined in advance. The Persians resolutely give chase but never catch them.

The first appearance of the Scythians in the *Histories* is as masters of hunting.[32] A group of Scythian nomads have taken refuge with Cyaxares, the king of the Medes, and he has "entrusted boys to their charge to be taught their language and the craft of archery." Every day they go hunting, then cook the game they have killed. Their function is that of bowmen and hunters. Now, what do the Scythians present Darius with in Scythia? A hunt, a strange hunt in which the roles of pursuer and pursued are switched, and in the last analysis the hunter becomes, in truth but without knowing it, the hunted.

One group, led by Scopasis, is instructed to *hupagein*, to lead the enemy to them; but in hunting terminology, *hupagein* means "to flush out the game."[33] Another of their orders, *hupopheugein*, means "to flee discreetly," but in hunting terminology this means "to escape from the hounds." The effect of this lexical confusion is that it becomes none too certain who is pursing whom: the Persians are hounds on the track of their quarry, but are they, perhaps, themselves being tracked?

In another phase of the war (representing the second series of orders given to the Scythian commander), as soon as the Persians give up his job is to pursue them, to hunt them down; Scopasis, now openly a hunter, must at this point attack, as the hound attacks the hare.

The other company of Scythians is also ordered to lure the Persians on and lead them astray, always keeping a day's march ahead

32. Hdt. 1.73. The text uses the word *ile*, meaning both band and herd. One day, when they had caught nothing in their hunt and Cyaxares had reproved them roughly for it, they had one of the children being educated among them served up as a dish for his table.

33. Hdt. 4.120. For all this hunting terminology, see P. Chantraine, *Etudes sur le vocabulaire grec* (Paris, 1956), and Xenophon *Cyn.*, with a (French) translation and commentary by Delebecque, *Traité de la chasse* (Paris, 1970).

of them. The verbs used are *hupexagein,* which through its prefix indicates that this movement is carried out surreptitiously, and *proechein,* "to keep ahead,"[34] but *proechein* is also used of a hound that is ahead of the hare, and we are presented once again with the same ambiguity: who is pursuing whom? The strategy is to lure the Persians out of Scythia (and, through this ruse, to force the neighboring peoples to enter the war): then, this being effected, suddenly to about-face and return to Scythia. Herodotus uses the word *hupostrephein,* which is usually applied to the hare: with hounds in its pursuit, the hare suddenly raises one ear, throwing itself off balance and swiveling itself around on the spot, and in this way it is able to elude its pursuers.[35] This cunning behavior of the hare, which is reminiscent of the sudden about-face the fox executes to fall upon its prey *(epistrephein),* sets us squarely in the semantic domain of *metis.*[36] The Scythians, a quarry full of *metis,* have all the makings of excellent hunters.

Up to this point we have been concerned with strategy. Let us now move on to the implementation of these plans *(ta bebouleumena),*[37] which the Scythians proceed to execute step by step.[38] The first step is to evacuate the women, children, and livestock to the north *(elaunein pros Boreo)*; in itself, the use of the verb *elaunein,* "to drive before one," to describe this precaution suggests that the entire convoy is regarded simply as a large herd being driven to a place of safety.[39] Then come the military operations proper, and here we again find, in connection with their execution, that same hunting terminology employed to describe their elaboration. When the Persians, who have lost their way, finally catch sight of the Scythians, they hurry on after them or, to be precise, "they march on in their tracks, *(kata stibon),*"[40] no doubt in the same way as one follows the quarry so as not to lose it, but also—and perhaps even more—so as not to become lost themselves.

34. Hdt. 4.120.

35. Xenophon *Cyn.* 5.32.

36. J.-P. Vernant and M. Detienne, *Cunning Intelligence in Greek Culture and Society* (Sussex, 1978), p. 40.

37. Hdt. 4.120–21.

38. Hdt. 4.122.

39. The term generally used to denote the action of sending women and children into shelter is *hupektithestai* (Hdt. 7.4, 41).

40. Hdt. 4.122.

Then comes the final ruse in the story. In this hunt across the space of Scythia the hunter, the pursuer, is never in control, while the pursued invariably is, being at times, in truth, the pursuer. The hunt ends in a mockery of a hunt.[41] At the very point when it seems that Darius is finally about to obtain what he has sought from the start, namely, a real battle, when the Scythians take up their positions in battle order facing the Persian army as if about to come to grips (*hos*), a hare starts up in between the two armies. As it passes before them, the Scythians immediately break ranks and, all thoughts of the Persians dismissed, set off in pursuit of the hare (*diokein*). They have found more diverting quarry: better a real hare than a false hare that is not even a real hunter. But this hare that starts up between the two armies evokes another one. When Xerxes' army has just crossed the Hellespont, a portent occurs "the meaning of which was easy to guess": a mare gives birth to a hare. It clearly signifies that Xerxes is about to conduct a most magnificent expedition of great pomp against Greece but that he will have to return to his own country in a hurry in order to save his skin.[42] Xerxes, naturally enough, pays it no attention at all. Darius, in contrast, finally realizes what paltry quarry he has seemed to the Scythians and that, as in the case of the hare, his only hope of escaping from his pursuers now is to flee, and to flee with cunning. The last point to note here is that it was not even as if the Greeks considered the hare as challenging quarry or particularly prestigious to hunt. For example, when Adonis hunts, his mistress Aphrodite assigns him "cowardly hares and timid deer, all creatures quick to flee before the hunter,"[43] not lions and wild boar. But to the Scythians even the hare seems a more interesting quarry than Darius.

After Herodotus, other authors suggested other reasons to account for the absence of battle between the Scythians and Darius. According to Ctesias,[44] Darius crossed the Ister and advanced a fifteen days' march into the Scythian interior, then the kings exchanged bows. The Scythian bow proved the stronger (*epikratestera*) and Darius took to flight but was in such a hurry that he destroyed his bridge even before the whole of his army had crossed. This theme of

41. Hdt. 4.134.
42. Hdt. 7.57.
43. M. Detienne, *Dionysus Slain* (Baltimore, 1979), p. 87.
44. Jacoby, *FGrH*, 688 Ctesias, F 13.

the unbendable bow is also present in the *Histories* but in the context of the south rather than the north, among the "long-lived Ethiopians": the king of the Ethiopians presents just such a bow as a gift to Cambyses, who is planning to attack him.[45] Ctesias thus transfers to the Scythians what Herodotus attributes to the Ethiopians, as though elements that belong to the representation of peoples who live on the margins of the world were altogether interchangeable: the bow may without difficulty move from the extreme south to the extreme north, for, either way, Scythia and Ethiopia are both "inaccessible spaces."[46]

As for Strabo, he attributes Darius's discomfiture not to the "Russian winter" but to the "desert of the Getae,"[47] a vast waterless plain where, having crossed the Ister, Darius and all his army almost die of thirst. Darius is, as it were, a prisoner trapped in this desert: the text uses the word *apolephteis*,[48] like an animal "caught in a trap." So the hunting metaphor surfaces again, but on this occasion no hunter lies in wait.

The Persian "Hoplites"

When the Persians invaded Greece, they represented a formidable power, as the Greeks both stated and repeated. But they also stated and repeated that, basically, the Persians did not know how to fight. When Aristagoras of Miletus comes to Athens in the hope of persuading the Assembly to intervene in Asia, he emphasizes that since the Persians employ neither spear (*doru*) nor shield (*aspis*), they will be easy to defeat.[49] Herodotus remarks: "What chiefly did them harm was that they wore no armour over their clothing and fought, as it were, naked against men fully armed."[50] In a striking

45. Hdt. 3.21: "The king of the Ethiopians counsels the king of the Persians: when the Persians can draw a bow of this greatness as easily as I do, then to bring overwhelming odds to attack the long-lived Ethiopians."
46. Cf. below, pp. 57ff.
47. Strabo 7.3.14. The expression *he ton Geton eremia* evokes *he ton Skuthon eremia*.
48. Strabo 7.3.14. The same word is to be found at 6.1.12 to describe Milo, who is the prisoner of the tree he aimed to chop down and who is caught in this trap as in a net.
49. Hdt. 5.97.
50. Hdt. 9.63.

example of an ellipsis, they are called *anoploi,* "without arms." Their weapons are not true weapons, the only true weapons being the arms of the hoplite.[51] "Without arms" means "armed with bows."[52] The Persians are indeed bowmen, even bowmen par excellence. As early as Aeschylus's *Persians,* the opposition between the spear and the bow is drawn several times. This inferiority in weaponry (fundamentally, a way of suggesting the Persians to be barbarians: to be *anoplos* is not to be a hoplite, not to be a citizen) is compounded by an inferiority in skill.

In his account of the battle of Plataea, Herodotus notes: "The Persians were neither the less valorous nor the weaker; but they had no armour [*anoploi*] and moreover they were unskilled [*anepistemones*] and no match for their enemies in craft [*sophie*]."[53] Thus, they would rush out in small groups against the Spartans—and were inevitably massacred. They understood nothing about the phalanx and were incapable of *taxis.* Without the orderliness which enables each soldier to fight in his proper place, standing "man to man,"[54] neither spears nor shields are truly arms. Being "without arms," inferior in *sophia,*" and "incapable of *taxis,*" the Persians did not know how to fight.

Persian children between the ages of five and twenty were taught "three things only, riding, archery and truth-telling."[55] So, as well as being bowmen, they were horsemen and, except at Marathon, the Persian cavalry played an important role during the Persian Wars, with its superiority never brought into doubt.[56] But Marathon was, precisely, "a purely hoplite battle. The cavalry, absent, through a

---

51. Hdt. 9.62.

52. The Persians' equipment is described at Hdt. 7.61: "They wore on their heads loose caps called tiaras, and on their bodies sleeved tunics of divers colours, with scales of iron like in appearance to the scales of fish, and breeches on their legs; for shields they had wicker bucklers, their quivers hanging beneath these; they carried short spears, long bows and arrows of reed, and also daggers which hung from the girdle by the right thigh." On the bowman-hoplite opposition, cf. Euripides *Heracles* 153, 164, and P. Vidal-Naquet, *Tragedy and Myth in Ancient Greece* (Brighton, 1981), p. 181.

53. Hdt. 9.62, 7.211.

54. Aristophanes *Wasps* 1081–83.

55. Hdt. 1.136.

56. A. E. Wardman, "Tactics and the Tradition of the Persian War," *Historia* (1959): 49–60.

stroke of luck, from the Persian side, played no part on the Athenian side either. The *hippeis* of Athens fought on foot."[57]

Not only do they not know how to fight, but the Persians can make neither head nor tail of the clash of two phalanxes. Mardonius says: "When they [the Greeks] have declared war against each other, they come down to the fairest and most level ground that they can find and there they fight, so that the victors come not off without great harm; and of the vanquished I say not so much as a word, for they are utterly destroyed."[58] Herodotus delights in collecting examples of the incomprehension of Mardonius, who has no understanding at all of the agonistic aspect of hoplite fighting and all that makes it ordered combat rather than the butchery he describes.[59]

There can therefore be no doubt that, in Greece, the Persians are regarded as barbarians, that is to say, as anti-hoplites. But in Scythia the army of Darius appears as a quasi-Greek army. How should this strange metamorphosis be understood? If the logic of the narrative leads to the Scythians being represented as Athenians of a kind, the Persians, for their part, ought to appear as barbaric warriors. But that is not the case. Herodotus tells us that when Darius crosses the Bosphorus he has with him an army of infantry and cavalrymen seven hundred thousand strong, not counting the naval army.[60] The Persians certainly do have a cavalry, but every time it encounters the Scythian cavalry it gets the worst of it and turns tail; it is strange, then, that the Persian infantry puts the Scythian cavalry to flight every time, for the latter are afraid of foot soldiers (*phobeomenoi ten pezon*).[61] So the Persians, born horsemen, are obliged to depend on their infantry, the very sight of which is enough to put the Scythians to flight.

Now, Herodotus notes that in the battle of Plataea the Lacedaemonians withdrew, keeping close to the slopes of Cithaeron "out of fear of the cavalry" (*phobeomenoi ten hippon*),[62] that is to say, of

57. P. Vidal-Naquet, "La Tradition de l'hoplite athénien," in his *Le Chasseur noir* (Paris, 1981).

58. Hdt. 7.9.

59. M. Detienne, "La Phalange," in Mauton, ed., *Problèmes de la guerre en Grèce ancienne* (Paris, 1968), p. 123.

60. Hdt. 4.87.

61. Hdt. 4.128.

62. Hdt. 9.56.

course, the Persian cavalry (even if it does include many other peoples as well as Persians). In the one case we have pure cavalry (the Scythians), in the other pure infantry (the Spartans). Faced with a Spartan, the Persian is a redoubtable horseman, for he does not obey the same rules; faced with a Scythian, however, the Persian is forced into being an infantryman. Moreover, when the Persians are in retreat from Scythia, Herodotus reports that the Persian army "was for the most part of infantry,"[63] and the reason that, despite being such poor quarry, the Persian army was successful in eluding its pursuers was partly that those pursuers were on horseback. Somehow the opposition cavalry-infantry here favors the Persian infantry, although Herodotus does not specify in what way.

If the Persians do not rate highly as horsemen in Scythia, they rate not at all as bowmen. Yet archery, along with horsemanship, constitutes the foundation of the Persian education. While in Greece the bowmen and horsemen are the Persians, in Scythia the horsemen and bowmen are the Scythians.[64] Why this switch in passing from one space to the other?

Why do the Persians lose their image as anti-hoplites and become instead quasi-hoplites? What does Darius really want when he crosses the Ister? To invade Scythia and thereby to force his adversaries to do battle with him: a pitched battle (*ithumachie*), in open country, in accordance with all the rules of hoplite combat. Darius explains his strategy clearly when he sends a cavalry officer as envoy to the king of the Scythians, to say: "Why will you ever flee? You can choose which of two things you will do: if you deem yourselves strong enough to withstand my power, wander no further but stand and fight; but if you know yourselves to be the weaker, then make an end of this running to and fro and come to terms with your master, sending him gifts of earth and water."[65] One thing or the other; there is no third option. I invade your territory so you must do battle to defend it and, if you are defeated, I become master of your territory.

---

63. Hdt. 4.136.
64. Hdt. 7.64 describes the equipment of the Sacae, but in Xerxes' "Grand Army" they were simply one of many groups of horsemen and bowmen: "The Sacae, who are Scythians, had on their heads tall caps, erect and stiff and tapering to a point; they wore breeches and carried their native bows and daggers and also axes, which they call 'sagaris.'"
65. Hdt. 4.126.

If you will not do battle, you thereby acknowledge your own inferiority and, in that case too, I become master of your territory;
acknowledge this, bring me earth and water and let us come to
terms. Darius's language here is that of "traditional strategy," according to Garlan,[66] that is, of course, Greek strategy: "When enemies
cross the frontiers of a Greek city, the first thing they normally have
to do is to confront a mass turn-out of the citizens and establish their
superiority in battle in open country."[67] In other words, Darius sees
Scythia as though it were a Greek city which he, also a Greek, is
attacking. He cannot make sense of the Scythian behavior, interpreting as a "running to and fro" (*plane*) what is in truth a deliberate and
confident course of action, and as retreat (*pheigein*), hence cowardli-
ness, what is in truth *hupophugein*, that is to say, a strategy of secret
flight and escape from the hound, hence a cunning type of combat.
One way of forcing the adversary to fight is for the invader to pillage
the territory.[68] But in this instance Darius would be hard put to it to
do so, since the Scythians have made a preemptive "pillaging" strike,
themselves blocking up wells and springs, ravaging the crops, and
sending their herds to a place of safety.[69] The King encounters no
"normal" behavior until he enters Budini territory. There he comes
upon their town of wooden constructions, already deserted, and
promptly sets fire to it.[70] Adopting traditional strategy, he might also
resort to the *epiteichismos*, that is, "establish a stronghold perma-
nently manned by a garrison;"[71] but again, that course turns out to be
hardly practical, since the Scythians are constantly on the move.
Thus, when Darius builds eight great fortifications on the banks of
the river Oarus, the Scythians, still behaving as cunning quarry,
escape from his laughable trap, which then stands in the path of
nothing but the desert winds.[72]

   Considering that Darius is a "traditional" strategist, it is hardly

---

66. Y. Garlan, *Recherches de poliorcétique grecque* (Paris, 1974), pp. 20–44.
   67. Ibid., p. 27.
   68. Ibid., pp. 22ff.
   69. Hdt. 4.120; on evacuation to safety, as current practice during the classical
and Hellenistic periods, cf. P. Ducrey, *Le Traitement des prisonniers de guerre dans
la Grèce antique* (Paris, 1968), p. 90 n. 4; an example of this type of operation is
provided by the way Alyattes waged war against Miletus (Hdt. 1.17).
   70. Hdt. 4.123.
   71. Garlan, *Recherches*, p. 33.
   72. Hdt. 4.124.

surprising that he fails to understand the meaning of the presents that Idanthyrsus sends him: a mouse, a frog, a bird, and five arrows. To his mind, these gifts can only be the symbolic equivalents of earth and water: if Idanthyrsus is sending him presents it means that he acknowledges his inferiority,[73] otherwise he would engage in battle— one thing or the other. But it is precisely to the extent that Herodotus portrays Darius as a "traditional" strategist that he can convey the "otherness" of the Scythian strategy: he had to dress Darius up as a hoplite in order to set the Scythian bowmen galloping. Garlan refers to this passage in Herodotus in a paragraph entitled "On a Few Exceptions that Prove the Rule" (of traditional strategy) and he concludes: "The astonishment and interest manifested by Herodotus with respect to the strategy of Darius's adversaries constitutes glaring proof of the extent to which Pericles' contemporaries had become accustomed to an opposite kind of strategy, which subordinated the survival of the community to the defense of its territory."[74]

That may well be. However, what strikes me most is the apparent incapacity of Herodotus's narrative to accommodate a model comprising three terms: the Greeks, the Persians, and the Scythians. Confronted with Greeks, the Persians are indeed "Persians," that is to say, people who do not know how to fight, anti-hoplites. But faced with the Scythians, they have no thought for anything but a pitched battle, the stake being domination of the territory, and they thus appear as (quasi-)hoplites, that is to say, as "Greeks." From a strategic point of view, the narrative thus encompasses no more than two terms: Greeks and Persians in Greece and, in Scythia, Scythians and Persians, that is, "Greeks." Greeks and anti-hoplites in one context; Scythians and quasi-hoplites in the other. If the Persians become "Greeks" in Scythia, it might be supposed that through a permutation of roles the Scythians might appear as Persians, that is, "anti-hoplites." And it is certainly they who are the bowmen and horsemen and consequently they who are the furthest from hoplite combat. Nevertheless, at no point does Herodotus stress or even suggest that the Scythians do not know how to fight. On the contrary, their strategy is described as a most intelligent invention (*sophotata*);

---

73. Hdt. 4.131–32. Another version of these gifts is recorded by Pherecydes in Jacoby, *FGrH*, 3 F 174: he lists a frog, a bird, an arrow, and a plough.

74. Garlan, *Recherches*, p. 29.

besides, they can hardly be represented as anti-hoplites, since it is they who in the end gain the upper hand and force the Persians to beat a retreat.

How to Fight Without Engaging Battle

If they are neither quasi-hoplites nor anti-hoplites, what *are* these Scythian fighters? That question goes to the roots of their strategy: not to engage in battle but to flee, retreat, hide. When, faced with Xerxes' invasion, the Athenians consult the Pythian oracle, the priestess tells the *theoroi,* to their consternation: "Wretches, why do you delay? leave your homes and the heights of your circular city, flee to the ends of the earth [*es eschata gaies*]."[75] When, returning with suppliant offerings, they consult her once again in the hope of obtaining a less catastrophic reply, she makes it very clear that they should not remain (*menein*), awaiting the impact of the Persian invasion—as the hoplite awaits the clash with the opposing phalanx—but instead withdraw and "turn their backs to the foe,"[76] at least for the time being. The Pythia thus advises the Athenians to adopt a "Scythian" strategy: not to engage in pitched battle, but, rather, to abandon the town and its territory. In this, her second reply, she adds that only a rampart of wood will be *aporthetos* (unravaged, unravageable).[77] How the oracle was interpreted is well known. Some believed it referred to the Acropolis, which used to be fortified by a wooden palisade;[78] they accordingly counseled abandoning the territory and lower town but defending the citadel. Others, notably Themistocles, maintained that it referred to ships and that what was needed was a naval battle; the territory, along with the town, should be abandoned and the city would transfer to its ships—indeed, become its ships.[79] Thus, as compared to hoplite combat where the essential is to "stand firm" (*menein*), the naval combat advised by the Pythia and the guerrilla warfare practiced by

75. Hdt. 7.140.
76. Hdt. 7.141.
77. A city's main claim to glory lay in being in a position to declare its territory to be *aporthetos;* cf. Garlan, *Recherches,* p. 20.
78. Hdt. 7.142.
79. Hdt. 8.61: this is the gist of Themistocles' retort to the Corinthian Adeimantus, who had taxed him with having become an *apolis* person.

the Scythians adopt the same position. Both begin with flight, and the rampart of wood is *aporthetos* just as the Scythians are *aporoi*.

Darius adopts a "traditional" strategy. Perhaps a comparison between Scythian strategy and Periclean strategy during the Peloponnesian War will prove illuminating. It may provide a way of apprehending the "otherness" of the behavior of the Scythians. Pericles' strategy was to avoid pitched battles, to abandon the territory, to defend the town, and to put his trust in the fleet.[80] He declared that the Athenians should as nearly as possible assume the condition of islanders, for an islander was one who "offered the enemy the least hold."[81] So it was always a matter of escaping, of being *aporos*. But the defense of a town clearly had no meaning for the Scythians. It is one thing to abandon the territory in order to defend the town, but if there is no town the very concept of territory loses its meaning. Possessing no town, are not the Scythians in effect also without territory? For them, there are only pasturelands.

As well as flight, the Scythians wherever possible employ surprise strikes against the Persians: rapid operations carried out on horseback just when the Persians are busy collecting their provisions, for instance.[82] With these commando raids, the Scythians may be seen as forerunners of the peltasts of the fourth century and Plato's *Laches* which, in the background, raises the question of the new forms of warfare, indeed mentions the Scythian strategy. Socrates asks Laches, a professional soldier, "What is courage?" Laches replies that the courageous man is "anyone who is willing to stay at his post and face the enemy and does not run away."[83] His definition is based on "a totally socialized concept of military courage which rejects all *techne*."[84] To demolish Laches' definition, Socrates begins by asking him if it is possible to take to flight yet still be courageous. Seeing Laches' confusion, he immediately provides him with an example: "Well, as the Scythians are said to fight, as much fleeing [*pheugontes*] as pursuing [*diokontes*]." Socrates goes on to say that one might also consider Homer's praise of the horses of Aeneas which, according to him, knew "how to pursue and to flee . . . full swiftly

80. Garlan, *Recherches*, pp. 44–65.
81. Thucydides 1.143.
82. Hdt. 4.128.
83. Plato *Laches* 191a–b.
84. P. Vidal-Naquet, "L'Hoplite athénien," *Problèmes de la guerre*, p. 174.

this way and that way." And Aeneas himself is praised as a "master of flight" (*mestora phoboio*). Laches' reply comes promptly: "And very properly too, Socrates; for he was speaking of chariots; and so are you speaking of the mode of the Scythian horsemen. That is the way of their cavalry fighting (*to hippikon*), but with Greek men at arms (*to hoplitikon*) it is as I state it." Thus, Socrates' objection does not affect the definition of courage, since neither this arm nor these people are Greek. Socrates then goes on to mention the tactical retreat of the Lacedaemonians at Plataea, it being of course hard to deny that they were Greek. So the Scythians are certainly known to be people who take to flight yet who pursue at the same time, as "masters of flight": did they perhaps fight in the manner of the Homeric heroes, whose chariots made it possible for them to move swiftly from one spot to another? That may be the implication of the comparison with Aeneas, but in Laches' view their behavior is explained simply by the fact that they are horsemen. The difference in their strategy is accounted for by the difference that separates *to hippokon* from *to hoplitikon*.

Another indirect way of understanding the otherness in the Scythian strategy is suggested by Photius. He notes: "The Eleans call the ephebes *Scythians* and the Spartans call them *Sideunes*."[85] According to Liddell-Scott-Jones, *Sideunes* denotes a boy of fifteen or sixteen years of age. The two terms are clearly not operating on the same level. In one case, the epithet refers to a distant people; in the other, it denotes an age-group. Why are the boys called Scythian? Pelikidis thinks that "the ephebes of Elis who served, as did the Athenian ephebes, in the country's frontier guards, were dressed and armed in the manner of the Scythians" and that this "explains their name."[86] This hypothesis of Pelikidis's is based on Plassart's research on the subject of the bowmen of Athens,[87] in which he tries to show that before 476 the bowmen and mounted bowmen of Athens were in truth Athenians dressed as Scythians and that their role was that of *hyperetai*, auxiliaries or orderlies.

---

85. Photius *Lexikon*, s.v. *sunephebos*: *tous de ephebous Hleioi men Skuthas kalousin, Spartiatai de sideunas*.

86. C. Pelikidis, *Histoire de l'éphébie attique* (Paris, 1962), p. 42.

87. A. Plassart, "Les Archers d'Athènes," *Revue des Etudes Grecques* 26 (1913): 151–213.

In the fifth century, Athens possessed a police force, which was formed in 476 and lasted for less than a century and was composed of Scythian bowmen bought by the city. Ever since the Persian Wars, a body of military bowmen had also existed. Before that, there had been no organized units of bowmen; however, the bow, which had been used in warfare in Attica ever since extremely ancient times, was the particular weapon of a number of Athenian auxiliary troops who served as orderlies to the hoplites, either mounted or on foot. Many of these orderlies, no doubt in imitation of the Ionians, wore the Scythian costume.[88]

If they were really Athenians, why the Scythian costume? It is probably here that Plassart's thesis is the least convincing. "In imitation of the Ionians," he says, and also suggests that it was "the fashion": "One day a few sons of the great families had the whim of adopting the colorful costume and weaponry of the Scythian *hippotoxotai* and, as these became fashionable, the Scythian equipment appears to have become quite widely adopted."[89]

Obviously it would be much more satisfactory if one could show that these young men (Plassart several times mentions their youth) were ephebes and that the Scythian costume was a kind of uniform of the *ephebeia*, However, there is (so far) no evidence to that effect. To make out such a case it would at the very least be necessary to review the whole body of figurative representations,[90] and that is not my intention at this point.[91] If, as Photius claims, the ephebes of Elis were known as "Scythians" and if, in Athens, there were or had been youths (ephebes?) who dressed as Scythians, the question that remains is whether Herodotus's Scythians were in some way regarded as ephebes. What I mean is, is there an image of the *ephebeia* at work, even slightly, in Herodotus's text, or could such an image provide a means for apprehending and gauging the otherness of the Scythians' behavior, in particular, their strategy? We must, however,

88. Ibid., pp. 212–13.

89. Ibid., p. 175.

90. This task has been undertaken by F. Lissarague; see his forthcoming book (Paris, 1988).

91. Similarly, in Hesychius's lexicon, we find *Skuthrax: meirax, ephebos,* and *meirax* means young girl, little girl (for example, in Aristophanes *Thesmophoriazusae* 410, *Ecclesiazusae* 611, *Plutus* 1071–79). Liddell-Scott-Jones notes that later on it also came to refer to a young boy.

proceed with extreme caution, since we know nothing about the *ephebeia* in the fifth century.

The Scythians claim to be youthful: "They say that their nation is the youngest in all the world" (*neotaton*).[92] Now, connection, if not equivalence, between *neotatoi* and ephebes is well known,[93] but I will not go so far as to conclude that the Scythians are a people of ephebes. Calling the ephebes of Elis "Scythians" might also be a way of referring to the ephebes' zone of activity: the ephebe "inhabited the frontier forts";[94] he was the *peripolos*, one who moved around the outside of the city and roamed the *eschatia*, just as the Scythian was the ever-mobile inhabitant of the frontiers of the world.

Finally, the Scythians fight as hunters; for them, combat is a hunt full of cunning ploys and sudden strikes, both attacks timed to coincide with the moment when the Persians are out foraging, and nocturnal attacks as well.[95] Now, cunning, ambushes, and nocturnal combat are all features of the behavior of the ephebe, who is both a pre-hoplite and an anti-hoplite.[96] Contrasted with the Persians who, in Scythia, are represented as being to all intents and purposes equipped as hoplites, the Scythians are certainly anti-hoplites of a kind, but not in the same sense as the Persians in Greece, who are there regarded as anti-hoplites first and foremost because they do not know how to fight. So the former are anti-hoplites because they fight in a cunning fashion, the latter because they "do not know how to fight."

These are no more than pointers; nevertheless, they serve to render the Scythian tactics employed against Darius more plausible. For if the shared knowledge of Herodotus's audience connected (however remotely) the words *ephebe* and *Scythian*, and the images of the ephebe and of the Scythian, this association—even if implicit—must have affected the way their mode of fighting was represented. Let me express it schematically (although, obviously, neither Herodotus nor any of his audience would have formulated it

92. Hdt. 4.3.

93. Pelikidis, *L'Ephébie antique*, pp. 47–49.

94. P. Vidal-Naquet, "Sophocles' *Philoctetes* and the Ephebeia," in *Tragedy and Myth*, p. 175.

95. Hdt. 4.128.

96. P. Vidal-Naquet, "Le Chasseur noir et l'origine de l'éphébie athénienne," *Annales E.S.C.* 5 (1968): 947–64.

like this, if, indeed, they formulated it at all). We are provided with a kind of matrix of intelligibility: they fight like people who would always fight in the manner of ephebes. The reader can see what that means (at any rate, let us suppose that he can), but *always* to fight in the manner of ephebes . . . that is a contradiction in terms, for it is well known that the *ephebeia* was a transitory phase. So this too could be a way for the narrative to convey something about their behavior while setting it at a distance—in short, to emphasize its otherness.

The Scythians' strategic choice, which strangely enough boils down to waging war to the exclusion of everything else but doing so without engaging in battle, is justified, from the narrative's point of view, by the refusal of the neighboring kings to fight alongside them. We have just seen how such a strategy could, implicitly or indirectly, be illuminated by comparisons with the Pythia's directives to the Athenians, Periclean strategy, the questioning of Laches, and the *ephebeia*. But the fundamental explanation for this strategy is the nomadism of the Scythians. In answer to Darius, the "traditional" strategist, Idanthyrsus, the nomad, replies: "this that I have done is no new thing or other than my practice in peace. But as to the reason why I do not straightway fight with you, this too I will tell you. For we Scythians have no towns or planted lands, that we might meet you the sooner in battle, fearing lest the one be taken or the other be wasted."[97] Consequently, "traditional" strategy, whether it involves temporary invasions or *epiteichismos,* has no effect on me.

That is why Darius is so absurd when he claims earth and water as his due, for my earth is wherever I roam, my water is that of all the wells at which I stop to drink. So Idanthyrsus proudly retorts: "Gifts I will send you, not (*anti doron*) earth and water but such as you should rightly receive."[98] Shortly afterward he does indeed send Darius a mouse, a frog, a bird, and five arrows. Darius, still trapped in his own way of thinking in terms of "one thing . . . or the other," clearly fails to understand the play on *anti:* to his mind, these gifts can only represent metaphors for earth and water and must therefore be a symbolic way of expressing submission, "for he reasoned that a mouse is a creature found in the earth and eating the same produce as men, and a frog is a creature of the water and a bird most like to a

97. Hdt. 4.127. But it would be a different matter were the Persians to discover the tombs of the kings, which are the true *omphalos* of Scythia.
98. Hdt. 4.127.

horse; and the arrows,—said he—signified that the Scythians sur-
rendered their fighting power." To make these metaphors coincide
with his own desires certainly involved a certain amount of distortion. Only Gobryas, his father-in-law, realizes that the presents are
no metaphors and on the contrary mean "unless you become birds,
Persians, and fly up into the sky, or mice and hide in the earth, or
frogs and leap into the lakes, you will be shot by these arrows and
never return home."[99] In other words, since you are men, there is for
you no way to escape, no *poros*.

Herodotus himself, speaking in the first person, explicitly draws
out the strategic implications of the nomadic way of life, presenting
what might be termed a theory of nomad warfare: "The Scythian race
has in that matter which of all human affairs is of the greatest import
made the cleverest discovery that we know; I praise not the Scythians
in all respects, but in this greatest matter they have so devised that
none who attacks them can escape, and none can catch them if they
desire not to be found." That gives the refusal to engage in battle
its full strategic force. He goes on to say: "For when men have
no established cities or fortresses but are still house-bearers and
mounted archers, living not only by tilling the soil but by cattle-
rearing and carrying their dwellings on waggons, how should these
not be invincible and unapproachable?"[100]

This constitutes the true basis of the Scythian strategy. The
narrative constraints tend to turn the Scythians into Athenians, so
the words of the Scythian delegates to the assembly of kings are close
enough to those of the Athenians or the "Greeks moved by the best of
sentiments." However, the demands of ethnology, tugging in the
opposite direction, make nomads of them. Herodotus's narrative
purveys both propositions simultaneously: the Scythians are "Athenians," yet at the same time they are quite the opposite, since they
are nomads. Idanthyrsus is no Themistocles, since the Athenians
live in a *polis* while the Scythians know nothing of such a life; that is
the measure of the irreducible distance between them. The truth is
that the Scythians are an *apolis* people by nature.[101] In contrast,
even with Athens captured and Attica occupied, Themistocles in-

---

99. Hdt. 4.132.
100. Hdt. 4.46. Thucydides (2.97.6) repeats this judgment on the military
superiority of the Scythians but does not connect it with their strategy.
101. On *apolis*, cf., for example, Aristotle *Politics*, 1.1.9–10.

sists, in the face of the allegations of the Corinthian Adeimantus, that he is not an *apolis* person. Athens continues to exist as a *polis*, in its ships.

When Xerxes decides to launch his great expedition, Artabanus, his uncle and the *mnemon* of the dynasty, reminds him that he once advised Darius against undertaking his campaign against the Scythians, "who have no cities anywhere to dwell in."[102] Later on, while Xerxes is contemplating his armies at Abydus, the two men return to the subject and Artabanus again puts forward reasons for fear which Xerxes tries hard to counter, pointing out in particular that "those against whom we march are no wandering tribes but tillers of the soil."[103] In the immediate context, the point of this remark is: provisioning will present no problems, for the countryside will provide for our needs; but it also has another implication, to wit: those whom we are attacking are men to whom the notion of territory means something, men over whom one can establish some hold, men with whom it is possible to fight in a pitched battle. Idanthyrsus is certainly no Themistocles, but Themistocles is at least as cunning as Idanthyrsus.

Poros and Aporia: A Story about Losing One's Way

To pass from one space to another involves crossing a river, a waterway, an inlet of the sea, or a desert: in a narrative, the action that dramatizes such a crossing is the building of a bridge. The operator for this crossing is thus the bridge, but it is "a difficult or dangerous operator,"[104] in that it establishes an intercommunication, a *poros* between two spaces with no common border. In the *Histories* it is surely true to say that any crossing by means of a bridge may invariably be read as a transgression. When Darius first informs queen Atossa of his plan, he tells her that he is resolved "to make a bridge from this to the other continent and so lead an army against the Scythians."[105] It is Mandrocles of Samos who is commissioned to

102. Hdt. 7.10.
103. Hdt. 7.50.
104. M. Serres, *La Distribution de quelque chose* (Paris, 1977), p. 200.
105. Hdt. 3.134.

join the two shores of the Hellespont by a bridge.[106] By this means, Darius and his army cross from Asia into Europe; but to reach the Scythians they are obliged to change from one space to another yet again, by crossing the Ister. The Ionians are entrusted with throwing this second bridge across the river.[107] Once the bridge is in place and the river is crossed, Darius orders the bridge to be destroyed, but Coes, the general of the Mytilenaeans, suggests leaving it in place, saying, "Seeing, O King, that you are about to march against a country where you will find neither tilled lands nor inhabited cities, do now suffer this bridge to stand where it is, leaving those who made it to be its guards." The argument may seem a strange one: what can the connection be between nomadism and maintaining the bridge? But of course, in the narrative, this intervention hints at what is to happen later, and Coes goes on to say: "Thus, if we find the Scythians and accomplish our will, we have a way of return; and even if we do not find them, our way back is safe; for fear has never yet been lest we be overcome by the Scythians in the field, but rather lest we should not be able to find them [*eurein*]",[108] for the very reason that they have no towns and no cultivation. In other words— and it is this that makes the episode so interesting—there can be no certainty that the bridge over the Ister will really be a *poros*, or, rather, it is to be feared that it may prove a false *poros* and that the *aporia* of the Scythians will remain unimpaired. In contrast, when Croesus crosses the Halys, he meets the Persians; when Cyrus crosses the Araxes he meets the Massagetae; when Xerxes crosses the Bosphorus, he subjugates the Thracians. Yet when he crosses the Ister he does not gain access to the Scythians; he believes the bridge to be a *poros* but in reality it is not.

The Scythian space is a space of "others," and no mere bridge will gain access there: that is the sense of Coes's words and also of Artabanus's remarks to his brother Darius, in which he points out the *aporia* of the Scythians.[109] They are remarks which he is later to repeat to Xerxes, his nephew, when the latter too decides to cross over into Europe.[110] That is also what is conveyed by Herodotus himself when he sketches out his theory of nomadic warfare: since

106. Hdt. 4.87–88.
107. Hdt. 4.89. Note that, nearly always, any engineering is Greek.
108. Hdt. 4.97.
109. Hdt. 4.83.
110. Hdt. 7.10.

they are *amachoi*, it is impossible to fight with such people, who have neither town nor walls nor agriculture, for they are inaccessible (*aporoi*): no *poros* leads to them.[111] So Scythia is a space of "others," and the mark of its otherness is its nomadism.

Not only is Scythia a space of "others;" it is also an "other" space, and the Ister marks the line between "this side" and "beyond," as the Persians are soon to find out. Once they have crossed the bridge, they enter a different kind of space the manner of whose organization totally baffles them, a strange world where, for them, there are no certain directions or reference points. When they find the Scythians, all they can do is "follow in their tracks" (*stibon*), coming to a halt if they lose the trail. It is therefore left to the Scythians, if and only if they so desire, to create a *poros* that will lead to them, thereby forcing the Persians to become hounds in a hunt. Furthermore, even as he pursues them Darius is incapable of telling in which direction he is going. Sticking to their plan, the Scythians in effect go straight ahead, but when Darius gets a message to Idanthyrsus, he reproaches him for his "wanderings" (*plane*).[112] To the Persians, who do not know the way, there seems to be no open route, while for the Scythians, who know their own space, there are not only paths to follow but also "shortcuts,"[113] a whole network of routes of communication. Thus, when the Persians, finally convinced of the *aporia*, decide to beat a retreat, they are incapable of orienting themselves, of finding their way, and are reduced to retracing their own tracks (*stibon*), those left by them on their outward journey.

It is at this point in the narrative that, through a reversal, the bridge truly at last becomes a *poros*:[114] not a path leading to the Scythians, but one that enables the Persians to escape from them. Without it, Darius would never have found a way out, for the Scythian space is one from which there is no return. That is what is explicitly stated by Herodotus the theorist of nomadism (in 4.46, as cited above): "in this greatest matter they have so devised that *none*

---

111. Hdt. 4.46.

112. Hdt. 4.120, 122, 135. In hunting terminology, *plane* is used to denote that the paths taken by the hare are not straight but interweaving; the word also denotes a hound's losing track of its quarry. *Plane* also appears to be associated with the geometrical idea of describing a circle.

113. Hdt. 4.136. Xenophon *Cyn.* 5.17: hares know the "shortcuts in a path" (*suntoma tes hodou*).

114. Hdt. 4.140, 7.10, where the bridge is specifically referred to as a *poros*.

who attacks them can escape [*apophugein*] and none can catch them if they desire not to be found." Such is the message of the gifts Idanthyrsus sends to Darius.[115] They are sent at the point when Darius, tired of vainly giving pursuit, has no idea what to do, when he is in "the midst of *aporiai* [*en aporiesi eicheto*]," and they appear as an answer to those *aporiai*. They are brought by the Scythian herald, who vouchsafes not a word of explanation, even when he is pressed for the meaning (*noon*) of these objects. Gobryas is the only one to interpret them correctly: offered to Darius when he is in the midst of *aporiai*, as they are, they signify that there is indeed no *poros* for him.[116]

Nevertheless, Darius does manage to escape. First, because the Scythians in pursuit miss him. By way of explanation for this surprising turn of events, the narrative introduces a reversal. The opacity of this Scythian space from which Darius has hitherto suffered now operates in his favor, while the Scythians' familiarity with their own space proves a disadvantage to them. They seek Darius where he is not; while he is painfully retracing his steps, the Scythians take a shortcut and thus reach the bridge before him.[117] They then turn back, looking for him wherever there is a possibility for him to find provisions and water, whereas Darius is, needless to say, quite incapable of devising such an itinerary. The bridge, which was nothing but a false *poros* at the beginning of the expedition, now becomes a true *poros* at the very moment when it is falsely purported to be cut. It is even because the Ionians pretend to cut it that it is able to play its role as an escape route out of Scythian territory.[118] The interplay between *poros* and *aporia* thus operates as a way of indicating a frontier: throwing a bridge across the Ister is not enough to reach the Scythians, because they inhabit a space that is "other."

115. Hdt. 4.127. "Idanthyrsus declares, 'Gifts I will send you, not [*anti*] earth and water, but such as you should rightly receive; and as for your boast that you are my master, to hell with you'" Idanthyrsus's speech ends with: "That is what the Scythians have to say to you [*he apo Skutheon rhesis*]," which is a proverbial expression (cf. Leutsch and Schneidewin, *Corpus Paroemiographorum graecorum*, vol. 1, p. 250), which Herodotus brings into his narration.

116. Another example of a space from which there is no return is the space of Libya: those who go there do so despite themselves (Hdt. 4.179) and those who wish to reach it lose their way in the wilderness, just as Cambyses' army did (3.26).

117. Hdt. 4.136.

118. Hdt. 4.139.

Three

Frontiers and Otherness

The question of otherness raises that of frontiers. Where does the break dividing the same from the other occur? The Scythians are nomads and, spatially, Scythia is an "other" space to the extent that it is an inaccessible place. As Darius learns to his cost, throwing a bridge across the Ister does not suffice for truly entering Scythia. He exhausts himself in this mockery of a hunt and emerges from it defeated, without ever even setting eyes upon his adversaries. However, this "otherness"—that is to say, the apparent absence of any fixed frontier—cannot be dissociated from the narrative of the war itself. It can only be understood in the context of the protagonists in this narrative. In one sense, the Ister certainly is a frontier (the Scythians do not seek to cross it, and when Darius crosses back over it in his retreat, he is saved). In another sense, though, it is not, for it does not provide "access" to the Scythians, whose *aporia* remains unaffected by it. Thus, even from a purely spatial point of view, the frontier may be understood in a number of ways.

Two other episodes in the Scythian *logos* make it possible to pose the question of the frontier, this time not in a geographical but in a cultural sense: first, the misadventures of Anacharsis and Scyles, both Scythians of high nobility; second, the story of Salmoxis, a figure of uncertain identity. The two texts offer two opposing approaches to the frontier theme. Anacharsis and Scyles in effect "forget" the frontier between the Greeks and the Scythians and suffer the consequences. In the Salmoxis episode, on the other

61

hand, the Black Sea Greeks attempt, by every conceivable means, to make it impossible to "forget" the distance which separates them from the Getae.[1]

The question of a cultural frontier leads to the organization of divine space: is the world of the gods affected by geographical and human frontiers? Also, these two texts afford us a glimpse of the narrator in operation. In the story of Anacharsis and Scyles he makes the addressee think that he is seeing the Greeks through the eyes of the Scythians, in the story of Salmoxis, in contrast, he shows the Getae as seen by the Black Sea Greeks. These two stories thus relate respectively to either side of that imaginary line traced by 'the frontier: in the first, the Greeks are seen through the eyes of "others," in the second, the "others" are seen through the eyes of the Greeks.

Anacharsis and Scyles:
Circumscribing a Transgression

The stories of Anacharsis and Scyles should be read together, and in relation to one another.[2] The destinies of Anacharsis and Scyles were "analogous" (*paraplesia*). That similarity is the justification for considering them together even if they are chronologically separated, Scyles having "lived long after Anacharsis." Herodotus presents them as two examples illustrating a rule of Scythian behavior and his narrative, which begins by setting out the rule governing such behavior, ends by calling it to mind: "As regards foreign usages,

1. Even if Herodotus considers Salmoxis as one of the Getae, rather than Scythian, and the Getae are Thracian, I think it is legitimate to consider as a single group the chapters devoted to Anacharsis and Scyles and those concerning Salmoxis. In the first place, the narrative of Salmoxis not only belongs to the Scythian *logos* but is included in the account of Darius's expedition against the Scythians. Having crossed the Bosphorus, the Persian army advances, making subject all the peoples it encounters on its march, and in particular the Getae, who are the only ones to put up a resistance, precisely on account of Salmoxis. On the whole, the *logos* wins out over the *ethnos*. Besides, several later texts (*Suda*, s.v. *Lucian*) declare Salmoxis to be Scythian. Moreover, the two episodes (that of Anacharsis and Scyles and that of Salmoxis) belong together insofar as they both raise the question of frontiers.

2. Herodotus 4.76–80. The episode is an example of ring composition. Cf. I. Beck, *Die Ringkomposition bei Herodot und ihre Bedeutung für die Beweistechnik* (New York, 1971).

the Scythians (as others) are remarkably loath to practise those of any other country, particularly those of Greece."[3] That is the lesson the addressee is specifically invited to learn from the two episodes.

Taking as my starting point this manifest organization of the text, I should like to suggest a hypothesis concerning the logic of this *logos:* are not the different codes which operate in these two stories to some extent homologous?

First, who are the protagonists in these two stories? In the story of Anacharsis, the cast, in order of appearance, consists of Anacharsis, the Cyzicenes (who are engaged in celebrating a festival), a Scythian (who denounces Anacharsis's behavior to the king), and, finally, King Saulius, who, Herodotus tells us, is in reality Anacharsis's own brother (it is he who kills Anacharsis). To this list we should add a divine personage: the Mother of the Gods. We may already at this point note that, like Dionysus in the other episode, the Mother of the Gods is simply the mute object of a cult: the narrative does not tell us whether or not these deities appreciate the cult of their new devotees.

Next, the story of Scyles: it involves Scyles, the Borysthenites (who worship Dionysus Bacchus), one particular Borysthenite (who reports the whole affair to the Scythians), the principal Scythians, "who saw him among the revellers . . . and told [*esemainon*]" the other Scythians about it, and, finally, Octamasades, Scyles's brother, whom the Scythians adopt as their leader; he it is who later puts Scyles to death.

Second, who are Anacharsis and Scyles? Herodotus is at pains to trace the genealogy of Anacharsis and produces a witness to bear him out: Tymnes, one who was in the confidence of the late King Ariapeithes.[4] Anacharsis is the paternal uncle of Idanthyrsus; Idanthyrsus's father is Saulius, so Anacharsis and Saulius are brothers.[5]

---

3. Hdt. 4.76. The text says "as others" (*kai houtoi*). As Legrand points out in a note to 4.76 of his translation, this *houtoi* probably refers to the Egyptians, of whom it is said, "The Egyptians shun the use of Greek customs and (to speak generally) the customs of other men whatever" (2.91). This piece of information in the text indicates, yet again, the links between the Egyptians and the Scythians, who are in a way paired.

4. Hdt. 4.76.

5. This is the first way that Herodotus tackles the genealogy of Anacharsis. Then, as if to substantiate it from a different angle, he approaches the question again: Anacharsis is the son of Gnurus. All that remains to be done is to show that Saulius is also a son of Gnurus, but Herodotus does not do so at this point.

The important point is that Anacharsis belongs to the Scythian royal family. His biography is given in a most summary fashion: "Anachar-sis, having seen much of the world [*gen pollen*] in his travels and given many proofs of his wisdom [*sophien pollen*], was comiong back to the Scythian country [*ethea*]."[6] It was also said of Solon that he had seen much of the world (*gen pollen*) and had shown much *sophie*.[7] In Herodotus, Anacharsis is not included among the Sages and is not related directly to Solon, but both were men for whom travel and *sophie* were linked.

Scyles is not just a member of the royal family, but is the king himself. He is, however, a bastard, one of his father's many illegiti-mate children. He is nevertheless different from his brothers, in that his mother was Greek; she was not native-born (*epichories*) but came from Istria,[8] and she "taught him to speak and read Greek."[9] Scyles is thus a double personage, half Scythian, half Greek; he is *diglossos*. When his father is assassinated, the kingdom passes to him, as does his father's wife. But Herodotus does not tell us how he came by the throne or how he qualified for the title despite the fact that his father had at least one legitimate son, Oricus;[10] no more did he, earlier, explain why Anacharsis did *not* obtain the throne, which instead passed to his brother.

A comparison between these two "biographies" enables us to make an observation about the logic of the narrative: the travels of Anacharsis and the bilingualism of Scyles occupy parallel structural positions in the two narratives and also serve the same function in their development. To travel and to be bilingual come down to the same thing; both are dangerous, for they lead to forgetting the frontier and thus to transgression.[11]

How do Anacharsis and Scyles move from one place to another?

6. For Herodotus the geographer, the earth is a continuous space and Anachar-sis has traveled through much of it. His fault is, precisely, to have forgotten that some frontiers cannot be crossed.

7. Hdt. 1.130.

8. Hdt. 4.78.

9. Ibid.

10. Ibid.

11. Confirmation of this equivalence is to be found in the tradition relating to Anacharsis. Diogenes Laertius (1.101) gives him a Greek mother and makes him bilingual, as if this element borrowed from the biography of Scyles could also "be attached" to him and as if it were necessary to reinforce his "traveling," which, on its own, did not suffice to set him apart.

What spaces do they cross? In the case of Scyles, the schema is quite simple: he moves to and fro between the *ethea* of the Scythians (the word denotes an animal's lair, one's habitual domicile) and the town of the Borysthenites, namely, Olbia. He leaves the Scythian space, a space more animal than human, where he feels ill at ease (he detests the Scythian life-style) and sets off for the town, but the narrative specifies that he leaves his train on the outskirts (*toi proasteioi*),[12] in that intermediary zone outside the domain of *ethea* but not yet in that of the *astu*. It is as if it were impossible for the Scythians to progress any further, for *they* are not bilingual. The narrative explicitly notes that Scyles, now on his own, then passes through the walls, which are the precise demarcation of this division in the spatial fabric, drawing the line between "this side" and "beyond." "Beyond," once the intermediary zone of the outskirts is crossed, is the Scythian space, the open range; "this side," once the door is closed (for the Scythians cannot even see what goes on within) is a Greek space, the space of the town. At the end of a month or more, Scyles makes the same journey in the opposite direction, with the same pauses.

But "as it had to be that evil should befall him,"[13] the story now becomes a narrative of his last journey of all. He gets back to the Scythian *ethea* but the Scythians, having seen what they were not supposed to see, rise up against him, whereupon he flees to Thrace. Because of what he has done, the Scythian space is now forbidden to him. The Scythians assemble on the banks of the Ister, ready for battle, and the Thracians do likewise, massing on the opposite bank. The Ister, then, clearly represents a frontier between the Scythians and the Thracians.[14] The two kings make a deal: "Return my brother to me and I will return yours." As soon as Scyles has crossed back over the Ister, he is executed. The text even specifies "on the spot," on that side of the river.[15] He can set foot in the Scythian space only to be met with death. These are the stages of Scyles' last voyage.

Anacharsis leaves the Scythian space altogether. After a long absence, he travels back to the *ethea* of the Scythians.[16] When he puts in to Cyzicus, the Milesian colony, he is still in Greek space;

12. Hdt. 4.78.
13. Hdt. 4.79.
14. On the Ister as a frontier, see above, p. 58.
15. Hdt. 4.80.
16. Hdt. 4.76.

then he lands in Scythia and immediately plunges into the wooded
region known as the Hylaia. A Scythian sees him and informs the
king, who, upon seeing the scene, immediately kills Anacharsis. In
this second case, the spatial schema is very simple: Anacharsis passes
from a Greek space into the Scythian space. Yet I think that two
questions are posed: (1) Is the Hylaia a completely Scythian space or
is it a particular, even marginal, part of that space? (2) What is the
position of the town of Cyzicus in relation to the "Greek space"? Is it a
particular part of that space? These are questions which cannot be
answered simply by examining the journeys from a geographical
point of view. The only possible way to tackle them is to take account
of the semantic content and the cultural codes.

Let us consider the action of the two stories: the narrative
concerning Anacharsis is much more starkly told than the other.
Having seen the Cyzicenes celebrating the Mother of the Gods,
Anacharsis vows that if he ever reaches home he will devote a similar
ceremony to her. On his return, he immediately fulfills his vow, as
piety demands. Yet Saulius kills him with an arrow.

The story of Scyles is more elaborate, but three principal points
can be noted. Each time Scyles returns to the town, his first action is
to shed the Scythian "robe" (*stole*) and adopt Greek clothing (*esthes*);
more generally, he adopts the Greek style of life (*diaite Hellenike*) in
every respect. The second point concerns his relations with women:
he receives the kingship and also his father's wife, Opoia, but he also
marries another woman, whom he installs in the house he has had
built in Olbia. There is a problem here: Opoia is described as *aste*,[17]
which the translators and commentators render as "native"; in other
words, according to them she is Scythian. The second wife is called
epichorie, that is to say, "local," but the translators and commentators explain that we should understand that she was born in the town
and so is Greek. So Scyles appears simply to have acted as his father
did before him. That is to say that the translators are here reversing
the usual meaning of these words and that, at the limit, their
meanings are interchangeable: *epichorie* means "native" but also "of
the town," and *aste* means "of the town" but also "native." All the
same, perhaps we should recall the beginning of chapter 78, which
stated that Scyles was born from a woman of Istria and definitely not

17. Hdt. 4.78.

from a native (*oudamos epichorie*), the opposition between the town and the country in this case being indicated by precisely the use of *epichorie*.

Might it not be that Scyles' actions are more complex than is assumed? He marries Opoia, a woman from the town but who lives in Scythian space;[18] then, in Olbia, he marries a woman who is *epichorie*, a native, but he has her live in the Greek space or, rather, within the enclosure of his vast residence, whose precise position is uncertain; it is not known whether it fully belongs to the spatial fabric of the city. The principle behind his actions might thus be confusion—to muddle up both people and spaces.

Finally, consider the religious domain: he practices the Greek religion and wishes to become an initiate (*telesthenai*) of Dionysus Bacchus. As in the case of Anacharsis, Scyles's piety occasions his death, for what is piety for the Greeks is the height of impiety for the Scythians.

From a logical point of view, then, the two accounts establish an equivalence between traveling and being bilingual. From that point on, the number and complexity of the sequences may vary but they all speak of confusion and its attendant dangers, above all in the religious domain; only death can put a stop to such disorder. We must now examine the two stories again, this time imbuing the various sequences with their full semantic content and tracing out the cultural codes that provide their context and are at the same time conveyed by them.

What is the Hylaia? In Greek the word means "wooded" but also "wild"; as is to be expected, the forest belongs to the border spaces and thus to wildness. But what is the situation in Scythia? According to Herodotus, the Hylaia is situated along the shore of the sea, bordered by the Borysthenites to the west and the territory of the "farming Scythians" to the north.[19] Its distinctive feature is that, in contrast to the rest of the country, it is covered with trees and, furthermore, trees of every kind. And it has another peculiarity: it was in the Hylaia that Heracles encountered the Mixoparthenos with whom he was then united; according to the Black Sea Greeks, the Scythian people were the issue of that union. These observations

18. Ibid. Would it be fanciful to detect a play of words in her name: *Opoia*, i.e., what, or of what sort, is my identity?

19. Hdt. 4.9, 18, 54, 55, 76.

provide justification for assigning the Hylaia a rather special place within the Scythian space; they do not, however, tell us enough to determine the meaning of its peculiarity with any precision.

When later texts refer to the Hylaia, they mention that it is thickly wooded. Pomponius Mela describes it as a place "where the largest forests in this country lie situated";[20] Valerius Flaccus adds, "Nowhere do the forests produce taller or bushier trees; arrows lose their momentum and fall back before reaching the treetops."[21] All the same, Saulius's arrow there found its mark and killed Anacharsis.

Just as, once its doors are closed, Olbia offers Scyles shelter to do things that the Scythians must not behold, similarly the Hylaia, into which Anacharsis plunges (*katadus*),[22] provides him with a hidden place where he can celebrate a cult which the Scythians refuse to recognize. But as well as the protection which this dense forest offers, has it not another aspect that makes it a suitable place for a celebration in honor of the Mother of the Gods? It is the only wooded region in the country; and the cult of the Mother is associated with trees and plants. Tradition has it that the Argonauts founded the cult of the Mother, at Cyzicus.[23] To atone for the murder of the hero Cyzicus, the Argonauts, on Mount Dindymus "under the shelter of some tall oaks, the highest trees that grow," established a sanctuary of the goddess, and Argus himself carved from a vine root the *xoanon* revered ever since that time.[24] It thus seems that within the Scythian space the Hylaia was the most suitable place for a "transplantation" of the cult of the Mother of the Gods.

In the story of Scyles the spatial pattern is simple: Olbia lies to one side, Scythia to the other. But why, in Anacharsis's case, is there first Cyzicus and then the Hylaia? Why both? Would it not be perfectly plausible for a Scythian to surprise Anacharsis in Cyzicus, engaged with the Cyzicenes (like Scyles with the Borysthenites) in celebrating a *pannuchis*, and subsequently to have him assassinated as he

20. Pomponius Mela 2.5.

21. Valerius Flaccus *Argonautica* 6.76.

22. Hdt. 4.76.

23. Neanthes of Cyzicus in Jacoby, *FGrH*, 84 F 39: "The Argonauts, journeying toward the Phasis, set up a temple dedicated to the Mother-Goddess of Mount Ida in the region of Cyzicus."

24. Apollonius Rhodius 1.1053–1152. On the coins of Heirapolis Castabala, Cybele is associated with the pine tree.

lands in Scythia? That is not necessarily a foolish question. Nevertheless, it seems to have been impossible for the narrative to adopt that story line: the distance separating Cyzicus from Scythia is too great, too much sea lies between them. At Cyzicus, Anacharsis "vowed . . . to this same Mother of Gods that, if he returned to his own country safe and sound, he would sacrifice [*thusein*] to her . . . and establish a nightly rite of worship [*pannuchis*]."[25] Such prayers would have been perfectly reasonable, since Cybele was also a "lady of the sea."[26] She was called upon in time of storm,[27] sailors made her *ex voto* offerings,[28] and "on the headlands" of the Mysian coastline her temples stood "like lighthouses of salvation."

From a spatial point of view we may thus regard the Hylaia as the double of Cyzicus in Scythian territory, the difference being that here Anacharsis no longer has the right to worship the Mother; his piety bcomes impiety. The comparison between Cyzicus and the Hylaia thus reinforces the latter spot's exceptional character, noted above: it is Scythian territory but it is also something else. Olbia, however, does lie outside the Scythian space, and the town walls symbolize that extraterritoriality. These walls block the view and conceal what is going on inside them, but they are not altogether beyond the Scythian territory: spying Scythian eyes can always look in from atop the walls. Through the metaphor of looking, the narrative conveys the spatial ambiguity of the Hylaia and Olbia: even when you are screened by the forest or the fortifications, a look, whether a chance one or one with intent to harm, may at any time discover you.

One more relationship should be considered: having posed the questions of the respective positions of Cyzicus and the Hylaia, and of Olbia in relation to the space of Scythia, we must examine that of the relation of Cyzicus and Olbia to the space of Greece. It is a question which, in truth, it is not possible to answer for the moment; but both were colonial towns. For Herodotus, Olbia is an "emporium" inhabited by "Greeks";[29] more specifically, the Borysthen-

---

25. Hdt. 4.76.

26. H. Graillot, *Le Culte de Cybèle* (Paris, 1912), p. 200.

27. Diodorus 3.55.8: Myrina the Amazon invokes her. Apollonius Rhodius 1.1098–99.

28. *Bulletin de Correspondance Hellénique* 23 (1899): 591.

29. Hdt. 4.2.

ites "say that they are Milesians."[30] In other words, Borysthenes is a
colony of Miletus and between the two cities exists an agreement of
reciprocal political rights. Cyzicus is also a colony of Miletus, and a
similar agreement probably existed between these two cities.[31] As to
the question of whether the Cyzicenes and the Borysthenites were
considered marginal peoples within the space of Greece, not on a
geographical level of course but from the point of view of the shared
knowledge, of the Greeks, there is so far no evidence on which to
base a reply.

What is the position of the Mother of the Gods and of Dionysus,
on the one hand in relation to the space of Scythia and, on the other,
in relation to the space of Greece? That is the next question. It boils
down to asking what it was that Anacharsis and Scyles did wrong.
How did they contravene the Scythian cultural codes (as conveyed to
us through Herodotus's narrative, of course)? In relation to the space
of Greece that means, why did they choose the Mother and Dionysus in preference to, for example, Apollo or Hera? So the
question to which these few chapters of the *Histories* point is that of
the place occupied by the Mother and Dionysus within the Greek
pantheon. Why are these two deities chosen by two non-Greeks and
why are they regarded by the Scythians as the symbols of Greekness?

First, though, let us be clear as to the voices making themselves
heard. The text is presented as a narrative (as is indicated in
particular by the use of the aorist, which serves to exemplify a
general rule expressed in the intemporality of the present tense).
This accounts for the dearth of indicators as to who is speaking:[32] in a
sense, it is the general rule itself speaking, and speaking of itself; but
at the same time it is the voice of destiny, a voice that belongs to
nobody, which nobody, not even the gods, can elude. The text

30. Hdt. 4.78.

31. On relations between Miletus, the metropolis, and its colonies Cyzicus and
Olbia, cf. F. Bilabel, *Philologus Supplement* 14, 1 (1920): pp. 46, 70, 120, 140. The
article by B. Bravo, "Une Lettre de plomb de Berezan: Colonisation et modes de
contact dans le Pont," *Dialogues d'Histoire Ancienne* (1974): 111–87, contains a wealth
of information on Olbia. See A. Wasowicz, *Olbia Pontique et son territoire* (Paris,
1975).

32. Narration (or narrative) in the sense in which it is defined by E. Benveniste,
Problems in General Linguistics (Coral Gables, 1971).

expresses this brilliantly at the end of the tragic story of Anacharsis: this man was destroyed, as has been recounted above (*hosper proteron eirethe*) and this impersonal speaker in effect embodies indestructible destiny. Or, again, this time in the Scyles story, when "it *had to be* that evil should befall him [*epei te de edei hoi kakos genesthai*]."[33] The no more than implied reference to the tragic code is thus a way for the text to suggest that to ignore a frontier is every bit as unreasonable as to seek to elude destiny.

All the same, the Herodotean "I" intervenes at two points. First, in chapter 76, to explain that Anacharsis was killed by his brother: "according to what I heard from Tymnes [*ekousa*], the deputy for Ariapeithes." This important information establishes a further connection between the destinies of Anacharsis and Scyles. It should be noted that to express the conclusion of the explanation, the narrator reverts to the third person and to the present tense ("*isto*," "he should know" that it was his own brother who slew him). This switch to intemporality perfectly conveys the idea that the result of what has been explained is hereby established definitively and, as an impersonal statement, may well resound even as far afield as the underworld.[34]

On the second occasion, Herodotus intervenes to report the *logos* of the Peloponnesians. Anacharsis is said to have been sent off on a mission by the king of the Scythians, to "learn the ways of Greece [*tes Hellados mathetes*];"[35] on his return to his own country, he is supposed to have declared that of all the Greeks only the Lacedaemonians "spoke and listened with discretion." Quite clearly, this *logos* is completely adventitious: it does not illustrate the general rule but on the contrary, contradicts it. Far from detesting the foreign *nomoi,* the Scythians seek to know them; and the figure of Anacharsis is simply used by the Lacedaemonians to make the point that they are superior to the rest of the Greeks, who are represented

33. Hdt. 4.79.

34. The fact that the murder of Anacharsis is committed by his brother makes it eminently "tragic." At the level of the action, equally, this constitutes a reference to the code of tragedy.

35. Hdt. 4.77. This is the first time that Anacharsis is represented as having set out to learn from the Greeks, and it is worth noting that Herodotus does not himself claim to vouch for this version of the adventures of Anacharsis.

as drudges devoid of talent. Having mentioned this tradition, Herodotus dismisses it as a fiction devised (*peplastai*) in Greece, by
Greeks, as a means of scoring points in their own Greek quarrels.

As well as the voice of the Peloponnesians, Herodotus records that
of the Scythians: "they say they have no knowledge of Anacharsis; this
is because he left his country for Greece and followed the customs of
strangers."[36] His error is mentioned again, in virtually identical
terms, at the beginning of chapter 78: *dia xenika te nomaia kai
Hellenikas homilias*, which could apply equally to Scyles. This,
then, is the explicit fault that these two figures commit.

To put it more precisely, it can be shown that both contravene the
Scythian cultural codes. The list of deities in the Scythian pantheon
includes neither Dionysus nor the Mother of the Gods. They have no
place there, even under other names.[37] We may be sure that were that
not the case, Herodotus would have been at pains to give the
translation. Furthermore, a basic rule of the Scythian religion is to
make no use of statues, altars, or temples except those dedicated to
Ares.[38] Now, how does Anacharsis celebrate his ritual in honor of the
Mother? He sounds a tambourine but also wears around his neck the
agalmata of the goddess. As for Scyles, as soon as he has entered
Olbia he offers up sacrifices "in accordance with the customs of the
Greeks," visiting temples and sacrificing upon altars.

In the case of Scyles, there is also the problem of initiation. It
appears that so long as he contented himself with visiting Olbia and
living there in the Greek fashion, the Scythians tolerated his transgression, which hardly amounted to more than his bilingualism.
When he departed from Olbia and dressed once again in the
Scythian costume to return to the *ethea* of the Scythians, that was
the end of it: there was no confusion, no "overlapping" of the *nomoi*
of one space onto the other. But initiation seems to have upset this
clear division. Why? Precisely because initiation makes a lasting,
irreversible change of status; it is meaningful only in the context
of a separation established between a "before" and an "after." So even
if Scyles readopts the Scythian costume as usual at the end of his

36. Hdt. 4.76.
37. Hdt. 4.59.
38. Ibid.; cf. below, pp. 188ff.

visit, he remains an initiate of Dionysus Bacchus for all that. The Scythians cannot tolerate that: it is an "overlapping" and thus must be punished.[39]

On the "Greek side," the solemnity of this initiation is indicated, in the narrative, by the intervention of the gods. To put it more clearly: the text appears to purvey two opposed points of view at the same time. On the one hand, this initiation is simply "the occasion, the pretext"[40] for punishing Scyles, for whom "it had to be that evil should befall him" in any case; on the other, it is something solemn, since immediately before it the god sends an "extremely impressive omen [*phasma megiston*]." However, this opposition is resolved to the extent that the two expressions do not operate on the same level: the first is an interruption arranged by the narrator, made by the anonymous voice of destiny and tragedy; the second is an assertion, within the narrative, of the importance of the initiation.

In Olbia, Scyles has had himself built a "great and costly" house surrounded by a wall of "sphinxes and griffons wrought in white marble."[41] There is something inappropriate and exaggerated about this mansion: it is more barbarian than Greek. The griffons, which appear to guard it, are creatures from the edges of the world. According to some, they are "the guardians of gold," which live between the Arimaspians and the Hyperboreans.[42] By erecting this enclosure, Scyles establishes his own difference within the city. And what is the omen that "the god," that is to say, Zeus, is about to send? It is a thunderbolt, which will strike the enclosure and reduce it to ashes.[43] What is Zeus trying to tell Scyles at the very moment when he is about to become initiated? Just as the thunderbolt, by destroy-

---

39. It seems hardly necessary to point out that this implicit logic of Scythian behavior refers the reader to the Greek world-view. It does, however, provide information about the status of this initiation.

40. Hdt. 4.79. The theme of destruction may be associated here with those of corruption and waywardness; the ambiguity increases the impact of the polysemy of this text.

41. Ibid. The use of the expression "which I have just mentioned" (which Herodotus has clearly borrowed) to refer to this house suggests that it must have been one of the interesting sights of Olbia.

42. Hdt. 3.116, 4.13, 27, 29.

43. Hdt. 4.79: *es tauten* seems to me to refer to the surrounding walls rather than the house itself.

ing this wall, does away with the separation between the two spaces, so the initiation, for which he is preparing himself, in a sense abolishes the distance between Greek space and Scythian space; and this transgression of one space upon another is a serious matter. But, needless to say, Scyles is incapable of fathoming the meaning of the omen and so goes ahead with the ceremony, which is to lead to his death.

Herodotus is at pains to describe the circumstances of the death in some detail. We have noticed the importance he attached in his narrative to establishing and recording the fact that Anacharsis was killed by his own brother, Saulius. The introduction of these two brothers is easily explained.[44] They are the closest relatives to Anacharsis and Scyles respectively, and they are also their doubles. But these are the doubles that represent the good side. In contrast to their brothers, they remained totally faithful to the Scythian *nomoi,* and it is consequently they who are the most appalled by the transgression. They are without doubt the best qualified to punish and eliminate the guilty ones, to whom the Scythian soil is henceforth forbidden ground.[45] Not content simply to execute them, the Scythians annihilate their very memory; they are wiped out, have never so much as existed, "and now the Scythians, if they are asked about Anacharsis, say they have no knowledge of him."[46]

Anacharsis and Scyles choose to honor two deities on whose account they meet their deaths: the Mother of the Gods, and Dionysus. Why this particular choice? Why those deities rather than any others? To the objection that the question is a pointless one since that was the choice the narrative made, I would suggest that it is worth attempting to understand what the Mother of the Gods and Dionysus represent in the *Histories* and in the fifth century; to put it in a more precise and unpretentious way, let me suggest that the Mother of the Gods and Dionysus appear in the very place where a number of cultural codes intersect and that Herodotus's narrative

44. The fact that in Scyles's case he is only a half-brother is not significant.

45. Ambushed by his brother, Anacharsis is shot with a bow and arrow, like a hunted animal, whereas Scyles is beheaded. Note that the punishment suffered by Scyles is that inflicted on perjurers (4.60), since perjury is a threat to the royal hearth.

46. Hdt. 4.76.

may enable us to formulate a number of hypotheses on the topography of that place.

Cyzicus and Olbia are situated on the very edges of the Greek space. Might we postulate a homology here and suggest that the same might be said of the Mother of the Gods and Dionysus?

The Mother is referred to as such only here, in this chapter of the *Histories:* even if we are told nothing more about her position, she is thus certainly linked with Cyzicus.[47] If, on the other hand, we accept an equivalence between the Mother of the Gods and the goddess of Mount Dindymus, it should be pointed out that she is also mentioned once by that name.[48] And if we also recognize, as the tradition does, the equivalence between the Mother of the Gods and Kybebe or Cybele, we must note that she is also mentioned in Book 5. There Herodotus tells us that the Ionians burned down Sardis and, in particular, "the temple of Kybebe, the goddess of that country [*epichories theou*]."[49] This "native goddess" belongs to the political space of Persia, "which burning the Persians afterwards made their pretext for burning the temples of Greece."[50] In the narrrative of the war, Cybele falls on the side of the Persians and is therefore one of the deities "who hold Persia for their allotted realm," to whom Xerxes prays before crossing the Hellespont.[51]

Finally, Cybele is one of only three gods for whom Herodotus suggests no equivalent "in the Greek language": in Herodotus's "dictionary" no translation is supplied for the name Kybebe.[52] In short, her only point of anchorage within the space of Greece is Cyzicus, and the only Greeks who devote a cult to her are the Cyzicenes.

47. On Cybele and Cyzicus, cf. W. Hasluck, *Cyzicus* (Cambridge, 1910). It is worth noting that Herodotus does not speak of a cult, an "initiation," or orgies in this connection. He mentions a festival (*orte*), a sacrifice (*thusein*), and a nocturnal watch (*pannuchis*); the word *pannuchis* is also to be found elsewhere meaning a vigil in honor of the Mother, in particular in Euripides *Helen* 1365.

48. Hdt. 1.80.

49. Hdt. 5.102.

50. Ibid. This reasoning is echoed at 6.101, when the Persians capture Eretria: the sanctuaries are burned down "in revenge for the temples that were burned at Sardis, . . . according to Darius's command."

51. Hdt. 7.53.

52. The other two are Pleisthorus (9.119) and Salmoxis (4.64).

Dionysus is much more widely known and figures in numerous pantheons. Which peoples, in the *Histories*, devote a cult to him? He is worshiped by the Ethiopians.[53] Elsewhere, it is stated that for the long-lived Ethiopians "and also those who dwell about the holy Nysa," "Dionysus is the god of their festivals [*anagousi tas hortas*]."[54] Apart from Ourania, he is the only god whose existence is recognized by the Arabs,[55] who call him Orotalt. Egypt is noted for his presence: if Osiris is translated "into the Greek language," he becomes Dionysus.[56] Moving from the south to the north, Dionysus is to be found among the Thracians, who revere him as they do Artemis and Ares.[57] A Thracian people, the Satrae, who have never been conquered by anyone, even "possess a place of divination sacred to Dionysus; which place is among the highest of their mountains . . . and it is a priestess that utters the oracle."[58] Even much further north, Herodotus tells us, the Geloni celebrate festivals in honor of Dionysus or, to be more exact, "they honor Dionysus every two years with Bacchic festivals."[59]

He is explicitly said to be present, in Greek territory, in Byzantium, where he has a temple,[60] and in Smyrna, where the inhabitants offer him a festival "outside the walls."[61] In Sicyon, Cleisthenes devoted tragic choruses to him.[62] Finally, he is invoked under the name of Iacchus, in the initiation ceremonies at Eleusis.[63] This brief list of the places where his presence is attested is not intended to suggest that he does not also appear elsewhere: after all, the *Histories* do not claim to be a monograph on the subject of Dionysus,

53. Hdt. 2.29.
54. Hdt. 3.97.
55. Hdt. 3.87.
56. Hdt. 2.144.
57. Hdt. 5.7. E. Rhode (*Psyché;* Paris, 1928) considers his origins to be Thracian. Besides H. Jeanmaire's, W. F. Otto's, and R. Kerenyi's classical books on Dionysos, see lastly M. Detienne, *Dionysos à ciel ouvert* (Paris, 1986).
58. Hdt. 7.111.
59. Hdt. 4.108.
60. Hdt. 4.87.
61. Hdt. 1.150.
62. Hdt. 5.67.
63. Hdt. 8.65. On the difference between Iacchus and Dionysus, cf. P. Boyancé, *Le Culte des Muses chez les philosophes grecs* (Paris, 1937), p. 26 n. 3.

on top of everything else. Honored in distant lands and revered in mainland Greece as well, he seems to be present everywhere.

To discover how his influence spread, who—according to Herodotus—received it from whom, we must pose the question of the god's origin. As always when it comes to origin, we must heed a number of voices: here, those of the Greeks, the Egyptians, and the narrator.

Dionysus (like Heracles and Pan) is considered by the Greeks as one of the most recent of the gods (*neotatoi*);[64] he is said to have been born from Semele, the daughter of Cadmus. Furthermore, as the Greek story has it, "now [*nun*], no sooner was Dionysus born than Zeus sewed him up in his thigh and carried him away to Nysa, in Ethiopia beyond Egypt."[65] For the Egyptians, on the other hand, Dionysus belongs to the third generation of the gods. First there were the eight, then the twelve, and finally those born from the twelve, who include Dionysus. They calculate fifteen thousand years to have elapsed between Dionysus and king Amasis.[66] As we have seen, there is an equivalence between Dionysus and Osiris. The Egyptians also say that "the rulers of the lower world are Demeter and Dionysus."[67]

The narrator, for his part, is totally opposed to the Greek version. In the first place, on the strength of the "inquiries" he has made, he believes that virtually all the *Ounomata* of the gods came to Greece from Egypt: *punthanomenos houto heurisko eon*.[68] Dionysus was introduced as follows:

I believe that Melampus learnt the worship of Dionysus chiefly from Cadmus of Tyre and those who came with Cadmus from Phoenicia to the land now called Boeotia. . . . It was Melampus who taught the Greeks the name of Dionysus and the way of sacrificing to him, and the phallic procession [*to ounoma kai ten thusien kai ten pompen tou phallou*].[69]

The Greek story consequently becomes untenable. Herodotus makes that very clear by pointing to the chronology: between

64. Hdt. 2.145.
65. Hdt. 2.146 and 3.111.
66. Hdt. 2.145.
67. Hdt. 2.123.
68. Hdt. 2.50.
69. Hdt. 2.49.

Dionysus, the son of Semele, and "myself," one thousand years at the ouside have elapsed, whereas according to the Egyptian calculation, fifteen thousand years separated Dionysus and Amasis.[70] Now, the Egyptians are quite "certain" (*atrekeos*), of their date "seeing that they had always reckoned the years and chronicled them in writing."

One conclusion to be drawn is that the Greeks are mistaken, for they have confused the time when they learnt of this god and the time of his birth. Another is that the Greeks came to know of Dionysus (and likewise Pan and Hermes) "later" (*histeron*) than the other gods.[71] Finally, no doubt Dionysus did have a foreign origin but, for Herodotus, that is true of most of the Greek gods.

On the evidence of the *Histories* alone, these then are the places where the Mother of the Gods and Dionysus are recognized, and that is who they are. If the Mother of the Gods does seem a truly marginal figure, the procession of Dionysus, in contrast, is (apparently) known everywhere, throughout the non-Greek space as well as the Greek one. But the interesting question that the text now raises is the manner in which Dionysus and the Mother of the Gods operated as criteria of Greekness not only for the Scythians and Greeks in the *Histories* but also for the actual addressees of this discourse, Herodotus's audience. When the narrator shows, in Book 2, that Dionysus is of Egyptian origin, he at one point uses an important *a contrario* argument: "I will not admit that it is a chance agreement between the Egyptian ritual of Dionysus and the Greek; for were that so, the Greek ritual would be of a Greek nature [*homotropa*] and not but lately introduced."[72]

In other words, one proof of the foreignness of Dionysus, in the narrator's view, is the fact (which he is content simply to state, without explaining or glossing it) that practices followed in the cult addressed to him are not *homotropa* with those of the Greeks: his cult is thus a reminder of his non-Greekness. That is the first proposition to be found in the *Histories*.

There is another, perhaps less explicit but equally interesting. It occurs in the passage on the Geloni. The Geloni live in the same territory as the Budini, but they have built themselves a wooden

70. Hdt. 2.145.
71. Hdt. 2.146.
72. Hdt. 2.49.

town with sanctuaries consecrated to Greek gods and "they honour Dionysus every two years with Bacchic festivals." The information given here is surprising, and Herodotus, who is well aware of this, is quick to explain the behavior of the Geloni: the reason is that "the Geloni are by their origin [*to archaion*] Greeks."[73] The construction of a *polis*, the establishment of sanctuaries, and the celebration of festivals in honor of Dionysus are thus all associated as so many actions which are no longer surprising once the reader is told that the Geloni had Greeks for ancestors. In this particular case, to look no further, Dionysus functions as a criterion for Greekness. Is there a contradiction between these two propositions? There is not, because they do not operate on the same level or refer to the same time: in one case it is a question of origins, in the other of the (narrator's) present time. Thus, even if the expression "to honour Dionysus with Bacchic festivals" was not initially in keeping with Greek practices, with the passing of time it may well have become a way of indicating Greekness.

At all events, Dionysus is a familiar figure along the shores of the Black Sea. That is frequently attested, but the fact remains that the testimony of Herodotus is the most ancient. Pippidi tells us, for example, that at Callatis there were not only *Xenika Dionysia*—that is to say, the ritual banquets organized in honor of Dionysus[74]—but also a public cult (*thiasoi*), a sanctuary consecrated to the god, and a month of Dionysus.[75] In short, his was an extremely active presence (well attested during the Hellenistic period), and that goes not just for Callatis but for the entire length and breadth of Scythia Minor.[76]

In a digression in the treatise on *Dance* attributed to Lucian, the author mentions the traditional custom of Bacchic dances in Ionia and in the Black Sea area: "The Bacchic dance has so enthralled the people of those countries that when the appropriate time comes round, they each and all forget everything else and sit the whole day

73. Hdt. 4.108.

74. D. M. Pippidi, *I Greci nello Basso Danubio* (Milan, 1971): "For the Greeks of Dobrugia, who had carried him with them aboard their ships, Dionysus was a national god, worshiped as a secular tradition, with titles that reappear in Megara and Asia Minor", p. 127.

75. D. M. Pippidi, "Xenika Dionysia à Callatis," *Acta Antiqua Academiae Scientiarum Hungaricae* 16 (1968): 191–95.

76. Cf. also G. M. Hirst, "The Cults of Olbia," *Journal of Hellenic Studies* 23 (1903): 24–53.

looking at titans, corybantes, satyrs and rustics [the performers in the festival of Dionysus]. Indeed, these parts in the dance are performed by the men of the best birth and first rank in every one of their cities, not only without shame but with greater pride in the thing than in family trees and public services and ancestral distinctions."[77] Did these dances already "enthrall" the people of Olbia when Scyles was anxious to become an initiate? Was the *thiasos* even then composed of the best families in the town? Unfortunately, Herodotus says nothing about its composition, being content simply to mention it—a fact that indicates that details were unnecessary and that every member of his audience would know exactly what he meant. Some scholars have wondered whether the *thiasoi* were reserved for women,[78] but men certainly participated at Olbia, since when the Scythians catch sight of Scyles he is taking part in the *thiasos*. As to whether the status of the *thiasos* was official, we may note that in Olbia everything took place quite publicly in the streets of the town.

This prompts one further remark. In support of the thesis that the place of Dionysus was considered to be outside the city itself, mention has often been made of the fact that even when the god has been adopted, he does not enter the town. When the places in which mysteries take place are mentioned, it is always a matter of a wild place in the *agros*; remember, too, that the people of Smyrna celebrate his festival "outside the walls [*exo teicheos*]";[79] and consider, finally, the name by which he is sometimes known, *propoleos*, "in front of the town." However, to return to Olbia, it must be admitted that here the initiation and procession take place inside the town; Scyles has seen to it that the gates are closed. When the Scythians, positioned up on the tower, behold the procession, Scyles is described, in a word, as "acting as a Bacchant," which means that the *pompe* demands that the initiates sing and dance in honor of the god.

As for the Mother of the Gods, who addresses a cult to her? Herodotus is content here too to do no more than mention the

77. Lucian *On Dance* 79.

78. On the obscurity of these early theories, cf. A. J. Festugière, *Etudes de religion grecque et hellénistique* (Paris, 1972), p. 14ff. The Thiasotai of the *Frogs* include both men and women.

79. Hdt. 1.150.

"Cyzicenes," a term which covers men as well as women. For Hasluck,[80] on the contrary, it is clear that the Greeks considered her cult to be "barbarian" and that her religion "was probably for the natives. . . . The Mother was always a foreigner to the Cyzicenes, though a foreigner that must be conciliated." Now, as proof that this cult was regarded as barbarian by Greeks, Hasluck cites the example of Anacharsis in the text of Herodotus; yet Anacharsis is assassinated by the Scythians precisely for having introduced a cult imported from Cyzicus! As to his second claim, the insertion of that "probably" no doubt dispenses him from substantiating it. Who else, then? According to a tradition which it is difficult to date and which is echoed in particular by the scholium to Aristophanes and by Iamblichus, the zealots of the Mother were recruited above all from among women and effeminate males.[81] Note also the legend recorded by the *Suda* and Photius on the origin of her introduction in Athens.[82] A certain Metragyrtes, having landed in Attica, began to initiate women into the cult. The Athenians killed him and threw him into the *barathros*. A *loimos* then followed. An oracle they consulted suggested that they build a hall and consecrate it to the Mother of the Gods. This is the explanation and justification for the construction of the Metroon,[83] which marks the appearance of Mother of the Gods in the agora. This Metroon later became the official depository for public documents. At the end of the fifth century the

80. Cf. Hasluck, *Cyzicus*, p. 215.

81. Scholium to Aristophanes *Birds* 1.877; Iamblichus *On the Mysteries* 3.10.

82. *Suda*, s.v. *Metragurtes* (Photius). See also P. Foucart, *Des associations religieuses chez les Grecs* (Paris, 1873), p. 64, for whom this takes place in the 430s. Plutarch *Nicias* 13 cites, among the unfavorable omens that manifested themselves before the Sicilian expedition, the following: "Then there was the affair of the altar of the twelve gods. An unknown man leaped upon it all of a sudden, bestrode it and then mutilated himself with a stone."

83. On the problem posed by the Metroon, see R. Martin, *Recherches sur l'agora grecque* (Paris, 1951), pp. 328ff., who writes: "considering that the literary tradition and the archaeological evidence [are more or less in agreement,] why not recognize that the deity may have been installed in the hypostyle hall of Eleusian character (which already stood in the agora and served as a meeting hall for the *Boule*), while the Council was at last given an independent meeting hall (the new building erected at the end of the fifth century)?" The earliest literary reference to the Metroon and its functions is to be found in a text by Chamaeleon of Pontus (Athenaeus 9.407c).

Mother had her own building on the agora, so it seems that the question of her "foreignness" was no simple matter:[84] sometimes rejected, sometimes a marginal figure, sometimes admitted to the very center of the city, she occupied a whole range of positions.

To close this excursus with an example of an extreme text, let us cite Clement of Alexandria:

> Blessings be upon the Scythian king. . . . When a countryman of his own was imitating among the Scythians the rite of the Mother of the Gods, as practised at Cyzicus, by beating a drum and clanging a cymbal and by having images of the goddess suspended from his neck after the manner of a priest of Cybele, this king slew him with an arrow, on the grounds that the man, having been deprived of his own virility in Greece [*anandron gegenemenon*], was now communicating the effeminate disease to his fellow citizens [*theleias nosou*].[85]

Anacharsis became a zealot of the Mother, a veritable Metragyrtes. Morevoer, there is no doubt in the mind of Clement of Alexandria that practicing the cult of Cybele is a criterion of Greekness—in other words, a failing. Anacharsis is in truth killed not for having introduced foreign *nomoi*, but for having become "effeminate" or, rather, for having lost his virility among the Greeks and for seeking to teach this "effeminate disease": so Cybele is Greek, and the Greeks are women!

The Scythians, for their part, totally reject the Mother and Dionysus, applying the rule set out by Herodotus. When Saulius sees Anacharsis, he promptly slays him, without a word, as if any explanation or justification were quite unnecessary: the crime is patently clear, the punishment immediate. In the case of Scyles the scenario is slightly different: Dionysus is not only foreign but induces madness—two excellent "reasons" for the Scythians to reject him. This raises the question of the relationship between Dionysus and *mania*. In the *Bacchae*, Pentheus is driven out of his mind by Dionysus, who leads him to the Citheron disguised as a woman,[86]

---

84. On the Mother of the Gods, see E. Will, in *Eléments oreintaux dans la religion grecque ancienne* (Paris, 1960), pp. 95–111, for whom the Great Mother arrived in mainland Greece from Ionia as early as the sixth century. Pindar mentions her and is interested in her cult: *Pythian 3* 77, fragments 48 and 63 Bockh. Cf. also A. Dupont-Sommer and L. Robert, *La Déesse de Hierapolis Castabala* (Paris, 1964).

85. Clement of Alexandria *Protreptica* 24.1.

86. Euripides *Bacchae* 1. 912ff.; H. Jeanmaire, *Dionysos* (Paris, 1970), pp. 105–56.

for the very reason that he persists in refusing to recognize him and wants "to break his neck." This is one type of *mania*, but there is another, that which afflicts Agave and her companions who are wandering over the slopes of the mountain, for they too have "outraged" Dionysus, "denying that he was truly god."[87] One might also cite the example of the daughters of Minyas at Orchomenae or that of the daughters of Eleuther at Eleutherae. Blinding, loss of reason, and *mania* are all punishments for refusing the god recognition.[88] Once this logic of *mania* is established, it is easy to understand why Pentheus, when discovered perched in his tree, dies for having seen "forbidden sights" and having pursued "what one should flee."[89]

In the case of Scyles however, the situation is in many respects reversed. Here it is the Scythian leaders who lie in wait at the top of a tower (*lathre*). They are the ones who see what they should not see, yet it is they who deal the death-blow; it is they who totally reject the god, yet they too who speak of *mania* and accuse others of madness. And when the Borysthenite seeks them out, he pretends to speak their language, as an expression of his scorn for them: he repeats the words that Herodotus ascribes to the Scythians in explanation of their conduct,[90] and even goes so far as to refer to Dionysus as a *daimon*.

The Scythians' failure to understand Dionysus might—and herein, perhaps, lies the cunning of the narrator—be a way of suggesting that the one who is mad is not the one we think it to be; that, in the last analysis, the real madmen are perhaps those who are the first to denounce madness in others. But this incomprehension on the part of the Scythians is also a ruse in another sense. What the Scythians interpret as *mania* in the performance of the *thiasos* may well give every appearance of *mania*, but the point is that it *is* only an appearance; in other words, *mania* is as different from *Bakcheuein* as those who reject Dionysus are from those who accept him. However, the Scythians are incapable of seeing beyond the appearances, so their discourse does not know what it is saying.

87. *Bacchae* 1.1297.
88. Boyancé, *Le Culte des Muses*, p. 65ff.
89. *Bacchae* 1.912.
90. Hdt. 4.79: "they say that it is not reasonable to set up a god who leads men on to madness." So this is clearly an intervention on the part of the narrator.

At this point we find ourselves back with the theme of the discourse of the ethnologist, which *does* tell the truth. It is the discourse of the one who knows, because he knows the circumstances and the results. The Scythians, for their part, do not differentiate between, for example, feathers and snow,[91] and call what they should call snow feathers, just because snowflakes "resemble" feathers; similarly, they cannot distinguish between being afflicted with *mania* and being a Bacchant, because the two appear to be one and the same thing.

Such, then, were the lives and deaths of Anacharsis and Scyles, and all because they forgot the existence of frontiers.

Salmoxis: The Getan Pythagoras

Who is Salmoxis or Zamolxis or Zalmoxis? (And this hesitation over the name is but the beginning of a long story of identity.) Is he a man, a *daimon*, or a god? We do not really know. When was he born? In Book 4, chapter 94, of Herodotus's *Histories*. When did he die? Is he perhaps still alive in Rumania? What are the main events in his career? He starts as a Getan, is then Dacian, and becomes a great priest or king "of much erudition in philosophy," as Jordanes tells us. With the arrival of the Romans, abetted by the advent of Christianity, he disappears from his own country but lives on in the traditions of the Goths (Getan = Goth). Alphonse the Wise regards him as someone who was "marvellously learned in philosophy." He then suffers a long eclipse before reappearing, this time in his own land, when, in Rumania, a movement of Thracomania developed, centered on Parvan and his followers. According to Mircea Eliade, "Zalmoxis is revered because he embodies the religious spirit of the Daco-Getae, because in the last analysis he represents the spirituality of the autochthonous ones, those almost mythical ancestors who were conquered and assimilated by the Romans."[92]

I will not pursue the story of Salmoxis, which would lead us along far distant paths where we should encounter not only Mircea Eliade and others but also the shades of shamans, strange and always disturbing figures—but will limit myself to considering Salmoxis's "birth." I will start by noting all the features that make Salmoxis a

91. Hdt. 4.31. Cf. G. Dumézil, *Romans de Scythie et d'alentour* (Paris, 1978), pp. 339–51.

92. Mircea Eliade, *De Zalmoxis à Gengis-Khan* (Paris, 1970), pp. 79–80.

kind of Getan Pythagoras. This portrait of him is one put together first and foremost by the Greeks of the Black Sea and the Hellespont, and Herodotus takes it directly from them: *punthanomai*, "I asked them and this is what they said."

Who is Salmoxis? To the Black Sea Greeks, there is no doubt about the answer: Salmoxis is an *anthropos*, a human being and not, as is suggested in chapter 94, either a *daimon* or a *theos*.[93] He is of Getan origin, a former slave. Similarly (still in the view of the Black Sea Greeks), Pythagoras is the son of Mnesarchus, a native of Samos, and was Salmoxis's master for a while. It is immediately clear how the Black Sea Greeks proceed where it is a question of "otherness": the one who was no more than a slave to the Greeks is regarded by the Getae as a divine being.

To give this observation its full meaning, we must at this point introduce another term, another country: Egypt. According to one tradition, Pythagoras (but also Solon, and Thales too) traveled to Egypt once in his life, to learn from the Egyptians,[94] the most ancient men in the world, or at least the most ancient after the Phrygians.[95] Their antiquity was the reason for their knowledge being greater than that of younger peoples. Pythagoras became the pupil of the Egyptian priests. But in the case of the Getae, the situation is at once reversed and Pythagoras appears as the master, in every sense of the word, of Salmoxis. Moving northward then, knowledge thus declines.[96] The decline is explained in part by the age of the peoples involved: if the Egyptians are the oldest, the Scythians are the youngest or "most recent of men,"[97] being no more than a thousand years old. In the chapter that Strabo devotes to Salmoxis, he too describes him as a slave of Pythagoras but also credits him with a journey to Egypt, where he may have acquired a knowledge of astronomy.[98]

93. Hdt. 4.94–96.

94. C. Froidefond, *Le Mirage égyptien dans la littérature grecque d'Homère à Aristote* (Paris, 1971).

95. Hdt. 2.2.

96. Hdt. 4.46: "We cannot show that any nation within the region of the Pontus has any cleverness."

97. Hdt. 4.7; here, once again, is evidence of the Greeks' fascination with Egypt and the problems it posed for them, for even if the Egyptians are "ancestors," they are still non-Greeks.

98. Strabo 6.5; note how, in a way, Pythagoras is used to "read" the Egyptian religion; cf. Hdt. 2.37, 81.

As well as the details of identity attributed to him by the Black Sea Greeks, Pythagoras has been assigned vaguer or more shifting personalities. A similar vagueness characterizes Herodotus's text concerning Salmoxis. In the first place, Pythagoras had known a number of previous existences and possessed the unique ability of remembering them.[99] If we are to believe some fragments, he had been, at the other end of the scale of beings, a veritable "god: an Apollo who came from the Hyperboreans."[100] But the description that best conveys this vagueness is perhaps that of *daimon:* "in between the gods and men, there is the divine man, the *daimon*, the intermediary, that is to say Pythagoras."[101] The *daimon* is not defined by any figurative representation or by any myth or ritual. In his work "on the Pythagoreans," Aristotle writes that there are "on the one hand the gods," "on the other, men," and, third, "beings like Pythagoras"; thus Pythagoras is one of the glorious representatives of the race of *daimones* and, it should be added, he is "a good *daimon*, full of love for men."[102]

In Herodotus, Salmoxis is described first as a *daimon*, then as a *theos*, then as an *anthropos;* so he too is said to occupy all three positions at the same time or to be one who continually passes from one to another. "Whoever dies goes to Salmoxis, a divine being [*daimona*]." That is what the Getae believe; the word *daimona*, which is placed in apposition, appears to be an intervention into the narrative on the part of the narrator; it provides an element of information which should make it possible for the Greek reader without any previous knowledge to know where to place Salmoxis. Between *para Salmoxin* and *daimona*, which to make any sense does not depend upon *nomizousi*, there is a pause. Salmoxis belongs to that category of intermediaries which we Greeks call *daimones*. In the next sentence, the narrator provides more information on the names of Salmoxis, who is also known by the Thracians as Gebeleizis, and the expression used is *ton auton touton* (some people name "this" same one Gebeleizis). The *touton*, which is not at all necessary (Herodotus could just as well have written *ton auton* or *ton auton*

---

99. Heraclides fr. 89 W (= Diogenes Laertius 8.4).

100. Diogenes Laertius 8.11; Iamblichus *Life of Pythagoras* 28.

101. M. Detienne, *De la pensée religieuse à la pensée philosophique: La Notion de Daimon dans le pythagorisme ancien* (Paris, 1963).

102. In Iamblichus *Life of Pythagoras* 31.

daimona) may be regarded as a hesitation on the part of the narrator. *Touton*, by its very vagueness, leaves every possibility open and, as it were, nuances the earlier statement: just as Salmoxis in fact has at least two names, so he may be a *daimon*, or a *daimon* of a kind, or even something else.

If the messenger dispatched to Salmoxis dies (he is tossed into the air to fall upon the tips of upright javelins), "they conclude that the god is favourable toward them." In contrast to the term *daimon*, the word *theos* is not introduced in an intervention on the part of the narrator, who is content (given the presence of *dokeei*) at this point simply to record the opinion of the Getae. To whom does *theos* refer here? Surely, to the one to whom the messenger is sent, that is, to Salmoxis; but at the same time, not without a measure of ambiguity, *theos* may denote gods in general, the deity, in rather the same way as our own expression "heaven" does. Since the text is careful not to make the sense clear, the listener or reader is bound to admit that the identity of Salmoxis is more uncertain than ever. The ambiguous use of the word *theos*, which refers either to Salmoxis alone or to heaven in general or to both at once (which is most probably the case), explains how it is that, a few lines further on, it is possible to pass on to another *theos* which this time denotes not only the god of heaven but specifically the Greek god of heaven.

The very evolution of the text thus expresses the vagueness of the identity of Salmoxis. The vagueness is not accidental, but is a constitutive element of his personality and is analogous to the vagueness we have noted with regard to the true nature of Pythagoras. It is, finally, a vagueness which the term *daimon* makes it possible both to express and to contain.

Another feature characteristic of the narrative is the use of a whole vocabulary of terms to denote knowledge. Salmoxis, who is the one who knows (*epistamenos*), is set in opposition to the Thracians, "people who live wretchedly [*kakobion*]" and are "not very clever [*hupaphronesteron*]." In his *Historia animalium*, Aristotle calls the goldfinches *kakobioi*:[103] they have a hard life, struggling to "find" their livelihood, that is to say, their food, whereas other birds, mentioned earlier, are represented as *eubiotoi* and *eumechanoi*. These find their livlihoods easily, thanks to their *dianoa* or "intel-

---

103. Aristotle *Historia animalium* 9.17.3.

ligence," as Aristotle puts it. To call a bird *kakobioi*, then, also means that it is not intelligent, that it does not know how to adapt to a difficult situation. The Thracians, similarly, are devoid of the practical intelligence which would enable them to make the most of their admittedly difficult situation; this deficiency is underlined and amplified by the use of the adjective *hupaphronesteron*, indicating that they are semi-cretinous.

In contrast, Salmoxis, despite his Getan origins, by virtue of having lived in Samos among the Greeks has managed to become a man who knows *epistamenos*, "he knows") *diatian Iada* (an expression that balances *kakobioi*), that is to say, he knows the "regimen" but also "the place where one lives" and the "mode of life" in Ionia; and he also knows *ethea bathutera*, an expression with Ionian and intellectual overtones.[104] He knows all the better for having had Pythagoras as master—Pythagoras who, as Herodotus notes, is a *sophistes* and by no means the least of them. The word was at that time in no way pejorative and carries none of the sense that Plato was later to give it. Its meaning was something like sage, poet, seer: sage, as in the expression the Seven Sages; in the fifth *Isthmian* the *sophistai* are poets;[105] in the *Rhesos*,[106] Orpheus is said to be *sophistes*. In Herodotus, the words *kakobioi*, *bathutera* (with this meaning), and *hupaphronesteron* appear only at this point. (That is not to suggest that the words are borrowed, but it seems a point worth noting.)

Salmoxis's wisdom is a pale reflection of that of his master, but is nevertheless enough to impress those yokels, the Getae. Pythagoras and the Pythagoreans were indeed men of great knowledge; theirs was a community of learned (*eidotes*) and educated (*pepaideumenoi*)[107] people. As early as the fifth century, the tradition seldom misses a chance to represent Pythagoras as a man of great learning.

---

104. Heraclitus in H. Diels and W. Kranz, *Die Fragments der Vorsokratiker* (12th ed.), 22 B 45, speaks of *bathun logon*. Pindar *Nemean 3* 53: Chiron is called *bathumetes; Nemean 7* 1: the Moires are called *bathuphrones*. The expression *bathuphron* is also to be found in Alcman. Solon 23.1 in Diehl, *Anthologia lyrica graeca*, writes ironically of himself: "Solon was a man who was neither clever [*bathuphron*], nor cunning [*bouleeis*].

105. *Isthmian 5*, 36.

106. *Rhesos* 949.

107. Iamblichus *Life of Pythagoras* 200.

Heraclitus cites him as an example of *polumathes* man,[108] and Empedocles and Ion of Chios describe him as the man who knows the most, almost too much.[109] So this opposition between knowledge and ignorance, between people who know and the common crowd, is certainly an element in the general representation of Pythagoras and the Pythagoreans. Herodotus's text plays on this opposition, echoing the tradition or, rather, chiming in with it.

A reading of these chapters of Herodotus reveals another constellation or series of three terms with a family resemblance, each of which implies the other two in an unequivocal fashion. They invite the reader to press on with this continuous to-ing and fro-ing between Pythagoreanism and "Salmoxism." The terms are immortality, courage, and the communal meal.

No sooner does Herodotus mention the Getae than he adds *athanatizontes* immediately after their name.[110] A few lines further on he returns to this adjective; and when he mentions the Getae in another book in the *Histories* he writes, for all the world as if it were a cliché, "the Getae who claim to be immortal [*Getae hoi athanatizontes*]."[111] Moreover, Herodotus is not the only writer to associate the Getan people with immortality or practices of immortality. Plato, Diodorus, Arrian, and Lucian, among others, all make the same connection.[112] It thus seems plausible to suppose that in the shared knowledge of the Greeks the Getae and immortality were associated, *hoi athanatizontes* being a somehow natural description for this northern people, which I would suggest translating as "the Getae who practice immortality,"[113] while the concept of immortality deliberately leaves the modalities of this association quite indeterminate. The text does not resolve the question of the relation between this immortality and Salmoxis. Is Salmoxis himself the only

108. Heraclitus, 22 B 40 (D.-K.).

109. Empedocles, 31 B 129 (D.-K.); Ion of Chios, 36 B 2 (D.-K.).

110. Hdt. 4.93.

111. Hdt. 5.4.

112. Cf. I. M. Linforth, "hoi Athanatizontes," *Classical Philology* 13 (1918): 22–33. Plato *Charmides* 156d. Diodorus 1.94. Arrian *Anabasis* 1.3.2. *Suda, Etym. Magn.*, s.v. *Zalmoxis* (Photius). Lucian *Skytes* 1.860, and *Assembly of Gods* 9.533.

113. Linforth, *Classical Philology*, p. 27, translates *athanatizein* as "make immortal and divine, deify" when it is transitive, and as "act the part of a being immortal and divine" when it is intransitive.

connection? Without him, would the Getae still be said to "practice immortality"? Chapter 95 appears to limit the immortality to the initiates of Salmoxism alone, but a few lines further on, the text mentions the Thracians (in general) mourning the "death" of Salmoxis. Moreover, at the beginning of chapter 94, we find the following: "As to their [the Getae's] claim to be immortal, this is how they show it: they believe that they do not die, but he who perishes goes to Salmoxis, a divine being." According to this definition, every one of the Getae is concerned and implicated: Salmoxis represents a mediation valid for them all.

This is the first time the word *athanatizein* appears in Greek literature, so we might assume that Herodotus invented it especially to describe the Getae and express their originality. However, I believe, quite to the contrary, that the word was part and parcel of the shared knowledge of the Greeks of the time and that Herodotus (for the first time or following others?) removed it from its context in order to apply it to the Getae. The fact that we find it used for the first time in the *Histories* is obviously not particularly significant, considering that our documentation on the texts contemporary with or earlier than Herodotus is no more than patchy, to say the least. Besides, the fact that he uses the expression as soon as the Getae appear, without feeling any need to explain or comment on it, seems rather to suggest that it was familiar to his audience. All Herodotus needs to do is pinpoint its significance in the world-view of the Getae, by introducing the figure of Salmoxis; there is no need for him to explain it.

If we accept that the word belongs to the domain of what is "well-known," if it indisputably indicates a connection with immortality even if the modalities of that connection remain vague, we must then ask to whom it applied in the ordinary way. To whom could the expression *hoi athanatizontes* apply if not to people who claimed to be specialists in matters of the Beyond and immortality? Now who, in Greece, could be more concerned with these problems than the Pythagoreans, those whose "entire life . . . appears to have been considered simply as a preparation for death"?[114] Hence Linforth's hypothesis (which is beguiling, even if there is no text to support it explicitly), according to which *hoi athanatizontes* is a nickname

---

114. P. Boyancé, *Le Culte des Muses*, p. 144.

designating the Pythagoreans: "The Greeks, observing that the Pythagoreans claimed to be able to remove the sting of death and insure for themselves and their associates eternal happiness beyond the grave, thereby putting on the divine and making themselves like the gods, applied to them the appellation *athanatizontes*."[115]

It could thus well be that this term, which the tradition tends to connect with the Getae, could have a value as a descriptive epithet or as a nickname,[116] reinforced to the extent that for a Greek listener it would also operate as a citation:[117] to say that the Getae practice immortality comes to the same thing as saying that they are Pythagoreans of a sort. If that is so, the shadow of Pythagoras is cast over this text from the very outset.

The Getae, in contrast to the other Thracians, who surrender to Darius without striking a blow, put up a resistance to the army of the Great King. Of course, they are then defeated but, Herodotus writes, they are "the bravest [*andreiotatoi*] and most law-abiding of all Thracians." Here we come upon the second element in the constellation of terms mentioned above: *andreia*. *Andreia* refers the reader to immortality which, in return, evokes *andreia*. Even if Herodotus does not make the link between the two terms explicit, he certainly associates them since, immediately after speaking of the Thracians "who practise immortality," he mentions their great courage.[118] But when other authors speak of the Thracians, they stress their "appetite for death";[119] for Pomponius Mela, for example, the Getae are *paratissimi ad mortem*, and he proceeds to give three reasons for this: *alii rediturus putant animas adeuntium, alii, etsi non redeant, non extingui tamen, sed ad beatiora transire, alii, emori quidem, sed id melius esse quam vivere.*[120] Under circum-

115. Linforth, *Classical Philology*, p. 31.

116. Cf. also the following fragment from the comic poet Aristophon: one of the characters in *The Pythagorean* says, "having descended into the lair of those below, he saw them all and noticed that the Pythagoreans were much more important than the other dead, for they were the only ones who enjoyed the privilege of eating with Pluto." The verb used is *sussitein* (= Diogenes Laertius 8.37).

117. A citation which, as M. de Certeau notes (*L'Ecriture de l'histoire* [Paris, 1975], p. 111), "is capable both of 'summoning up' a referential language which here operates as a reality, and also of passing judgment on it as a piece of knowledge."

118. Hdt. 4.93.

119. Cf. E. Rohde, *Psyché* (trans. Paris, 1928), p. 291.

120. Pomponius Mela 2.2.

stances such as these, fighting becomes a pleasurable pastime and dying a sought-after objective. Chapter 94 provides an *a contrario* confirmation of this connection between immortality and courage: when the Getae dispatch a messenger to Salmoxis, they toss him into the air so that he lands on pointed javelins; if the messenger does not die from being impaled upon the javelin tips, they reproach him for being *kakos*, cowardly (not "wicked," *"méchant,"* as Legrand's French translation has it). The only possible explanation for his refusal to die—that is to say, his rejectioin of immortality—is that he is a coward.

Warfare and the practice of *andreia* may, at first sight, seem not to have much to do with Pythagoreanism. But reflection on such a figure as Milo of Croton suggests that more caution is called for here. The man was an athlete, six times victor at Olympia, a daunting warrior, commander-in-chief in the war against the Sybarites in 540, and also an eminent Pythagorean, since it was under his roof that Pythagoras and his disciples met together. And we are prompted to reconsider the question by the words reported by Aristoxenus, according to which "one should fight not with words but with actions, for it is just and sacred to make war when one fights man to man";[121] and, equally, by the following extremely militaristic precept: "It is fine to die from wounds received face on, whereas the contrary is a disgrace."[122] Detienne, indeed, has shown that Milo is no less Pythagorean than Pythagoras himself and that their behavior, far from being opposed, is in truth complementary, for each represents one of two different trends in the movement. Pythagoras, the "exstatic magus, the sage bent on purification, the man-god who is beyond suffering from hunger or thirst," indicates an "insistence upon individual salvation," while Milo, "one of the first citizens of the city, an athlete, a warrior, a hearty eater of meat," represents an "urge to reform the city,"[123] or Pythagoreanism as a political movement.

It was a reform that the Pythagoreans were not content simply to dream about. They made considerable efforts to promote it, not just by proclaiming it but also by preparing for it in and through their

---

121. In Iamblichus *Life of Pythagoras* 232.
122. Iambl. *Life of Pythagoras* 85.
123. Cf. M. Detienne, *V Convegno di studi sulla Magna Graecia* (Naples, 1966 [1969]), pp. 149–56, and "La Cuisine de Pythagore," *Archives de Sociologie des Religions*, 29 (1970): 146–48.

own social behavior. They developed a style of life and a series of institutions that constituted a veritable system of education and "collective training." To counter *truphe*, Sybaritism, it was necessary to promote the virtues of *sophrosune, andreia, arete.* What better way of doing so than through a series of institutions, taken from the model of warrior societies—namely, communal meals, fraternities, and gymnastic exercises? The Spartan Megillus declares: "Communal meals and the gymnasia are well devised to foster courage and temperance."[124] Or consider the following words, this time on the lips of the Athenian of the *Laws*: "Do we not assert that the communal meals and the gymnasia were devised by the lawgiver with a view to war?"[125]

The connection between courage and immortality is reinforced, on the level of social practice and institutions, by the connection between courage and the communal meal. Thus, the communal meal functions as a breeding ground for *andreia*. And so, through its complex relationship to the other two terms, we reach the third term in the constellation: the communal meal. Immortality, courage, and the communal meal, three terms that are mutually evocative, each of which refers to the other two, are three elements in a single constellation. We have considered the connections first between immortality and courage, then between courage and the communal meal. Now we must establish the link between the first and the third of these elements, in other words, we must tackle the question of the feasts of immortality.

When he had become free and rich, Salmoxis returned to his own country; there he commissioned a banqueting hall to be built, where he could entertain certain of his fellow-countrymen. In short, he introduced the practice of communal meals and seems to have used them as one of the bases of his activities. What he had set up for himself was an *andreon*, that is, a "hall for men."[126] Beyond the

<hr/>

124. In Plato *Laws* 633a.

125. Ibid.

126. *Andreon* in Herodotus means "men's hall." 1.34: after he has a dream, Croesus has the weapons móved *ek ton andreonon*, to avoid the possibility of his son wounding himself. 3.77–78: The (Persian) conspirators enter *eis ton andreona* to kill the magus Smerdis. 3.121, 128: Polycrates of Samos lies in the *andreon* in the company of Anacreon of Teos; the furnishings of the *andreon* were consecrated in the Heraion after the murder of Polycrates.

Herodotean context, this word refers the reader to Cretan and Spartan practices:

> In Crete, the term *andreon* denotes the public premises where members of the *hetairiai* would congregate, but it also signifies the *hetairiai* themselves and the meals at which they met. The Spartan expression, for the more recent period at least, appears to have been *phiditie*, the meaning of which is uncertain. The expression *andreion* had been used in Sparta, as in Crete, in more ancient times. [127]

As we have seen from the Pythagorean society of Croton, the communal meals were an important element in life lived according to the precepts of the philosopher of Samos, and Boyancé, on reading Herodotus's text, thought he had discovered in it the first and most precious allusions to those communal meals which constituted the most important feature of Pythagorean life as described by Aristoxenus. [128] But so far we have only encountered communal meals in connection with the figure of Milo, those designed to foster *andreia*, those with a political function. We have not followed the other orientation of Pythagoreanism and come across communal meals seen as an important moment in religious life, a feast of immortality. I do not, of course, mean to suggest that there were two separate kinds of communal meals, but it is perfectly possible to lay the emphasis on one aspect rather than the other, either on the figure of Milo or else on that of Pythagoras. Aristoxenus of Tarentum, who claims to have been an initiate in one of the last Pythagorean communities of Phlius (in the fourth century) tells us that toward evening, after taking a bath, the members of the sect would share a communal meal; the meal was preceded and followed by libations, sacrifices, and offerings. [129] A text was then read aloud by the youngest disciple, after which the oldest member took over to make a number of recommendations. The company then broke up and each man returned to his home.

Salmoxis, who sets up communal meals with a religious purpose, invites to them "the chief amongst his fellow citizens [*ton aston tous protous*]." [130] The expression is somewhat surprising: here are Getae

127. H. Jeanmaire, *Couroi et Courètes* (Paris, 1939), pp. 85, 423, 483.
128. Boyancé, *Le Culte des Muses*, p. 134.
129. Iamblichus *Life of Pythagoras* 96–100.
130. Hdt. 4.95.

who, as soon as the word *andreion* and communal meals are mentioned, become citizens, just as if they lived in a town of Ionia or
southern Italy, meeting together at a feast presided over by a
banquet master. It is not really important to know whether the
expression should be taken literally (Herodotus having "forgotten"
that the Thracians knew nothing of life in a city), or metaphorically, or
whether it is perhaps an ironic or derisory transposition. What is
interesting here is that the mention of a communal meal should have
led to these particular words: communal meals bring together only
"respectable people," and Salmoxis, who is fully aware of that, does
not issue his invitations indiscriminately.

By making this point, the text refers us to the communal meals of
the Pythagoreans and, more generally, to Pythagorean politics. Who
attended these meetings? To whom was the teaching of Pythagoras
addressed? The aristocratic tendencies of Pythagoreanism have long
since been noted.[131] Having settled in Croton, Pythagoras "laid
down a constitution for the Italian Greeks and he and his followers
were held in great estimation, for, being nearly three hundred in
number, so well did they govern the State that its constitution was in
effect a true aristocracy."[132] Delatte considers this piece of information vouchsafed by Diogenes Laertius to be a rather inaccurate
summary of a passage from Timaeus in which it is stated that the
society, which was three hundred members strong, organized itself
as a *hetairia* in Croton and set itself to defend institutions established to discourage democratic movements.[133] The Pythagoreans
thus relied on the support of the aristocracies of cities and recruited
their members from among them: once again we encounter the
figure of Milo, the representative of an aristocratic family of Croton.

Immortality has thus led us to courage and courage to communal
meals but, far from succeeding one another, these three terms, all on
the same level, form a constellation, that is to say, a recognizable
composition in which a number of by no means exclusive features of
Pythagoreanism—and so also of Salmoxism—fall into place.

Within the *andreion* that he has set up in this fashion, Salmoxis

131. A. Delatte, *Essai sur la politique pythagoricienne* (Paris, 1922), and more
recently K. von Fritz, s.v. *Pythagoras, R.E.* (1936), C 171–300.
132. Diogenes Laertius 8.3.
133. A. Delatte, *La Vie de Pythagore de Diogène Laërce* (Brussels, 1922), p. 154.
The passage from Timaeus is in Iamblichus *Life of Pythagoras* 254.

proceeds to instruct the best of his fellow-citizens; the verb used is *anadidaskein*, which, the Thesaurus tells us, means *redoceo, iterum doceo, edoceo* (to teach again, to pass on knowledge or to teach thoroughly). To this definition Liddell-Scott-Jones adds "to teach otherwise or better." So this verb, used to define Salmoxis's activities, can mean both that he was teaching all over again, that is to say, passing on the teachings of Pythagoras and giving a thorough exposition of them, and also that he was teaching them in his own fashion. It is a polysemy worth underlining, and one which we should certainly not seek to minimize by choosing one meaning in preference to another, for it is within this very polysemy that the theme of "otherness" operates.

The doctrine of Salmoxis is summarized by—once again— the Black Sea Greeks: "He taught them that neither he nor his guests nor any of their descendants should ever die but that they should go to a place where they would live for ever and have all good things."[134] These few words are a mixture of statements that are quite unexceptional and vague, and claims that are quite exorbitant: what is this place to which the elect will go, what is this felicity that they are to enjoy, what is the meaning of this promise which includes not only those eating together but also their "descendants"? This indeterminate place where Salmoxis's "fellow-citizens" are to go is certainly reminiscent of the Pythagoreans' Islands of the Blessed, those goals of the ultimate journey which are none other than the sun and the moon, but that is not sufficient justification for making an identification between the teaching of Salmoxis and that of Pythagoras. However, as early as the fifth century we may refer to readings of the teaching of Salmoxis that are of a more Pythagorean nature, that is to say, more explicitly Pythagorean. Hellanicus of Mytilene, the historian of the last quarter of the fifth century, states in his *nomima barbarika*[135] that Salmoxis instituted "mysteries" among the Getae and that the dead go to join Salmoxis, but also that they return (*exein de authis*); in short, Salmoxism taught something very similar to metemsomatosis and involved a sect of initiates.[136]

The writings of the emperor Julian give an interesting reading of

134. Hdt. 4.95.
135. *Suda*, s.v. *Zamolxis.*
136. Cf. also Pomponius Mela, cited above in connection with the relationship between *andreia* and immortality.

this change of place from which the fellow-guests of Salmoxis benefit. The change of place is in fact represented as "moving home": "They believe that they do not die but simply change their residence."[137] Now, the themes of *metoikesis* and moving home are both Pythagorean ones.[138] The disciples, to borrow Iamblichus's expression, exchanged long *akousmata* "on the removal from earth [*peri metoikeseos tes enteuthen*].[139]

One more text may be included in this collection of explicitly Pythagorean interpretations of Salmoxism. This time it is not concerned with initiation or with the voyages of souls, but with dietary practices. Concluding his account of Salmoxis, Strabo remarks: "the Pythagorean doctrine of abstention from eating any living thing still survived [among the Getae] as taught by Zalmoxis, who is supposed to have learned it from Pythagoras."[140] The dietary regime of the Getae, which excluded all "murder," that is to say, the eating of meat, was thus taken directly from the teaching of Pythagoras.

These few examples taken from the sources show that it is possible to provide a reading of Salmoxism that is wholly Pythagorean but, returning to Herodotus, we need to point out a few anomalies. It is quite a hazardous undertaking since, in the first place, our only information on Pythagoreanism comes in snippets and fragments, so we are a long way from possessing a clear picture of what he represented in the fifth century and, second, Herodotus is one of our earliest sources of evidence (if not the first) certainly on Salmoxis but also on Pythagoras. In brief, Salmoxis's recommendations are very simple: feast with me and you will never know death but will live forever. However, that is not at all what Pythagoras teaches. Far from denying death, the Pythagoreans, on the contrary, seem inclined to regard their whole lives as a long preparation for death.[141] There was, moreover, a full Pythagorean ceremonial of death, which took

137. *The Caesars* 327d.

138. F. Cumont, "A propos des dernières paroles de Socrate," *Compte Rendu de l'Académie des Inscriptions et Belles-Lettres* (1943): 122 n. 4.

139. Iamblichus *Life of Pythagoras* 85; cf. also *Apologia of Socrates*, 40e: *Metoikesis tei psuchei tou topou ton enthende eis allon topon.*

140. Strabo 7.3, 5.

141. Boyancé, *Le Culte des Muses*, p. 134: "Perhaps . . . we know enough about it to establish that all in all the Pythagorean life was truly a preparation for death, and also that the Pythagoreans were noted for their claims to know of rites that assured them of preferential treatment in the beyond."

the form of an *anagoge*, that is, both a (sea) crossing and an ascension, with the Islands of the Blessed as destination. "A passage of Iamblichus compares the rites that accompanied the last moments of a Pythagorean with those attending a departure on a sea voyage. . . . They entailed a ritual observation of the flight of birds, and a religious silence was supposed to be observed during the last moments."[142]

There is, thus, an ascetic side to the Pythagoreans' communal meals which appears to be totally lacking in the banquets of Salmoxis. By way of confirmation we need only recall Aristoxenus's description of a day in the life of a Pythagorean. Their daily communal meals, extremely austere affairs, are simply preparations for that meal to be shared with Pluto to which the comic poet Aristophon mockingly refers, which will take place only after death. What a Pythagorean would say is that the fate of each individual after his death will depend on how he has lived. But Salmoxis goes much further, for he teaches that neither his guests nor their descendants (*hoi ek touton*) will ever die. This inclusion of the descendants raises problems. They put one in mind of those Orpheotelestai mentioned in Plato's *Republic*,[143] the charlatans who beat a path to rich men's doors "and make them believe that they . . . can expiate and cure with pleasurable festivals any misdeed of any man or of his ancestors." In the one case it is the ancestors, in the other the descendants, but either way this is the world of charlatans.

This mention of descendants openly undermines the text by introducing a note of derision. So now the implication of "after his own fashion" is uppermost in the verb *anadidaskein*, and it is heavily ironical. "Salmoxis teaches after his own fashion" implies, "just imagine what a creature such as he can have understood and retained from the doctrine of Pythagoras which, furthermore, he is teaching to such simple-minded people as the Getae." An alternative is possible, namely, that the mention of descendants says as much about Pythagoreanism as it does about Salmoxism and that in this case *anadidaskein* stresses the fact that this is a readoption, a repetition of the master's teaching, so the derision is intended to cover both Salmoxis and Pythagoras. The Black Sea Greeks are mocking the pair of them by mocking the one through the other.

142. Ibid., p. 137, and Iamblichus *Life of Pythagoras* 257.
143. *Republic* 364b.

If we accept that the addition of "descendants" introduces a note of derision, we are bound to examine the text anew to determine whether it is possible to distinguish other expressions that are, as it were, in quotation marks, or other clashes of tone. Once he has built his *andreion*, a term that refers to Crete and its warrior societies, Salmoxis receives his guests there like an innkeeper at the door of his kitchen: the Greek word used is *pandokeuein*. One cannot help being struck by the discrepancy between the two words. They do not belong to the same world; where we expect to find the host of a banquet, we discover an innkeeper, whose first concern, according to the most common image of him, is to fleece his clients by extorting as much money as possible from them in the shortest possible time.[144]

The description of the Getae whom Salmoxis chooses to share his meal as "the chief amongst his fellow-citizens" is somewhat surprising. Its presence here may indicate the narrator's "forgetfulness" of local color (for the Getae did not live in cities) but, on the other hand, it may equally well be prompted by the context. The concept of communal meals evokes the idea of "the chief amongst his fellow-citizens," and vice versa. However, the expression jars in association with the eating-hall of an inn. If the derisory overtone of *pandokeuin* can hardly be denied, we may also take it that the expression "the chief amongst his fellow-citizens" is there as an *antiphrasis:* if this were Greece it would indeed be a matter of the town's chief citizens, but among these pitiful yokels . . . The narrator pretends to believe them to be what they ought to be in order to suggest that in fact they are nothing of the kind. This could well be another deliberate undermining of the text and, once again, the derision pierces through.

The term *sumpotai* may also operate on two levels. It may denote a guest, one who takes part in a meal in an altogether normal fashion. But equally it may apply to a drinker, a man with no qualms regarding wine. To which category do Salmoxis's guests belong? According to some sources of evidence, the Pythagoreans did not drink wine at all.[145] In that case, at whom can the possible irony be aimed? These questions bring us back to that of the possible meanings of *ana* in *anadidaskein*.

144. *Laws* 11.918d ff.

145. Iamblichus *Life of Pythagoras* 69; see also Alexis *Tarentins* in Athenaeus 4.161b, and Aristophon in Athenaeus 4.238c–d.

The exaggeration introduced by the mention of the "descendants" of Salmoxis's guests finally returns us to the expression *athanatizontes*, on which we have already dwelt at some length. Linforth reads into it an irony, that extends to Salmoxism as well as to Pythagoreanism. These Getae are, in truth, quite remarkable practitioners of immortality. They maintain no less than that in order not to die the first thing to do is to die. That is substantiated by the fact that in chapter 94 the messenger is briefed on his mission to Salmoxis while he is "still alive [*eti zoonti*]." Perhaps we should be better advised to translate the expression *hoi athanatizontes* as, not "those who practice," but "those who fake," "fakers of immortality."

Clearly, then, the various terms that we have examined interact with the shared knowledge of the fifth-century Greeks in a way that is by no means unequivocal or constant. These words and expressions may take on a number of different meanings vis-à-vis one another, and each reader may combine them in a number of different ways simultaneously. In the interplay between these words and expressions with their shifting meanings, derision may be suggested and, at the same time, "otherness."

The story of Salmoxis, as told by the Black Sea Greeks, runs as follows:

While he was doing as I have said and teaching this doctrine, he was all the while making himself an underground chamber. When this was finished, he vanished from the sight of the Thracians and descended into the underground chamber where he lived for three years, the Thracians wishing him back and mourning for him for dead. Then, in the fourth year, he appeared to the Thracians and thus they came to believe what Salmoxis had told them.[146]

This *katabasis* of Salmoxis is one of the sequences in the story that have most prompted comparisons between Salmoxis and Pythagoras, for Pythagoras was also a man who used the *katabasis*, a specialist in underground living. Hieronymus of Rhodes credits him with a descent to the underworld where he meets, in particular, the souls of Homer and Hesiod,[147] but most significant is the account given by Hermippus, according to which Pythagoras secretly builds himself an underground house, exactly as Salmoxis does.[148] He then

146. Hdt. 4.95.
147. Diogenes Laertius 8.21.
148. In Diogenes Laertius 8.41.

descends to his new dwelling; his old mother, who is the only one let into the secret, passes down to him tablets recording the most important events that meanwhile take place. After a while, the master reappears, haggard and emaciated, declaring that he has just returned from Hades. When he also tells of all that has happened in his absence, his disciples are convinced he is divine.

Delatte thinks that one "ought" to associate these two texts,[149] but he does not elucidate in what sense this is an obligation. According to others, Hermippus plagiarizes the Herodotean account or even "boldly reworks" it. Burkert holds that the theme of the underground house does not belong to the "Salmoxis tradition" but is a "Greek motif," as is proved by the fact that, according to Strabo, the high priest of the Thracians lives not in a cave but on top of a mountain. He does not think that Hermippus derives his story entirely from Herodotus, since his account includes elements that are not to be found in Herodotus, in particular the presence of Pythagoras's mother. He then comes up with the remarkably bold suggestion that we are here presented with an extremely ancient theme which is no longer understood and which Hermippus "rationalizes" as best he can: this mother, Hermippus claims, is not Pythagoras's own mother at all, but is really the divine Mother—in other words, Demeter, whose devotee Pythagoras has become.[150]

A comparison of these two episodes in the life of Salmoxis by Herodotus and in that of Pythagoras by Hermippus shows that the two may be read together.[151] Salmoxis refers us to Pythagoras; Pythagoras refers us to Salmoxis. But as to claiming one of the sequences to be the origin and model of the other simply on the grounds that it is earlier—that would be altogether too presumptuous, considering how little we know about these matters.

At the beginning of this inquiry we set out to understand Salmoxism in the light of Pythagoreanism. That was a legitimate undertaking (despite the fact that no systematic account of Pythagoreanism exists), but an inadequate one. This study has shown us that if

149. Delatte, *Vie de Pythagore*, p. 245.

150. W. Burkert, *Lore and Science in Ancient Pythagorism* (Cambridge, Mass., 1972), pp. 158–59.

151. In Hermippus's account, Pythagoras returns from the Beyond bearing a message (and it is this message that occasions the belief in him), whereas in Herodotus's text there is no message as such; belief in Salmoxis is occasioned by his presence alone.

"Salmoxism" may be read through Pythagoreanism, Pythagoreanism, in its turn and similarly, may be read through "Salmoxism."

Finally, we must tackle the question of Herodotus the ethnologist:
how did the Black Sea Greeks regard Salmoxis, and how does the
traveler record their view? The Greeks know things about which the
Getae, who have never left their homeland, are ignorant or, rather,
whose existence they do not even suspect. The Greeks are people of
knowledge. They know much more about Salmoxis than even the
most knowledgeable of his disciples will ever discover. So, at the very
outset they assume the ignorance of these "others" who, quite
literally, do not know what they are saying.

Second, the Black Sea Greeks, installed on the margins of the
Greek world, undertake a long detour to give an account of a
religious phenomenon on their own doorstep. They call upon the
figure who is geographically more distant from them than any other,
Pythagoras, the man of the West, if not the Far West. In order to
defuse the "otherness" of the Getae, in order to come to terms with
the threat represented by this strange and elusive figure whose
nature is none too clear to them (is he a god, a *daimon*, or something
else again?), they turn to one who, far away to the west, had acquired
in the shared knowledge of the Greeks the position of an intermediary, an intermediary who no doubt also conveys a charge of "otherness"—in his case, though, the otherness is no longer "savage," but
accounted for, recognized, docketed. The Greeks play off what is
near against what is far away (what is near being in this case what is
further away).

Between themselves and Salmoxis, whom they cannot look in the
face and to whom they cannot listen, since he says nothing worth
hearing, they set up a third term, a milestone on the road to
intelligibility. Pythagoras can then be reckoned as the origin of the
actions and words of Salmoxis and as providing the true version of
them. In a process such as this, the relationship between the two
reads from Pythagoras to Salmoxis; in other words, Salmoxism is
interpreted entirely through Pythagoreanism and is considered
purely and simply as a plagiarism of it.

To the Black Sea Greeks, it is truly unthinkable that the relationship might equally be read from Salmoxis to Pythagoras, since they
are separated from the Getae by the boundary of the Greek world.

Their account expresses this in a particularly uncompromising and brutal fashion: Salmoxis was Pythagoras's slave. Even if Aristotle's reflections on those who are slaves "by nature" were yet to come, the fact remains that the slave and the free man belonged to two different worlds which, in the normal course of things, did not overlap. In Athens, for example, a freed slave obtained the status of metic, but a metic he then remained, as did his descendants, with no chance of ever becoming citizens. Given that the two are not even on the same level, the implication could not possibly be reversed.

Nevertheless, the otherness which is reduced, channeled, and exorcised in this way can still operate in the text in and through the interplay of polysemy. Recall the *anadidaskein*, the significance of "in his own fashion," the "innkeeper" treating the "chief amongst his fellow-citizens" to a meal in his *andreion*, the "descendants" promised immortality on the strength of the draught of wine knocked back by their parents: so many words and expressions in which a Greek could detect derision. This derision would introduce a certain distancing between Salmoxis and Pythagoras, which would really simply be a way of repeating, in a different key, that Salmoxis was the slave of Pythagoras.

All this discourse of the Black Sea Greeks depends on an "I" ("I made inquiries," *punthanomai*) who, in indirect speech, reports what they say. Up to now we have proceeded as if there was nothing to separate the Black Sea Greeks from their own words, but in reality Herodotus the interpreter mediates.[152]

After concentrating on chapter 95, the only one to record the point of view of the Black Sea Greeks, we must now move on to consider the passage devoted to the Getae in its entirety, taking first the relationship between chapters 94 and 95 and between Salmoxis the *daimon* and Salmoxis the charlatan. Some commentators consider the problems easily resolved: chapter 94, which explains how, at fixed dates, a messenger is dispatched to Salmoxis and what procedures must be followed depending on whether the message is delivered or not, is a description of the ritual; whereas chapter 95, in which the story of Salmoxis is recounted, is devoted to the myth. Mircea Eliade writes as follows: "The gods' reappearance in the myth

152. Furthermore, Herodotus was a citizen of Thurii, the new Sybaris. To evoke Salmoxis through Pythagoras may also be a way of reaching an "Italian" public.

corresponds, in the ritual, to the reestablishment of practical communication between Salmoxis and the faithful. It is a symbolic (because ritual) repetition of the foundation of the cult."[153]

The main argument for imposing such a classification on the text used by these authors is based on calendrical considerations. They point out that a messenger is sent to Salmoxis every four years and that Salmoxis remained in his underground hideout for four years. However, the Greek states that a messenger is sent to him *dia penteteridos*, every fifth year, in other words, at the end of every four years; as for his life underground, it lasted *ep' etea tria*, that is, for three full years, with Salmoxis making his reappearance in the fourth year. The ritual and the myth are thus one year out of step. Perhaps the Getae, who are "not very clever," have made a mistake in their calculations—always supposing that they even know how to count.

However that may be, chapter 94 can hardly be made to support such a commentary. A messenger is dispatched to Salmoxis and the description of this appalling mission employs the most pedestrian and neutral vocabulary possible.[154] The murder of the messenger is described with an almost technical precision: at no point is he regarded as a sacrifice. Now, Herodotus is quite capable, when he sees fit, of describing as sacrifices barbarian practices apparently considered scandalous by the Greeks; consider the example of the funerary feasts of the Issedones, in the course of which they eat their own dead parents.[155] But chapter 94 is presented as a description, as accurate as possible, of the Getan practices surrounding their deity; it is a narrative or, to be more precise, a description, but—and herein lie its originality and its difficulty—a description which postulates no witness, a narrative with no narrator, or at least none made explicit. No mediator, nobody with extra knowledge, intervenes to provide the listener or reader with the last word in the story. The author appears to make no intervention; at least there is no sign that he does (in contrast to chapter 95: "I tell what the Black Sea Greeks say"). Nor is there any reference to sources, just a narrative which, in the immediacy of the present tense (this is how . . . ; it is like this . . .) gives direct access to and an immediate transcription

153. Mircea Eliade, *De Zalmoxis*, p. 57.

154. The only word to be vaguely connected with ritual might be *penteteris;* as for *apopempein*, it is perhaps more solemn than the simple *pempein*.

155. Hdt. 4.26.

of what the Getae have always (at least ever since Salmoxis was Salmoxis) thought, believed, and done and will continue to think, believe, and do forever.

This narrative is thus, as it were, a zero degree of interpretation. It simply presents a slice of the beliefs of the Getae; they may seem obscure, but that is how it is. But perhaps we may wonder whether, in reality, a more subtle form of authorial comment is not involved. In the first place, it was certainly not by mere chance that Herodotus composed this chapter at this particular point: positioned at this juncture, just before the words of the Black Sea Greeks, it is bound to produce a particular kind of effect—one that will assuredly undergo modification as the reader proceeds to the end of the sequence.

Within this chapter itself a certain amount of exegesis is going on. The text repeatedly indicates that these are the beliefs of the Getae (*nomizousi, phamenoi, dokeei, nomizontes*). This insistence reflects the narrator's desire to stand back, to dissociate himself, to disclaim all personal responsibility; but by the very action of keeping his distance he sets those beliefs at a distance, and this absence of any positive authorial comment is, for all that, still an authorial comment of a kind. Besides, all the repetitions of "they believe" scattered through the text simply confer a minimum of coherence on the behavior of the Getae. To toss a man onto spikes and draw the conclusion that if he dies the god is favorably disposed is absurd, if not monstrous, but the moment it is seen as a matter of belief, the behavior makes sense even if it remains abominable. What we have here amounts to the beginnings of an exegesis.

The narrator makes two other detectable interventions in the text, which operate on a slightly different level. "This same Salmoxis is also Gebeleizis, as some of them call him." Salmoxis has no name in the Greek language.[156] Very often Herodotus writes that this or that native god is this or that god in Greek: Hestia, for example, is called Tabiti in the Scythian language, while Zeus is known as Papaios.[157] In the case of Salmoxis, however, his "otherness," far from being reduced by a reference to what is familiar, is to some extent increased: from Salmoxis we pass to Gebeleizis, an even stranger-sounding name. The fact that the Getae themselves refer to him by

156. Diogenes Laertius (8.1) mentions the Zalmoxis-Cronos equivalence, which he incorrectly attributes to Herodotus.
157. Hdt. 4.59.

two different names simply serves to emphasize the uncertainty surrounding his identity. The narrator shows, or shows off, his own knowledge at the same time as he bewilders his addressee even further, if that be possible.[158]

His second intervention takes the following form: "Moreover, when there is thunder and lightning these same Thracians shoot arrows skyward as a threat to *the god,* believing in no *other* god but their own [*oudena allon theon nomizontes einai ei me ton sphete-ron*]." This sentence poses a problem: the word *theos,* which appears twice, refers to a different god each time. As Rohde has pointed out, if the god they threaten were to be understood as "this god" (as Legrand translates into French), in other words Salmoxis, the reason given for their behavior by the narrator would be strange, if not absurd: they threaten him because he is the only one that they believe in.[159] It makes much more sense to take the threatened god to be, not Salmoxis, but the god of heaven (that is, something as vague as our "heaven"). And this is where it becomes interesting, for *that* god is Greek: to speak of thunder and lightning as *ho theos* is to adopt a Greek point of view. When the thunderbolt falls on Scyles's house in Olbia, Herodotus writes: "the god hurled his thunderbolt [*ho theos*]."[160] This passage, which is surreptitiously written from the Greek world-view, forces the narrator to intervene to make it quite clear that, apart from Salmoxis, the Getae have no gods and that for them the "god of heaven" does not exist. By providing this piece of information he reintroduces the Getae's world-view, but does so by setting it in contrast to that of the Greeks. Simultaneously, he suggests that in shooting their arrows at the sky, the Getae do not know what they are doing; anyway they are ridiculous to do it, since between this earthly world and the world of the gods there can be no such communication and, in truth, their behavior can only be explained by their ignorance. Moreover, there can be no doubt that, to Herodotus, this religious chauvinism is totally ridiculous, since he

158. Linforth, "Greek Gods and Foreign Gods in Herodotus," *University of California Publications in Classical Philology* 9 (1926): 1–25. Only three deities elude all assimilation: Pleistorus (a deity of the Apsinthian Thracians), Cybele, and Salmoxis.

159. *Psyché,* p. 286 n. 2.

160. Hdt. 4.79.

believes that the world is "one"[161] and that the gods are the same everywhere, even if the same gods are not everywhere recognized.[162]

Finally, does the ritual which every four years makes it possible to reestablish communications between the Getae and their god say anything about "otherness"? At all events, it certainly takes the form of an *antiphrasis*. How is this unfortunate messenger treated? He is tossed onto the points of three javelins or spears, whereas in normal practice the javelins would be thrown at him. Furthermore, the javelins are used in a vertical position, whereas normally they are deployed horizontally. The Getae's use of their spears is thus doubly abnormal. In order to reach Salmoxis, the messenger has to fall onto the spikes. The play made with this reversal orients the ritual and perhaps suggests the meaning of its "otherness."

So chapter 94 turns out not to be a zero degree of interpretation, after all. It is simply presented as if it were, which is quite a different matter. We have noticed how (indirect) indicators as to who is speaking break through the text, sketching in an exegesis. This chapter reveals an "other" Pythagoras who, if Pythagoras and Salmoxis truly imply one another, is, as it were, the other side to Pythagoras.[163]

Whose are the various voices heard speaking in these few chapters? In chapter 93 we are still involved in history and the "narration of events."[164] The situation completely changes at the beginning of chapter 94: the narration of events is left behind and the present tense takes the place of the aorist. But if we are no longer involved in a narration of events, no more are we in the sphere of "it is said that" (*legetai*); we are, rather, in that of the *esti*. The chapter begins with the expression *tonde ton tropon* ("in this manner"), suggestive of a

161. Hdt. 4.45: "Nor can I guess for what reason the earth, which is one, has three names," etc.

162. P. Veyne, *Comment on écrit l'histoire* (Paris, 1971), p. 141: "The gods are the same (in antiquity) for all men. At the very most, each people names them in its own language; that is to say, the names of the gods can be translated from one language to another in the same way as common nouns." Cf. below, pp. 244ff.

163. It should be added that everything in Pythagoras's teaching that concerns abstention from "murder" is the polar opposite to this human "sacrifice."

164. G. Genette, *Figures III* (Paris, 1972), p. 186.

stage direction, and the expression is in effect reiterated, a few lines further on, with *hode* ("this is how"). This is the vocabulary of description, then, or, rather, of what is manifest, for there is no suggestion of any witness in these descriptions. This chapter could be called a "narration" insofar as "it excludes every 'autobiographical' linguistic form";[165] in it we find nothing but verb forms in the third person, which postulate neither a speaker nor a hearer.

New voices are introduced at the beginning of chapter 95. We leave behind description which is static and fixed and requires no observer or reporter as intermediary, to enter the world of the *legetai*. The immediacy of the *esti* is replaced by the distancing of reported speech.[166] If "every utterance assuming a speaker and a hearer" can be defined as discourse,[167] this chapter is discourse; but, cast as it is as if it were being reported, it is discourse presented as a narration and (almost) ends up by becoming one. I think that is what accounts for the sudden reappearance of the aorist at the end of the chapter, the aorist which, since it is "the tense of the event outside the person of a narrator,"[168] is normally excluded from discourse. Finally, the chapter closes with the words "Such is the Greek story about him [*tauta phasi min poiesai*]." They indicate a stage direction and remind us that this is reported speech; and, in accordance with the pattern of ring composition, they balance the *punthanomai* of the opening. This rationalizing and positivist discourse does its best to minimize the "otherness" of Salmoxis, and it is presented as discourse that tells the truth—the truth the Getae would certainly be incapable of telling, the truth they do not even suspect about their beliefs. It is the last word to chapter 94 and also the last word on the whole story of Salmoxis.

Then, in chapter 96, we hear mainly the voice of the "I," who

165. E. Benveniste, *Problems in General Linguistics*, vol. 2 (Coral Gables, 1971), p. 206.

166. Ibid., p. 209: "Historical utterance can on occasion merge with discourse to make a third type of utterance in which discourse is reported in terms of an event and is transposed onto the historical plane; this is what is ordinarily called 'indirect speech.'" The free indirect style increases the difficulty.

167. Ibid.

168. Ibid., p. 208: "[In the narrative] the events are set forth chronologically, as they occurred. No one speaks here; the events seem to narrate themselves. The fundamental tense is the aorist, which is the tense of the event outside the person of a narrator."

intervenes to comment on what is said by the Black Sea Greeks. The definitive, self-confident words which did their best to do away with an "otherness" in too close proximity are cleverly challenged by Herodotus, who reintroduces a measure of doubt and uncertainty and ruins their pretensions to being the last word on the subject. The balancing of the expressions *oute . . . oute, eite . . . eite* reflects a desire to avoid making any final choice and to leave some room for "otherness": neither "I do not believe" nor "I am quite convinced," but "either he was a man" or "he was a *daimon.*"

Taken as a whole, Herodotus's procedure could be summed up as follows: a chapter in which the "otherness" is great, seemingly as great as could be (chapter 94), is followed by a chapter in which it is practically dismissed (chapter 95). Then comes the final intervention on the part of Herodotus himself, chiefly concerning the statements of the Black Sea Greeks but also relating to chapter 94 (since it returns to the question of whether Salmoxis was a *daimon*). It implies that the answers suggested to the question of Salmoxis by the Black Sea Greeks may be quite misleading: "I think he [Salmoxis] lived many years before Pythagoras." This *dokeo moi* completely undermines their arguments, suggesting that they may have quite missed the point about Salmoxis's "otherness." By denying that theirs is a discourse of the truth and by refusing to recognize chapter 95 as giving the last word on chapter 94, Herodotus reestablishes between the two reports a relationship which is no longer one-way but reversible.

Salmoxis may be a man or a *daimon*, he may have been the former and now be the latter, or he may be something else again; in the last analysis, the mark of his "otherness" is this open-endedness. I believe that is the sense of Herodotus's final *chaireto*, that third-person imperative, "farewell," or "that is enough of that."[169]

Frontiers and Otherness

Anacharsis and Scyles both met their deaths as the result of transgressing a frontier. The one, in the Hylaia, celebrated the mysteries of the Mother, alone; the other, inside the walls of Olbia, became an

169. The above pages are a slightly reworked version of an article that appeared in *Annali della Scuola Normale Superiore di Pisa* 8, 1 (1978): 15–42.

initiate of Dionysus Bacchus. This "forgetfulness" of the Scythian *nomoi* must be punished, by virtue of the rule which the narrator has stated: the Scythians refuse to adopt foreign *nomoi*. In short, the narrative of their misfortunes is just one more illustration of the great general law that "custom rules the world."[170]

The story of Anacharsis and Scyles, just as much as that of Salmoxis, hinges on the interplay between the near and the far. Dionysus, who is recognized within the walls of Olbia, is not at all understood outside them, and Bacchanalian "revels" are interpreted by the Scythians as "being mad." The spatial proximity is transformed into a cultural distancing. In a similar fashion, the Greeks of the Black Sea, attempting to give an account of Salmoxis, their neighbor, appeal to Pythagoras, admittedly a Greek but a compatriot who in spatial terms is very distant from them and whose behavior is extremely strange. Confronted with Salmoxis, whose identity escapes them and who is surrounded by rituals which are unfailingly disturbing to them, the Black Sea Greeks make a detour by way of Pythagoras. By doing so, they manage to *translate* Salmoxis into Greek (Salmoxism should be understood in relation to Pythagoreanism) and also to mark out the distances or construct a view of his otherness (Salmoxis is a man, he used to be Pythagoras's slave, all in all he is a charlatan, and the Getae are really not very clever). In this way it is possible to cross the frontier even while reinforcing it.

But, in an implicit fashion, the near and the far also operate on another level. From the point of view of Herodotus's addressee, what does the choice of the Mother of the Gods and Dionysus tell us? Both are certainly important deities of Cyzicus and Olbia, which are situated on the margins of the Greek world. But, as we have seen, it is much too simplistic to assume a direct homology between a representation of geographical space, on the one hand, and a representation of divine space, on the other; to suggest that the geograph-

170. Hdt. 3.38: "When Darius was king, he summoned the Greeks who were with him and asked them what price would persuade the to eat their fathers' dead bodies. They answered that there was no price for which they would do it. Then he summoned those Indians who are called Callatiae, who eat their parents, and asked them (the Greeks being present and understanding by interpretation what was said) what would make them willing to burn their fathers at death. The Indians expressed their horror and begged Darius not to speak such words of evil omen. Such is the strength of custom; and it is, I think, rightly said in Pindar's poem that 'Custom rules the world.'"

ical marginality is matched by a similar marginality where the gods are concerned, that the Mother and Dionysus stand, in relation to the rest of the Greek pantheon, in the same position as Cyzicus and Olbia in relation to the rest of the Greek world. To do so would be to overlook their capacity to move from those margins into the interior and to be present in several places at once.

All the same, so that their radical rejection (on the part of the Scythians) may be as meaningful as possible to Herodotus's addressee, perhaps these two powers, the Mother and Dionysus, should be seen both as Greek and, at the same time, as close to the Scythians. The fact is that they must be perceived to be Greek by the addressee if the behavior of the Scythians is to make sense and in order to illustrate the general rule put forward by the narrative. But they must also be recognized to be close to the Scythians not only geographically but culturally, if their rejection is to astonish and take on its full meaning. These are deities that it ought to be possible for them to accommodate easily (by reason of their origin, the rituals they entail, their "barbaric" aspect); yet these are the very deities that they reject utterly (as Greek). In this way, the explicit moral of the story is further reinforced: truth lies on this side of the frontier, error beyond it.

In the narrative of the misfortunes of Scyles, the narrator does not directly intervene to counterpoint the opinions he ascribes to the Scythians. It is left up to the reader to appreciate the extent to which they confuse *mania* and *bachkeuein*. The Salmoxis episode presents a richer structure and is therefore even more interesting. The discourse of the Black Sea Greeks seems to be truthful discourse that is sure of itself, that records the true facts of the case (Salmoxis is a charlatan), that knows more about the Getae than they do themselves.[171] But it is then overlaid by a direct intervention from the narrator which, in effect, ruins the reassuring and reductive explanation given by the Black Sea Greeks and reopens the question of the identity of this figure. The *chaireto* is also saying, "it is for you to decide."

---

171. The fact that it is possible to regard Salmoxism as an avatar of Pythagoreanism rebounds upon Pythagoreanism: it is a mirror effect. From the point of view of the general knowledge of the Greeks, comparison between the two is bound to be at least admissible, even if it is made by the distant citizens of Olbia and even if Salmoxis was Pythagoras's slave.

Four

The Body of the King: Space and Power

The Sick Body

The king is suffering, the king is sick, so he sends for the diviners to cure him. The diviners set to work and soon tell him the cause of his illness: a perjurer. The remedy: cut off his head. To put it another way, the royal indisposition is a symptom of perjury and it does not appear to be possible to find any other cause for it, for the diviners "for the most part tell him that such and such a man . . . has forsworn himself."[1] It is perjury that always and more than anything else physically affects the king. When a Scythian commits this crime the king immediately feels the painful effects: a number of strange relationships between the king and his subjects stem from this.

Herodotus here describes a situation that is the reverse of the well-known one involving a just king. A good and just king ensures the prosperity of his country: the land brings forth rich harvests, the herds proliferate, and the women produce "children like their parents."[2] In contrast, a bad king, one who commits a crime, who allows himself to indulge in *hubris* or is not mindful of justice, causes a *loimos:* famine spreads, the herds do not reproduce, and the women are barren. But in both these cases, it is the king, whether good or bad, who influences his subjects and country; the possibility

1. Herodotus 4.68.
2. Hesiod *Works and Days* 225–37; cf. *Odyssey* 9.109–14.

of this influence being reversed so that the subjects influence the person of the king is never even considered as a possibility.[3] Yet that is exactly what seems to happen among the Scythians, where a subject who is criminal and unjust may harm the king. In all logic, loyal subjects should, in contrast, promote his health and increase his prosperity.

The Blood of the Oath

How do the Scythians swear an oath? "They take blood from the parties to the agreement by making a little hole or cut in the body with an awl or knife [*machaira*] and pour it mixed with wine into a great earthenware bowl, wherein they then dip a scimitar and arrows and an axe and a javelin; and when this is done, the makers of the sworn agreement themselves, and the most honourable of their followers, drink of the blood after solemn imprecations [*kateuchontai*]."[4] In the *Toxaris* Lucian describes a similar blood-brothers' ritual: each of the two contractors makes a cut in his finger and lets the blood flow into a single container, and, before drinking, each of them dips the tip of his sword into it.[5]

Folklorists such as H. Gaidoz of France, ethnographers such as J. Frazier, classicists such as G. Glotz,[6] or sociologists such as the Durkheimian G. Davy[7] have noted many examples of blood covenants. But the first scholar to have advanced a theory concerning

3. On the various royal rites, see R. Roux, *Le Problème des Argonautes* (Paris, 1949). On the Persian side, note the following prayer of King Darius: "May Ahuramazda bring me help, together with all the other gods, and protect this country from the enemy army, bad harvests, and lying."

4. Hdt. 4.70. An oath was taken among the Lydians (1.74) with similar cutting of the body and licking of the blood. Among the Arabs (3.8), the palms of the contractors' hands are cut with a stone, but the blood is not drunk.

5. Lucian *Toxaris* 37. G. Dumézil, *Légende sur les Nartes* (Paris, 1930), p. 165, gives the following description of the ritual of the oath of brotherhood: "The two contractors fill a bowl with spirits or beer, toss in a silver coin and each then drinks three times, swearing to keep faith. The formulae pronounced are, for example: 'May this drink become poison, may this silver become anger, if I do not love you more than a brother,' or 'I swear by this silver, by this gold, to keep faith.' (The Ossetians considered silver 'as something sacred, possessing the power to punish')."

6. G. Glotz, *La Solidariteé de la famille en Grèce* (Paris, 1904), p. 160.

7. G. Davy, *La Foi jurée* (Paris, 1922), pp. 33–81.

these practices is Robertson Smith. In his opinion, there can be no kinship except by blood and no bond except by kinship and that is the basis of the blood-covenant, the alliance through blood. "Contractors who can only be linked as kin and who are not naturally related by kinship, if they wish to be linked, render themselves kin artificially. Since kinship means sharing the same blood, they must, through a rite of communion which may take various forms, share in each other's blood."[8] This is how Smith introduces the idea of communion, which is central to his own idea of sacrifice and which he then proceeds to develop more fully.

According to Glotz, "the ordeal is an oath in action, the oath an ordeal in words,"[9] but the Scythian oath appears, through its ritual, to be an ordeal both in action and in words. At any rate, the oath, a combination of action and words, represents an anticipated ordeal. In his study of the oath in Greece, Benveniste points out that there are solid grounds for "identifying the *horkos* with an object: whether it be a sacred substance or the scepter of authority, the essential element is always the object itself rather than the act of speech." In this case, it is a mixture of neat wine and blood that is the consecrating "object . . . that contains the power to punish any failure to honor the word given."[10]

The wine is mixed with "the blood of the contractors [*ton to horkion tamnamenon*]." What is the significance of this expression, when no mention is made of the sacrifice of any victim? The formula *horkia tamnein* is only to be found in Homer, in a few archaic Ionian inscriptions, and in Herodotus,[11] where it means both "to sacrifice victims" and also "to conclude a pact." *Horkia* "originally designated the *horkia iereia*, then came to signify the 'ceremonies of oath-taking,' while *horkion* on its own came to mean 'pact.'"[12] So in the text with which we are concerned, *horkion* and *horkia* simply mean

8. W. R. Smith *Marriage in Early Arabia* (Cambridge, 1885), pp. 56–59, and *Lectures on the Religion of the Semites* (London, 1914).

9. In C. Daremberg and E. Saglio, *Dictionnaire des antiquités* (Paris, 1887), s.v. *jusjurandum*.

10. E. Benveniste, *Vocabulaire des institutions indo-européennes* (Paris, 1969), vol. 2, p. 168.

11. See the references in J. Casabona, "Recherches sur le vocabulaire des sacrifices en grec," diss. Paris, 1967, pp. 212ff.

12 Ibid., p. 214.

"pacts," "oaths."[13] But why this combination of *horkia* and *tamnein*? According to Casabona, the expression initially denoted "the rite that consisted of cutting victims into pieces when oaths were sworn and—at the time of the constitution of the Homeric formulae, at any rate—no doubt essentially when military pacts were sealed."[14] Subsequently, when that custom had fallen into disuse, the expression was taken to mean "to slaughter victims" and, in Attic particularly, the word *temno* was related to the rite in which animals' throats were "cut." The important thing was making the blood flow from the animal's cut throat. It was not so much a matter of sacrifice in the strict sense of the term as of "a kind of blood libation."[15] Now, the Scythian oath was also based on a kind of blood libation or, to be more precise, the blood was first poured into a bowl, where it was mixed with wine.[16] Furthermore, this "libation" was not obtained from the blood of an animal victim but from the human contractors in person. This, of course, is the first fundamental difference between the Scythian ritual and a Greek oath: the contractors are in effect their own victims. Admittedly, they do not cut their own throats, but they do "make a little hole" (*tupto*) with an awl or "cut" themselves with a *machaira*. It is therefore reasonable to suppose that even if *horkia tamnein* simply means "to swear an oath," as Casabona believes, the expression is nevertheless not out of place in the context of blood-letting: blood is involved and it flows — not very much, perhaps (*smikron*), but it does come from them. We may also take it that these cuts or incisions they inflict upon themselves operate as so many reminders, by virtue of the scars they leave: the Scythians record their acts of commitment upon their bodies.

Wine, and in particular wine that is neat, is connected with the

13. Casabona notes that Herodotus uses *omnumi* for this type of private oath, p. 214. The only exception appears to be the Scythian oath, sworn between two private individuals: could it be that the public/private distinction is not applicable to Scythian society?

14. Ibid., p. 219.

15. J. Rudhardt, *Notions fondamentales de la pensée religieuse et actes constitutifs du culte dans la Grèce classique* (Geneva, 1958), p. 282. Cf. also L. Gernet, *The Anthropology of Ancient Greece* (Baltimore, 1981), p. 171.

16. The scene parodying the swearing of oaths (Aristophanes *Lysistrata* 181ff.) certainly refers to this chapter of Herodotus. For an explanation (albeit an extremely moderate one) of this passage, see Casabona, "Recherches," pp. 323–26.

oath.[17] In the swearing of oaths, wine is poured out, and in daily life the ritual of oath-taking can even be reduced to a simple libation. "Through wine, one is tied by the bonds of an oath," runs one inscription[18]—wine which, to judge from virtually all the examples, is not to be consumed but is all spilt at once.[19] Now we come to the second aberration in the Scythian ritual: wine is used in the ceremony as in "normal" practice, but instead of being a libation, it is a drink; instead of spilling it all, those involved in the ritual drink it.

The most fundamental deviation from the Greek ritual relates to the quality of the blood and the way it is used. This is human, not animal, blood. Furthermore, simply to make it flow from an animal's throat and to cover the victim with it do not suffice. It must be mixed with wine and drunk; wine and blood are mixed in a great bowl, as wine and water are mingled in a Greek crater. Herodotus does report one case in which Greeks drink human blood: they are the Greek and Carian mercenaries in the service of the pharaoh Amasis. Before engaging in battle against the Persians, they slaughter two children and collect their blood in a crater; then, having added wine and water, each man takes a drink of it.[20] Herodotus rationalizes this sacrificial scene, explaining it as an act of vengeance: the two children were the sons of Phanes. This Phanes, a native of Halicarnassus, was one of Amasis's mercenaries who had left his employer and offered his services to Cambyses. His former comrades held this against him and made a point of killing his children before their father's very eyes. The charge of monstrosity which could be leveled at this sacrifice, which is both propitiatory and connected with an oath, is thus answered by ascribing the act to vengeance.

The *Seven against Thebes* provides another example of the connections that exist between blood and oath-swearing. The messenger tells Eteocles:

> There were seven men, fierce regiment commanders,
> Who cut bulls' throats into an iron-rimmed
> Shield, and with hands touched the bulls' blood,
> Taking their oath by Ares and Enyo,

17. Homer *Iliad* 2.339ff. 13.245ff., 4.158ff.
18. Gernet, *Anthropology*, p. 169.
19. For example, *Iliad* 3.296.
20. Hdt. 3.11.

By the blood-thirsty god of Battle Rout,
Either to lay your city level
With the ground, sacked, or by their death to make
A bloody paste of this same soil of yours.[21]

This ritual is already "sweetened" (the blood comes from a bull and it is smeared on the hands, not imbibed), but Aeschylus nevertheless ascribed it to the seven monstrous warriors attacking the seven gates of Thebes. Blood is always a fearsome beverage, but the blood of a bull is particularly so, since it passes for a poison: to drink the blood of a bull is to kill oneself, and to force somebody else to drink the blood of a bull is to force him to commit suicide. But Glotz believes that "the legendary suicide by the blood of a bull is really simply an ordeal distorted by people who no longer understood it."[22] In other words, in the case of the oath, the wording might have been something like: "May this blood become poisonous to me if the oath which I swear is false." An extreme and mythical example of what a liquid affected by a false oath can do is provided by the waters of the Styx: when a god swears a great oath, he spills out the contents of the golden ewer in which the waters have been collected; if he is a perjurer he falls down, inert, and remains so, without breathing, for a year.[23] Herodotus does not record the words pronounced during the ceremony: he says nothing about the invocation, the promises, or the prayer. All we know is that "there were many prayers [*kateuchontai polla*]." Did they, in the manner of the Ossetians, say: "May this drink become poisonous to me?" It seems probable. In any event, the action of dipping weapons into the bowl appears to suggest that if the oath is false, they too will become poisonous and will, without fail, strike down the perjurer.

To the Greeks, a perjurer was certainly a criminal. He was a man who swore a false oath or, to be more precise, as Benveniste explains,

21. Aeschylus *Seven against Thebes* 42–48; cf. also Xenophon *Anabasis* 2.2.10: the mercenaries dip not their hands but their swords into a shield filled wtih blood. "These oaths they sealed by sacrificing a bull, a boar and a ram over a shield, the Greeks dipping a sword in the blood and the barbarians a lance." The kings of Atlantis also drink a mixture of bull's blood, wine, and water (Plato *Critias* 119d ff.).
22. G. Glotz, *L'Ordalie dans la Grèce primitive* (Paris, 1904), p. 112, where the examples are collected.
23. Hesiod *Theogony* 135ff.

one who added (*epi*) an oath (*horkos*) to a statement or promise which he knew to be false.[24] For him there could thereafter be no rest or salvation, as the Pythia explains to Glaucus, who comes to consult her to find out whether through a false oath he can keep money entrusted to him which he would prefer not to return: "But an oath has a son, anonymous, with neither hands nor feet. Yet swiftly he pursues him [the perjurer] until he seizes him and destroys all his descendants and all his house. The descendants of the man who keeps his word will enjoy a better fate."[25]

The perjurer thus causes his own ruin and that of his *oikos*; a kind of *loimos* descends upon him and his. But the important point is that his punishment is a matter for the gods, not for men. Demosthenes states that a perjurer commits an injustice, an impiety against the gods (*adikei tous theous*);[26] and, in truth, "no ancient Indo-European code provided sanctions against a perjurer. His punishment was reckoned to come from the gods, since they were the guarantors of the oath."[27] Yet the Scythians, strangely enough, did provide such a punishment. Having been identified by the diviners, the perjurer was beheaded. They did not leave it to the gods to wreak vengeance and reestablish the order that had been upset in this way—at least, they certainly did not in the case of a false oath sworn "by the royal hearths [*basileias histias*]," swearing by the royal hearths being "their greatest oath [*megiston horkon*]."

Imprecations against perjury usually promised perjurers sterility for their women and the extinction of their hearth.[28] Thus, Glaucus, as a punishment for having considered not returning what had been entrusted to him, beheld his hearth (*histia*) annihilated: "There is, at this day, no descendant of Glaucus, nor any household that bears his name; he and his have been utterly uprooted from Sparta."[29] A close

24. Benveniste, *Vocabulaire*, p. 170.

25. Hdt. 6.86. This declaration echoes a few lines in Hesiod: *Theogony* 231–32, *Works and Days* 219, 282ff., 321ff.

26. Demosthenes 48 (*Against Olympios*) 52.

27. Benveniste, *Vocabulaire*, p. 175. Cf. Glotz, *Solidarité*, p. 574. Lycurgus: "a perjurer cannot evade the attention of the gods nor avoid their vengeance" (*Against Leocrates* 79–80).

28. For imprecations against the perjurer, see Rudhardt, *Notions Fondamentales*, p. 208 n. 4.

29. Hdt. 6.86.

link thus exists between the oath and the hearth: whoever commits perjury puts his hearth in danger, brings destruction down upon his own hearth. But among the Scythians, the perjurer, through an astonishing transference, damages not his own hearth but the king himself. The king immediately falls sick (*kame*) and suffers (*algeei*). No doubt this only happens when an oath has been sworn "by the royal hearths," but why does the impiety, the injustice toward the royal hearths, immediately rebound upon the person of the king? Why is it made manifest in the body of the king?

The Body of the King: Hestia and Nomadism

The first question this poses is that of the royal hearth and, more generally, that of Hestia's place in the Scythian pantheon. Curiously enough, Hestia occupies the place of paramount importance among the Scythians. It is to her, in preference to all other deities, that they address their prayers. Next in importance come Zeus and Ge.[30] Idanthyrsus, the king of the Scythians, testifies to the supremacy of Hestia in his reply to Darius. When the Great King bids him submit, he answers that where masters (*despotes*) are concerned, he recognizes only two: "Zeus, my forefather, and Hestia, queen of the Scythians."[31] So Hestia, being the *basileia* of the Scythians, is also their *despotes*. And what is the king in relation to Hestia? Is his position in relation to the Scythians the same as hers in relation to the other gods, perhaps? That would make him, in a sense, analogous to Hestia.[32] And we should remember that in cases of perjury through swearing by the royal hearths, it is he who is affected and who suffers.

On the subject of Hestia, Herodotus adds that in the Scythian tongue Hestia is called Tabiti.[33] Dumézil notes that this is the only

30. Hdt. 4.59: "The only gods whom they propitiate by worship are these: first and foremost Hestia, and secondly Zeus and the Earth, whom they deem to be the wife of Zeus; after these, Apollo, and the Heavenly Aphrodite, and Heracles and Ares"; cf. below, p. 174. Hestia is seldom mentioned in the *Histories*: the only people mentioned in connection with her, apart from the Scythians, are the Egyptians, of whom we are told simply that they know nothing of her.

31. Hdt. 4.127.

32. Idanthyrsus nevertheless mentions that Zeus is his ance

33. Hdt. 4.59.

name whose meaning is immediately clear: she is called Tabiti, which means "the one who heats"[34]—that is to say, her name is almost identical to that of the luminous Indian Tapiti, the daughter of the sun. If Hestia is the *basileia* of the Scythians, we have seen that swearing by "the royal hearths [*tas basileias histias*]" was the most solemn of all oaths for a Scythian. So Hestia is the hearth. Dumézil, citing this same Herodotean text, points out that among the Ossetians "the hearth is the holy place par excellence: the most solemn oath is sworn 'by the hearth,' while holding onto the iron chain suspended above the hearth."[35] As for the importance of the royal fire, we find that it is emphasized in Iran during the Sassanid period: the king had his own personal fire, lit when he came to the throne and extinguished when he died. The years of his reign were counted from the time it was first lit.[36] Herodotus does not say that it was the same for the Scythian kings, but the example helps us to understand that the royal fire may have constituted a point of reference, marking a point in time and the beginning of a period for contracts.

Why does the text refer to "royal hearths" in the plural? We know from the chapters devoted to the origins of the Scythian people that there were three kings: if each king had a hearth it is not strange to find "royal hearths," in the plural. All the same, chapter 68 only mentions *the* king of the Scythians ("when the king of the Scythians is sick"), as if he were the sole sovereign. So, in the immediate context, these plural hearths belong to one, sole, singular person. But there is another possible explanation: the same person has several *successive* hearths. As a nomad, the king moves from place to place and his hearth moves with him; alternatively, simpler still, the plural may reflect the royal "we."

But there is an association here that we must find suprising: Hestia and nomadism. How can a nomad revere Hestia above all else? Hestia is connected with space and its representations; she

34. G. Dumézil, *Romans de Scythie et d'alentour* (Paris, 1978), p. 143. Dumézil suggests a connection between the Indian Tapati, daughter of the sun; the Ossetian Acyruxs, also a daughter of the sun; and Herodotus's Hestia-Tabiti.

35. Dumézil, *Légendes sur les Nartes*, p. 154. Cf. his *Religion romaine archaïque* (Paris, 1966), p. 318: "Among the modern Ossetians, the last descendants of the Scythians, it is also the fire spirit who is mentioned at the end of the 'general prayer' addressed to fourteen gods or spirits, which provides a framework for all special liturgies."

36. G. Widengren, *Les Religions de l'Iran* (trans. Paris, 1968), p. 351.

relates to the terrestial expanse, she is even an "expression"[37] of space, but her domain is that of human beings with fixed abodes, not of nomads. The *Homeric Hymn* puts it as follows:[38] "Hestia, in the high dwellings of all, both deathless gods and men who walk on earth, you have gained an everlasting abode and highest honor. Glorious is your portion and your right [*geras kai time*]." The house is Hestia's allotted place among both gods and men and, as the *Homeric Hymn to Aphrodite* states, there she "is enthroned in the midst of the house"[39] and there she is unmovable. So she is the center of domesticated space and, that being the case, this center represents the values of fixity, immutability, permanence.[40] Now, the point is that Scythians, precisely, do not have fixed houses; they are "house-bearers" (*phereoikoi*), who carry their dwellings on waggons (*iokemata epi zeugeon*).[41]

The fixity of the hearth, the rootedness of the home: these concepts are unfamiliar to the Scythians, who are constantly engaged in driving their herds before them, moving on from one encampment to the next.

All things considered, it would seem logical if, among nomads, Hestia's role should be reduced, even dispensed with, while that of her "neighbor," Hermes, ought to be important, even the most important of all. However, if Hestia is, curiously enough, the principal Scythian deity, equally surprisingly Hermes is altogether absent from their pantheon.[42] Yet Hermes is the master of the *agros*, the lord of the land reserved for pasturage, far away from cultivated fields, and of the open spaces where wild animals are hunted.[43] And surely the whole of Scythia, an area of *eschatia*, is a land of *agros*. Hermes' specialty is that of moving from one place to another. "To

37. J.-P. Vernant, "Hestia-Hermes," *Myth and Thought among the Greeks* (London, 1983), pp. 127–76.

38. *Homeric Hymn to Hestia* 1.1–3.

39. *Homeric Hymn to Aphrodite* 30.

40. Vernant, "Hestia-Hermes," p. 126: "Hestia represents not only the center of the domestic sphere: fixed in the ground, the circular hearth denotes the navel which ties the house to the earth. It is the symbol and pledge of fixity, immutability and permanence."

41. Hdt. 4.46.

42. On Hermes, in addition to the analyses by J.-P. Vernant in "Hestia-Hermes," see L. Kahn, *Hermès passe* (Paris, 1978).

43. P. Chantraine, *Etudes sur le vocabulaire grec* (Paris, 1956), pp. 34–35.

Hermes, the outside, escape outward, movement, interchange with others."[44] Yet the Scythians give no recognition to the son of Maia, while all in all, for a Greek it was Hestia and Hermes who expressed spatial relationships. These two powers formed a couple:

> by virtue of their polarity, the Hermes-Hestia couple represents the tension which is so marked in the archaic representation of space: space requires a center, a nodal point with a special value, from which all directions, each different qualitatively, may be channeled and defined; yet at the same time space appears as the medium of movement, implying the possibility of transition and passage from any one point to another.[45]

Hestia "centers" space and Hermes "mobilizes" it.

From these two figures who express space (Hestia together with Hermes), the Scythians appear to have selected Hestia on her own, as if they set a higher value on the center, at the expense of opportunity to move outward and mobility, despite the fact that they are people who do not know the meaning of staying still.

What should we make of the fact that it is Hestia, not Hermes, whom the Scythians revere? In the first place, this is a royal Hestia. She is constantly linked with the king: "As Queen of the Scythians, she is 'the royal hearth.'" So her position depends on that of the king and her power depends on that of the sovereign. This mention of the royal hearth refers back to a bygone age in Greece, when no city hearth as yet existed and the hearth of the royal household played the role of primary importance: "The preeminent value of the royal hearth still survives, here and there, in the memory of poetry."[46] In tragedy, the royal hearth and the city hearth are sometimes opposed or confused.[47] But in Scythia there can be no such duality, for since the sole power is royal power there is no common hearth apart from the royal hearth. In that sense Hestia truly is the *basileia* of the Scythians.

Moreover, the royal hearth is the place and the object of the most solemn of oaths, the most binding oath, the one that, if perjury is involved, may cause the king to sicken. In Greece, in contrast,

44. Vernant, "Hestia-Hermes," p. 130.
45. Ibid.
46. L. Gernet, "Political Symbolism: The Common Hearth," *Anthropology.*
47. E.g., Aeschylus *The Suppliant Women* 365ff.

Hestia is not numbered among the deities generally invoked when oaths are sworn.[48] All the same, during the classical period there was, we know, one oath sworn by Hestia Boulaia: Aeschines writes that Demosthenes "swore by Hestia Boulaia [*ten Hestian epiomose ten Boulaian*] that he congratulated the city for having entrusted this mission to men who . . . ."[49] So within the precincts of the Boule existed an altar to Hestia and she was involved on certain occasions; but there was nothing comparable to the central role played among the Scythians by the royal hearth, which was both the guarantor and the medium for the most solemn contracts. Within the space of Scythia the royal hearth represented and functioned as a sort of junction: when two Scythians wished to make an agreement, this was where they came. Through the oath, the royal Hestia truly was the center of Scythian society and in this respect conforms to the Hestia mentioned by J.-P. Vernant, the Hestia who "provides a center" for space. Yet, to the extent that it is she who authorizes meetings and exchanges, she who is where oaths are sworn, she also, in part, represents escape outward and mobility, "as though Hestia already belonged to Hermes."[50]

Dumézil noted that among the Ossetians the most serious of all oaths was sworn by the hearth, and he compared this information with Herodotus's text, remarking, however, that "the custom has simply been democratized or decentralized among the Ossetians, who have retained neither a king nor any unity."[51] Among them, any hearth can be invoked equally well to guarantee a commitment, and there is no need to call on the "agent of exchange" represented by the royal hearth; this is a society that has been "democratized" or "decentralized" or, at any rate, where there is no dominant royal power. In contrast, Herodotus's Scythia is characterized by the

48. The most frequently invoked deities are Zeus, Apollo, Demeter, or Zeus, Poseidon, Demeter; cf. Rudhardt, *Notions fondomentales*, p. 204.

49. Aeschines 2 (*On Embassy*) 45; Harpokration, s.v. *Boulaia*; A. Preuner. *Hestia-Vesta* (Tübingen, 1864), pp. 118ff.

50. Vernant, "Hestia-Hermes," p. 159: "the polarity that is so marked a characteristic of all the goddess's relations with Hermes is such a basic feature of archaic thought that it appears as an integral attribute of the hearth-goddess, as though Hestia already belonged to Hermes."

51. Dumézil, *Légendes sur les Nartes*, p. 155.

presence of the king as the center of power. His hearth is the place through which contracts must pass, and it provides the point of reference for all social relations. At the limit, individual Scythians have no hearth of their own; their only true hearth is that of the king.

The diviners declare that "such or such a man (naming whoever it is of the citizens [*ton aston*]) has forsworn himself by the king's hearth." This statement contains one quite astonishing word: it is, clearly, *astoi*, city-dwellers or citizens. The fact is that as soon as we find ourselves in this context of oath-swearing and the royal hearth, the Scythians must be *astoi*. The procedure of oath-swearing and the invocation of the royal hearth turn the Scythian society into a *koinonia* of *astoi*,[52] as if their nomadism no longer counted. They suddenly become a fixed and centered community; that constantly shifting world of theirs is forgotten. It is fascinating to note how Herodotus presents the royal hearth as the hearth of the city—the hearth that guarantees the contracts of the *astoi*—and how it assumes the role of *Hestia koine*, the common hearth of the city. At the same time, however, we are presented with the strange relationship that exists between it and the person of the king, and this turns it into something quite other than the hearth of the *astoi*.

In this connection between the body of the king and the social body which obtains among the Scythians, the royal body extends until it finally swallows up the social or political body. It is a notion whose strangeness compares to that of a theory elaborated much later, in medieval England, in relation to the double nature of the king. Kantorowicz has explained this duality of the royal body: "The king has two bodies, the one whereof is a body natural, consisting of natural members as every other man has, and he is subject to passions and death as other men are; the other is a body politic, and the members thereof are his subjects."[53] The two bodies are at the same time completely distinct and perfectly united. But in the case of the Scythian king, a fault on the part of the body politic (a perjury) affects the king's natural body (he suffers). By calling into question the foundation for the possibility of a contract, the crime of perjury

52. The same "forgetfulness" occurs in connection with Salmoxis (Hdt. 4.95), who invites the chief among the *astoi* to the communal meals that he organizes among the Getae.

53. E. H. Kantorowicz, *The King's Two Bodies* (Princeton, 1957), p. 13.

attacks the king physically. Perjury is thus a form of regicide. In Greece, perjury puts one's own health in danger; and if, in Scythia, it strikes at the hearth of the king, is not that a way of saying that, in the last analysis, the only real hearth there is that of the king? The figure of the king is so dominant that he is the only person truly to possess a hearth. So, in the fullest sense, Hestia is the one who provides a center for the space and unites the Scythians.

As for nomadism, the presence of Hestia, which transforms the Scythians into *astoi*, seems to have eliminated it. But perhaps it lives on in that plural form we mentioned just now: why the royal hearths? Because the king is constantly on the move between one hearth and the next, even if each one is the same as the last, and Hestia thus provides a center not so much for the geographical as for the social space. The Scythian people thus perhaps resemble one of the constellations that pass across the heavens: although they are always changing position, each of the stars that goes to compose them remains at a constant distance from every other.

How to Produce the Truth

To discover the causes of his sickness, the king calls in the diviners. As men of knowledge and power, they are the administrators of the truth: their skill enables them to know the true cause of the king's sickness, that is, to point out who, of all the Scythians, is the perjurer. Their knowledge thus confers on them the power of life and death over the Scythians, but there is another side to the coin: they too risk their lives. If, at the end of the exercise, they are bound to admit they have been *pseudomantis*, "lying diviners," they are executed. There are many of them, and "they divine by means of many willow wands. . . . They bring great bundles of wands, which they lay on the ground and unfasten, and utter their divinations [*thespizousi*], laying the rods down one by one; and while they yet speak they gather up the rods once more and again place them together."[54] Another category of diviners, the Enareis, use lime-tree bark, which they "plait and unplait" in their fingers. Ammianus Marcellinus, similarly, writes of the Alains: "They divine the future

54. Hdt. 4.67.

by a strange method; they cut up very straight sticks and, at a given moment, they arrange them in a particular way, uttering secret formulae: in this way they discover what is going to happen."[55] In the 1880s, the Russian scholar Vs. Miller, in his *Ossetian Studies* (1881–1887), was the first to illuminate Herodotus's text by establishing a connection between these procedures and the customs of the modern Ossetians.[56]

So it is the patterns formed by the sticks or the way they move that enables the diviners to decode the answer to the question posed. But in his description of this procedure, Herodotus cannot prevent himself from ascribing more importance to what is said than to what is seen, so that the manipulation of the rods is, finally, simply an accompaniment to the words that are pronounced. It is first and foremost the words that count: "they utter their divinations [*thespizousi*]."[57] To establish a connection between the two levels, Herodotus simply coordinates them through *ama*, meaning "at the same time": "while they yet speak, they gather up the rods once more and again place them together." The two activities are juxtaposed, not really articulated: the rods certainly do not dictate the words; as for the words, what need have they of rods? By using the Greek oracular vocabulary of divination, Herodotus thus stresses what is heard

55. Ammianus Marcellinus 21.2.24.

56. Dumézil, *Romans de Scythie et d'alentour*, pp. 212ff: "Among the Ossetians, sorcerers are held in high esteem . . . S. Y. Koviev tells us: 'Each sorcerer has four little rods with one end split. These enable him to divine the meaning of all events. The sorcerer approaches the sick man, sits on the ground, and asks for a cushion of a particular color and a sheet or clean carpet which he spreads out, meanwhile reciting a particular formula. He takes the four rods from his pocket, places them on the ground in two pairs, each joined at the split ends. As for the two free ends of each pair, one rests on the cushion, the other is held by the sorcerer. Holding one end of each pair in each hand, the sorcerer loudly pronounces the names of a number of spirits who may have sent the sickness. With each name, he asks that if it be the correct one, either the pair of rods on the left or the pair on the right should rise up and, of course, at the moment chosen by the charlatan, cleverly and imperceptibly he himself lifts the pair that is supposed to rise.'"

57. R. Crahay, "La Bouche de la verité." in *Divination et rationalité*, ed. J. P. Vernant (Paris, 1974), p. 204: "*Thespizo* appears, albeit somewhat obscurely, to be connected with *theos*, god, and with a verb implying 'declaring,' attested in the form of *ennepo*, the aorist being *espon*. (See also *thespesios*: with a divine voice.) The word thus appears to mean 'to pronounce divine words.' Similarly, *chrao*, 'from *chre*' (it is necessary, it is normal) appears to be a verb implying 'saying' and meaning 'to say *chre*.'"

rather than what is seen, without thinking of connecting the two. For a Greek, divination was first and foremost an oral procedure.[58] Introducing this Greek schema serves both to reduce and to devalue the "otherness" of the Scythian custom, for the Scythian divination is interpreted in terms of the Greek and meanwhile it is reduced and devalued, since the lime-tree bark or willow rods apparently serve no purpose.

The diviners are summoned by the king to make their diagnosis. There appear to be no doctors in Scythia and no medicine apart from divination. Not that the text stresses that fact in any way, for recourse to diviners in cases of sickness is presented as going without saying. Simply, since the king is involved, it is necessary to send for the diviners "most in repute." It is, however, worth noting that when the Great Kings fall sick, they turn not to magi but to doctors. Cambyses sends for an Egyptian doctor to cure his eyes, and Darius turns to Democedes of Croton to treat his foot.[59] Does the Scythian way of proceeding really go without saying, or does Herodotus only pretend to present it as doing so? Whatever the case may be, divination is the functional equivalent of a diagnosis. To name the perjurer is to indicate the cause for the king's sufferings (*dia tauta algeei o basileus*): that is why your daughter is dumb!

To locate the cause of the evil is also to condemn the guilty party, so the diagnosis is a form of judgment and the divination also functions as an ordeal. The diviners are, in their own way, truly "masters of the truth,"[60] and their words combine divination and justice. Greece also was familiar with this form of justice which resorted to divination. In Mantinea, as late as the fifth century, "in an affair of sacrilege, a tribunal composed of a mixture of priests and

58. J.-P. Vernant, "Paroles et signes muets," *Divination et rationalité*, p. 18: "The Greeks set a high value on oral divination. Rather than techniques for interpreting signs and procedures involving chance, such as the throwing of dice, which they regarded as minor forms, they preferred what R. Crahay has called 'oracular dialogue,' in which the words of the god respond directly to the questions of those consulting him. This preeminence of the word as a means of communication with the beyond is in line with the basically oral character of a civilization in which writing is not only a recent phenomenon but, by virtue of its entirely phonetic character, functions as an extension of the spoken language."

59. Hdt. 3.1, 130.

60. M. Detienne, *Les Maîtres de vérité dans la Grèce ancienne* (Paris, 1967), pp. 29–50.

judges fixes the sanction which may be inflicted upon the guilty, but has the verdict depend upon an oracle."[61] Of course here, the fact that sacrilege is involved is relevant to the use of this archaic procedure, which Glotz describes as "an ordeal without suffering." As they pronounce their formulae and shuffle their rods in order to discover the sacrilege embodied in the perjurer, the Scythian diviners are likewise operating a kind of "ordeal without suffering": it is not a matter of discovering truth of a historical nature, which could be done by holding an inquiry. Instead, through "the correct application of the procedure, ritually carried out,"[62] the truth is declared; it is not proven. It is used as proof but cannot itself be proven. This ancient type of proof, divination, is, furthermore, decisive:[63] if the second batch of diviners, through their divination, confirms the "diagnosis" of the first batch, the perjurer must forthwith (*itheos*) be put to death. The sentence is automatically determined by the outcome of the divination. Similarly, in the opposite case, when a majority of diviners pronounce in favor of the innocence of the man denounced as perjurer by the first group of diviners, the first diviners must automatically die (*dedoktai*). That is how it is; there is no appeal against the sentence, and the divination, once more, provides the decisive proof.

Thus, where the king is concerned, divination is at once a diagnosis, an ordeal, and an archaic type of proof, but it is also more. The moment the perjurer is brought before the diviners, the setting suddenly changes and we find ourselves in a court of law with a trial taking place. From this point onward, the perjurer or the one whom divination has declared to be such is regarded as "the accused": he is "arrested" and "brought up."[64] What does he do? Like any accused, he begins by denying the charge: no, he is not a perjurer. His denials

61. Glotz, *L'Ordalie*, p. 5. It is also worth noting the Megarean custom, mentioned by Theognis (543ff.): "I must give each party their fair due by resorting to diviners, to birds and to burning altars, so as to avoid making a shameful mistake."

62. Detienne, *Maîtres de vérité*, p. 49.

63. Gernet, *Anthropology*, p. 222.

64. Hdt. 4.68: "Forthwith the man whom they allege to be forsworn is seized and brought in, and when he comes the diviners accuse him, saying that their divination shows him to have forsworn himself by the king's hearths and that this is the cause of the king's sickness; and the man vehemently denies he is forsworn. So when he denies it, the king sends for twice as many diviners; and if they too, looking into their art, prove him guilty of perjury, then straightaway he is beheaded and his

transform the confrontation into a trial for, on hearing his plea, the king summons other diviners, twice as many in number.

By challenging the legitimacy of the action against him, the accused forces the king to intervene and assume the position of judge in charge of the course of the proceedings. Here again, the Scythian king plays an astonishing role. He is at once the patient about whose body the doctor-diviners gather and also the one presiding over a court sitting in judgment upon an attack against his "body politic." With this new distribution of roles, the diviners are no sooner brought face to face with the accused-perjurer than they become prosecutors and adopt a legal vocabulary. They "convict" him of perjury (*elegkhousi*)—*elegkhos* being sufficient proof for conviction—they "condemn him, after convicting him" (*katadesosi*), or else they "find him innocent" (*apolusosi*). All these expressions belong to the legal *agon* in which speech becomes a dialogue seeking to convince or convict.

But the limits of the *agon* are soon reached, for there can be no real dialogue. In his defense, the accused can do no more than "plead not guilty" and "vehemently deny" (*deinologein*); there is no way for him to prove his innocence by demonstrating it. The diviners, men who know, use divination as evidence, but to the extent that this knowledge cannot be questioned and this evidence "cannot be put to any positivistic use,"[65] it continues to function as proof in the archaic sense of the term. In their attempt to win a conviction, the diviners do no more than invoke their divination, "saying that their divination shows him to have forsworn himself [*epiorkesas phainetai en tei mantikei*]," or that "they can see in the divination [*esorontes es ten mantiken*]."[66] This time Herodotus stresses the ocular nature of the divination, to make it quite clear that it cannot be questioned. In other words, this Scythian "court" is not the Areopagus of the *Oresteia*, whose task it is to pass judgment, not in accordance with oaths sworn, but on the basis of evidence and the testimony of witnesses. This is no "investigation."

---

goods are divided among the first diviners; but if the later diviners acquit him, then other diviners come and yet again others. If then the greater number acquit the man, it is decreed that the first diviners shall themselves be put to death."

65. Gernet, *Anthropology*, p. 170.

66. Hdt. 4.68. An equivalent use of this verb is to be found at 7.219, where the diviner Megistias, "having *esidon es ta ira*, announces that . . . "

This strange court has one more important surprise to spring on us. In the end, the rule of majority decision is observed. If the majority of the diviners condemn the accused, he is beheaded; if the majority pronounce him innocent, he is released.[67] The application of such a rule puts one in mind of the procedure of multiple oaths. We know of a murder law from Cyme (in the Aeolid): "If the prosecutor on the charge of murder produces a certain number of his own relatives as witnesses, the defendant is guilty of murder."[68] Aristotle cites this law as an example of the naïveté but also of the simplicity and barbarity of the legislation of past times. Other cases are also known, in particular in Crete, where an oath sworn in a group in this fashion was decisive.[69]

This procedure, well known in ancient legal systems, indicates a kind of turning point since it reveals, rather naïvely, the need for proof, but it partakes of a primitive concept of justice: neither "witnesses to the truth" nor "witnesses to credibility," as has sometimes been understood, the co-swearers, by their collective willingness, are not affirming a fact but are rendering a decision concerning the "law." That is, if they are numerous enough, they assure the "victory" of the familial party they represent.[70]

Although a comparison with this procedure may throw some light on how the Scythian "court" functioned, significant differences remain between the two. The Scythian diviners do not represent any "family party," and above all they swear no oath; there is no co-swearing of an oath, simply co-divination.[71]

67. We should note one problem about Herodotus's description of these events: the king sends for three diviners, then six. If the six confirm the divination of the first three, the man is executed; if they challenge it, the king sends for others, until a majority opinion emerges. But is there not already a majority when the first group of six makes its pronouncement? Or perhaps each *group's* vote counts equally.

68. Aristotle *Politics* 2.5.10–12. 1269a (*plethos ti marturon*).

69. The custom was simply to fix the necessary number of co-swearers; the rule of the majority was also sometimes applied, as a (fragmentary) clause in the Gortyn code indicates. Victory went to the party on whose side the greatest number swore (*niken d'otera k'hoi p* [*lies o*] *mosonti*). See G. Sautel, "Les Preuves en droit grec archaïque," *Recueils de la Société J. Bodin* 16 (1965): 135–41.

70. Gernet, *Anthropology*, p. 192.

71. To complete the picture, we should also remember that the diviners, by drawing lots, divided up (*dialagchanousi*) the possessions of the condemned man among themselves. What was the significance of this drawing of lots? It is the only time this verb is used in Herodotus.

All in all, this text, albeit simple in appearance, is a difficult one. The few comparisons we have considered have shown that in this production of the truth, divination functions at once as an ordeal, as a proof, and as evidence. Of course, part of the difficulty stems from the fact that Herodotus takes good care not to provide details: for example, is the king cured once the perjurer has been executed? If the presumed perjurer finally turns out to be innocent, do the diviners have to discover another? But the rapidity of the sequence of events helps to create an impression of "otherness." It is one way the traveler can suggest distancing. The text is difficult to understand because it is difficult to imagine how Herodotus's audience may have received it. How was this trial regarded? As some bizarre procedure? As an archaic way of revealing the truth? Or, on the contrary, as a procedure to which one might oneself resort, under some circumstances? After all, in Mantinea, even in the fifth century, in a matter of sacrilege the judgment depended on an oracle. In any event, it provides evidence of the close interrelation among divination, pre-law, and law.

The sickness of the king sets in action a procedure for producing the truth, the result of which is to "prove" that the perjurer is a true perjurer and the diviners are true diviners,[72] or, alternatively, that the perjurer is not a true perjurer and the diviners are false diviners (*pseudomantis*). In either case, the end result is one or more executions. The perjurer is beheaded (*apotamnousi ten kephalen*), in other words, he is treated as an enemy, for the Scythians beheaded their enemies.[73] To cut off his head is to consider him no longer to be a Scythian. We already know of one example of a famous Scythian who suffered this assuredly humiliating death: Scyles, traitor to the Scythian *nomoi*, was beheaded by order of his own brother.[74] So the perjurer is an enemy and a traitor and the death inflicted on him confirms that to swear falsely by the royal hearths is to undermine the very basis of the Scythian *koinonia*. As for diviners who ultimately turn out to be "masters of falsehood," they too must be eliminated. The ritual of their death is strange and unique: they are not treated as enemies but undergo a nomad death. "Men yoke oxen to a waggon

72. The expression *alethemantis* is applied to Cassandra (Aeschylus *Agamemnon* 1241).
73. Hdt. 4.64.
74. Hdt. 4.80.

laden with sticks and make the diviners fast amid these, fettering
their legs and binding their hands behind them and gagging them;
then they set fire to the sticks and drive the oxen away by frightening
them."[75] The diviner who has revealed himself to be a bad doctor,
incapable of diagnosing the sickness of the king, incapable of producing the truth, is expelled, away from the royal body. He is not
insulted, beaten, or stoned, but burned. He goes to annihilation out
on the steppes, where his ashes will be dispersed: a *pharmakos*, but
one who is charged only with his own "fault," he dies for having been
a *pseudomantis*, a master of falsehood. Before a dead king is buried,
he is paraded before his subjects; an individual passes among his
relatives before he is buried; but the diviner is tossed onto a wagon,
to be consumed in the flames. His charred body will have no burial
and nobody will come to gather up his ashes. He is wiped out; the
steppes are like the sea.

Masters of truth and masters of accusation as they are, the diviners
are also the king's doctors, but only at the peril of their own lives.
Their power may be great but their frailty is no less so. This
combination of strength and frailty is the mark of the ambiguity of
their status vis-à-vis the power which they serve and which has need
of them. Such ambiguity is in no way surprising to the Greeks, who
were quite familiar with the question of relations between the
diviner and the sovereign: witness the figure of Tiresias.[76] Moreover,
the ambiguity of their position is further reinforced since, among the
many Scythian diviners, there are some, the Enareis, who are
"androgynous."[77] But here again the story of Tiresias, who was first a
man, then a woman, then a man again, serves as testimony to the fact
that the Scythian diviners simply belong to that same category of
mediators whom the Greeks were prone to represent to themselves
as ambiguous beings.

75. Hdt. 4.69.
76. Detienne, *Maîtres de vérité*, p. 50 n. 111. On Tiresias, see L. Brisson, *Le
Mythe de Tirésias* (Leiden, 1976). On the status of witchcraft, cf. M. Auge, "Les
Croyances à la sorcellerie," in *La Construction du monde* (Paris, 1974), pp. 52–70.
77. A number of texts mention the Enareis: Hdt. 1.105, 4.67; Hippocratic Corpus
Airs, Waters, Places 22: here the Enareis are men who have become impotent and
who live and dress as women, but there is no suggestion that they are diviners;
Aristotle *Nicomachean Ethics* 7.7. See also L. Brisson, "Bi-sexualité et médiation en
Grèce ancienne," *Nouvelle Revue de Psychanalyse* (Spring 1973): 27–48.

The king's sickness demonstrates that the royal person is the central figure in a despotic power in which the royal body and the social body tend to become confused. At the same time that he is the patient by whose sickbed the solicitous gather, he is also the judge who, from start to finish, controls the entire procedure: he is the dealer of death. The centrality of this power is expressed through the position held by Hestia and by the fundamental role played by the royal hearths.

The Dead Body: The Kings' Funerals

> *And I will tell you of another great marvel: when the bodies of these Great Khans are brought to these mountains for burial, even if they be forty or more days distant, all the people who are met on the way are put to the sword by those bringing the body. And as they kill, they say: "Go and serve your lord in the other world!"*
>
> Marco Polo, *Description of the World*, chap. 69

Funerary rites have always been considered choice morsels by observers, travelers, and ethnologists. To those who know how to see, they tell much about the life of the tribe, ethnic group, or society involved. To those who know how to listen, they make it possible to piece together the system of representations of the group to which the man or woman whose funeral is being celebrated belonged.[78] So the question which now arises is, what place does Herodotus's discourse allot to the death of "the other"? What is the pertinence of this figure in the rhetoric of otherness, if we take the funeral rites of the Scythian kings to represent an example par excellence of it?[79]

Death is a sign of otherness and is an important factor in the ever-renewed tension between what is the same and what is other: it produces a manifestation of difference. It could be said, "Tell me how you die and I will tell you who you are." But even as it makes its mark as a discriminator, it is also a category and a subject for classification.

78. E. Durkheim, *Les Formes élémentaires de la vie religieuse* (Paris, 1912), pp. 557ff.

79. Hdt. 4.71–73.

It is quite possible for the observer to construct a table of funerary customs ranging across the spectrum from extreme sameness to extreme otherness. In his treatise *On Mourning*, Lucian recognizes the pertinence of such distinctions when he declares that "the Greek burns, the Persian buries, the Indian covers with glass, the Scythian eats, and the Egyptian salts" the body.[80]

Death and the Civic Space

Death is connected with space. It is even an element in the representation of space: what does a community do with its dead? Are they kept in the house? Are they put in a special place? In this sense, the otherness of death and the otherness of space are probably two sides to a single coin.

Where did the classical city put its dead? As a rule they were not buried inside the town.[81] There were obviously a number of exceptions: for instance, the rule does not appear to have obtained in the case of children; Pausanias mentions the presence of tombs inside Megara;[82] and a necropolis has been found inside the walls of Tarentum. And then there is Sparta, which marks out its difference on this point too: "In order to do away with all superstitious terror, he [Lycurgus] allowed them to bury their dead within the city and to have tombs of them near the sacred places."[83] Faced with this strange fact, Plutarch rationalizes as follows: if Lycurgus defied normal practice, it was clearly with pedagogical motives. In this way "he made the young familiar with such sights and accustomed to them, so that they were not confounded by them and had no horror of death as polluting those who touched a corpse or walked among graves."[84]

But another category also constitutes an exception to the rule:

80. Lucian *On Mourning* 21. Note that Lucian attributes to the Indians (preservation under glass) what Herodotus records as being the practice of the Ethiopians (3.24) and to the Scythians what Herodotus attributes to the Indians. So this is a constellation of terms that are distributed among "the others" in a number of ways; the stock of characteristics is fixed but their distribution is variable.
81. D. Kurtz and J. Boardman, *Greek Burial Customs* (London, 1971), pp. 91ff.
82. Pausanias 1.43.2.
83. Plutarch *Life of Lycurgus* 27. Lycurgus is thus doubly opposed to the general rule: he permits burials not only within the town but also close to the temples.
84. Ibid.

that of the heroes. Where does the city bury them? We must make a rapid digression to consider this question in order to understand the funeral ceremonies for the Scythian kings. The city tends to honor a hero by giving him a grave in the agora.[85] Adrastus, of whom Cleisthenes wished to be rid,[86] was lodged in the agora of Sicyon; similarly, in 476, Theseus was officially installed "right in the center of the town," in the Theseion.[87] Another category, close to that of the heroes, also often favored with the honors of the agora was that of the city founders, such as Battus at Cyrene,[88] and, later, Themistocles at Magnesia on the Meander and Brasidas at Amphipolis.[89] A scholium to Pindar even suggests this to have been the general rule: "*Oikistai* are habitually buried in the town centres."[90]

One other possible resting place for heroes was the town walls and, in particular, the gates to the town. For example, Aetolus the son of Oxilus was buried in the very gateway of Elis.[91] And then there is the tomb of the prince of Eretria, excavated by C. Bérard, which "is neatly fitted into a series of *heroa* for the most part situated within the city walls, with a view to providing a supernatural defense for the gates. . . . At Eretria, the shades of the prince in tomb 6 and his warriors guarded the western gate facing Chalcis, the city's rival."[92]

Finally, there was a third place where it was sometimes considered advantageous to install a hero: on the frontiers of the territory. Coroebus, the first Olympic victor, thus rests "on the frontiers of Elis [*epi toi perati*],"[93] and his tomb is said to "mark the limit [*horizei*]" of

85. It is possible to reconstitute the list on the basis of the information provided by E. Rohde, *Psyché* (trans. Paris, 1928), pp. 132–34; F. Pfister, *Der Reliquienkult im Altertum* (Giessen, 1912); R. Martin, *Recherches sur l'agora* (Paris, 1951), pp. 194ff.

86. Hdt. 5.67.

87. Plutarch *Life of Cimon* 8, *Life of Theseus* 36; A. Podlecki, "Cimon Skyros and Theseus, Bones," *Journal of Hellenic Studies* 91 (1971): 141. The other mythical kings of Athens, when they have a special place allotted to them, are accommodated on the Acropolis: e.g., Erechtheus, Cecrops, Pandion.

88. Pindar *Pythian V* 87ff.

89. Thucydides 1.138, 5.11.

90. Scholium, to Pindar *Olympian I* 149.

91. Pausanias 5.44.

92. C. Bérard, *Eretria III, l'Heroon à la porte de l'ouest* (Bern, 1970), p. 70, and "Recupérer la mort du prince: héroïsation et formation de la cité," *La mort, les morts dans les sociétés anciennes*, ed. G. Gnoli and J. P. Vernant (Cambridge, Paris, 1982), pp. 89–107.

93. Pausanias 8.26.3.

the country; another Coroebus, the son of Mygdon, is buried "on the borders [*en horois*] of Phrygia."[94]

These few examples will suffice to show that heroes may be buried equally well in the agora, in a town gateway, or on the frontiers of the country.[95] Thus, from the point of view of the representation of the territory, an equivalence exists among the three places. For the primary function of a corpse honored in this way is to mount guard, to defend the territory or ensure victory for it. For example, Herodotus gives a detailed account of the vicissitudes of Orestes' remains.[96] The Spartans were repeatedly defeated in battle by the Tegaeans. Such regularity could only be occasioned by the hostility of some god, so they consulted the Pythia, who promised them victory on the day when they would bring home the bones of Orestes: they would then "become the protectors of Tegaea." After searching for a long time, a Spartan by the name of Lichas finally discovered the bones in Tegaea itself, in a blacksmith's forge. He brought them back to Sparta, where they were buried on the agora, "and ever after this time the Lacedaemonians got much the better of the men of Tegaea in all their battles." In similar fashion, Theseus was brought back to Athens from Skyros. In Plutarch's opinion, the reason why this was considered desirable was above all because his armor-clad ghost had appeared to the soldiers at Marathon.[97] When Cimon took possession of the island, he was "ambitious to discover the grave of Theseus and eventually found the coffin of a man of extraordinary size, a bronze spear lying by its side, and a sword."[98]

Conversely, the city might wish to rid itself of a hero whom it believed to be damaging it. Cleisthenes was anxious to "eject" Adrastus from the agora of Sicyon because he was an Argive, for Cleisthenes was at war with Argos. Having Adrastus there in the agora was like harboring a traitor in the very heart of the city. The Pythia did not approve of Cleisthenes' plan, so he was obliged to give it up and tried instead to get Adrastus to depart "of his own free will" through the following ruse: close to the prytaneum, also on the

94. Pausanias 10.27.1.

95. In the cases of the two Coroeboi, it is a matter of the territory, not the city.

96. Hdt. 1.67–68. For a more detailed account of these peregrinations, see Rohde, *Psyché*, p. 133.

97. Plutarch *Life of Theseus* 36.

98. Pausanias 1.15.3.

agora, he installed Melanippus, another hero, whom he considered to be Adrastus's worst enemy.

A hero may thus be very closely bound to a territory: when the Tegaeans "lost" Orestes, they also lost their military supremacy and, eventually, dominion over the territory. By the same token, the Spartans acquired what the Tegaeans had lost. The hero can thus be seen as the territory's metonym. That being so, it is altogether understandable that the Pythia should wish to have a say, or even the last word, in these matters.

Finally, there are those who are buried in secret places. Thus, Periander, the tyrant of Corinth, no doubt worried about his posthumous future, devised a ruse: "He ordered two young men to go out at night by a certain road which he pointed out to them; they were to kill the man they met and bury him. He afterwards ordered four more to go in pursuit of the two, kill them and bury them."[99] The first person the two young men encountered was, needless to say, Periander himself. He clearly wished to avoid what subsequently happened to his nephew Cypselus as soon as he was overthrown, namely, having his tomb violated. Nicholas of Damascus writes: "The people threw the corpse of Cypselus beyond the frontier, leaving it unburied, violated the tombs of his ancestors and emptied out the bones."[100] We should note that detail: "beyond the frontier." The corpse, instead of being beneficent, may, on the contrary, become a kind of *pharmakos* which is expelled from the territory.

In contrast to such an egoistical and tyrannical reason for having a secret burial place, there might be an altruistic and heroic reason: to prevent the possibility of enemies of the city, knowing where a protector-hero was buried, from seizing his bones and thus ensuring their own superiority. This is the reason alluded to by Plutarch when he writes that the heroes have "secret" tombs "which are difficult to find."[101] The most telling example is that of Oedipus at Colonus.[102] When he is on the point of death he sends for Theseus, who is to be the only one to know the precise spot where he is to die. The blind man then acts as Theseus's guide, leading him to the exact place of his "tomb":

99. Diogenes Laertius 1.96.
100. Jacoby, *FGrHist*, 60 F 60.
101. Plutarch *On the Pythian Oracle* 27.
102. Sophocles *Oedipus at Colonus* 1518ff.

I'll lead you to the place where I must die;
But you must never tell it to any man,
Not even the neighbourhood in which it lies.
If you obey, this will count more for you
Than many shields and many neighbours' spears.[103]

This army of reinforcements offered by Oedipus will make it possible to protect Athens from the ravages which the "children of the earth" might otherwise inflict on her. Banished from Thebes, Oedipus is now the one who is best placed to protect Attica against Thebes. He is transformed from a *pharmakos* into a protector-hero.[104] In this way the secret burial place, like the secret password for a garrison in time of siege, renders the offered protection more effective.

This digression on the tombs of the heroes may help us to gain a better understanding of the funeral rites of the Scythian kings. They can be implicitly referred to this spatial schema while at the same time they make it function differently.

The Tomb and Eschatia

Where are the kings buried? Among the Gerrhi.[105] The Gerrhi live in the land of the Gerrhus and are the most distant (*eschata*) of the peoples ruled by the Scythians. To reach this country, it is necessary to travel up the Borysthenes River, that is, northward, for forty days. The destination marks the point at which the Borysthenes becomes unnavigable and beyond which it is unexplored. Further up (*to katuperthe*) its exact course is not known, nor yet what peoples it passes through. It is also at this point that the Gerrhus tributary diverges from the Borysthenes, eventually to flow into the Hypaki-ris.[106] The Gerrhus thus delimits a zone of *eschata* beyond which stretch great expanses about which nobody has any information,[107] not even any based on hearsay, and it is here, in this peripheral zone, that the Scythians bury their kings. Why here? In their case, unlike that of the heroes, it is not a matter of installing them so that they can

103. Pausanias knows of two tombs of Oedipus: one is situated in the Areopagus, within the very walls of the Sanctuary of the Semnoi (1.28.7); the other at Colonus, where there was a *heroon* devoted to Perithoos, Theseus, Adrastus, and Oedipus.
104. J.-P. Vernant, *Tragedy and Myth* (Brighton, 1981), pp. 87ff.
105. Hdt. 4.71.
106. Hdt. 4.56; cf. map, p. 16.
107. Hdt. 4.53.

protect the northern "frontier" of the country against invasion from wild or particularly bellicose peoples, since nothing is known of what lies beyond. I believe that they are placed here not to protect but themselves to be protected, just as the body of a hero is protected by being given a secret burial. For the Scythians, the north is a protection, a refuge; that is made clear enough at the time of Darius's invasion. One of the precautions taken then is the evacuation of the women, the children, and most of the herds: "all these they sent forward, charged to drive ever northward."[108]

Even installed on the margins of Scythia, the kings are still linked with the "territory"; were they not, it would be hard to see why they should be protected. That is certainly the meaning of the words of Idanthyrsus, the king of the Scythians, when he sends Darius (who cannot understand why he refuses to engage in battle against him) the following message: "Find the tombs of our fathers and try to destroy them. Then you will know whether we will fight you for those graves or no. But until then we will not join battle unless we think good."[109] Idanthyrsus clearly sees a link between the royal tombs and the country. To find and violate the former would be to strike at the latter. To find the tombs of the kings would be the equivalent to finding the tomb of a hero in Greece and thereby acquiring (an at least virtual) dominion over the territory.

During his lifetime the king occupies a central position, as is indicated by the fundamental place of Hestia, the "queen of the Scythians," and also by the importance of the oath sworn by "the royal hearths." His position is, in the most precise sense, that of center, but it is a mobile center.

Then what is the explanation for the fact that, once dead, he is carried off almost to the limits of the known world? No doubt it is partly because, to the Scythians, the north is a zone of refuge; but there is also another, more fundamental, reason: to wit, nomadism. A city buries its heroes in its agora, in its gateways, or on its frontiers; positioned as they are, these tombs mark out a particular space and help to create a representation of the civic territory. However, as Idanthyrsus reminds Darius, the Scythians have "neither towns nor cultivated land"; instead, they are a people with pastures and encampments. Their territory is an area of pastureland, not an

108. Hdt. 4.121.
109. Hdt. 4.127.

ordered space. How should they treat their dead kings, who occupy a central position and represent a central point, when no agora exists to receive their bodies? The text tells us that once the king is dead, the Scythians "load" (*analambanousi*) his body onto a wagon. We are not told where it is—the point being, precisely, that it is nowhere, there is no institutional place for it; the king can die anywhere. While alive, he is a mobile circle whose circumference is everywhere, its center nowhere. The compromise elaborated between the exigencies of nomadism and a functional centrality is represented by an "excentric" fixed point: the tomb will be situated in the margins. Having no towns or cultivated land to defend, the Scythians have no need to engage in a pitched battle against Darius, who, if we pursue this logic, is not an invader. If, however, he finds the royal tombs, he does become an "invader," against whom it is then necessary to fight. So the space of the pastureland is not a totally undifferentiated space. It includes a nodal point that represents it metonymically. Herodotus makes this metonymy explicit: to bury their king, the Scythians dig a "great four-cornered pit [*tetragon*]" in the country of the Gerrhi. A bit further on in the text, the narrator mentions that the Scythian territory is, by and large, square: "Scythia, then, being a four-sided country . . . "[110] To establish the burial space of the Scythian kings, Herodotus thus adopts the Greek schema that establishes the relationship between the civic space and the tomb of a hero, but since nomadism is the operator in the case of the Scythians, what was at the center remains at the center, yet becomes "excentric." Herodotus conceives of this burial space in the same terms but operates a displacement: for the city, the zone of the *eschata* is what is furthest from the center, but for the Scythians it is precisely the *eschata* that is regarded as the center. Moreover, it is this excentric place, this point fixed on the frontier, that makes it possible for the space of Scythia to be seen as nomad space. The very logic of the narrative thus demands that these tombs be placed, not within the Scythian "territory" (which would be to deny its nomadic character), but on the borders (which confirms it to be an undifferentiated space with no fixed point of reference).

Before this space of death is reached, a number of strange and impressive ceremonies take place, ceremonies which appear to comprise a striking element of otherness. In Greece, the ceremony

110. Hdt. 4.101.

of *prothesis* normally took place between death and the funeral rites: the corpse, having been washed and dressed by the womenfolk—either his closest relatives or women over sixty years of age—was displayed on a bed. This display, which took place the day following the death, usually lasted for one day. "The purpose of the *prothesis* was not only to confirm death, but also to provide an opportunity for the performance of the traditional lament and for the friends and the family to pay their last respects."[111] But among the Scythians we find no procedure analogous to the *prothesis*. Quite the contrary: the king's body is borne on a wagon from one people to another; each people receives it and then passes it on to the next, until finally it reaches the Gerrhi, who are the last of all. So his subjects do not come to him to pay their last respects; rather, he pays each of them a last visit. This procedure, then, is the exact reverse of the *prothesis*. The explanation is once again found to be connected with the Scythians' nomadism. The central figure of the king can only be a mobile one; the wagon traveling northward, but en route making a round trip (*perielthein*) to visit each of his subject peoples in turn, is, as it were, the expression of this role. Furthermore, this long procession, to which Herodotus does not refer with the usual term *ekphora*, would put his audience in mind of the funeral rites of the great families of the past;[112] and it was precisely against the *hubris* that those manifested that the city had sought to react by imposing a common model for all funerals.

Confirmation that it is Scythian nomadism that provides the explanation for this inverse *prothesis* is to be found in the treatment even of ordinary corpses: they too are placed on wagons and sent to visit their relatives. Just as the king passes from people to people, the ordinary man is moved from house to house or, rather, from wagon to wagon, "doing the rounds [*periagousi*]" of his relatives (*philous*). It took forty days for the king to reach the Gerrhus; the corpses of ordinary individuals were also moved around (*periagontai*) for forty days before being buried.[113]

111. Kurtz and Boardman, *Greek Burial Customs*, p. 144.
112. M. Alexiou, *The Ritual Lament* (Cambridge, 1974), p. 7: "Attic vase painting confirms that, in the geometric and archaic periods, the ekphora had been a magnificent, public affair, with the bier carried on a waggon and drawn by two horses, followed by kinswomen, professional mourners and armed men."
113. Hdt. 4.73. I think it better to translate *philous* as "relatives."

Mutilate, Embalm, Strangle

Each in turn, all the peoples of the Scythian "empire" take part in this funeral procession. What form does their required participation take? "Those that receive the dead man at his coming do the same as do the Royal Scythians; that is, they cut off [*apotamnontai*] a part of their ears, shave [*perikeirontai*] their heads, make cuts round [*peritamnontai*] their arms, tear [*katamussontai*] their foreheads and noses, and pierce [*diabuneontai*] their left hands with arrows."[114] We must imagine not only the procession advancing from one people to the next, but also all the mutilations that take place wherever it passes: an ineffaceable wake stretches from the country of the Royal Scythians all the way to that of the Gerrhi. The narrator gives us absolutely no information as to the identities of "those that receive the dead man": the entire scene is described using the intemporal present tense and with not the slightest indication as to who is speaking.

The vocabulary used to describe these scenes is not without interest for, on the whole, it applies generally to the barbarian world, in which the infliction of mutilation was a form of the exercise of power.[115] The Great Kings, and sometimes the pharaohs, practice mutilation, and it is also a feature of certain rituals connected with warfare, in particular among the Scythians. A clear link exists between mutilation and the sphere of law.[116] Thus, in the city no mutilation is practiced: the bodily integrity of the citizen must be preserved. Torture is reserved for slaves, in circumstances where their evidence is required or when the truth has to be extorted from them. It is interesting to note that exclusion from the *polis* is inseparable from exclusion from truthfulness. Conversely, to practice mutilation is to place oneself beyond the sphere of law, and among the Scythians neither law nor even pre-law holds any sway. Thus, mutilation, self-mutilation, even beating one's breast on the

114. Hdt. 4.71.
115. *Katamusso* is a hapax in Herodotus. *Perikeiro* is also used in 3.154, when the Persian Zopyrus mutilates himself. *Peritamno* is used, in particular at 4.64, in the description of the Scythian method of scalping, and at 2.162, in connection with the mutilation of an Egyptian by the pharaoh. *Apotamno* can be used in the same register (the cutting off of an arm, nose, ears, or head).
116. L. Gernet, *Recherches sur le développement de la pensée juridique et morale en Grèce* (Paris, 1917), and Glotz, *Solidarité*.

occasion of funerals, is initially a feature of areas outside the city. As well as the Scythians, the Egyptians may be mentioned: "All the women of the house . . . roam about the city beating themselves, with their garments belted about them and their breasts showing, and with them all the women of their kin; and they too, for their part, beat themselves, their garments belted likewise."[117]

Such practices also point to an ancient past, a time before, when the city was not yet truly a city. In Athens, for example, they were a relic of the period before the legislation of Solon. When Epimenides came to Athens and became friendly with Solon, "he made the Athenians . . . milder [*praoterous*] in their rites of mourning . . . by taking away the harsh and barbaric practices in which their women had usually indulged up to that time."[118] The nature of these "harsh and barbaric" practices is made clearer a bit further on in the text: "Laceration of the flesh by mourners, and the use of versified lamentations and the bewailing of anyone at the funeral ceremonies of another he forbade."[119] In the world of epic, on the other hand, such "excessive" manifestations of mourning were perfectly acceptable: following the death of Patroclus, Achilles and the Myrmidons abandon themselves to prolonged weeping and "find some solace in their tears."[120] And before setting fire to the funeral pyre of his friend, Achilles does not hesitate to make him an offering of his own locks.[121] Similarly, in the world of tragedy, the chorus of *The Suppliant Women* can declare: "Our nails cut furrows down our cheeks; / We have poured dust over our heads."[122]

Such manifestations of mourning put one in mind of earlier times, but they are also particularly associated with women. In the city, women are a source of danger; if the lawgiver is not careful, they may at any time introduce excess into funeral ceremonies. They no doubt

117. Hdt. 2.85. "Mourning includes a whole series of ritual actions (scattering dust, scratching, wounding) which express both the statutory grief of the relatives and the social loss of status which, through the ban, affects them, with the effect of debasing them in a religious sense" (Gernet, *Recherches*, p. 218).

118. Plutarch *Life of Solon* 12.8.

119. Plutarch *Life of Solon* 21.6. Not "affected laments" (*plaintes affectées*), as the French Flacelière translation has it, but "versified lamentations." Cf. E. Reiner, *Die rituelle Totenklage* (Stuttgart, 1938), p. 4.

120. Homer *Iliad* 23.6ff.

121. Homer *Iliad* 23.140.

122. Euripides *The Suppliant Women* 836.

have their special part to play at different moments in the ceremony, but it is important to establish limits which they must under no circumstances exceed. The law of Iulis, for example, lays down which women are authorized to enter the house of the deceased and states that the *ekphora* must take place "in silence."[123] In the case of the Scythian kings, Herodotus does not say whether the funeral procession was accompanied by weeping and lamentations, but it appears to have taken place in total silence.

While the participants in the funeral procession mutilate themselves, the king's corpse is, in contrast, the object of particular honor, for it is embalmed: "His body is cut open and cleansed and filled with cut marsh-plants and frankincense and parsley and anise seed, and sewn up again."[124] Such an operation is altogether surprising, and the plants used by the Scythian embalmers do not reappear anywhere else in the *Histories*, except for frankincense, which is also used by the Egyptian specialists in embalming.[125] As for the method, it "is reminiscent" of the ritual of sacrifice to Isis, in the course of which the victim was filled with *aromata*. Why these plants? They are among the *aromata*, known for their "pleasant smell";[126] their function is the same as that of the fragrant plants which the Egyptians slip into the stomach of the sacrificial victim. But one of them, parsley, also appears in Greece in a funerary context.[127] The soldiers of Timoleon who catch sight of mules laden with parsley take this to be an evil omen since "we are generally accustomed to wreath the tombs of the dead with parsley"; there was even a proverb according to which "one who is dangerously sick 'needs only parsley.'"[128]

Pliny also mentions "parsley consecrated at funeral meals."[129]

123. *Recueil des inscriptions juridiques grecques*, 1st fasc., no. 2, p. 11: "The women who have attended the ceremony will return from the monument ahead of the men. . . . In the house of the deceased, after the body has been removed, no other women should enter apart from those who are already defiled."

124. Hdt. 4.71.

125. Hdt. 2.86. Frankincense also appears at 1.183, 2.40, 6.97.

126. K. Lembach, *Die Pflanzen bei Theokrit* (Heidelberg, 1970), pp. 35, 44.

127. J. Murr, *Die Pflanzenwelt in der griechischen Mythologie* (Groningen, 1969).

128. Plutarch *Life of Timoleon* 26. Timoleon replies that it is in no way an ominous sign, since parsley has been used for crowns in the Isthmian games. Cf. also E. Leutsch and F. G. Schneidewin, *Corpus Paroemiographorum graecorum*, vol.2, p. 639.

129. Pliny *HN* 22.44.113.

While a connection between parsley and death may thus exist for the Greeks, the fact nevertheless remains that in this context the Scythians operate a considerable displacement, since they use it to embalm the corpse of a king.

Before the embalming another operation is carried out, that of "coating the body in wax." The practice is unusual but not unique: it is also customary among the Persians, who "before they bury the body in the earth, . . . embalm it in wax."[130] It is also attested in one case in Sparta. Thus, the Scythians' way of preparing the body of their king refers the reader to Egypt, to the Persians, and finally (but outside the context of the *Histories*) to Sparta, with certain differences in each case. The question is, is it possible to assign a particular meaning to those differences? Among the Persians, it seems that all corpses were covered with wax. In Egypt, embalming could be contracted by the payment of a *misthos*:[131] there were three tariffs, and a mummy might even possess a certain value, since the mummy of one's father could be used as a pledge to guarantee a debt.[132] As for the Greek city, it rejected embalming utterly: a corpse was simply washed, anointed with oil, and dressed and adorned by the closest relatives or by women over sixty years of age.

The body of the Scythian king was sent off on a wagon, and when this long, inverted *prothesis* was completed, the funeral ceremony, as such, was conducted. It is not easy to comment on the gruesome splendor of this silent scene: what impact did it make upon the Greek audience? The charge of "otherness" that it carries is pronounced, and the speechlessness of the scene, which unfolds like some silent movie, must certainly have been matched by the silence of a "spectator" left speechless.

In Athens on the occasion of public funerals held to honor dead soldiers, the ceremony was a celebration of the city through the words of an appointed orator. Loraux has shown how much more important speech was than vision, in the context of the "fine death," that of the *andres agathoi*.[133] At such funerals, spectacle was reduced to the minimum; what counted was speech. Among the Scythians, in contrast, nobody says a word; there is no official

130. Hdt. 1.140.
131. Hdt. 2.86.
132. Hdt. 2.136.
133. N. Loraux, *L'Invention d'Athènes* (Paris, 1980).

pronouncement upon the death, no lamentations on the part of the king's subjects to express the bereavement of the community. Rather, the corpse is paraded on a wagon, as a spectacle, just as the body of the Persian Masistius, also paraded on a cart, is said to be "worth the viewing."[134] Why this silence? It can be explained by the Scythian nomadism. The city represents a full *koinonia* and has forged a thoroughly political form of speech to express and commemorate itself. Nomads are just the opposite, for they are hardly even a "community": what could they possibly have to say, commemorate, or celebrate?

But, in truth, the situation is probably more complex. Although the Scythians do not raise their voices and they pronounce no words, they *do* speak, but in their own fashion—with and through their bodies. By mutilating themselves, they record the Scythian law upon their bodies, turning these into a celebration and a funeral speech for the dead king. Through the scars they will bear, their bodies will become memorials.[135] Moreover, these mutilations are not the result of a haphazard excess of violence. On the contrary, they are a part of the funerary ceremonial: they must be carried out at the moment when the corpse is received, and the parts of the body where they must be inflicted are quite specific (the head, the arms, the left hand). Furthermore, to obey this etiquette is to acknowledge not only the power of the king but also that one is Scythian: "The best way of testifying to oneself and to others that one belongs to the same group is to imprint the same distinctive mark upon one's body."[136] The visible sign speaks of belonging. Every body marked in this way makes its contribution to the composition of the "coat-of-arms" of the Scythian kings. In Greece, it is the public slaves who are branded with the city's arms;[137] for a Greek, is it not royalty which, in the last analysis, always blocks the word, whether spoken or written? Thus, the Scythians can speak only through their bodies and then only to declare that they are subjects.

The mutilation of the subjects is offset by the embalming of the king. Indeed, it is only in relation to one another that the two

134. Hdt. 9.25.
135. P. Clastres, *La Société contre l'état* (Paris, 1974), pp. 5, 152ff.
136. Durkheim, *Formes élémentaires*, p. 333.
137. P. Ducrey, *Le Traitement des prisonniers de guerre dans la Grèce antique* (Paris, 1968), p. 215.

operations can be fully understood. The abasement of the former corresponds to the exaltation of the latter. The lot of the deceased is to become a "fine corpse" (the viscera are replaced by aromatic plants, wax prevents decomposition); that of the subjects is *aikia*, self-wounding, degradation for their bodies. In contrast, the city forbids both mutilation, by which it is horrified, and embalming, by which it is disgusted, as two types of behavior marked by *hubris*; it is the orator's speech which makes a citizen's death a "fine death."

The Scythians thus form a community whose emblem is, as it were, constituted by the marks they inflict on themselves; but it is interesting to note that they are perhaps never so much a community as at the moment of the king's death, and that the king is perhaps never so much a king as when he is dead. Durkheim and others have shown that ceremonies of mourning are the means whereby a community demonstrates that it is not damaged, even that it will emerge from this trial stronger than before. As for the Scythians, they seem truly to exist as a community only at the moment of these funeral rites. The progress of the corpse on its cart, followed by the long procession of mutilated men which grows longer after each halt, represents their true constitution. Up to this point they were nothing but separate bands of nomads. The text records this change when it notes that once the ceremony is completed, "they *all* build a great barrow of earth, vying zealously with one another to make this as great as possible":[138] at this moment they form a community and because that is so, the various groups that compose it experience some kind of a sense of emulation.

The royal *sema*, out there on the *eschata*, represents the Scythian territory and marks its center. It thus becomes a spatial point of reference but also, in a curious way, a temporal point of reference of a kind, marking a point of beginning. It is "after a year has passed [*eniautou*]" that the second ceremony must be performed. In contrast, between the king's death and his funeral two months may have elapsed or, equally, six. There was no fixed period for that; to put it more precisely, time did not enter into the arrangements. But from now on the Scythians have a temporal point of reference at their disposal.

Once he is dead, moreover, the king is at last provided with a

138. Hdt. 4. 71.

proper house: a huge space is arranged for him and he is assigned a large team of servants—all of which puts one in mind of the house of the Great King. From this point on in the narrative, the emphasis is laid on fixity. To construct the awning of branches set up over the corpse, Scythians "plant" spears in the earth. To "raise" the macabre ring around the tomb, as one raises a monument, they "plant" posts in the ground and these then serve to support the stuffed horses, each of which is, furthermore, tethered by a peg.

In his lifetime, the king roams through Scythia on horseback; when he is dead he makes his last and longest journey on a wagon. Once he is buried, that is the end of it: the horses are stuffed and the wagons are dismantled, for wheels are used to set up the ring of horsemen and these can only be the wheels of the wagons. They are cut in half through the middle, arranged on the ground flat side down,[139] and used as supports to hold up the horses. The wagon is thus taken to pieces and its "principle" of mobility, namely, the wheels, is transformed into its opposite, an instrument of immobility. It is the end of all the traveling; the nomadism is over. In life the king was a mobile center; in death he becomes a fixed but "excentric" center of a ring which is itself immobile.

The description of the funeral rites, bewildering as it is, incorporates a number of elements that differ from Greek practices. For instance, Solon forbids "the burial with the dead of more than three changes of raiment";[140] the law of Iulis specifies that the three shrouds should not be worth more than one hundred drachmas and lays down the quantities of wine and oil (three *congai*) that it is lawful to use. Set alongside the profusion of the Scythian funerary furnishings, these prescriptions are striking.[141] There is also a contrast in the size of the monuments, for the burial mounds of the classical and even the archaic period are a far cry from the construction raised for the kings; and another contrast in the nature of the constructions, for the Scythian monument is built with natural materials including, in addition to earth, a sheet of leaves, wooden spears, and beams, and a

139. Hdt. 4.72.
140. Plutarch *Life of Solon* 21.
141. The disparity in social status is not enough to account for the difference. One is referred to the aristocratic funerals from which the city wished to preserve itself.

screen of reeds, while the Greek tombs are made of stone, bricks, and sometimes even plaster, and they constitute a proper building.[142]

The most striking contrast, however, lies in the actions performed around the tombs. The Scythians strangle (*apopnigei*) a concubine, a cupbearer, a cook, a groom, a messenger, horses—in short, the entire normal entourage of a barbarian king. In the first place, strangulation is a non-Greek form of execution or murder;[143] so that is one difference. Furthermore, in Scythia strangulation is the normal mode of sacrificing.[144] The action the Scythians perform on their kings' tombs is therefore a sacrifice: the strangling of these people corresponds, in the city, to Solon's prohibition against sacrificing an ox to the dead,[145] or to the stipulation at Iulis: "in sacrifice, follow the custom of your ancestors." The contrast between the two practices could hardly be greater: the prohibition against slaughtering an ox is counterbalanced by a human sacrifice. We must turn all the way back to the epic, that is to say, to a distant past, to find another human sacrifice on a funeral pyre: to Achilles, of course, who sacrificed twelve Trojans in honor of Patroclus (but did so by putting them to the sword),[146] together with four mares and two pet dogs.

Then comes the second phase, in a way the most enigmatic: the ceremony that takes place at the end of one year. This is an immense sacrifice (fifty people are strangled), with the creation of a setting which, to us, seems to belong to some fantastical description. Those sacrificed are, again, members of the king's household.[147] The image

---

142. Kurtz and Boardman, *Greek Burial Customs*, pp. 79ff., 105ff.

143. Apries is strangled by the Egyptians (Hdt. 2.169). The Babylonians smother women (3.150). The Scythians strangle sacrificial animals (4.60). Arkesilas, the son of Battus I, is strangled by his brother (4.160). Cf. Gernet, *Anthropology*, "On Capital Punishment."

144. Hdt. 4.60.

145. Plutarch *Life of Solon* 21.

146. Homer *Iliad* 23.175. In both cases it is a matter of giving pleasure to the deceased: whether it is his friends or his enemies who are sacrificed, the purpose is identical.

147. They are Scythian by birth. Those who serve the king do so at his express orders; the Scythians have no bought servants (*arguronetoi therapontes*). This is an interesting piece of evidence on slavery, for it shows that for Herodotus a slave was normally bought and was not *eggenes*.

of the circle, already mentioned, appears once again in this funerary context: the royal *sema* is at the center of his fifty servants who surround him in a macabre ring of stuffed figures.

After the funeral ceremony comes the ritual of purification, as is to be expected.[148] But while such a ritual may be expected, the form that it takes in this instance is much less so. Yet the enigmatic nature of these steam-baths to some extent disappears as soon as one realizes that they are structured by an opposition between water on the one hand and fire and smoke on the other. The whole chapter hinges on the expression *anti loutrou*: for them, this purification stands in lieu of a bath, but at the same time it is the opposite of a bath. Some scholars, Meuli for one, believe that this ceremony stems from the procedures of ecstatic religions.[149] Hemp is a type of hashish, so we appear to find ourselves in a context of shamanism.

In Greece, water is repeatedly used in funerary rites, in particular for purification following burial. For instance, the law of Iulis stipulates that "those who are defiled should wash their entire bodies with much water and will then be pure." The same is true for Athens.[150]

However, this opposition between water and fire-and-smoke does not explain the behavior of the Scythian women, who are here for the first time distinguished as a group. They smear their faces and bodies with a paste made from various plants mixed with water. Legrand suggests that Herodotus is here confusing funerary rites with cosmetic care.[151] Yet, after this operation the women are declared to be pure (*katharai*).[152] Besides, consider the ingredients used to make this paste: they "pound on a rough stone cypress and cedar and frankincense wood, pouring water also thereon." That is altogether astonishing when one remembers that Scythia is quite devoid of wood, except in the region known as the Hylaia. And the presence of frankincense is even more surprising: incense came from the country of aromatic plants, namely, Arabia, which was "the only country" in the world that produced incense, myrrh, cassia, cinnamon, and

148. Hdt. 4.73–75.

149. K. Meuli, "Scythica," *Hermes* 70 (1935): 122.

150. Scholium to *Clouds* 838.

151. P.-E. Legrand, *Hdt.* 4.73, n. 4.

152. *Katharai kai lamprai;* but the sense of purity certainly cannot be entirely excluded.

laudanum,[153] a country which was baked and rebaked by the sun, whereas Scythia was known as a cold country. This paste, composed of precious woods, was characterized by the essential feature of aromatic plants, its "sweet smell."[154] The cypress is sometimes recognized by its "sweet smell,"[155] as is the cedar.[156] This purification ceremony thus belongs as a whole to an aromatic context: on the side of the men, the quasi-aromatic fumes given off by the smoldering hemp (but what kind of communication do they set up?); for the women, an ointment made from aromatic woods.

One last feature underlines the strange nature of this ceremony. When the Scythian males are in this "vapour bath" they are said to "howl with joy [*agamenoi oruontai*]".[157] A kind of double meaning is involved here: on only one other occasion does Herodotus use *oruontai* in connection with people, to wit, those living in central Persia who, when bringing their complaints before the Great King, "cry and howl."[158] Generally, the word is applied to animals (dogs, wolves), in particular wild animals. Many commentators have suggested amending it, mainly because of the presence of *agamenoi*, while Meuli regards it as yet another sign of the trancelike atmosphere surrounding the ceremony.[159] In any event, since this word does not normally belong to the vocabulary of purification, it is bound to occasion surprise, although at the same time it should be remembered that Herodotus several times noted that the Scythians lived in *ethea*, "lairs."

So this is a scene of purification that does not involve the use of water: this is its fundamental difference. Furthermore, (on the side of the women at least) it takes place in a decidedly aromatic context. To interpret the significance of these differences, we must examine other scenes of a similar type.

153. Hdt. 3.107.
154. Hdt. 4.75.
155. Homer *Odyssey* 5.64; Jacoby, *RE*, article "Kypressus," in particular its funerary significance.
156. Theocritus *Epigrams* 8.4.
157. Hdt. 4.75.
158. Hdt. 3.117.
159. Meuli, "Scythica," p. 125.

The Spartan Kings

The grandiose and in some respects unique funeral rites of the Scythian kings point to a number of connections with Sparta. It is therefore worth pondering whether the funeral rites of the Spartan kings might not be classed as a case of otherness where death is concerned, indicating that there might be a divide even within Greece itself.[160]

In tackling this question Herodotus explicitly proceeds on the basis of a number of comparisons which make the context in which he situates such ceremonies clear beyond any doubt: "The Lacedaemonians have the same custom at the deaths of their kings as have the barbarians of Asia."[161] A little further on he notes a resemblance to Persian customs: the new king cancels out debts just as the Great King "at the beginning of his reign forgives all cities their arrears of tribute."[162] Then, immediately after the passage on the funeral rites, he introduces a new comparison: "Moreover, the Lacedaemonians are like the Egyptians in this *too* in that . . . ."[163] The *kai tade* indicates clearly that where funeral rites are concerned the Egyptians belong to this same configuration. And the Scythians may also be associated with the barbarians of Asia, the Persians, and the Egyptians. The Spartans, then, find themselves in a company that is, to put it mildly, characterized by "otherness."

Herodotus says nothing definite about how the corpse is treated, except that there is an *ekphoria* on a display bed and that there has to be a corpse to display there, whether it be a real or a false one. The fact is that "if a king has perished in war, they make an image of him, an *eidolon.*" The importance attached to the king's corpse is also conveyed by the rule according to which the remains of a king who has died abroad are repatriated. Plutarch explains that "it was the Spartan custom, when men of ordinary rank died in a foreign country, to give their bodies funeral rites and burial there, but to carry the bodies of their kings home."[164] How was it possible to bring

160. On the difference between Athenian and Spartan funerals, see Loraux, *L'Invention d'Athènes,* pp. 45–47.
161. Hdt. 6.58.
162. Hdt. 6.59.
163. Hdt. 6.60.
164. Plutarch *Life of Agesilaus* 40.4.

the king back? By carrying out a kind of embalming process, using honey or wax. Thus, when Agesilaus died on his way back from Egypt, "his body was coated with honey and taken back to Sparta to be buried."[165] According to Plutarch, the Spartans, having no honey, in fact "coated his body with wax."[166] Another example is that of king Agesipolis, who was brought, preserved in honey, home from Chalcis.[167] This use of wax or honey puts us in mind of the Persians and Scythians. It is the only known Greek example of embalming, even of a temporary kind.

Who took part in the funeral rites? When the king died, horsemen rode throughout Laconia to announce the news (*periaggelousi*). In the town, women went the rounds (*periiousai*), beating saucepans; two free individuals from each household (one man and one woman) were obliged to bear the marks of mourning (*katamiainesthai*); *perioikoi* were required to attend the funeral, and so were helots. Tyrtaeus had already noted, in connection with the helots, "They and their companions are required to mourn their masters each time the sinister destiny of death strikes."[168] Herodotus makes another remarkable observation: great promiscuity prevails on the occasion of funerals, since men and women are "intermingled" (*summiga*). Such a thing ran totally contrary to the customary legislation, whether we take that to be the laws of Solon, the law of Iulis, or even the measures prescribed by Plato in the *Laws:*[169] men and women are kept separate.

Also, these funerals are despotic in character: they are governed by compulsion. It is "necessary" (*anagke*), it is "required" (*dei*), "on pain of severe penalties," that a predetermined number of individuals, representing the people as a whole, should assemble at Sparta. The horsemen cover the length and breadth of Laconia, the women make the rounds of the town, and people gather from every side. A scholium to Pindar provides another example with a similar gist, but this time it concerns not the Spartans but the Corinthians. In the past, the Megarians, then subject to Corinth, had been forced to

---

165. Diodorus 15.93.6.
166. Plutarch *Life of Agesilaus;* C. Nepos *Agesilas* 8.7.
167. Xenophon *Hellenica* 5.3.19.
168. Tyrtaeus, fr. 5 Diehl.
169. Plato *Laws* 12.958d ff.

travel to Corinth to attend the funeral of a Bacchiad king.[170] The movements occasioned by these funerary ceremonies completely confirm the spatial inversion represented by the Scythian *nomos* of the inverted *prothesis*. By contrast, in Sparta and Corinth, the king is a fixed and central point around which people gather, not—as in Scythia—a mobile point that makes the rounds of his subjects.

To summon the people to mourn, women "beat upon saucepans," just as in Egypt, men and women, traveling to Boubastis to celebrate the festival of Artemis and mingling in the ships conveying them, "clap their hands."[171] At the beginning of the funeral ceremony, probably in the agora of Sparta, the participants "wail in lengthy lamentation [*oimogei diachreontai apletoi*]." *Oimoge* is a word more generally associated with tragedy, but Herodotus applies it only to the Persians. The Persians "lament loud and long" when Cambyses is sick.[172] When, at Susa, they learn of the defeat at Salamis, they "lament loud and long";[173] and at the death of Masistius, they cut their hair and beards and the manes of their horses and "lament loud and long."[174] So this is a non-Greek context, and it is interesting to note the suggestion of a similarity between the Spartans and the Persians in this connection.

These statutory lamentations naturally stand in opposition to the legislation of other cities and in particular to the laws of Athens which, ever since Solon, had prohibited the funeral lament (*threnos*) or had laid down a code for its use, limiting it to women.[175] For examples of the protracted wailing which brought "satisfaction," it is necessary to turn back to epic. As we have noted, the Scythians knew nothing of the *threnos*. For them, funeral rites were all spectacle, purely visual; speech played no part at all. The funeral rites of the Spartan kings also inclined chiefly to spectacle and to the visual but did include an element of speech, albeit almost inarticulate, to wit, this "endless wailing" which was required from the participants. In

170. Scholium to Pindar *Nemean VII* 155.
171. Hdt. 2.60.
172. Hdt. 3.66.
173. Hdt. 8.99.
174. Hdt. 9.24.
175. On this question of the *threnos*, see, most recently, Loraux, *L'Invention d'Athènes*, pp. 44–50; Pollux 6.202.

contrast to these two types of ceremony, let us for a moment recall the burial of the Athenian soldiers who had fallen in battle. This was a ceremony in which speech was very much to the fore while the visual was reduced to a minimum. The corpses themselves were not displayed, only the bones, and even that *prothesis* was probably a tribal rather than an individual affair;[176] all that mattered was the voice of the orator, itself the voice of the city. A comparison of these three ceremonies suggests a functional equivalence between the funeral speech in Athens, the lamentations in Sparta, and the inverted *prothesis* in Scythia. But the differences between the three societies are expressed, precisely, in the discrepancies in the three manifestations (which range from seeing to listening and from a maximum to a minimum degree of *koinonia*).

The Lacedaemonians (Spartans, *perioikoi*, helots, men and women alike) "wail" and also "violently strike their foreheads." This practice, too, ran counter to the laws of Solon and refers us to the non-Greek world, where it was customary to strike oneself or to scratch one's face during funeral ceremonies. Among the Scythians, mutilation and embalming went together, and to mutilate oneself was to acknowledge oneself, and to be acknowledged by others, as a Scythian. In Athens, neither practice was customary: the city celebrated itself through the mouth of its official orator, by recognizing the dead to have been worthy of it. Sparta represents an intermediary state: it practiced no systematic embalming and no real mutilation, but the city did select a number of individuals who were delegated to mourn and thereby manifest their membership in the Lacedaemonian collectivity while acknowledging a certain dependence on the king.

Through their lamentations, however, the Lacedaemonians declare that the king who has just died "was the best," and this they do every single time. The only articulate statement produced by this city is, in the last analysis, no more than a formula, always the same one, which must be pronounced but which has no meaning, since it is repeated at every royal burial. In any case—and this constitutes yet another difference from the funeral speech—what is celebrated is the king or, rather, the institution of royalty, that is, of hereditary

176. Thucydides 2.34.

monarchy, not the city as such.[177] Furthermore, it is an exaggerated formula, as we realize when we compare Solon's law which "forbids speaking ill of the dead."[178] The gap between not speaking ill of the dead and declaring the deceased to be the best king ever was one that the Spartans did not hesitate to cross.

To complete our examination of these Spartan funeral rites, which present both resemblances to and also differences from those of the Scythian kings, let us consider the positioning of the tombs. Since the Spartan king is the fixed point around which people gather, it comes as no surprise to find him buried inside the city; furthermore, Sparta, in contrast to other Greek cities, displays no disinclination to bury the dead inside the city walls. According to Pausanias, the Eurypontidai had their tomb at the end of the Alphetis way leading from the agora, while the Agiadai were accommodated to the west of the agora.

If there are two sides to death, the death of the Spartan kings is closer to the death of "others," and Herodotus draws attention to its otherness by giving it a spatial reference. He likens these funeral rites to the practices of the barbarians of Asia in general—the Persians, even the Egyptians; and we may certainly add the Scythians to that list. When Xenophon came across such evidence of otherness in the fourth century, he was to treat it quite differently. Instead of interpreting it, so to speak, "horizontally," he did so "vertically," noting that at their deaths the Spartan kings "were held in honour not as mere men but as heroes."[179] It was one sign, among many others, that the image of the king had changed.

The Leader Must Have Heads

The Scythians first appear in the *Histories* in the guise of masters of hunting in the service of Cyaxarus. When Darius invades Scythia, the war they wage against him is one in which they are now quarry,

177. M. I. Finley, "Sparta," *Problèmes de la guerre en Grèce ancienne* (Paris, 1968), pp. 143ff.

178. Plutarch *Solon* 21.1; Demosthenes *Against Leptines* 104, *Against Boetos* 2.49.

179. Xenophon *Constitution of the Lacedaemonians* 15.9 and *Hellenica* 3.31: *ouk hos anthropous, all' hos heroas tous Lakedaimonion basileis protetimekasin;* or, on the subject of Agis, *etuche semnoteras e kat' anthropon taphes.*

now hunters, and in the end they prefer chasing a hare over engaging in battle with him. Warfare, for them, is simply an extension of hunting, and they use the same methods for both.[180]

Head-hunting

But when we read the chapters devoted to the customs of war,[181] this image is noticeably changed. The Scythians no longer appear as huntsmen hunting and fighting all at once, but as "made for war"; and if warfare remains a hunt, it is a man-hunt or, to be precise, a head-hunt. The Scythian warrior

carries to his king the heads of all whom he has slain in the battle; for he receives a share of the booty taken if he brings a head but not otherwise. He scalps the head by making a cut round it by the ears, then grasping the scalp and shaking it off the skull. Then he scrapes out the flesh with the rib of an ox and kneads the skin with his hands and, having made it supple, he keeps it for a napkin, fastening it to the bridle of the horse which he rides and taking pride in it.[182]

Beheading, scalping, tanning . . . .

Who in the *Histories*, apart from the Scythians, practices decapitation? Let us, for the moment,[183] leave aside beheading as a method of execution and punishment—that is to say, as a form of the exercise of power—and concentrate on the decapitation of corpses.

The Tauri decapitate their enemies and take their heads home with them to set on poles, high above their houses.[184] When the seven conspirators enter the palace to assassinate Smerdis, the usurper, they kill the Magi and cut off their heads.[185] Artaphernes and Harpagus crucify Histiaeus of Miletus, then decapitate him and send his head to Darius.[186] After Thermopylae, Xerxes, passing

---

180. Hdt. 1.73.
181. Hdt. 4.64–66.
182. Hdt. 4.64.
183. Cf. below, p. 333.
184. Hdt. 4.103. They say that in this way they have "guardians" to watch over their houses. The custom is therefore different from that of the Scythians.
185. Hdt. 3.79.
186. Hdt. 6.30.

among the corpses, has Leonidas's head cut off and orders it to be "impaled".[187] The verb here (*anastaurosai*) is the same as that used to describe the custom among the Tauri. One more example is provided by the people of Amathus, a city in Cyprus. Onesilus had tried to start a revolt against the Great King; when the people of Amathus refused to join him he besieged their city, but without success. When the revolt was crushed by the Persians and Onesilus was killed, the people of Amathus cut off his head and hung it over their gateway. Revenge and derision: the town would now be "protected" by the one who had been incapable of seizing it. However, Herodotus goes on: "and the head being set there aloft, when it was hollow a swarm of bees entered it and filled it with their cells. On this an oracle was given to the Amathusians (for they had enquired concerning the matter) that they should take the head down and bury it and offer yearly sacrifice to Onesilus, as to a hero. This the Amathusians did, and have done to this day."[188] Thus, the intervention of the bees condemned the practice, and as a result of the words of the oracle Onesilus passed from excessive infamy to the highest honor: his head, treated as though it were his intact body, was buried and he acquired a status equivalent to that of a hero or of a protector of the city.[189]

As for the Persians, although they do occasionally do such things, it is not usual practice for them. Herodotus in fact makes it clear that he regards the treatment meted out to Leonidas as proof of Xerxes' anger against him, for generally "the Persians are of all men known to be the most inclined to honour valiant warriors." Herodotus totally condemns the action, saying that Xerxes "outraged the body" or, to put it more strongly, "submitted him to treatment which contravened the *nomos* [*parenomese*]."[190] All in all, the only real decapitators are the Tauri and the Scythians.

They are perhaps even more notorious as people who practice scalping. The verb used is *skuthizo*, with the compounds *aposku-*

---

187. Hdt. 7.238.

188. Hdt. 5.114.

189. Cf. above, pp. 134–38ff.

190. Hdt. 7.238. This passage should, of course, be compared with 9.78, in which Pausanias refuses to do as Lampon suggests and have the corpse of Mardonius impaled (crucified) in retaliation for Leonidas: "that would be an act more proper for barbarians than for Greeks, and one that we deem matter of blame even in barbarians."

thizo and *periskuthizo*, which may mean specifically "to scalp."[191]
Aposkuthizo is glossed by the *Suda* and by Stephanus of Byzantium
as "to cut out and remove the skin of the skull with the hair." But it
can also mean "to shave completely." Thus, Hecuba tells Helen: "You
should walk submissively in rags of robes, / Shivering with anxiety,
head Scythian-cropped";[192] similarly, in Athenaeus *aposkuthizein*
means to cut someone's hair as an insult to him.[193] Strabo mentions a
Thracian tribe, the Saraparae—which means, more or less, "those
who cut heads"—a savage mountain people who "practise scalping
and decapitation [*periskuthistes kai apokephalistes*]."[194]

The Scythian makes himself a kind of "napkin" (*cheiromaktron*)
out of the scalp. The Greek means "hand-towel."[195] After being
treated, the scalp becomes a kind of towel. The Scythians appear to
have been well known for this practice since there seems to existed
an expression *skuthisti cheiromaktron;* it is to be found in a fragment
of Sophocles, *skuthisti cheiromaktron ekkekarmenos* (or *ekdedar-
menos*), "the head shaved [or, scalped] to make a napkin in the
Scythian manner."[196] Hesychius uses the expression and explains it
by referring to the Scythians' custom of scalping their prisoners.[197]
Such expressions, snippets of which one comes across, like sea-
wrack on a beach, in the entries of the lexicographers, testify that the
Scythians' reputation as scalpers was firmly established.

Reinach has collected the classical texts that provide information
on this practice of decapitation among the Celts and "neighboring or
related peoples." It is attested among the Germans, the Alemanni,
and the Dacians, in Iberia, in Scythia (Reinach cites the chapter in
Herodotus), and, of course, in Gaul,[198] for which two sources are

191. *Skuthizo* on its own (late) means "to drink with excess," "to shave" (Euripides *Electra* 241, "razor-cropped in the Scythian manner") as a sign of mourning
(G. Kaibel, *Epigrammata graeca*, 790–98) and "to speak Scythian."
192. Euripides *The Trojan Women* 1026.
193. Athenaeus 12.524f.
194. Strabo 11.14.14.
195. Aristophanes 1.521 Kock; Xenophon *Cyropaedia* 1.3.5.
196. *Tragicorum graecorum fragmenta*², 432 = Athenaeus 9.410c.
197. K. Latte, ed., *Lecikon*, s.v. *Skuthisti cheiromaktron; hoi Skuthai ton
lambanomenon (polemion) on tas kephalas ekderontes [esan] anti cheiromaktron
echronto* (Copenhagen, 1953).
198. A. Reinach, "Les Têtes coupées et les trophées en Gaule," *Revue Celtique*
(1913): pp. 38–60; F. Benoît, "Le Sanctuaire aux 'esprits' d'Entremont," *Cahiers
Ligures de Préhistoire et d'Archéologie* 4 (1955): 38–70.

cited. One is Diodorus, the other Strabo, both of whom summarize Poseidonius of Apamea, who had traveled in Gaul at the time of the Roman conquest. The following few lines of Diodorus illustrate the customs of the Gauls and at the same time testify to the differences between the Gauls and the Scythians:

They cut off the heads of the enemy fallen and attach them to the necks of their horses. As for the bloodstained remains, they give them to their grooms and carry them off as booty, performing a triumphal march and singing a hymn of victory; as for their trophies, they nail them to their houses as is done with certain animals killed in hunting. As for the heads of the most renowned enemies, they embalm them carefully with the oil of cedars and preserve them in a chest.[199]

As well as manufacturing napkins, the Scythians, clearly most industrious in this respect, are skilled at making drinking bowls from skulls. This special treatment is reserved for their "worst enemies." Herodotus provides us with the trade secrets: "Each saws off all the part beneath the eyebrows and cleanses the rest. If he be a poor man, then he does but cover the outside with a piece of raw hide, and so makes use of it; but if he be rich, he gilds the inside of it and so uses it for a drinking cup. Such cups a man makes also of the head of his own kinsman with whom he has been at feud and whom he has vanquished in single combat before the king."[200] An echo of these special skills is to be found in Strabo, citing Apollodorus and Eratosthenes: the Black Sea was called *Axenos* on account of its storms and also because of the cruelty of the tribes in the region, in particular the Scythians, who "sacrifice strangers, eat human flesh and drink from skulls."[201] Similarly, Pliny mentions the Man-eaters

---

199. Diodorus 5.29.5. For example, to refer to the heads, Diodorus uses the word *akrothinion*, meaning "first fruits"—to be precise, the top of the pile of booty—and these "first fruits" are fixed by the Gauls to the doorways of their houses, whereas in Scythia the heads are taken to the king.

200. Hdt. 4.65. Herodotus provides no explanation at all as to why this treatment is reserved for the worst enemies and for relatives (who may thus, it seems, be included in the category of worst enemies). Note, too, how the difference between rich and poor is expressed in Scythian society. The Scythians are alone in their practice of drinking from skulls. The Issedones (4.26) preserve the skulls of their dead relatives; they clean them, strip them bare and gild them, and use them as *agalmata* in their yearly ceremonies in honor of the dead.

201. Strabo 7.3.6.

who live a ten days' march north of the Borysthenes and "drink from human skulls, the scalps of which they wear as napkins, on their chests."[202] The image evokes our worthy Scythian craftsmen.

Herodotus mentions another special feature in their treatment of their enemies' corpses, one the tradition does not appear to have picked up. They use scalps stitched together to make themselves cloaks (*chlaines*) resembling the "capes of shepherds."[203] They also practice flaying: "Many too take off the skin, nails and all, from their dead enemies' right hands and make thereof coverings for their quivers" and "there are many too that flay the skin from the whole body and carry it about on horseback stretched on a wooden frame."[204] What can be the purpose of these bogeys paraded about in this fashion? Herodotus makes no suggestions, simply noting that they are displayed (*peripherein*). Perhaps the warrior shows them off as a sign of his valor.

But it is the head that qualifies him to share in the booty. If the warrior brings no head, he forfeits his right to booty. Considering that the king presides over the distribution, this behavior is reminiscent of the Homeric distribution of booty: the booty is what is set down "in the middle"; all the objects thus become *xuneia keimena*, objects made common property,[205] which it is the king's duty to apportion. But in Homer, simply having taken part in the operation (the sacking of a town or a raid) seems to have been enough to entitle a warrior to a share of the booty. When, after the sack of Ismarus,

202. Pliny *HN* 7.2.12. Cf. also Aristotle *Politics* 7.2.132.9b17.
203. Hdt. 4.64: Kataper baitas, baite = a shepherd's cloak, a garment made from animal skins. Note the effect of this comparison: the Scythians are shepherds who wear garments made from skins, but in this case they are human skins. Dumézil (*Légendes sur les Nartes*, p. 153) compares this chapter to the incident in the life of Batraz where "he assembles the wives and daughters of the Nartes and orders them to sew him a coat from the skin of the heads which he gives them; whereupon the unfortunate women begin to wail: 'It is the skin of the head of my father,' said one, 'of my fiancé', 'of my brother,' said the others."
204. Apodeiro, "flaying," here means the flaying of a corpse (Hdt. 5.25). Darius had a royal judge flayed. But at 2.40, 42 and 4.60, 61, it is a matter of "flaying" a sacrificed animal. Similarly, except for this example and 7.26, where it is a matter of the "skin" of Marsyas the Silenian, *ekdeiro* means the flaying of an animal (2.42, 7.70). The presence of the imperfect *en* indicates an intervention on the part of the narrator in his account.
205. *Iliad* 1.124; Detienne, *Maîtres de vérité*, pp. 84–85.

Odysseus distributes a share to each of his men, he requires no additional proof of their actions or valor.[206] Furthermore, the booty made common property does not account for *all* the booty, for each warrior endeavors to seize his own "individual" booty: to wit, the arms of the enemy he has overcome. Although Herodotus does not specify how the distribution was organized—was all the booty divided up by the king? Was it enough to bring along a single head? Or were the shares proportional to the number of heads presented?—he yet again represents the king as the central and dominant figure on whom all transactions depend.

To underline the contrast, we may compare this Scythian method of distribution with that of the Greeks—after Plataea, for example: Pausanias laid down that the booty was not to be touched and ordered the helots to collect all the precious objects; then, once the tenth part had been set aside for the gods, "they divided the remainder and each people received according to its desert."[207] So Pausanias played an important role here, at least in the organization of the distribution, which was based on the criterion of "merit." The actual booty was allotted people by people; only the prizes for *aristeia*, valor, were awarded individually.

The Arithmetic of Aristeia: Drinking Wine, Drinking Blood

A decapitated head entitles a warrior to a share of the booty, but it is also the sign of his *aristeia:* the warrior keeps the scalp "for a napkin, fastening it to the bridle of the horse which he himself rides and taking pride in it [*agalletai*].[208] Having prepared for the effect that he means to create (with the sentence ending with *agalletai*), the narrator intervenes and explains how it is possible to take pride in so abominable an action: "he is judged the best man [*aner aristos*

---

206. *Odyssey* 9.39–42.
207. Herodotus 9.81. On the question of booty, see W. K. Pritchett, *The Greek State at War* vol. 1 (Berkeley and Los Angeles, 1974), pp. 53–84. On the distribution `" ~~v be interesting to recall the rule that obtained in the army of the Ten
                cquired by a soldier out marauding on his own belonged to
                ne entire army set out, if an individual went off by himself and
                Jecreed to be public property" (*Anabasis* 6.6.2–10).
                ie *Greek State at War*, vol. 1, pp. 76–290.

kekritai] who has most scalps for napkins."[209] So in the last analysis, taking scalps is simply a way of proving oneself to be a "man of courage." The same goes for the skulls fashioned into drinking cups: "if guests whom he honours visit him, he will serve them with these heads and show how the dead were his kinsfolk who made war upon him and were worsted by him; this they call manly valour [*tauten andragathein legontes*]."[210]

The fundamental "otherness" of Scythian behavior can be reduced to this, the manner of their quest for *aristeia*, and we may use it to gauge the difference between their concept of *aristeia* and the Greek one. As a matter of fact, Herodotus pays considerable attention to this question of the prizes won for valor and is at pains, after each battle, to report who received such prizes. The *Histories* contain no fewer than twenty-three examples of such awards.[211] *Aristeia* is no longer manifested through individual exploits, as it used to be in archaic combat. Instead, it results from a strict observance of the rules of hoplite warfare: fighting in position, holding one's place in the phalanx. Xerxes, unable to make anything of all this, can only scoff when Demaratus explains to him that the law, the *despotes*, of the Lacedaemonians always bids them do the same thing: "They must never flee from the battle before whatsoever odds, but abide at their post and there conquer or die."[212] The distinction between the two forms of *aristeia*, the old and the new, is illustrated clearly in the behavior of two Spartans, Aristodamus and Poseidonius, during the

---

209. Hdt. 4.64.

210. Hdt. 4.65. L. Robert, *Laodicée du Lycos* (Paris, 1969), p. 307 n. 2: "The word *andragathia*, like *andreia*, does not mean 'merit' in any vague sense but quite specifically physical courage (of athletes, etc.) and above all military courage, and *andragathia* refers to great exploits in warfare, not simply merits."

211. Pritchett, *The Greek State at War*, vol. 1, p. 285, sets out a table of the *aristeia* in Herodotus. Herodotus is the only historian to consider the matter with such care: is that perhaps, as J. de Romilly suggests, because "his model remains the epic"? (*Histoire et raison chez Thucydide* [Paris, 1956], p. 113). In any event, Herodotus believes it his duty to find out the names of those who showed the greatest courage. Thus, he knows, even if he does not record them, the names of all those who fell at Thermopylae: "their names I have learnt for their great worth and desert [*hos andron axion genomenon*], as I have learnt besides the names of all the three hundred" (7.224).

212. Hdt. 7.104; M. Detienne, "La Phalange," in *Problèmes de la guerre en Grèce ancienne*, p. 128.

battle of Plataea. Which was the braver of the two?[213] According to
the Spartans, Aristodamus had certainly accomplished great exploits
(*erga megala*) but he had "pressed forward . . . from his post," "in
frenzy" (*lusson*), as a man seeking death,[214] whereas Poseidonius had
proved himself a man of courage without abandoning himself to *lussa*
or courting death: he was, thus, the more courageous.[215]

The Scythians attach scalps to the reins of their horses, and the
one who has the most is deemed the most courageous. In Greece,
however, *aristeia* must be recognized by the city or cities before it
may proclaim itself. Thus, after the battle of Salamis the *strategoi*
take a vote to decide on the prizes for valor.[216] Finally, one more
contrast: in Scythia the scalps are both the direct manifestation of
aristeia and at the same time its symbol (they are considered as so
many decorations). In Greece, a greater distance is set between
aristeia on the field of battle and its recognition by the city: the
prizes allotted for bravery take the form of either a choice portion of
the booty, money, a wreath, or simply a speech of praise.[217] Thus, on
his return to Sparta, Eurybiades, the commander of the fleet at
Salamis, received an olive wreath as his prize for bravery.[218]

The Scythian *aristeia* might be said to resemble Homeric *aristeia*
in that it is an individual exploit, but in that respect alone. The
fundamental difference is that Homeric combat is never a head-
hunt, despite the fact that certain warriors—Dolon, Hippolochus,
and Coos, for example—are finally beheaded.[219] The decapitation of
a fallen warrior appears only in the form of a threat, in Book 17 in
particular, when Hector, to outrage the corpse of Patroclus, "wanted
to behead him" and "give it to the dogs of Troy."[220] But although
Euphorbus and Hector resolve on such a deed, and Iris talks of it, it

213. Hdt. 9.71.

214. Aristodamus, the sole survivor from the three hundred, had lived in Sparta
ever since, in shame and degradation (*oneidos kai atimie*).

215. Herodotus, for his part, considers Aristodamus to have been by far the
braver.

216. Hdt. 8.123; W. K. Pritchett, *The Greek State at War*, vol. 2 (Berkeley and
Los Angeles, 1974) p. 288.

217. Ibid., p. 289.

218. Hdt. 8.124.

219. C. Segal, *The Theme of the Mutilation of the Corpse in the Iliad* (Leiden,
1971), p. 20.

220. *Iliad* 17.126–27.

nevertheless remains no more than a threat. The Greeks do not hunt for heads but seek to obtain a trophy, a sign of victory and a mark of valor, by seizing the arms of the warriors whom they kill: "In Homer's Greece, armour replaced heads,"[221] but a trophy is certainly needed if their renown is to spread.

Finally, the mutilation of the corpse, which is decapitated and flayed, is presented by Herodotus purely as a mark of *aristeia*, not as a manifestation of *aikia*, outrage. The mutilation is considered only from the point of view of the living, not at all from that of the dead. "To mutilate a body is to distress its soul"[222] and prevent it from avenging itself: this is the explanation for outrages done to corpses, in particular the ritual of *maschalismos*.[223] According to Gernet, "there may be a number of explanations for the practice of *aikia*. Through it, a group or individual avenged their own people; through it too the power of the dead enemy could be annihilated [*maschalismos*] . . . and through it also a warrior doubled his own power, his own courage."[224] But among the Scythians, mutilation in war represented first and foremost the arithmetic of *aristeia*.

Among the Scythians, then, the scalp was invariably both a mark and a symbol of *aristeia;* in Greece, in the fifth century at least, *aristeia* was proclaimed through a vote to allot the prizes for bravery. However, in Scythia there also existed a symbolic procedure for recognizing *aristeia:* "Once in every year, each governor [*nomarch*] of a province [*nome*] mixes a bowl of wine in his own province, whereof those Scythians drink who have slain enemies. Those who have not achieved this do not taste this wine but sit apart, dishonoured; and they consider this a very great disgrace. But those who have slain not one but many enemies each have two cups and drink of them both."[225] So to have killed gives one the right to drink, to have killed "many enemies" gives one, not the right to drink a great deal, but simply a double ration, while not to have killed at all relegates one to a position outside the community. The governor,[226] who can only be the representative of the central power, is the banquet

---

221. M. I. Finley, *The World of Odysseus* (London, 1962), p. 138.
222. Glotz, *Solidarité*, p. 63.
223. Rohde, *Psyché*, pp. 599–603.
224. Gernet, *Recherches*, p. 216.
225. Hdt. 4.66.
226. This is the only time that this figure appears in the whole Scythian *logos*.

master or, rather, the assessor of *aristeia;* the scalps bestow a right to wine, blood bestows a right to wine.[227]

On this occasion, at least, the Scythians appear as drinkers of wine but, in Herodotus as in the general tradition, their relations with wine are no simple matter, since they are also represented sometimes as drinkers of blood, sometimes as drinkers of milk.

In the *Histories*, wine is considered a "civilized" drink. When Croesus is preparing to attack the Persians, a Lydian who enjoys a great reputation as a *sophos* advises him not to do so, pointing out that there can be nothing to gain and much to lose by marching against people who dress in leather, never eat their fill, and "have no use for wine, but are water-drinkers";[228] in other words, there is no point in attacking real savages. In the fable that Cyrus displays to the Persians to persuade them to revolt against the Medes, wine again has a role to play. Having gathered them together, on one day hè makes them clear a field of thistles; on the next he serves them a rich banquet with much wine. The moral is that they will live as on the second day if they pay attention to him, as on the first day if they remain enslaved by the Medes.[229] Finally, wine is the only present Cambyses offers to the king of the long-lived Ethiopians that finds favor in his eyes and is not considered to be a trap. The Ethiopians, for their part, are drinkers of milk:[230] "He was vastly pleased with the draught and asked further what food their king ate and what was the greatest age to which a Persian lived. The Fish-eaters told him their king ate bread, showing him how wheat grew, and said that the full age to which a man might hope to live was eighty years. Then, said the Ethiopian, it was no wonder that their lives were so short, if they ate dung; they would never attain even to that age were it not for the strengthening power of the draught—whereby he signified to the Fish-eaters the wine—for in this, he said, the Persians excelled the Ethiopians."[231]

Wine is a civilized drink, to be included among the *agatha*, but it

227. Dumézil, *Romans de Scythie et d'alentour*, pp. 227ff., compares this crater to a bowl that appears in the legend of the Nartes; this bowl of the Nartes, the *nartamongae*, which had the power of revealing the truth, by making a sign confirmed or negated the Nartes' claims about their exploits.

228. Hdt.1.71.   229. Hdt.1.126.
230. Hdt. 3.23.   231. Hdt. 3.22.

may also serve to trick those not familiar with it. It thus has a role to play in the scenario devised by Croesus to get the better of the Massagetae.[232] Since the Massagetae have "no experience of good things" (*agatha*), Croesus suggests that Cyrus should advance into the country of the Massagetae, prepare a great banquet with all kinds of dishes (*sitia pantoia*) and many craters of neat wine (*oinou akretou*) and then retire, leaving behind only soldiers of inferior caliber. It will then be easy to surprise the Massagetae "full of wine and food" and accomplish "mighty deeds." The plan depends partly on the fact that the Massagetae are "drinkers of milk";[233] not only will they now drink wine but, their ignorance rendering the trick doubly effective, they will drink it undiluted. After the disaster, Tomyris, the queen of the Massagetae, sends word to Cyrus telling him that he has conquered not by strength, in a proper battle, but through a trick leading to great slaughter and that he owes his success to wine, which is a cunning *pharmakon*.[234] And wine certainly does possess all the ambiguity of a *pharmakon*, being either a poison or a remedy, depending on whether or not one knows how to use it.

When Tomyris had defeated the Persians, she sought out Cyrus's corpse and plunged the head into a skin filled with human blood, and she "spoke these words of insult to the dead man: 'Though I live and conquer you, you have undone me, overcoming my son by guile; but even as I threatened, so will I do, and give you your fill of blood [*aimatos koreso*].'"[235] This was the queen's answer to the ruse of the banquet organized by Cyrus; but this time, instead of wine, human blood is served. The scene is based on the assumption that it is easy to pass from the one drink to the other. In Tomyris's eyes, Cyrus the drinker of wine is in truth a drinker of blood, so he will be served blood just as if it were undiluted wine.

Drinking wine, drinking blood: there is one context in which the two actions are associated or confused, that of oath-swearing, when wine, neat wine, and blood are mixed together.[236] The Scythians

232. Hdt.1.207.   233. Hdt.1.216.
234. Hdt. 1.212.   235. Hdt. 1.214.
236. K. Kircher, *Die sakrale Bedeutung des Weines im Altertum* (Giessen, 1910), pp. 82ff.; Gernet, *Anthropology*, p.168: "The one is the equivalent of the other [wine and blood]; both belong to the same group, which is clearly opposed to the group composed of milk-and-honey libations."

swear an oath by mixing wine and blood in a bowl and drinking it. The equivalence between the two also manifests itself in the customs of war: "A Scythian drinks of the blood of the first man whom he has overthrown."[237] So a young Scythian is not a full warrior until he has completed this rite of initiation; but later, on the occasion of the annual ceremony, whether or not the warriors drain a cup of wine depends on whether or not they have slain enemies. They pass from blood (the first time) to wine (each year) and wine is the symbolic equivalent of blood. At the same time, however, this transition to the symbolic level clearly indicates the distance separating the first time from those that follow. The first time is repeated, but in such a way as to indicate that it will never again be the same: from blood, the warriors pass on to wine.

In some circumstances, then, Scythians drink blood, in others they drink wine; and they also drink milk. As early as chapter 2, Herodotus explains how they obtain their milk.[238] In fact, tradition often represented them as drinkers of milk: Strabo collects all the references to the practice from Homer down to Ephorus. The *Iliad* mentions "the lordly Hippemolgi who drink mares' milk,"[239] and a fragment of Hesiod identifies this people with the Scythians.[240] Aeschylus, in a lost play, mentions "the Scythians who eat mares' cheese and know *eunomia*."[241] And finally, Hippocrates also recognizes the Scythians to follow a diet based upon milk and cheese.[242] Alongside this current of opinion which associates the drinking of milk with justice and *eunomia*, there also developed an image of the Scythians as a cruel people, cutting off heads and drinking from skulls. Reflecting on this double tradition, Ephorus attempted to make sense of it by making a geographical and ethnic distinction: on the one hand, there were the "good" Scythians who, as the sacred formula had it, abstained from all living creatures (*ton zoon apechesthai*), drank milk, and were known for their justice;[243] on the other, the "bad" ones, the eaters of human flesh.[244]

237. Hdt. 4.64.   238. Hdt. 4.2.
239. Strabo 7.3.7; *Iliad* 13.5–6.
240. Hdt. 7.3.7.
241. Nauck, fr. 198.
242. Hippocratic Corpus, *Airs, Waters, Places* 18.
243. Strabo 7.3.9; cf. P. Vidal-Naquet, "Valeurs religieuses et mythiques de la terre et du sacrifice dans l'Odyssée," *Annales E.S.C.* 5 (1970): 1287.
244. Ephorus does not specify what they drink. It may be blood, or wine, but equally it may be milk.

On the one hand, Scythia is seen as a country ignorant of the vine, that is to say, of the delights of civilization, but, more important, also of its soft luxuries. In his play entitled *The Bacchae*, Antiphanes writes that because of the drunkenness of women, a man who marries is an unfortunate wretch "except in Scythia, the only place where the vine does not even grow."[245] Similarly, when a Greek asks Anacharsis whether flutes exist in Scythia, he replies, "No, nor yet vines."[246]

But, on the other hand, there is the tradition, beginning with Herodotus and still being echoed by Athenaeus, that represents the Scythians as inveterate drunkards. Not content to drink wine on the occasion of the swearing of oaths or at their annual ceremony, they drink "like fish." To drink "in the Scythian fashion" is a proverb which refers to the drinking of neat wine.[247] The expression, used in this sense, is mentioned early on by Herodotus, when he is recounting the fate of the Spartan king Cleomenes. The Lacedaemonians claimed that Cleomenes went mad because he learned from the Scythians (who had come to Sparta to propose an alliance against Darius) to drink undiluted wine. From that day on they themselves, when they wished to drink "purer" (or less diluted) wine, said that they were going to drink "in the Scythian manner."[248] Anacreon, Chamaileus of Heraclea in his book *On Drunkenness*, and Achaius, in *Aethon*, all speak of drinking "in the Scythian fashion" or of "Scythian drink."[249] So to drink wine is the mark of a civilized man, but to drink wine undiluted is the mark of a savage and represents a transgression. One dabbles in this transgression as soon as one alters the normal ratios of wine and water. "To drink in the Scythian fashion" is not necessarily to drink totally undiluted wine, but to add less water to it than usual. Only Cleomenes drank totally undiluted wine, and he went "mad" (*manenai*). Pure wine is a dangerous beverage.

245. Athenaeus 10.441d.

246. Diogenes Laertius 1.104. There are a number of comments about wine and drunkenness in the chapter devoted to Anacharsis.

247. Leutsch and Schneidewin, *Corpus Paroemiographorum graecorum*, vol. 2, p. 166: *Episkuthison: epi ton akratoi chromenon; hoi gar Skuthai akratopotai.*

248. Hdt. 6.84. We may also note that the Scythians rejected Dionysus on the pretext that he made men mad.

249. Anacreon, in *Poetae lyrici graeci*, fr. 63 (= Athenaeus 427a–b). Chamaileus (Athenaeus 427b) also tells the stories of Cleomenes and Achaius: *Tragicorum graecorum fragmenta*[2], 748 (= Athenaeus 427c).

Pondering the etymology of the word *skyphos*, Athenaeus proposes, among other suggestions, that it should be derived from *skythos* since the Scythians have such a reputation for getting drunk; and, he adds, Hieronymus of Rhodes, in his work on *Drunkenness*, even writes that "to get drunk is to behave like a Scythian [*to methusai skuthisai*]";250 so *skuthizo* means "to shave one's hair off" but also "to become drunk."

Plato has one final touch to add to this picture of Scythian drunkenness. It applies to men as well as to women. The Athenian of the *Laws* declares: "You [*Lacedaemonians*], as you say, abstain from it altogether, whereas the Scythians and Thracians, both men and women, take their wine neat and let it pour down over their clothes and regard this practice of theirs as a noble and splendid one."251

Occasional drinkers of blood, constant drinkers of milk, excessive drinkers of wine: such are the Scythians. It is pointless to seek to reduce these traditions for, in truth, they are essential to the *aporia* of the Scythian character. We need only think of Polyphemus, the Cyclops: he is a drinker of milk and an eater of cheese, but also an eater of men. He is familiar with "wine of our own made from the grapes that our rich soil and the timely rains produce" but he does not know how to drink and behaves like a drunkard. When Odysseus offers him wine, he drains it at a draught, neat, and asks for more.252 So in his case, the two beverages milk and neat wine simultaneously mark out a savage.

War is a hunt and, first and foremost, a head-hunt. Warfare is an habitual occupation, and the Scythians are made for war. But—and here is what is so astonishing—warfare appears as an organized and codified activity. Among nomads, who rate very low on the score of

250. Athenaeus 11.499f.

251. *Laws* 637e. The Scythians' relations to wine are also the subject of one of the Aristotelian *Problemata* (3.7): the Scythians love wine because they are both "hot" and "dry", whereas children, who are also "hot" but are "wet", do not like it.

252. *Odyssey* 9.353ff.: "I handed him another bowlful [*kissubion* = drinking bowl, milking pail] of the ruddy wine. Three times I filled it up for him; and three times the fool drained the bowl to the dregs. At last . . . the wine fuddled his wits" (360–62). The wine was a present from Maron, the priest of Apollo at Ismarus: "When they drank this red and honeyed vintage, he used to pour one cupful of wine into twenty of water" (9.208–10). On the other hand, when drunk "neat, it was a drink for the god" (9.205), a remark which should be taken literally: mortal men are unable to tolerate it.

koinonia, such elaborate social organization indeed seems surprising. Yet whenever Herodotus comes to report on the customs of war, the space of Scythia is no longer an undifferentiated pastureland but is organized into separate zones, each with an administration: the territory is divided into nomes with a nomarch or governor appointed over each one. Ares, who is the object of a special cult and particular sacrifices, often human ones,[253] has a sanctuary in each nome, which must be attended every year. The organization of space is complemented by a regular ordering of time: once every year the sanctuary of Ares is refurbished and he is honored there by sacrifices, and once every year a "banquet" is held by the nomarch to celebrate the enemies slain by each warrior; furthermore, there is a symbolical significance to this official ceremony.

Finally, in these customs connected with warfare, the central place falls to the king. He presides over the distribution of booty, allotting shares only against decapitated heads. As "master of the banquet" (through the intermediary of his representatives, the nomarchs), he allots a cup of wine (or two) to whoever has slain enemies in the course of the year. As "master of justice," he must preside over all judiciary duels: when two related Scythians have a quarrel, they engage in single combat in the presence of the king, and the victor makes a drinking cup of the skull of his foe. So here again it is the king who authorizes the decapitation: the leader must have heads!

As the leader of the hunt against Darius and as war leader, the Scythian king is certainly a *despotes*: for the Greeks of the fifth century, royalty was despotic and a barbarian leader was bound to be royal. In life he was the mobile center of power. In death he became the excentric center of the territory, his corpse a point of anchorage: the Scythian people were tied to his dead body like a ship at anchor. During his lifetime, his hearth was the foundation for all (contractual) exchanges and through it the Scythians were constituted as a social body. Any betrayal to his hearth caused him to fall sick, just as if the royal body and the social body were indeed two yet also one; to cure him, it was necessary to behead the perjurer. At his death his body was embalmed and the Scythians mutilated themselves. Through

253. Hdt. 4.62.

this ceremony which left its marks on their bodies, they acknowledged themselves to be Scythians and subjects: their bodies upon which the royal coat-of-arms was incised reminded them that they formed a social body and, through this mnemonics of power, the royal body and the social body were strangely woven together.

Five

Space and the Gods: The "Self-Cooking" Ox and the "Drinks" of Ares

What gods do the Scythians worship? What are their relations with them? Or, to put the question another way, how do nomads communicate with their gods? If the Scythians implicitly and insistently make the Greeks face the question: "How is it possible to be a nomad?" we may suppose that in one way or another nomadism must also leave its traces in the divine space and must, at some point, stamp its mark upon the relations that the Scythians maintain with their gods.[1] Take the example of sacrifice: to the city, blood sacrifice is fundamental. Through the slaughter of an animal and the commensality that it introduces, the city acknowledges itself to be a community of eaters of meat. If sacrifice is indeed linked with the political order of the *polis*, for which it is the basis and at the same time the expression, if it truly is "the corner-stone of the religion of the city,"[2] what can be the nature of sacrifice among nomads? Seen in this perspective, sacrificial practices become a means of probing human groups, establishing the differences between them, suggesting wherein their "otherness" lies.

But before turning, with this question in mind, to the two chapters that Herodotus devotes to sacrifices among the Scythians,[3]

---

1. This text appeared in a slightly different form in M. Detienne and J.-P. Vernant, *La Cuisine du sacrifice en pays grec* (Paris, 1979), pp. 251–69.
2. J.-P. Vernant, "Between the Beasts and the Gods," in his *Myth and Society* (Brighton, 1980), p. 161; cf. also J.-L. Durand, "Le Corps du délit," *Communications* 26 (1977); 46–60.
3. Herodotus 4.61–62.

let us take a look at their pantheon: "The gods whom they propitiate [*hilaskontai*] by worship are these: Hestia first and foremost and secondly Zeus and Earth, whom they deem [*nomizontes*] to be the wife of Zeus; after these, Apollo, the heavenly Aphrodite, Heracles and Ares. All the Scythians recognize [*nenomikasi*] these as gods; the Scythians called Royal sacrifice also to Poseidon."[4] The first thing to strike us about this pantheon is its paucity: it comprises no more than seven names (eight, for the Royal Scythians). Actually, the pantheons of all barbarians (with the exception of the Egyptians) are limited to a small number of deities.[5] As for the many other gods revered by the Greeks, Herodotus does not say whether they are completely unknown to the Scythians, but at all events they do not "propitiate" them, that is to say, they do not offer up sacrifices to them. Only the case of Dionysus is made clear: we know from the story of Scyles that the Scythians rejected him absolutely. Furthermore, the composition of this pantheon is curious. As conceived by the Scythians, the divine hierarchy is significantly different from the theogonies most current in the Greek world—those of Homer and, above all, Hesiod. Hestia, who is generally considered as the daughter of Rhea and Cronos, hence sister to Zeus,[6] is here set in the position of a primordial deity. I have tried to account for her strange presence among a nomad people by relating the centrality of Hestia to the centrality of the royal power.[7] But the most surprising association is that of Earth and Zeus who do not ordinarily belong to the same divine generation. Usually, the generation of Cronos comes between Earth, the offspring of Chaos, and Zeus. Conscious of the "heretical" character of this idea, the narrator intervenes to make it clear to his readers that it is not he who is responsible for this mistake and that there is a logic behind the Scythians' error: "They deem Earth to be the wife of Zeus." This affords some coherence to their idea, which can accordingly no longer be condemned as ludicrous, but becomes simply erroneous, and understandable in view of the Scythians' ignorance.

Their pantheon is thus characterized by paucity and confusion:

4. Hdt. 4.59.
5. I. M. Linforth, "Greek Gods and Foreign Gods in Herodotus," *Univ. of Calif. Publ. in Class. Phil.* 9 (1926): 6–7.
6. Hesiod *Theogony* 454.
7. Cf. above, pp. 119ff.

they had no Homer or Hesoid to establish the theogony in a definite form and sketch in the characters of the various gods. [8] Just as those ancestors of the Greeks, the Pelasgians, until just the other day[9] were ignorant of the parents from whom each of the gods was born or whether they had all existed forever and what they were like, similarly the Scythians are ignorant: they think that Hestia came before Earth and that the latter is the wife of Zeus. All the same, unlike the Pelasgians, who until they learned them from the Egyptians did not know the "names" (*ounomata*) of the gods, the Scythians do know how to name them.[10]

The Scythians pray to their gods, offering sacrifices to them, but this cult does not imply either that they made statues (*agalmata*) or that they used altars (*bomous*) or built temples (*neous*).[11] So they have no special places in which to address the gods. What can be the meaning of this absence? The narrator does not tell us. However, the appearance of this triad—statues, temples, altars—elsewhere in the *Histories* may suggest a possible approach to the problem. The Persians, similarly, are not in the habit of setting up statues, temples, or altars. Now, in their case, the narrator does intervene to add that not only do they not do such things but they consider it to be "madness" (*morie*) to do so, and Herodotus explains: "I suppose because they never believed the gods, as do the Greeks, to be in the likeness of men [*anthropophueas*]."[12] But although this explanation may be valid for the Greeks and for the Persians, who sacrifice to the sun, the moon, fire, and so forth, it will not do for the Scythians who, on the contrary, seek to propitiate such gods as Hestia, Zeus, and Apollo.

Some distance away from the Scythians, to the north, live the Budini. They live in a town constructed entirely out of wood: the walls and houses are wooden and so are the sanctuaries, "for there are among them temples of Greek gods [*Hellenikon theon*], furnished in Greek fashion [*hellenikos*] with statues and altars and

8. Hdt. 2.53.

9. Herodotus believes Hesiod and Homer to have lived four hundred years earlier than himself.

10. Hdt. 2.52.

11. Hdt. 4.59.

12. Hdt. 1.131.

shrines of wood."[13] In other words, temples, statues, and altars are signs of Greekness and may function as a criterion of Greekness. Moreover, it is by no mere chance that the Budini know how to use them, for in former times they were Greek. These three elements may thus assume the role of differentiating factors. The lack of fixed places of worship is truly a mark of the otherness of the religious practices of the Scythians.

The same triad recurs again, this time on the lips of the Egyptian priests. The priests of Heliopolis explain to Herodotus that the Egyptians are the first to have given the twelve gods their names and the first to have "assigned to the several gods their altars and statues and temples."[14] All these things are inventions of the Egyptians taken over by the Greeks, and not to know of them is, in a sense, to be living in a bygone age. The difference involved is then termed "primitivism." The Scythians appear never to have known what the Greeks learned from the Egyptians. I say "appear" not to have known because we do come across the exception of Ares, to whom it *was* customary to build sanctuaries and who *was* normally represented by an *agalma*.[15] In his myth, Protagoras goes even further: not to set up temples or fashion representations of the gods is not only to live in a "bygone age" before this Egyptian invention, but to live beyond the pale of humanity: "And now that man was partaker of a divine portion, he in the first place, by his nearness of kin to deity, was the only creature that worshipped gods and set himself to establish altars and holy images."[16] Whoever fails to honor the gods denies the divine *moira* which is man's special property.

The Ox

People of the frontier lands the Scythians may be, yet they do perform sacrifices. But in their case, their spatial remoteness does not, in return, afford them any particular proximity to the gods. They do not have the gods to share their meals, as Homer's Ethiopians do;

---

13. Hdt. 4.108. In the definition of *to Hellenikon* given by the Athenians at 8.144 we find, precisely, mention of buildings for the gods and sacrifices: "the shrines of gods and the sacrifices that we have in common [*theon idrumata te koina kai thusiai*]."

14. Hdt. 2.4.

15. Hdt. 4.59.

16. Plato *Protagoras* 322a.

unlike Herodotus's Long-lived Ethiopians, they have no Table of the Sun to provide them with ready-boiled meat dishes every day.[17] Nor do they possess, as do the Cyclopes, the faculty of not having to worry about Zeus and the other gods and so of ignoring all sacrificial practices. Plain mortal men and eaters of meat are the Scythians.

The first comment to be vouchsafed by the narrator concerns the uniformity of the sacrifices: all the Scythians sacrifice to all the gods (except Ares) in accordance with the same ritual.[18] The formula used is the same as in the case of Egyptian sacrifice: all the Egyptians behave in the same way with the heads of sacrificed animals and they all practice the same libations of wine;[19] but differences appear between one sacrifice and another when it comes to the extraction of the entrails and the cooking. By way of an example, Herodotus reports on the ritual in honor "of the deity they hold to be the greatest [*daimona megisten*]." That means that the ritual varies depending on the deity invoked. What does the uniformity of Scythian practice suggest? A certain ignorance on their part of the particular requirements of each god and a certain absence of differentiation in their pantheon, perhaps?

Since the Scythians set up no temples or altars, no sacrificial space is marked out; apparently, any place in the territory is as good as any other.[20] The ceremony opens with the leading-in of the victim (how, is not known).

The victim itself stands with its forefeet shackled together; the sacrificer stands behind the beast and throws it down by plucking the end of the rope; as the victim falls, he invokes whatever god it is to whom he sacrifices. Then, throwing a noose round the beast's neck, he thrusts in a stick and twists it and so strangles the victim, lighting no fire nor consecrating the victim, nor pouring any libation.[21]

---

17. Hdt. 3.18. See Vernant, *La Cuisine*, pp. 239–49.

18. Hdt. 4.60. J. Casabona, "Recherches sur le vocabulaire des sacrifices en grec," diss. Paris, 1967, p. 61 shows that in Herodotus *erdo* is equivalent to *poieo*: "one may see in the way Herodotus employs *erdo*, even with a religious meaning, one of those Homerisms in his language to which the ancient critics refer."

19. Hdt. 2.39.

20. The Persians (Hdt. 1.132) who, similarly, do not set up temples or altars, nevertheless choose "a pure place [*khoron katharon*]" in which to sacrifice. Their space is thus separated into zones of varying quality.

21. Hdt. 4.60: *kai apopnigei, oute pur anakausas oute katarxamenos out' epispeisas.*

In this first phase in the slaughtering of the animal, the narrator explicitly points out three omissions, indicated by the repetition of *oute:* the omissions of fire, first fruits, and libations represent three differences from sacrifice in the *polis.* The fact that it is these three points that are also mentioned, either together or separately, when Herodotus describes other sacrificial practices indicates that he regarded them as criteria of difference. The Persians, similarly, "when about to sacrifice, do not kindle fire."[22] So this means that the fire in question is that which is lit on an altar before the victim is put to death. The libations in question, absent from the Scythian ritual, are probably the libations of wine sometimes dispensed even before the killing takes place.[23] The Egyptians, for example, not only set up altars and light a fire but also "pour wine on the altar, over the victim . . . then they cut its throat."[24] Moreover, strangely enough, the Scythians themselves, although omitting libations when sacrificing to the rest of the gods, include them in honor of Ares. In this case, wine is poured over the head of the victim before the throat is cut, but the victim is a human one.[25] The narrator's comment points to one last pertinent feature: the absence of *katarkhesthai.* Legrand in his French translation writes *sans consacrer de prémices* (without consecrating first fruits), just as if Herodotus had written *aparkhesthai.* Now *aparkhesthai* occurs a number of times in the *Histories* with the precise meaning of "first fruits": once the meat is cooked and before starting their meal, the Scythians set a portion aside as first fruits.[26] The Libyans, before slaughtering the victim, cut off the tip of an ear as the first fruits.[27] What might *katarkhesthai* mean, if it is not in fact a doublet of *aparkhesthai?* Herodotus uses the word on two occasions in addition to this one: when the Tauri sacrifice prisoners, they begin by "consecrating" (*katarxamenoi*) them, before finishing them off.[28] Similarly, when Heracles is on the point of

22. Hdt. 1.132.
23. According to Casabona ("Recherches," p. 249) *epispendo,* in Herodotus, means "to pour libations onto something, and denotes a gesture rather than a ceremony. It is the equivalent of *kataspendo,* which Herodotus uses in a different sense."
24. Hdt. 2.39.
25. Hdt. 4.62.
26. Hdt. 4.61, and cf. 3.24.
27. Hdt. 4.188.
28. Hdt. 4.103.

being sacrificed, he too is "consecrated": "When he came to Egypt, the Egyptians crowned him and led him out in a procession [*pompe*] to sacrifice him to Zeus; and for a while (they say) he followed quietly, but when they began his consecration [*katarkhonto*], he resisted and slew them all".[29] Heracles revolts at the point when it becomes clear to him that he is not the hero of the festival but the intended sacrificial victim; his crowning and the procession were ambiguous, but once the "consecration" begins, the ambiguity vanishes. If it could alert Heracles to his true situation, what gestures identified it? When Nestor offers a sacrifice to Athena, he starts by sprinkling lustral water and barley grain (*katerkheto*), next he addresses a long prayer to Pallas, then he plucks a few hairs from the victim's head and tosses them into the fire (*aparkhomenos*).[30] Thus, *katarkhesthai* means to "consecrate," that is, to "sprinkle lustral water and barley grain," and *aparkhesthai*, which occurs soon after, refers to the plucking of a few hairs which are then burned. So the Scythians know nothing of "consecration," and this ignorance is extremely significant. In truth, the sprinkling of water and the scattering of grain over the victim were designed to obtain its consent to the sacrifice. By shaking its head from right to left, it accepted being sacrificed. This was how the ritual rid itself of the element of violence and the participants could in advance disculpate themselves from the accusation of murder.[31] So the presence or absence of "consecration" is the mark of all that separates a "non-violent" sacrifice from a "violent" one—and Scythian sacrifice is violent.

The absence of "consecration" also has another meaning and, at another level, this too indicates the difference of the Scythians: the Scythians cultivate no crops. Now, "the practice of sacrifice stresses this similarity between sacrificial animals and cultivated plants, by incorporating barley and wine into the ceremonial killing and burning of the ritually sacrificed animal."[32] So this omission is also a mark of the nomadism of the Scythians: how could they have barley at their disposal when they neither sow nor cultivate?

In their sacrifices the Greeks associate cultivated plants and domesticated animals. The Scythians know nothing of cultivated

29. Hdt. 2.45. For Herodotus, all this is "nonsense" recounted by the Greeks.
30. *Odyssey* 3.445.
31. Durand, "Le Corps du délit," pp. 51–59.
32. Vernant, "Beasts and Gods," p. 182, and *La Cuisine*, pp. 58–63.

plants but they sacrifice domesticated animals nonetheless. They do not go so far as to sacrifice wild animals. They thus retain only the second term from the couple composed of cultivated plants–domesticated animals. Herodotus tells us specifically that they sacrifice the ox and the smaller livestock (*probata*), but also the horse. The presence of this third animal is another point that differentiates their practice from that of the Greeks, who were not in the habit of sacrificing horses and, at all events, would never do so in a blood sacrifice followed by a meal provided by the victim. For the Scythians, however, the ox, the smaller livestock, and the horse seem to have been regarded as equivalents which could perfectly well be substituted for one another.[33] The only people in the *Histories* to sacrifice horses, apart from the Scythians, are the Massagetae: they sacrifice horses to the sun.[34] Pausanias also attributes this practice to the Sauromatae who, he claims, cut the throats of mares and ate them. To sacrifice horses might, at a pinch, be acceptable, but to eat them was altogether aberrant.[35]

The animal is taken by surprise and slaughtered without any attempt to gain its consent. It stands, its forefeet hobbled, with the sacrificer positioned behind it, unseen. "He throws it down by plucking the end of the rope; as the victim falls, he invokes whatever god it is to whom he sacrifices. Then, throwing a noose around the beast's neck, he thrusts in a stick and twists it and so strangles the victim."[36] Thus, instead of the *pelekus*, the axe used to decapitate the ox,[37] or the *makhaira*, the knife with which its throat is cut, the Scythians use a rope and a piece of wood, a lasso (*brokhos*) which they employ as a garrot. For,—and this is the most scandalous aspect to this sacrifice—the animal does not have its throat cut, and its blood is not shed. Instead, it is smothered. Greek sacrifice, involving a meal, is blood sacrifice; Scythian sacrifice certainly involves a meal,

33. P. Stengel, *Opferbraüche der Griechen* (Leipzig, 1910), pp. 155ff.

34. Hdt. 1.216. Strabo repeats this information (11.8.6). Furthermore, quite exceptionally, on one occasion the Persians sacrifice horses: in order to obtain good omens, magi cut the throats of some white horses in the waters of the river Strymon (7.213).

35. Pausanias 1.21.6.

36. Hdt. 4.60.

37. The absence of *pelekus* may be connected with the absence of cultivated land. Durand ("Le Corps du délit," p. 49 n. 5) points out that the axe may be regarded as an instrument for clearing land.

since it ends with the eating of the meat, but it is not blood sacrifice.

What is the meaning of this aberrant type of killing? Not only is strangulation not often employed in sacrifice, it is not even a current mode of execution. There is one instance of it among the Egyptians,[38] one among the Babylonians,[39] and one by a son of Battus:[40] in other words, it is practiced by non-Greeks, under particular circumstances, or by a "tyrant." In his list of the members of Xerxes' army, Herodotus mentions one people, the Sagartians, who in combat use not weapons of iron or bronze, but the lasso; all the same, the Sagartians do not strangle their human or animal prey but simply immobilize the victim in this manner, later killing it with a dagger. However, and the point is by no means without significance, it is specifically stated that these people are nomads.[41] Outside the *Histories*, strangulation or hanging seems to be the worst of all deaths: it is the fate of the servants disloyal to Odysseus. Telemachus promises them a death which will not be "honourable" (*katharos*). "The women held their heads out in a row and a noose was cast around each one's neck to despatch them in the most miserable way. For a little while their feet kicked out, but not for very long."[42] In tragedy, this death (*ankhone*) is imbued with the maximum degree of horror. For example, Andromache, ready to die to save her son, exclaims: "I'm in your hands, to mangle, murder, bind, hang by the neck."[43] And Oedipus tells the chorus-leader that he has committed "things deserving worse punishment than hanging" (or "things for which the guilty are strangled"?).[44] Strangulation seems to be regarded as a particularly "violent" form of killing.

Not only do the Scythians fail to remove all elements of violence

38. Hdt. 2.169. Apries is strangled by the Egyptians, who defeat him after rising against him.

39. Hdt. 3.150. When the Babylonians rise in revolt, they strangle the women.

40. Hdt. 4.160. Arkesilas is strangled by his brother.

41. Hdt. 7.85.

42. *Odyssey* 22.471–73. This death seems to be the feminine equivalent of that inflicted on Melanthios, who suffered the amputation of his nose, ears, sexual organs (which were given to the dogs), hands, and feet (474–77).

43. Euripides *Andromache* 412.

44. Sophocles *Oedipus Rex* 1374: *erga esti kreisson' agchones eirgasmena*. There is probably a connection between hanging and blood or the fear of blood, as in Aeschylus *The Suppliant Maidens* (788): "And willing would I be, / Fated to die hanging / Before a hated husband should touch me."

from their sacrifices, they accentuate them by their mode of slaughtering the victim. What should we make of the absence of blood? Is it possible to assign a precise meaning to this absence? Let us examine the other non-Greek sacrificial practices mentioned by Herodotus. It seems that the Egyptians "cut the throats" (*sphazousi*) of their victims, after lighting a fire and sprinkling libations;[45] whereas the Scythians strangle, light no fire, and pour no libations. The Libyans "wring the neck of the victim" [*apostrephousi ton aukhena*]"—perhaps to strangle it, by breaking the cervical vertebrae. The text says nothing about the preparations for the sacrifice. Are there libations? Is a fire lit? All Herodotus tells us is that they snip off a piece of the animal's ear, as first fruits, and toss it over their shoulder:[46] they remove a piece of the ear instead of a few hairs from the animal's head, and they throw it over their shoulder instead of into the fire, as is normally done with the hairs. The gestures seem to imply that there is no fire. But the most important point is that this type of slaughtering is practiced by nomadic Libyans, people who lead a similar kind of life to that of the Scythians. Unfortunately, this observation is too tenuous to warrant our assuming a connection between strangulation and nomadism, thereby at a stroke establishing the meaning of this absence of blood. As for the Persians, the last group whose sacrificial customs are mentioned, we are told nothing about the way they kill their victims, although Herodotus does note that they light no fire and dispense no libations.[47]

In Greek sacrifice, the blood flows for the gods. It is collected in a special vessel and poured onto the altar and the earth round about. It "flows down the walls built by man to mingle with the earth of the divine domain upon which they stand."[48] Since the Scythians have neither sanctuary nor altar upon which to sacrifice, there is no consecrated place for them to sprinkle; so, as one can see, they have no need to spill blood. Their aberrant ritual is at least coherent with their nomadism.[49]

45. Hdt. 4.39.

46. Hdt. 2.39. *Omon* is a conjecture; the manuscripts give *domon*.

47. Hdt. 1.132: no altar, no fire, no libation, no flutes, no fillets, no barley . . . yet the Persians are not presented as nomads, even if they do include a number of nomad "tribes" among them: the Dai, the Mardi, the Dropici, the Sagartii (1.125).

48. Durand, in *La Cuisine*, p. 139.

49. Practically speaking, the meat of an ox that had not been bled would be inedible. This detail about the blood makes it all the easier to see that with Ares one passes into a different kind of space: for Ares, blood must flow.

After the slaughtering come the cutting up and the cooking: "Having strangled and flayed the beast, the sacrificer sets about cooking it"; "when they have flayed the victim, they strip the flesh from the bones."[50] After the flaying, which takes place immediately after death, they (it is not known who) divide the animal into two parts: the flesh, *krea*, on one side, and the bones, *ostea*, on the other. The only opposition that is relevant is that between *ostea* and *crea*. Furthermore, these *ostea* are then used as fuel: it is they that are used to cook the animal. The aberrations of this ritual are quite clear. In the first place, this sacrifice does not set aside the gods' share: in particular, the *meria*, thigh bones, which are normally smeared with fat and burned on the altar.[51] Furthermore, far from being burned on the altar for the gods, the bones are burned underneath the animal, as fuel. All this is scandalous, as is indirectly confirmed by the rationalization, very Toynbean in its own way, used by the narrator to explain the matter: Scythia is very poor in wood, so the Scythians "invented" (*exeuretai*) the idea of using the bones of sacrificed animals instead. By this means, the aspect of their behavior that is scandalous to a Greek is rendered comprehensible, if not admissible. That this is just a rationalization we sense through the narrative's ambiguity on the subject of wood supplies in Scythia: although the country is, overall, short of wood, it does contain one region, the Hylaia, that is covered with forests;[52] the sanctuaries of Ares are built entirely from wood and they measure no less than three stades squared;[53] finally, when it comes to punishing the false diviners, a cart is filled with wood and then set alight.[54]

The absence of any *meria* is compounded by a second absence, which is implied in the division of the animal into no more than two parts, *ostea* and *krea*; there is no mention of the *splankhna*, the viscera. Now, "the consumption of the viscera necessarily constitutes the first phase of the sacrifice."[55] The viscera, threaded onto skewers,

50. Hdt. 4.60, 61.
51. J. Rudhardt, *Notions fondamentales de la pensé religieuse et actes constitutifs du culte dans la Grèce classique* (Geneva, 1958), p. 262.
52. Hdt. 4.76.
53. Hdt. 4.62.
54. Hdt. 4.6.
55. Aristotle *PA* 661b1 ff. and 673b1 ff.: the *splankhna* are the "vital" parts of the animal and comprise the liver, the lungs, the spleen, the kidneys, and the heart. Cf. M. Detienne, *Dionysos Slain* (Baltimore, 1979), pp. 77–78, and Vernant, in *La Cuisine*, pp. 139–50.

are set to roast and are eaten while the *meria* are burning on the altar.
Recalling the example of Telemachus's arrival in Pylos, Detienne has
shown that there were two circles of eaters in a sacrifice. The smaller
one comprised the "co-eaters of the *splankhna*"; the larger and less
tightly knit one was made up of the general participants in the
sacrificial meal. But it was certainly the consumption of the *splankhna* that ensured "maximum participation" in the sacrifice. Now, this
necessary phase is totally absent from the Scythian ritual: there is
none of this concentrated commensality among the co-eaters of the
splankhna, and the sacrificer appears as an isolated figure.

No *splankhna,* no spit, no roast. This sacrificial model seems to be
defined by its deficiencies and to be an altogether impoverished
ritual. The roasting phase, which normally precedes the boiling,
does not take place at all, for the Scythians practice no form of
cooking other than boiling (*hepsesis*):[56] "They throw the flesh into
the cauldrons of the country, if they have such: these are most like to
Lesbian craters save that they are much bigger. Into these, then,
they throw the flesh and cook it [*hepsonsi*] by lighting a fire beneath
with the bones of the victims."[57] This is the first mention of a truly
sacrificial instrument: a cauldron in which the meat is set to simmer,
even if it is a cauldron that looks more like a large crater. However, in
no time at all even this seemingly firm ground gives way. The
narrator goes on to say: "If they have no cauldron, they cast *all* the
flesh into the victims' stomachs, adding water thereto, and make a
fire beneath the bones, which burn extremely well. The stomachs

---

56. Here we confront the question of the cultural significance of what is boiled
and what is roasted. Detienne writes: "Just as cooking distinguishes man from the
animal who eats his food raw, boiling separates the truly civilized man from the
bumpkin condemned to roasting" (Dionysos Slain, p. 79). We should thus expect the
Scythians to practice roasting rather than boiling, but that is not at all the case: they
know nothing of roasting (apparently) and are familiar only with boiling. Similarly,
when the Persians make sacrifices, they boil the meat (Hdt. 1.132); but they also
know about roasting, a technique they use on the occasion of their anniversary
meals. Among the Ethiopians (3.18), the Table of the Sun is where the boiled meats
are set out. No details are provided about Libyan sacrifice. As for Egyptian sacrifice,
no information is explicitly given, although it appears from other indications (2.77) that
the Egyptians were familiar both with roasting and with cooking by boiling. The
Indians should also be mentioned: they live on plants (*poiephagousi*) and boil grain
together with the husks, which they also eat (3.100); their food is either raw or
boiled. As for the Massagetae, when they sacrifice their old men and mingle their
flesh with that of the *probata,* they boil the lot (1.216); they are consumers of milk.
    57. Hdt. 4.61.

[*gaster*] easily hold the flesh when it is stripped from the bones; thus an ox serves to cook itself [*heauton*] and every other victim does likewise."[58] When in Menander's *Dyskolus* one of the characters, who is on the point of sacrificing a sheep, realizes that he has forgotton his cauldron, he decides, after attempting in vain to find one, to roast all the meat instead.[59] But faced with the same absence of a cauldron, the Scythians, who know nothing of roasting, use the animal's own stomach instead of a *lebes*. This use of the *gaster* as a cooking pot is clearly surprising. It is true that Prometheus covers over the flesh and fatty entrails with the ox's stomach,[60] but his action is designed to deceive and make the part that is really the better look as if it is inedible; the *gaster* may be used as a container but that does not make it a substitute for the *lebes*. To present the Scythian practice to the reader, the narrator resorts to a rationalization similar to the one used earlier: since they have no wood they burn bones; when they have no cauldron they use the animal's stomach. But why should they not have a cauldron, if such a thing exists and is one of the instruments of sacrifice? That is really just a way to get around the profound strangeness of this cooking operation. Once the cauldron has disappeared, we are left with this astonishing image of the ox cooking itself, the ox that is "self-cooking."

Once the flesh is cooked, the last phase of the sacrifice follows, the meal, about which Herodotus tells us nothing: "When the flesh is cooked, the sacrificer takes the first fruits of the flesh and the entrails and casts it before him."[61] We learn nothing of the banquet itself. Are the pieces of meat shared out? By whom, between whom, in what fashion? In the city, it is fundamental that "each one should taste the animal,"[62] but in this case there is room to wonder whether a

58. Hdt. 4.61.

59. Menander *Dyskolos* 456, 519.

60. *Theogony* 538–39; cf. Vernant, "*Beasts and Gods*," p. 179. The suitors (*Odyssey* 18.44–45) have on their fire the "stomachs (*gasteres*) of goats, stuffed with fat and blood)–a kind of black pudding. Metrodorus, in Jacoby, *FGrHist.*, 43 F 3, reports that the people of Smyrna, originally Aeolians, sacrifice a black bull to Boubrostis; after cutting it up, they cook the whole lot inside its own skin (*autodoron*), so this is something quite different (a holocaust).

61. Hdt. 4.61. *ho thusas ton kreon kai ton splagchnon aparxamenos.*

62. Porphyry *On Piety*, fr. 18. The only occasion that Herodotus mentions a *dais*, or banquet, is in connection with the Egyptian sacrifice. He says nothing about the Libyans; among the Persians, he specifies that the sacrificer "carries away the flesh and uses it as he pleases" (1.132).

communal meal takes place at all. If, as the account of the Bouphonia suggests, sacrifice is a political operation, those who know nothing of the *polis* would also know nothing of the communal meal, and nomads less than anyone else. I therefore believe that the silence here indicates an absence: there is no equal distribution, no commensality, no true community. Even the gesture of the sacrificer poses a problem. It is customary to scatter a little of the food before himself,[63] but the composition of these first fruits is surprising: flesh (*krea*) and viscera (*splankhna*); the flesh is cooked, but what about the viscera? Normally, by this stage of the sacrifice they would already have been consumed by "the co-eaters of the *splankhna*" while the meat was simmering. Besides, it has already been stated that the animal was divided into two parts, the bones and the flesh. There was no mention of the viscera—not of the extraction nor of the cooking nor of the eating of them. Should we, then, assume that these *splankhna* have been treated as if they were ordinary meat, in other words, boiled along with the rest? If so, this constitutes yet another aberration. The eventual appearance of the *splankhna* thus simply adds to the confusion of the ritual. If some of the viscera *are* consecrated, that can only happen at the beginning of the sacrifice, when they are extracted and even before the flaying of the victim, not at the end when the more general meal should be beginning. The Scythians make no distinction between the first phase, of the *splankhna*, and that of the *krea*.

All in all, the Scythian ritual is characterized by a number of absences: the absence of a place of sacrifice; the absence of any preparatory phase (fire, first fruits, libations); the absence of blood. Moreover, it makes no provision for any share for the gods (*meria*) or for the *splankhna* phase, and it leads up to no final sharing out of the meat and no banquet. It makes no use of the indispensable instruments of sacrifice, which are inseparable from the Greek identity:[64] the knife, the spits, the cauldron (which is known but not considered necessary). It is a violent sacrifice: the animal, whose assent is not sought, is, furthermore, strangled. Compared with the Greek model

63. Curiously enough, Rudhardt (*Notions fondamentales*, p. 220) uses this Scythian example to show that this is normal Greek practice.

64. Hdt. 2.41: the Egyptians, with their different sacrificial customs, would not "kiss a Greek man or use a knife or a spit or a cauldron belonging to a Greek, or taste the flesh of an unblemished ox that has been cut up with a Greek knife."

of sacrifice, this ritual appears impoverished and confused. It does not ensure either mediation between men and gods or communication between men. It is not possible to assign a single, unequivocal meaning to each of these absences, but all of them at least hint that the Scythians do not cultivate crops and do not really form a community. So it is all the more interesting to note that throughout these chapters Herodotus in effect speaks only of the sacrifice of the ox. We know that the Scythians also sacrifice smaller livestock and horses, but we are told only about the sacrifice of the ox. The choice of the ox proves two things: (1) that the scene of reference constantly present is that of the civic sacrifice; and (2) that to represent the Scythians sacrificing an ox is, at a stroke, to make them seem as distant as possible, for the ox is precisely the last animal that they ought to sacrifice. If the ox and the *polis* are indissolubly associated, whoever is *apolis* should not be sacrificing an ox. Under these circumstances, to choose to represent them engaged in sacrificing an ox is to make the aberrations in their behavior, culminating in the image of the "self-cooking" ox, all the more evident to the audience.

Such, then, is this sacrificial ritual. By the time it is completed, it has incorporated a ceremony that hardly rates as a sacrifice at all to a Greek but which, set alongside the image of the Scythians as "beings made for war," may seem even overly sacrificial. The first time they appear in the *Histories* as masters of hunting in the service of Cyaxares, king of the Medes, the Scythians have no compunction, in order to avenge an injustice, about serving up to him one of the children in their charge, disguised as game and "prepared" as game.[65] In contrast, when Astyages, also in an act of vengeance, kills the son of Harpagus, he treats him as he would a sacrificial animal, in the way he cuts him up and cooks him, before he serves him up to his father.[66] Both are cannibal meals, but in the one a (human) *victim* is consumed, in the other (human) *game*. The Scythians, who appear to know about nothing but hunting and so only about wild animals, are ignorant of the procedures of sacrifice. In the opinion of Lucian, even if the Scythians are not totally ignorant of sacrifices they at any rate reject them all, considering them to be "unworthy," "too mean" (*tapeinas*), and preferring to "offer men to Artemis and by so doing to

65. Hdt. 1.73: *hosper eothesan kai ta theria skeuazein.*
66. Hdt. 1.49: "when Harpagus' son came, Astyages, king of the Medes, cut his throat and, tearing him limb from limb, roasted some and boiled some of the flesh."

gratify the goddess."[67] The Scythians are a violent, warlike people and so they are represented as serving up or sacrificing human beings. In Herodotus too, as well as making animal sacrifices, to one particular god they offer human sacrifices—not, as in Lucian, to Artemis (who does not even figure in their pantheon), but to Ares. To Ares they sacrifice (*thuousi*) their prisoners of war.

The "Drinks" of Ares

There are indications that Ares represents a special case from the moment that he is first named in the Scythian pantheon: the narrator gives a "Scythian translation" for the names of all these gods except Ares. If there is no Scythian equivalent for Ares, could it be that his name is not "Greek"? An entire tradition, from the *Iliad* onward, connects him with Thrace: he goes to Thrace, returns to Thrace, or lives in Thrace.[68] Further to the northeast, he is associated with the Amazons, whose father he is said to be.[69] In the *Histories*, his presence is quite discreet: he is revered in Thrace, where his position is of the first importance, above both Dionysus and Artemis;[70] in addition, he is firmly established in Egypt in the town of Papremis, where festivals are organized in his honor. As well as sacrifices, the ceremony here incorporates a strange battle fought with clubs in which, Herodotus believes, "many die of their wounds."[71] In the Greek world, on the other hand, he appears in only two oracles, where he symbolizes battle: "Impetuous Ares, swift driver of Syrian horses" and "Ares who reddens the sea with blood."[72]

---

67. Lucian *On Sacrifice* 13.

68. *Iliad* 13.301; *Odyssey* 8.361; Sophocles *Antigone* 970, *Oedipus Rex* 196.

69. Apollonius Rhodius *Argonautica* 2.989ff.: the Amazons "loved only fatal immoderation and the works of Ares, for they were descended from Ares and the nymph Harmonia who bore him warlike daughters."

70. Hdt. 5.7.

71. Hdt. 2.63: one group defends the entrance to the temple while another endeavors to gain entry. According to the local inhabitants, the origin of this battle was as follows. This was where the mother of Ares lived, Ares having been brought up apart from her; having reached manhood, he returned, anxious to visit—be united with (*summeixai*)—his mother. The servants tried to prevent him from entering; hence the battle. There was, moreover, an oracle devoted to Ares, also in Egypt (2.83) and there was yet another in the land of the Pisidians (Thracians) (7.76).

72. Hdt. 7.140, 8.77.

In Scythia he is honored in two ways. Like the other gods, he is offered animal sacrifices; but Herodotus does not say whether, as for the other gods, these victims are strangled. [73] All we know is that he is offered the smaller livestock or horses, but not the ox. However, he alone of all the gods is entitled to something more and occupies a position set apart.

Every district in each of the kingdoms has in it a sanctuary sacred to Ares, to wit a pile of faggots, sticks three furlongs broad and long, but of less height, on top of which there is a flattened four-sided surface; three of its sides are sheer but the fourth can be ascended. In every year a hundred and fifty waggon-loads of sticks are heaped upon this; for the storms of winter ever make it sink down. On this sacred pile there is set for each people an ancient scimitar of iron [*akinakes*] which is their image [*agalma*] of Ares. [74]

With Ares, we pass from an undifferentiated space to a space that is organized, set out geometrically, and administered. Whereas there are no special sacrificial places for the other gods, Ares has a sanctuary in every "district." These *marae,* where he is so impressively lodged, once again introduce the problem of wood. [75] For the other gods, there is no wood at all to spare, to the point where bones must be used for fuel. Ares, on the other hand, is favored with huge piles of wood. This is one reason why Dumézil regards Ares, like the Batraz of the Ossetians, as a "bully." [76] Similarly, wherever he appears temporality is introduced, that is, time is organized and calculated: "every year" it is necessary to repair his sanctuaries and "every year" he is offered animal sacrifices, whereas no attention is paid to any periodicity for offerings to the other gods. Furthermore, his sanctuary is a metonymic representation of the space of Scythia: the shape of Scythia is square, the royal tomb is dug out in a square, and the temple of Ares is constructed as a square. [77] Finally, as yet another mark of his special status, he is entitled to an image (*agalma*): he is present on the terrace of his temple in the form of "an

73. Hdt. 4.62: *thusias . . . prosagousi probaton kai hippon* (cf. Casabona, "Recherches," p. 135).

74. Hdt. 4.62.

75. It is, furthermore, wood that he does not use, since in the sacrifices made to him cooking plays no part. These are *marae,* by analogy with Polynesian sanctuaries.

76. G. Dumézil, *Romans de Scythie et d'alentour* (Paris, 1978), pp. 31–32.

77. Hdt. 4.62, 71, 101.

ancient scimitar of iron [*akinakes*]."⁷⁸ All the same, this *agalma* is a
scimitar, no more, whereas normally, particularly in the *Histories*,
the *agalmata* of the gods take the form of statues, as, for example, at
Papremis, where this same Ares has an *agalma* that is a statue.⁷⁹ Does
this difference in the figurative representation of the god betoken yet
another difference between the Scythians and others? If an absence
of temples and figurative representations is a sign of a certain
primitivism, then Ares turns out to be the least primitive of all the
Scythian gods, the very Ares who, in Greece and of all the Greek
gods, could be regarded as one of the most primitive. Here he stands
as a god of organized space, he who is generally associated with the
frenzy and confusion of battle and with his own children, Fear and
Rout. From the Scythians he receives special honors, he of whom
Sophocles wrote that of all the gods he was "a god unhonoured
among gods [*apotimos en theois theos*]."⁸⁰ Finally, this Scythian
Ares, who is a figure of order, fits into a wider context which confers
meaning on him: he refers to matters of war and consequently also to
the figure of the king, who, as I have tried to show, holds the central
position in this world of nomads where the place at the center ought
to be empty.

Of all the Scythian gods, Ares alone is entitled not only to animal
victims but to human victims: "Of all their enemies that they take
alive, they sacrifice [*thuousi*] one man in every hundred, not according to their fashion of sacrificing sheep and goats, but differently."⁸¹
Apart from the Scythians, the only people to practice human
sacrifice, in the *Histories*, are the Tauri and the Thracian Apsinthians. The Tauri sacrifice castaways, and Greek prisoners cap-

---

78. Hdt. 7.54, where the *akinakes* is defined as a Persian sword. A link also exists
between iron and Scythia. On a number of occasions, the chorus of the *Seven
against Thebes* associates the two: "the one who shakes the dice, the foreigner
Chalyb, Scythian colonist, a bitter divider of possessions, iron-hearted steel" (726–
30). "Bitter the reconciler of their feud [between Eteocles and Polynices], stranger
from the Black Sea, whetted steel come from fire, a bitter and evil divider of
possessions, Ares, who made their father's curse come true today" (942–46). There
is, then, a connection among Scythia, iron, and Ares. In the light of all this it
becomes easier to understand how the Scythians come to be regarded as being
"made for war" and that a scimitar should represent the *agalma* of Ares.

79. Hdt. 2.63.

80. Sophocles *Oedipus Rex* 215.

81. Hdt. 4.62.

tured at sea, to Iphigenia,[82] and the Thracians offer up to Pleisthorus (*theos epikhorios*), among others, the Persian Oiobazos.[83] So this is a rare and doggedly non-Greek practice. Outside the *Histories*, too, the act is rare, albeit attested.[84]

Sacrifice to the other gods included no libations. The sacrifice to Ares incorporates a libation of wine poured over the heads of the victims. It also provides for throat-cutting (*aposphazein*),[85] whereas the other ritual was characterized by a strange absence of blood: "They . . . cut their throats over a vessel; then they carry the blood up on to the pile of sticks and pour [*katakheousi*] it on the scimitar." On the one hand neither blood nor libations, on the other both blood and libations: the gestures of pouring libations and letting blood seem to go together. While Ares is "drinking" this blood, the bodies of the victims are subjected to more violence: mutilation. Their right shoulders and arms are cut off and tossed into the air, "and presently they depart, when they have sacrificed [*aperxantes*] the rest of the victims; the arm lies where it has fallen and the body apart from it."[86] Following this kind of *maskhalismos*, these sacrificed bodies suffer one last outrage: no funeral. They rot where they lie, in pieces, without burial and hence, in the eyes of the Greeks, denied the means of acceding fully to the status of the dead.[87] Such is this sacrifice, altogether in conformity with the image of the Scythians as beings made for war. Just as it is the custom for the Scythian warrior, on killing his first enemy, to drink his blood and each year subsequently, in accordance with the arithmetic of *aristeia* recognized by the nomarch, to drink wine, similarly, in each nome, Ares "drinks" the blood of the prisoners.

82. Hdt. 4.103.

83. Hdt. 9.119.

84. P. Ducrey, *Le Traitement des prisonniers de guerre dans la Grèce antique* (Paris, 1968), pp. 204–5: it was a sacrifice made in honor of the dead (Patroclus, Achilles, Philopoemenes), or before a battle (the three Persians said to have had their throats cut on the altar by Themistocles).

85. *Aposphazein*: Casabona, "Recherches," p. 167, indicates that the word is used only twice in connection with sacrifice: here and in Aristophanes *Thesmophoriazusae* 750; but cf. Detienne in *La Cuisine*, p. 223 n. 3.

86. Hdt. 4.62. On the meaning of *aperxantes*, see Casabona ("Recherches," p. 65), for whom *aperdo* is an equivalent of *apergazomai*.

87. J.-P. Vernant, "La Mort héroïque," *Actes du Colloque sur l'idéologie funéraire* (Ischia, 1977).

Is Ares a figure of order, or a figure of disorder? The truth is that the reason Ares can occupy the central position within Scythian space is that in Greece itself he is a marginal figure.[88] Thus, when Athenian ephebes swear their oath they invoke Ares (among other powers); when the Spartan youths set out to fight at the Platanistes, they sacrifice a dog to Ares Enyalius, by night. Ares is the father of the Amazons, and Lucian calls him "the god of women [*theos gunaikon*]," despite the fact that women are normally banned from fighting. In Tegaea the women, on their own, sacrifice to an Ares known as *gunaikothoinos*, an Ares of the banquet. In Sparta, again (according to Apollodorus of Athens), a man is sacrificed to him. The same marginality may be detected in his personal behavior: adultery—perhaps even incest—does not scare him.[89] Marginal: that is certainly what Sophocles means when he calls him "the god unhonoured among the gods," the god without *time*.

88. Cf. Roscher, *Lexikon*, s.v. *Ares*.

89. Cf. Supra n. 71, if one accepts that *summeixai* might mean "to be united" with his mother.

Conclusion

The Question of Nomadism

How can one be a nomad? The answer, according to the tradition, is, simply by being a Scythian. It assumes an equivalence between the two terms: Scythians are nomads, nomads are Scythians. The shared knowledge of the Greeks retained those characteristics in its image of the Scythian, and they came to provide the "true" image of the Scythian: such is the making of exoticism. Of course, there were not really two clearly defined stages, a first image followed by a second that overlaid it. The processes of exoticism were at work the moment the word *Scythian* was pronounced "for the first time."

When Prometheus tells Io of the long path on which his sufferings have led him, he speaks of the country of the "nomadic Scythians":

> First turn to the sun's rising and walk on
> Over the fields no plough has broken: then
> You will come to the nomadic Scythians
> Who live in wicker houses built above
> Their well-wheeled waggons; they are an armed people,
> Armed with the bow that strikes from far away:
> Do not draw near them.[1]

In similar fashion, the parasitic poet of the *Birds* (trying to get himself given a coat) cites Pindar and refers to the "Scythian nomads": "For among the Scythian nomads, far from the troops [*alatai straton*], there is one who wanders without any woven

1. Aeschylus *Prometheus Bound* 707–12.

193

garment;"[2] and Pindar spoke of a "house carried on a cart." In general, Strabo notes, "the ancient [*archaioi*] Greeks" embraced "the known inhabitants of the north under the single designation, Scythians [or nomads, to use Homer's term]."[3] The *nomad* entry in the *Suda* tells the same tale, defining *Nomades* as *Boskomenai agelai*, "herds which move about, grazing," *kai ethne skuthika*, "and Scythian peoples."[4] The Scythian is certainly the nomad.

But for Herodotus, the matter is not quite so simple. While the Scythians certainly are nomads, they are not the only nomads in the *Histories;* several other peoples also follow this way of life. A number of Persian tribes (*genea*) are nomads; certain Indian peoples (*ethnea*) are nomads; so too, further north, are the Massagetae whom Cyrus attacked; to the east of the Tanais and neighboring the Scythians, the Budini and the Man-eaters are also nomads. To the south we find Libyan nomads, moving over a vast territory stretching from Egypt to Lake Triton; and there is one mention of Ethiopian nomads.[5] What all these peoples share in common are their ignorance of ploughing and sowing and the fact that they do not dwell in houses. But that aside, *nomoi* vary widely among them. In the first place, their dietary regimes vary: many are consumers of milk (the Libyans, the Massagetae, the Scythians) but not all are; the majority consume

2. Aristophanes *Birds* 941–42; scholium to *Birds* 942–43. Pindar, fr. 105 b 1 Snell. Also Hippocratic Corpus *Airs, Waters, Places* 18.

3. Strabo 1.2.27.

4. *Suda*, s.v. *Nomades.* Stephen of Byzantium *Ek ton ethnikon*, ed. Meineke, s.v. *Skuthai: ethnos thrakion; ekalounto de proteron Nomaioi;* that is to say, people of the pasturelands, but also people who move on from one pasture to the next. Aristotle (PA 682b7) defines the *nomadikos bios* of insects as those that, in order to find their food, have to move outside (*dia ten trophen anagkaion ektopizein*). For a comprehensive study, see E. Laroche, *Histoire de la racine 'Nem' en grec ancien* (Paris, 1949). On the meaning of *nemo/nemomai* in Herodotus, see pp. 18–21, and on the meaning of the four derivatives *nome, nomeus, nomos, nomas*, see pp. 115–29; for example, p. 117, "definitively, the *nomos* referred to nothing more than a pastureland for animals or a habitat for men without recognized frontiers (ever since Herodotus, the *nome*, as an administrative zone, was regarded as a technical term . . . the compounds *nomarches*, etc., do not present any problem. Herodotus, IV, 66, etc.). The suggestion that *nomos* is derived from *nemo*, 'I divide up,' can only be a late interpretation introduced at a time when *nemo* could also be applied to territorial divisions, that is to say, during the fifth century B.C."

5. Herodotus 1.125, 215, 216, 2.29, 3.98, 99, 4.106, 109, 181, 186, 190.

their food cooked, but not all do (the Indians and the Budini eat it raw); the majority, but not all, are eaters of meat (some Indians are vegetarian, and the Budini eat pine-needles); as for the Man-eaters, they are eaters of men but they are stated to be an exception and, of all the northern peoples mentioned by Herodotus, their customs are the most savage (*agriotata*). Sexual customs also vary: some practice marriage, others do not; some have only one wife, others do not; some, the Indians for example, "make love in public," "like animals," others do so in private. The Libyans bury their dead "like the Greeks." The Scythians do so in a different fashion but do bury them. The Indians and the Massagetae sacrifice (*thuousi*) old men and then feast (*kateuocheontai*) on them,[6] yet one and all are nomads. So while nomadism may be a way of life, it is one that accommodates many different rules of life. Aside from the common differentiating feature, ignorance of agriculture, the nomads in Herodotus are not the same the world over, nor do they behave in a similar manner whether in the north or in the south. Moreover, compared with other nomads, Scythians seem relatively "un-nomadic." Their mode of life is not the one that is the most different (from the Greek model of existence): they are monogamous, cook their food, and make sacrifices.

One of a number of groups of nomads, the Scythians are not just nomads nor invariably so. Remember the first version of their origins, the one "told" by the Scythians themselves:[7] they are already established when they receive the golden objects (which include a yoke and a plough), which the youngest of the brothers carries off "home" with him. In short, they are not represented as nomads. It is true that in the last analysis Herodotus probably does not endorse or even take into account this story which is in any case a story more of the origins of royal power than of those of the Scythian people themselves.

As for the second version, the one recounted by the Black Sea Greeks, which—like the first—has more to do with the origins of royalty than with the origins of the Scythian people, the narrator does not personally accept that either. However, unlike the first

6. The Issedones (Hdt. 4.26) also make a banquet out of their dead parents, but they are not nomads.
7. Cf. above, pp. 19ff.

version, this one does not raise the question of agriculture and in no
way implies the Scythians to be a settled people. It simply states that
Scythes remained sole master of the territory which his two brothers, Agathyrsus and Gelonus, were obliged to leave. All in all, this
story produced by the Black Sea Greeks does not contradict the
shared knowledge of the Greeks, for whom a Scythian is a nomad.

But elsewhere and most categorically, Herodotus states that the
Scythians are not solely nomadic. The statement comes at the point
when he is about to carry out a survey of Scythia, listing all the
peoples who live there: "as far as we have been able to hear an exact
report of the furthest lands, all shall be set forth."[8] His intention is to
report *everything* that can be gleaned from *akoe*, provided the
information is treated accurately (*atrekeos*). Moving on from Olbia,[9]
first we come upon the Callippidae, who are "Scythian Greeks," and
beyond (*huper*) them are the Alazones: both peoples "sow and eat
wheat [*speirousi kai siteontai*]." Still further on dwell "Scythian
tillers of the land [*aroteres*]," who sow wheat but do not eat it.[10] This
first group is followed, further to the east and beyond the Borysthenes, by "farming Scythians [*georgoi*]"[11] From an agricultural
point of view, how do the *aroteres* differ from the *georgoi*? Probably
in the following respect: the *aroteres* sow and plough, while the
georgoi sow but do not plough; in other words, not only do they not
eat bread but they do not even produce wheat. After all, what the
narrator says of the "nomad Scythians" to be found across the river
Panticapes is that they "sow nothing nor plough [*oute ti speirontes
ouden oute arountes*]," that is to say, they eat no bread, produce no
wheat, and, furthermore, know nothing of any form of agriculture.

This list thus circumscribes nomadism: the country (*chore*) of the
nomads stretches from the Panticapes to the Gerrhus, over the

8. Hdt 4.16: *All' oson men hemeis atrekeos epi makrotaton hoioi te genometha
akoe exikesthai, pan eiresetai.*

9. Hdt. 4.17–20.

10. How can it be that people sow wheat, yet do not eat bread? The answer is that
they sell it. Living close to Olbia as they do, the Scythians "know about" wheat but
are not eaters of bread for all that.

11. The *georgoi* live in a territory that stretches northward for eleven days' river
travel (ten days' at Hdt. 4.53) and eastward for a four days' march, that is to say, as far
as the river Panticapes. We are explicitly told (4.53) that the Borysthenes (their
western boundary) provides excellent pasturelands and that whatever is sown along
its banks grows extremely well.

distance of a fourteen days' march. Beyond the Gerrhus, and the last to be named, come the "Royal Scythians": "They are the best [*aristoi*] and most in number [*pleistoi*] of the Scythians, who deem all other Scythians their slaves." How do they live? We are given no details. They are simply the Royal Scythians—that sums them up; they are the power. Passing from west to east, we thus find four successive groups of Scythians. The first three are defined by their relationship to agricultural labor, the last by its relationship to power. Any anthropologist basing his research on the oral tradition (*akoe*) would conclude from this list that the Scythians are not nomads.

The *Histories* thus seem to diverge from the shared knowledge of the Greeks. The Scythians are represented as just one of many nomad peoples; above all, they are not purely nomadic. Yet, seen from the point of view of the *logos* as a whole, the image of the Scythian is that of the nomad. In the end, the Scythians turn out to be nomads after all, even nothing but nomads. Here are a few examples. At the very beginning of the *logos*, they are presented as nomads, and their nomadism is invoked as an explanation (which explains nothing) for an aberrant practice: the reason why the Scythians blind their prisoners is that "they are not tillers of the soil, but nomads."[12] One mark of strangeness is explained by another that is familiar to everyone and whose implications are wider. According to the version of origins that Herodotus favors, "nomad Scythians" traveled from Asia to Europe, where they took possession of a "desert."[13] When Darius, having crossed the Ister, marches eastward in "pursuit" of some of the Scythians, he ought, in the normal course of things (that is to say, in accordance with the ethnographical list of tribes), to pass successively through the lands of the Scythian ploughmen, cultivators, nomads, and, finally, Royals, before coming to the region of the Sauromatae. On the contrary, however, we are told explicitly that in this entire trek there has been nothing to pillage, for "the land was uncultivated [*chersos*]."[14] It is as though when the account of the war starts the space changes and becomes nothing but pastureland: now an undifferentiated space of wasteland stretches all the way from Ister to the frontiers of the Sauromatic territory. The Scythians' way of coping with the Persian invasion is to

12. Hdt. 4.2.
13. Hdt. 4.11.
14. Hdt. 4.123.

"send forward . . . ever northward . . . the wagons in which their children and wives lived."[15] Now they are nothing but nomads. Finally, when Idanthyrsus sends his reply to Darius, he speaks purely and simply as a nomad: "this that I have done is no new thing or other than my practice in peace . . . for we Scythians have no towns or planted lands."[16] Except in the passage that includes the ethnographic survey and the list of tribes, we are presented with a people who are exclusively nomadic. What is the reason for this transition from "not exclusively nomads" to "nothing but nomads"? Why, in particular, does the presenter of Darius's war portray them as nothing but nomads?

Clearly, the shared knowledge of the Greeks, for whom *Scythian* and *nomad* are equivalent terms, has something to do with it. But that is not a sufficient explanation. Once we notice that as soon as the account of the war begins they are represented purely as nomads, we are led to ponder once again the question of narrative constraints. As we have seen,[17] these constraints consist of all the pressures at work to turn the Scythians into "Athenians" and the Scythian War into a repetition of the Persian Wars, which serve as a model for understanding it. However, there comes a point when this tendency to assimilate the Scythians and the Athenians, in particular as the defenders of liberty, runs up against an insuperable obstacle: the one group is autochthonous and lives in a *polis*, the other knows nothing of agriculture or city life. This is the point at which the purely narrative constraints (Scythians-quasi-Athenians) clash with the demands of the ethnological discourse (nomadism). It is clear that such a distinction exists and that there is a particular level at which it operates.

But I think that we should go even further and consider that another effect of the narrative constraints themselves is to see the Scythians as nothing but nomads. The fact is that it is important that the Scythians should win this war. It is a repetition of the Persian Wars; when a Great King crosses from Asia into Europe, there can be no question of his having left his own domain with impunity. On the

15. Hdt. 4.121.

16. Hdt. 4.127. Note, too, that in the story of Scyles the Scythians are represented as nomads.

17. Cf. above, pp. 35f.

other hand, it would hardly be plausible to have them engage in pitched battle against the Persian army, perhaps partly because the latter is infinitely superior to them, but also because there is no precedent for such a thing in the tradition. In other words, the Scythians' only advantage is their *aporia*, the fact that there is no *poros* by which to reach them, so they remain impossible to seize. The Athenians, for their part, depend on their rampart of wood, that is to say, their navy; the Scythians possess the surest of ramparts, their *aporia*.[18] From a structural point of view, the *aporia* of the one group and the fleet of the other occupy the same place and, at a particular point, play the same role in the narrative. Thus, the *aporia* is an element implied in the account of the war and is among the operative narrative constraints. Now, people who are *aporoi* must be nomads, so nomadism is at work in the narrative.

If the Scythians are *aporoi*, they can only be nomads, and if they are nomads it necessarily follows that they are *aporoi*. It is on the combination of these two propositions that the ethnological discourse of the narrator proceeds to concentrate. By ethnological discourse, I mean Herodotus's theoretical effort to come to terms with nomadism. For Herodotus, strategy provides the theoretical link between the two propositions at the same time as it provides the basis of nomadism; *aporia* is a strategic choice at least as much as it is the result of a way of life. This *aporia* is postulated by the shared knowledge of the Greeks (Scythian-nomad), is required by the narrative (the Scythians must escape from Darius), and is rationalized in Herodotus's ethnological discourse (nomadism is a way of life but also a strategy whose image, in spatial terms, is that of *aporia*). In *aporia*, the respective demands and constraints of the shared knowledge, the narrative, and the ethnology are fused together.[19]

18. Aeschylus *Eumenides* 700–703: Athena, installing the Areopagus, says: "You may deserve and have / Salvation for your citadel, your land's defence, / Such as is nowhere else found among men, neither / Among the Scythians, nor the land that Pelops held." One should understand that the defense of the Sycthians is, precisely, their *aporia*.

19. Remember, too, that in sacrificial practice they appear as nomads *and nothing else*: in this case, ritual does not reflect the distinction between the Scythians who are ploughmen or cultivators and those who are nomads; they are all equally ignorant of agriculture.

Power and Space

Sesostris condemned to hard labor the prisoners he had taken in the course of his wars of conquest, and by so doing he transformed the space of Egypt:[20] a country formerly negotiable by carts and horses was transformed into a territory crisscrossed by a network of canals. In the normal course of events, royal power stamps its mark on the space it governs: it orients it and gives it a fixed form, dividing it up and distributing it, setting up monuments there to testify to its presence. Conversely, pastureland and undifferentiated space are abhorrent to it. That being so, how is it possible for the Scythians to be both herdsmen and subjects at once? Or, what is a nomad king? Can such a hybrid be viable? Is not the very combination a contradiction in terms?

At this point let me suggest a double hypothesis: the barbarian is royal or despotic; and, in the *Histories*, the model par excellence of all barbarian power is provided by the Great King. What is said of the Egyptians, namely, that "they could never live without a king,"[21] in effect goes for all other barbarians or non-Greeks (the slight difference between these two terms accommodates the tyrant, who is both Greek and royal, in other words, both Greek and non-Greek). Here is the second hypothesis: nomad power is unthinkable. That being so, the Scythians, who are indisputably barbarians, can know of only one kind of power, royal power—which is indeed the case. However, the minute the figure of a king appears among them in the narrative, they can no longer be "nomads." At least, that is how I see it.

How is the king represented?[22] First, as a man who is sick as a result of the strange interchanges which take place between the body of the king and his subjects, between the royal body and the social body. He falls sick because a Scythian has sworn a false oath by the "royal hearths." Hestia, the first deity in the pantheon, is the "queen" of the Scythians and the "royal hearth" is the guarantor of the relations between Scythians and their foundation. If the central presence of Hestia-Tabiti is indeed a sign of the centrality of the royal

9.
ιudena gar chronon hoioi te esan aneu basileos diaitasthai.
ι. 112f.

power, it equally clearly indicates that it cannot possibly be a nomad power, either in theory or in practice.

When the king dies, he becomes perhaps even more of a king than when he was alive. He is buried among the Gerrhi, on the frontiers of Scythia, and his "house" there becomes the real center of the territory, as is proved by Idanthyrsus's words to Darius: find the tombs of our kings and we will engage in battle with you. In other words: for all that you have crossed the Ister, you have not discovered any *poros* to reach us, but if you discover the tombs, you will effectively threaten our "territory" and then we will fight. To be a real invader, Darius must not simply cross the Ister (which is all he believes to be necessary) but also find the tombs of the kings. In other words, the true *poros* is not the bridge but the tombs. The royal tomb thus truly counts as a center: in effect, it is the fixed and unmoving point which makes it possible for the Scythian space to constitute itself as a territory (ruled by a power) but at the same time, by reason of its location at the frontier, it enables the space of Scythia to function as a nomad space. There can be, then, no territory without a center, or without a power, but the effect of using nomadism as an operator at work in the narrative is to make that center a tomb and also "excentric." Furthermore, the dead king, who obliges the Scythians to acknowledge themselves as such by mutilating themselves, by the same token forces them to admit to being his subjects. These gestures of recognition and remembrance marked on the body turn them into a "community" and abolish their dispersion as nomads, which obtained before the funeral rites. The existence of a power is a denial of nomadism.

Finally, the king is a war leader. He is the one to whom heads must be brought to earn a share in the booty. More generally, as soon as it is a question of warfare, the space of Scythia changes: abruptly we pass from an undifferentiated expanse to a space that is contained, divided, and organized (with its nomes and nomarchs, annual rites and ceremonies). Ares, who is present in his sanctuaries, is the strange image (*agalma*) representing this warlike order: heads are brought to the king, prisoners offered to Ares. As the masters of warfare, the king and Ares between them thus create a space differing hardly at all from the Egyptian nomes or the Persian satrapies. Military power and nomadism thus appear to be mutually exclusive, and these portraits of the Scythian king exercising his despotism all establish a separation between power and nomadism. A nomad power is something inconceivable; if it is a power, it cannot be nomad.

Yet, when we pass from the account of Scythian *nomoi* to that of Darius's war, as soon as Idanthyrsus makes his appearance it is quite clear that he *is* a nomad king and he explains that he is waging a nomad war: we, who do not possess towns or cultivated fields, have no cause to engage in pitched battle. How should we explain his words? So far as the narrative of the war goes, the Scythians can be *nothing but* nomads and, above all, Idanthyrsus is introduced quite simply as the spokesman of nomad warfare. He explains to the Persians, who can make neither head nor tail of his words, that the Scythians' behavior is not "madness" at all but deployment of a strategy. By having Idanthyrsus speak, the narrator addresses the Persians who, in Scythia, behave like Greeks and quasi-hoplites but, through them, his target is above all his addressee. And it is precisely here, in his strategic explanation for nomadism, that Herodotus's great originality lies. In the last analysis, the only way to conceive of nomadism in a positive fashion is to regard it as a strategy. He is quite alone in suggesting this theory; it was not really taken up by later writers, who continued to define nomadism in a purely negative fashion. That is why, explicitly indicating it to be his own opinion, using "I," he says that "the Scythian race has in that matter which of all human affairs is of the greatest import, made the cleverest discovery that we know": nomad warfare is a method "so devised that none who attacks them can escape and none can catch them if they desire not to be found."[23] In other words, it is an *aporia*. Seen in this perspective, the only one that attributes any positive element to it, nomadism in the last analysis is not a way of life and in addition a strategy but, rather, a strategy which is in addition a way of life—a strategy which imposes a way of life.

What is it that makes it possible for Herodotus to produce such a theory, in which the strategy functions as a model of intelligibility? To answer that question, we must take into account what the shared knowledge of the Greeks said about strategy around 440–430 and

23. Hdt. 4.46.

what was being put forward as strategic theory not (or not yet) part of that shared knowledge. I have shown that structurally the *aporia* is to Darius's expedition against the Scythians what the Athenian fleet is to Xerxes' operation against the Greeks: the two occupy the same position in the narrative. But apart from the narrative reason, what is the basis for that equivalence? I believe the metaphor of insularity to be implicitly present or, to be more precise, that insularity functions as a metaphor for nomadism. The notion of insularity makes it possible to conceive of nomadism in a positive fashion. In the last analysis, being a nomad is like being an island-dweller.

At this point, if we step outside the *Histories* we are inevitably faced with Periclean strategy. In contrast to traditional strategy, which subordinated the defense of the town to that of the territory,[24] the new strategy favored abandoning the territory and not engaging in pitched battle, defending only the town and placing all reliance on the navy. Now, the discourse of this strategy makes use of the metaphor of insularity. Athens must become like an island and the Athenians must become like islanders. In his speech to the Athenians in 432, Pericles declares: "Reflect, if we were islanders, who would be more invulnerable [*aleptoteroi*]? Let us imagine that we are, and acting in that spirit let us give up lands and houses but keep a watch over the city and the sea. . . . If I thought you would listen to me, I would say to you 'Go yourselves and destroy them [the lands and houses] and thereby prove to the Peloponnesians that none of these things will move you.'"[25] The islander presents no hold to seize upon, he is unseizable, *aporos*. To be an islander is thus to be *aporos* just as to be a nomad is to be *aporos*. Although they cannot be islanders, the Athenians are sailors, and they entrench themselves behind their ramparts; the *aporoi* Scythians, unable to be islanders or sailors, or, equally, to entrench themselves, can only be nomads. Thus, insularity, the metaphorical transcription of Pericles' strategy, may also be used as the metaphorical principle of intelligibility for a

24. Cf. Y. Garlan, *Recherches de poliorcétique grecque* (Paris, 1974), pp. 44ff.
25. Thucydides 1.143.5. The same metaphor is to be found in pseudo-Xenophon's *Constitution of the Athenians*: "If they exercised control of the sea living on an island, it would be possible for them to inflict harm, if they wished, but so long as they ruled the sea, to suffer none,—neither the ravaging of their land nor enemy invasion." (2.14).

way of life that, without it, could be defined only by its deficien-cies.[26] It is insularity that implicitly informs Herodotus's theory of nomadism. We may note an instance of it at work in the measures taken by the Scythians at the time of Darius's invasion: the Scythians send their wives, children, and herds off to the northern regions, just as the Athenians evacuate their families and possessions to the safety of the islands. Above all, the Scythians implement Pericles' plan to the letter, by taking it on themselves to ravage their own pasturelands and block their own wells, but what would be the good of such a precaution in a country with as many water-courses as the canals in Egypt?

The idea that nomadism is first and foremost a strategy, even a deliberate strategic choice, is nowhere expressed more clearly than by Arrian of Nicomedia, the historian of the second century A.D., in a quite astonishing text. In a fragment of his *Bithynica* he both operates a reversal and at the same time carries it to its logical conclusion. In the first place, the Scythians are not or, rather, have not always been nomads. Second, it was for strategic reasons that they decided to become nomads:

> In the past, the Scythians used to eat bread, ploughed the land, lived in houses and had towns, but when they had been defeated by the Thracians, they changed their customs and swore never again to build houses, never again to furrow the earth with a plough or to build towns or amass riches, but to use wagons as their dwellings, the flesh of wild animals as their food and milk as their drink so as to have as their only possessions the livestock which would follow them in their peregrinations from one country to another. It is thus that they changed from being farmers and became nomads.[27]

The Words to Express It

Even if their strategy of *aporia* is the only Scythian invention Herodotus admires, that admiration is genuine. Through that inven-tion, nomadism becomes a conceivable notion and is no longer simply an aberrant way of life which can only be defined by its deficiencies. Without it, there are no words to express nomadism. It

26. By "metaphorical principle" of intelligibility I simply mean that its mode of operation is metaphorical.

27. Arrian, fr. 54 vol. 2, p. 218 Wirth.

could only be defined through an accumulation of negatives: nomads eat no bread, do not plough, do not sow, do not live in houses; to pray to their gods, they have no statues, no temples, no altars; and when they sacrifice they light no fires, consecrate no first fruits, pour no libations, do not cut the animal's throat, and so on. Under those circumstances, nomadism is no more than the sum (always incomplete) of its deficiencies and the nomad is the very image of one who is *apolis*. That is why Greek anthropology was to represent nomadism as a form of primitivism: the earliest times of humanity were nomadic. Thucydides, among others, suggests just that in his *Archaeology*.[28] When Odysseus lands among the Cyclopes in Euripides' *Cyclops*, he asks Silenus: "Who is their leader? Do they have a democratic state?" and Silenus replies, "They are nomads; nobody listens to [obeys] anybody about anything."[29]

The exchange is probably a reworking of Homer, but it also plays on the theme of the inconceivability of a nomad power.

Aristotle makes a remark about nomads that is both symptomatic of this impossibility of expressing nomadism and also interesting in the way it gets around the difficulty: "The idlest [*argotatoi*] men are nomads, for to procure food from domesticated animals involves no toil and no industry, but as it is necessary for the herds to move from place to place because of the pastures, the people themselves are forced to follow along with them, as though they were farming a live farm [*hosper georgian zosan georgountes*]."[30] In the first place, nomads know nothing of *ponos*, agricultural labor; they live, to all intents and purposes, in a time before Prometheus.[31] They live a life of leisure in a golden age, except that in their case it is not the earth that spontaneously produces everything necessary for them but their herds. The herds occupy the same place here as the earth does in representations of the golden age; Aristotle's phrase simply employs a substitution at that point. And, to create an image of the life of these men who know nothing of agricultural labor, Aristotle cannot resist using a specifically agricultural metaphor: season after season, they move from place to place "as though they were farming a

28. Thucydides 1.2; cf. T. Cole, *Democritus and the Sources of Greek Anthropology* (Ann Arbor, 1967) p. 29.
29. Euripides *Cyclops* 119–20: *Nomades akouei d'ouden oudeis oudenos.*
30. Aristotle *Politics* 1256a31–35.
31. Hesiod *Words and Days* 42ff.

live farm." There could be no clearer way of conveying the impossibility of conceiving of nomadism: being at a loss for words, Aristotle adopts a different code and resorts to a metaphor which, in the last analysis, simply reiterates, in redundant fashion, that nomadism is not good to think with.

Moving still further from Herodotus, we find increasingly rigid formulations, syntagmas in which nothing is examined at all. For instance, Nicholas of Damascus, in the first century B.C., in his *ethne sunagoge* describes the Libyan nomads as follows: "They count the time not in days but in nights."[32] We are left with nothing but an impoverished inversion. And ultimately, as synonyms for nomads the lexicographers simply give "savages," "barbarians."[33]

32. Nicholas of Damascus in Jacoby, *FGrHist*, 90 F 103.
33. *Suda*, s.v. *Nomadon*; Hesychius *Lexikon*, ed. Latte, s.v. *Nomadon* or s.v. *Nomades: emerai ai phtinontos tou menos.*

Part Two

Herodotus, Rhapsode and Surveyor

Introduction

Generalizing

We have as it were tracked down the name *Scythians* and assembled the collection of predicates that constitute it. This has involved a reading pursued step by step through the space encompassed by the *Histories*, a reading based on the practice of systematic differentiation. The *logos* constructs a picture of the nomad that makes his "otherness" conceivable: we pass from an overwhelming otherness which, to the addressee, is quite opaque, such as that encountered in chapter 2 of Book 4 (they blind their prisoners *because* they are nomads),[1] to an otherness that makes sense (nomadism is in the first instance a strategy); from a "false" intelligibility which only has the effect of doubling the strangeness, to an intelligibility that is true, one that makes sense to a Greek of the 430s B.C.

If it was our purpose to list all the "others" in Herodotus, this would be the point at which to take account of all the other peoples and other *logoi:* first, the Egyptians, whom the Greeks found even more fascinating than the Scythians and whose position in the *Histories* is both symmetrical with and the converse of that of the Scythians; then the Libyans, a partly nomadic people who are mentioned immediately after the Scythian *logos;* the Indians, the last of men out toward the east; and finally the Persians, with the emblematic figure of their Great King. By undertaking, as a first step at least, a similar kind of reading based on systematic differentiation

1. Hdt. 4.2; G. Dumézil, *Romans de Scythie et d'alentour* (Paris, 1978), p. 309.

it might be possible to determine what a fifth-century Greek's imaginary notion of their otherness might have been. But, quite aside from the fact that tracking down the Scythians has already involved encounters with, for example, the Egyptians and also the Persians, perhaps elaborating a general theory would be more fruitful: instead of moving to and fro between the narrative and the Greeks' shared knowledge in regard to the figure of the Scythian, and instead of studying the "others" whom the narrative successively presents, let us consider how it constructs them.

Assuming the narrative to be indeed deployed between a narrator and an addressee who is himself implicitly present in the text, our aim will be to see how it "translates" the "other" and how it gets the addressee to believe in the "other" whom it is constructing. To put it another way, we shall be seeking to discover the rhetoric of otherness at work in the text, to determine some of the figures it employs, and to dissect some of its procedures; in short, to note the operative rules in the fabrication of the "other."

However, while this work of discovery and analysis, which at best should produce a more or less complete inventory of static (rhetorical) figures, may be indispensable, more remains to be done. These figures are activated by the narrator, who makes his own interventions in a number of ways, from inside his narrative: any reading of the text must therefore attend to all the indicators as to who is speaking, for it is they that organize the rhetorical figures for the addressee and they, ultimately, that endow them with a definite persuasive power. In the *Histories* everything is above all played out within an area bounded by the following four indicators, or four operations: "I have seen," "I have heard," and "I say," "I write."

Because of the attention that must be paid to these indicators, we cannot be satisfied with a structuralist reading of a narrative such as the *Histories*, a reading which involves first selecting the subject matter, assuming a homogeneous text, and then manipulating the combinations of the utterances among themselves. For this narrative does not develop in a linear fashion, with each sentence following on from the one before, to end up by forming a system of transformations before the very eyes of the reader-commentator. On the contrary, it contains a whole series of different levels and breaks in continuity between the successive utterances and these are marked out precisely by the interplay of all the indicators as to who is speaking. Only by paying attention to this vertical dimension of the text and by asking ourselves, "Who is speaking to whom and how?" can we successfully pose the highly complex question of how the text achieves its effect.

Six

A Rhetoric of Otherness

Difference and Inversion

To speak of the "other" is to postulate it as different, to postulate that there are two terms, *a* and *b*, and that *a* is not *b*. For example, there are Greeks and there are non-Greeks. But the difference only becomes interesting when *a* and *b* become part of a single system. Until they do, we have a simple non-coincidence. But once they do, there are points of differentiation and hence a determinate and significant difference between the two terms.[1] For example, there are Greeks and there are barbarians. Once the difference is said or transcribed, it becomes significant because it is caught up in the systems of language and writing. It is at this point that the business of connecting the "other" with the "same," a movement as continuous and indefinite as that of waves breaking upon the shore, begins.

On the basis of the fundamental relationship established between two sets by the significant difference between them, a rhetoric of otherness may be developed, to be used by narratives that tell, primarily, of "others," travelers' tales in the widest sense of the expression. A narrator who belongs to group *a* tells the people of *a* about *b;* there is one world in which one recounts, another that is recounted. How can the world being recounted be introduced in convincing fashion into the world where it is recounted? That is the problem facing the narrator: a problem of translation.

1. J.-F. Lyotard, *Discours, figures* (Paris, 1971), p. 142.

To translate the difference, the traveler has at his disposal the handy figure of inversion, whereby otherness is transcribed as anti-sameness. It is not hard to see why travelers' tales and utopias frequently resort to this method, since it constructs an otherness that is transparent for the listener or reader; it is no longer a matter of *a* and *b*, simply of *a* and the converse of *a*. It is, furthermore, not hard to see why in utopian discourse this is the most favored of all figures, for the purpose of such discourse is invariably to speak of "sameness."

The *Histories* resort to this a number of times. Two examples will suffice to show the extent to which it represents a constant temptation for a narrative that purports to tell of the "other." The first step is to mention the difference, the second to "translate" or "apprehend" it by bringing into play the schema of inversion. Our first example is a familiar one: Egypt. The Egyptians live in an "other" (*heteros*) climate, on the banks of a river which is different (*allos*) from all other rivers and "so have they made all their customs and laws of a kind which is for the most part the converse of those of all other men."[2] When it comes to ways of life, a difference is converted into an inversion. Furthermore, such an utterance lays claim to universality: the inversion refers to the rest of the human race. But as soon as Herodotus starts to accumulate examples of inversion, it becomes apparent that in the expression "all other men" who should in fact be understood first and foremost are the Greeks: "Among them the women buy and sell, the men abide at home and weave; and whereas in weaving all others push the woof upwards, the Egyptians push it downwards. Men carry burdens on their heads, women on their shoulders. Women make water standing, men sitting."[3] The so-called universality of the rule is a way for the narrative to mask the procedure of inversion, to obliterate the trademark (we, the Greeks/ the converse of the Greeks) more than a way of suggesting an equivalence between saying "all other men" and "Greeks" or of suggesting that the extent of the two terms is the same.[4]

2. Herodotus 2.35.

3. Hdt. 2.35. Cf. C. Froidefond, *Le Mirage égyptien dans la littérature grecque d'Homère à Aristote* (Paris, 1971), pp. 129–36, and above all, S. Pembroke, "Women in Charge: The Function of Alternatives in Early Greek Tradition and the Ancient Idea of Matriarchy," *Journal of the Warburg and Courtauld Institute* 30 (1967): 17.

4. Here are some other examples of inversion. There are two statues in front of the gateway to the sanctuary of Hephaestus; the Egyptians call the one on the side of

The inversion may also be masked by eliding the second term in the opposition. We then have an inversion presented as a difference (while all the time it implicitly functions simply as an inversion). Such is the case in the description of the Scythian climate,[5] where, imperceptibly, recourse to the schema of inversion confers intelligibility on a climate which in the first instance is presented purely as an excess of winter, in the course of which the sea becomes a thoroughfare for wagons. The principle of inversion is thus a means of communicating otherness, by making it easy to apprehend that in the world in which things are recounted it is just the same except that it is the other way around. But it may also function as a heuristic principle: it thus becomes possible to understand, to explain, to make sense of an otherness which would otherwise remain altogether opaque. The inversion is a fiction which "shows how it is" and makes it possible to understand: it is one of the figures of rhetoric which help to elaborate a representation of the world.[6]

When describing Egypt, Herodotus thus moves on "naturally" from pointing out a difference to affirming an inversion. In the

---

Boreas the summer, the one on the side of Notos, the winter (Hdt. 2.121). Recourse to inversion also makes it possible to comprehend the effects of the sun among the Indians (that is to say, in the Far East): "Now, in these parts, the sun is hottest in the morning, not at midday as with all other man universally, but from sunrise to the hour of market-closing [a specific reference around which the entire schema of inversion is articulated]. Through these hours it is hotter by much than in Greece at noon, so that men are said to remain plunged in water at this time. At midday the sun's heat is well-nigh the same in India and among other men. As it grows to afternoon, the sun of India has the power of the morning sun in other lands; with its sinking, the day becomes ever cooler."(3.104). Our next example also concerns the sun, but this time the sun in southern Libya: the source of the sun, for the Ammonians. "Water . . . is warm at dawn and colder at market-time and very cold at noon; and it is then that they water their gardens; as the day declines the coldness abates till at sunset the water grows warm. It becomes ever hotter and hotter till midnight, and then it boils and bubbles; after midnight it becomes ever cooler until dawn" (4.181). And then there is the example of 1.133, 140, concerning the way Persians make decisions regarding drunkenness.

5. Cf. above, pp. 27ff.

6. In Herodotus, inversion is not used, as in the *dissoi logoi*, to inspire doubt: if two opposite forms of behavior are respectively considered equally correct in two different places, then either everything is correct or nothing is. Of course, this use of inversion, as a figure of the rhetoric on what is other, refers us to the schema of archaic Greek thought, which G. E. R. Lloyd calls "polarity": *Polarity and Analogy* (Cambridge, 1966).

sixteenth century, Jean de Léry was able to proceed otherwise: from the unlike to the new. "This country of America in which, as I *deduce*, everything to be seen, whether it be the way of life of the inhabitants, the form of the animals or in general whatever the earth produces, being *unlike* what we have in Europe, Asia, and Africa, may well be called a *new* world from our point of view."[7] Subsequently, of course, the "newness" may be partially converted into an inversion (in relation to what is to be found in the world over here).

However, it should not be assumed that the use of the rhetorical figure of inversion is enough to generate the whole of Herodotus's ethnography: for example, the inversion between the Greek *nomoi* and the *nomoi* of others; the inversion between the north of the *oikoumene*, where phenomena are explained by the cold, and the south, where they are explained by the heat.[8] In the first place, although there are certain "others" who are given a privileged position (Egyptians, Scythians, Persians), the *Histories* introduce many more besides. Now, if all their respective *nomoi* were the reverse of those of the Greeks, in the last analysis they would all have the same *nomoi*—which is not at all the case. Besides, our reading of the Scythian *logos* has shown that the rhetorical figure of inversion is certainly too narrow to account for many of the Scythian *nomoi*. It would not make sense to say that Scythian sacrifice is the reverse of civic sacrifice.[9] One sequence in the ritual (for example, the bones burned as fuel beneath the altar) may fit into the schema of inversion, but that does not mean that the preceding or the subsequent sequences necessarily follow the same model. Similarly, the funeral rites of the Scythian kings are organized spatially in accordance with the schema of inversion: the *eschata* takes the place of a center and the normal *prothesis* (display of the corpse) is replaced by a reversed *prothesis* (the dead king "visits" his subjects).[10] But plenty of the ceremony's features do not fit into the figure, which does not directly account for the way that the corpse is treated or for the self-inflicted mutilation of the participants, or for the human sacrifices by strangulation, or for the still ring of dead horsemen astride their stuffed

7. J. de Léry, *Histoire d'un voyage fait en la terre de Brésil*, ed. Contat (Lausanne, 1972), p. 28.

8. In contrast to what M. Panoff writes: *Ethnologie, le deuxième souffle* (Paris, 1977), p. 38.

9. Cf. above, pp. 176f.

10. Cf. above, pp. 141ff.

mounts. Inversion, functioning as a switching mechanism, gives meaning to a particular practice or form of behavior, a meaning that may be either explicit or implicit. In the traveler's tale, it thus effects an operation of translation: it is one of the procedures that make it possible to pass from the world recounted into the world where things are recounted.

But what about the features that do not fit into the inversion? Do they have a meaning? Do they even make sense? Or is their meaning precisely that they do not make sense, that they remain alien or mark out limits? Are they untranslatable? Even if they resist efforts to make them intelligible (when the traveler cannot or will not translate them), that does not mean that they are abandoned beyond the bounds of verisimilitude; on the contrary, it might be thought that their verisimilitude lies precisely in their apparent meaninglessness. The particular verisimilitude (of these features unaffected by inversion) perhaps lies in their being presented in the narrative as "idiotic"; they offer no hold, and this absence of purchase operates as a guarantee of their authenticity (you could not possibly invent such things). They offer no hold, passing like meteors across the traveler's tale, and their lack of purchase operates as a guarantee of their otherness, as is shown by the funeral ceremony in honor of the Scythian kings.

One last case, that of the Amazons,[11] also prompts reflection on inversion. The Greeks saw a polarity, that is to say, both a disjunction and a complementarity, between war and marriage: one was the lot of men, the other that of women. War and marriage, respectively, marked the fulfillment of a young man and a young woman.[12] Imagining an inversion of roles meant transferring women from the sphere of marriage into that of war and excluding men from the latter. Women would then hold a monopoly over the warrior function. What about marriage? There were two possible solutions. One was for women to reject marriage and live without men. That is the one recorded by Strabo: the Amazons spend most of their time among themselves and have relations with men from a neighboring people, the Gargarians, only once a year.[13] Their sexual intercourse

---

11. J. Carlier, "Amazones," in *Dictionnaire de Mythologie* (Paris, 1981).

12. J.-P. Vernant, "City-State Warfare," *Myth and Society* (Brighton 1980), p. 24.

13. Strabo 11.5.1.

takes place in the dark and with whoever first happens by, "and after they [the men] have made them pregnant, they [the Amazons] send them away and the females that are born are retained by the Amazons themselves, but the males are taken to the Gargarians to be brought up; and each Gargarian to whom a child is brought adopts the child as his own, regarding the child as his son because of his uncertainty." The second solution is that they do marry but their menfolk perform all the "women's work." That is the schema used by Diodorus Siculus: the men stay at home, take care of the children, and do what they are told.[14] However, the richness of the polarity between war and marriage is such that it remains present in Diodorus's narrative: so long as the Amazons engage in war they remain virgins, but as soon as they produce children they stop fighting. So, for the schema of an inversion of roles to continue to function despite this anomaly, we must assume there to exist in the city of the Amazons the little matter of a division between war and politics, for although they no longer fight, they do act as magistrates and concern themselves with "communal affairs" (*ta koina*)—quite on their own, of course, without the men, who are neither hoplites nor citizens. In other words, war is the business of virgin-Amazons, therefore of an age-group which goes through the equivalent of a period of *ephebeia*, which is brought to an end by marriage. The Amazons are ephebes of a kind.

14. Diodorus 3.53. "We are told that there was once in the western parts of Libya, on the bounds of the inhabited world, a race which was ruled by women and followed a manner of life unlike that which prevails among us. For it was the custom among them that the women should practise the arts of war and be required to serve in the army for a fixed period, during which time they maintained their virginity; then, when the years of service in the field had expired, they went in to the men for the procreation of children, but they kept in their hands the administration of the magistracies and of all affairs of the state. The men, however, like our married women, spent their days about the house, carrying out the orders which were given them by their wives; and they took no part in military campaigns or in office or in the exercise of free citizenship in the affairs of the community by virtue of which they might become presumptuous and rise up against the women. When their children were born, the babies were turned over to the men, who brought them up on milk and such cooked foods as were appropriate to the age of the infants; and if it happened that a girl was born, its breasts were seared that they might not develop at the time of maturity; for they thought that the breasts, as they stood out from the body, were no small hindrance in warfare; and in fact it is because they have been deprived of their breasts that they are called by the Greeks 'Amazons.'"

But Herodotus's text on the Amazons is considerably more complicated, for while the polarity between war and marriage is certainly at work, it operates differently, producing not war *or* marriage but war *and* marriage.[15] The passages in Diodorus Siculus and Strabo introduce only the Amazons ("it is said that the Amazons," etc.) and the Greeks, who are present in the background or stationed in the wings. But in Herodotus a larger cast is introduced on stage: the Amazons, the Scythians, the youngest of the Scythians (the Sauromatae), and the Greeks who, at the limit, may appear only in the shape of an absentee, the spectator, in relation to whom everything is organized. The relationships among the various characters are thus necessarily more complex. In Strabo and Diodorus, they are no more than dual: Amazons and (Greeks);[16] the schema of inversion is thus easy to apply. In Herodotus, relations are established between at least three terms: Amazons, Scythians, and (Greeks), so there is a relationship between the Amazons and the Scythians, one between the Amazons and the Greeks, and one between the Scythians and the (Greeks). This triangular arrangement of the stage makes one suspect that the schema of inversion is unlikely to be applicable in any simple fashion. However, that does not prevent the text from accommodating elements of inversion in certain sequences.

Furthermore, this text is not a description of the Amazons and their customs presented in an intemporal present tense.[17] It tells of the origin of the Sauromatae people, to whom the Scythians come to ask for aid in countering Darius's invasion. It is therefore constructed on the basis of a before and an after: it tells first of the origin of the Amazons and how they escaped from the Greeks by killing them, then of the encounters between the Scythians and the Amazons and of the birth of the Sauromatae, and finally of the way of life of the Sauromatae. This temporal progression contributes to the complexity of the text by making it impossible for it to be organized purely and simply on the basis of an inversion.

Having escaped from the Greeks, the Amazons arrive in Scythia and set about doing what they usually do—pillaging. "They seized the first troupe of horses they met and, mounted on them, they

15. Hdt. 4.110–17.
16. The parenthesis indicates that the Greeks may not be explicitly present.
17. On the present tense and description, cf. below, p. 254.

raided the Scythian lands. The Scythians could not understand the matter,[18] for they knew not the women's speech nor their dress nor their nation, but wondered whence they had come and supposed them to be men all the same age; and they met the Amazons in battle." It goes without saying that the Scythians decide to make war on these bellicose strangers, since they take them to be a band of men "all the same age," an age group and no doubt, given that these warriors are beardless, a young one.

Following that initial misunderstanding, they proceed to behave in accordance with all the rules. However, "the end of the fight was that the Scythians got possession of the dead and so came to know that their foes were women. They therefore consulted among themselves and decided under no circumstances to continue to kill them." So, as soon as it became clear that these were women, killing them became out of the question: the text postulates that women are excluded from the world of war and the Scythians thus implicitly "reason" as Greeks do. They decide not to kill any more of them but "to send to them their youngest men [*neotatoi*] of a number answering (as they guessed) to the number of the women . . . for they desired that children should be born of the women." So it is that the polarity between war and marriage surfaces again: with women one makes not war, but children.[19]

To implement their plan, they dispatch "the youngest" of the Scythian men who throughout the narrative are consistently referred to as an age-group (the youths, the youngest). Why do the Scythians make the strange decision to appeal to their "ephebes"?[20] In Greece, there is normally a separation between marriage and the *ephebeia*. An ephebe does not marry, and if he does it means that he is no longer an ephebe; one cannot be both an ephebe and also

18. *Sumbalesthai*: they had nothing at their disposal that could serve as an element of *comparison*; they were confronted with the unknown.

19. This whole narrative depends on an initial *legetai*, "it is said," and the construction of indirect speech makes it virtually impossible to distinguish between the opinions of the Scythians and interventions on the part of the narrator. Are the Scythians themselves justifying their behavior, or is the narrator, who is explaining it to his listeners by implicitly bringing into play the schema of war/marriage? It seems to be both.

20. Of course, it is I who am calling them ephebes. The text refers to them only as "youths." Introducing a concept such as that of the *ephebeia* into this story increases its intelligibility for a Greek listener. That is the most that I am suggesting.

married, for that would be to telescope two events which ought to succede one another, or, rather, two sequences, for a man passes from the one to the other before becoming a full adult. Conversely, however, one "cannot" be an ephebe and refuse to marry: the trouble with Hippolytus is that he tries to refuse to marry. Being an ephebe is a transitory stage and by rights it should lead to marriage.

But the Scythians appear to be combining marriage with the *ephebeia;* the *neotatoi* are, on the strength of that status, given orders to marry the Amazons.[21] Why is that? One obvious and simple answer is that since all the adult Scythians are already married, they are the only men available. Besides, the text does not make it clear whether, once married, they are still counted as *neotatoi,* so we do not know for sure whether the two sequences are really telescoped. That aside, the fact remains that it is as ephebes that they are entrusted with their mission. Faced with this band of young girls, they are marked out not for combat but for marriage. The Amazons' way of life, based on hunting and pillage, is more suited to ephebes, accustomed as these are to the border areas, than to adults. It is an implicit element which shows how, almost imperceptibly, in the course of the narrative a shift has taken place between the Scythians and the Greeks: confronted with the Amazons, the Scythians tend to change into Greeks. To "overcome" the Amazons, they are advised to adopt a cunning mode of behavior, this too being more in accordance with ephebe practices than with the rules governing adult life:

They bade these youths encamp near to the Amazons and to imitate all that they did; if the women pursued them, then not to fight but to flee; and when the pursuit ceased, to come and encamp near them. . . . When the Amazons perceived that the youths meant them no harm, they let them be; but every day, the two camps drew closer to each other. Now, the young men, like the Amazons, had nothing but their arms and their horses and lived as did the women, by hunting and plunder. (Hdt. 4.100–117)

The mainspring of this ruse is imitation. The fact is that if these were

---

21. The narrative emphasizes the marriage aspect. The Scythians send out as many young men as they reckon there to be girls; each man then stays with the woman with whom he first made love. In short, care is taken to make a clear distinction between this and the model of promiscuity in which couples make love "like animals"; here, it is a matter of a monogamous, legitimate marriage.

men, the Scythians would fight them; if they were merely women, they would rape them; but they are warrior women. Faced with a logical monster that is both man and woman at the same time, the only possible approach, according to the elder Scythians, is that of imitation. To this end, those most resembling them are chosen (or those whom the women most resemble), namely, the "ephebes," those who, through their very status still, for the time being, combine features of both masculinity and femininity. The ambiguity of their position thus renders them at the same time very close to yet very distant from the Amazons. To overcome or seduce these female warrior virgins, male warrior virgins are detailed to approach them.

If there are ephebic elements at work in the text, the latter is also organized not by a simple schema of inversion but by elements of it. Of course, the *ephebeia* leads naturally to inversion, given that the latter is one of its constitutive elements.

The seduction scene is presented, overall, as an anti-seduction scene, since the Scythians operate out in the open, in the middle of the day, when the Amazons go off individually, on their own, to perform their natural functions—all conditions that stand in opposition to Greek custom.[22] But the most interesting point is that this scene is in no sense one of rape. The Amazon girl consents: "She made no resistance but allowed him to do his will [*perieide chresasthai*]." One does not violate an Amazon; it would be a contradiction in terms.

If it is the ambiguity of their status that qualifies the ephebes for this encounter with the Amazons, their marriage with the latter does not reveal them to be adult men. Quite the contrary. It appears to be the feminine side of their nature that is thereby reinforced. Consider the scene where they propose that the Amazons should leave the "border regions" and come with them to live a "normal life"—a scene which, as goes without saying, can only be understood in relation to the Greek model of marriage and provided that one recognizes that the Scythians have turned into Greeks. The Amazons reply that they could not possibly live like Scythian women and there can be no question of their doing so, but they add: "'Go to your parents and let them give you the allotted share of their possessions and after that let

---

22. Making love in this way, in broad daylight and for all to see, is a transgression against the usual practices of the city.

us go and dwell by ourselves.' The young men agreed and did this."
So here it is the husband—not, as is customary, the bride—who
brings the dowry. The second anomaly is that a young bride normally
comes to live in the house of her husband. She leaves the paternal
oikos to enter that of her husband. But the Amazons refuse to do
this.[23] Of course it is impossible for them to introduce their husbands into their own *oikoi*, since they have no place of their own, but
they decide to go and live "elsewhere," beyond the river Tanais,
which marks the eastern border of Scythia. Just as a bride crosses the
threshold of the house in her husband's arms—and the text plays on
this analogy—so here the Amazons have their husbands cross the
Tanais and they take them away, beyond Scythia, to a land that is both
a new territory and a no-man's-land.

When the Scythians realize that the Amazons are women they
decide to have children by them, but one may well wonder whether,
in the end, it is not the Amazons who thereby manage to ensure their
own line of descent. In Strabo, for example, we are told that the
Amazons, a society without men, only concern themselves with
their female children; they do not undertake to rear their sons. The
schema of inversion leads quite logically to this position. In Herodotus, we are not told that the Amazons or their female descendants
concern themselves only with their daughters. It is even said that the
Sauromatae are a people among whom the male and the female parts
of the population live together. All the same, the only rule of
upbringing mentioned concerns the girls alone: "In regard to marriage, it is the custom that no virgin weds until she has slain a man of
the enemy; and some of them grow old and die unmarried because
they cannot fulfill the law." Far from dissociating war and marriage (as
is the case in Strabo and Diodorus), here the Sauromatae connect the
two. To gain the right to pass on from the state of virginity it is
necessary to kill a man, to have shed a man's blood. They must justify
their name of *oiorpata*, "killers of men," according to the Scythian
etymology reported by Herodotus. A requirement such as this puts
one in mind of the ritual through which a young man is received into
the warrior caste: for example, when a Scythian kills his first man, he
drinks his blood; thereafter, to celebrate the enemies slain in the

23. The text stresses the point that it is the husbands who leave the paternal
oikos: "We are in fear and dread at the idea of dwelling in this country, seeing that
not only have we separated you from your fathers but we have done much harm to
your land," the Amazons say.

course of the year, it is enough to drink a symbolic draught composed of wine mixed with water.[24] Far from being opposed to marriage (in Diodorus, Amazons cease to make war once they lose their virginity), war qualifies a young woman *for* marriage, but just as in order to be a warrior it is not enough simply to wage war, so too it is not enough for a young woman of the Sauromatae to wage war in order to be married: she must also accomplish an exploit. A male candidate for the status of warrior must bring in a scalp,[25] and a female candidate for marriage must kill a man.

As for the Amazons themselves, marriage with the Scythian "ephebes" does not in the least deter them from combining making war and making love: mature women they may now be, but they are no less warriors on that account. So far as their way of life goes, marriage does not mark a break between a "before" and an "after." Their need to continue to make war is in fact the reason they give for refusing to live in Scythia: "We could not dwell with your women; for we and they have not the same customs [*nomaia*]. We shoot with the bow and throw the javelin and ride but women's work [*erga gunaikeai*] we have never learned; and your women do none of the things whereof we speak but abide in their wagons, busy with women's work and never go out hunting or for anything else. So we and they could never agree." The Scythian women, who are assigned "women's work," are very much like Greek women. They live in their wagons just as Greek women live in their houses. So here the shift mentioned above again takes place. Confronted with the Amazons, the Scythians turn into quasi-Greeks. In relation to the Scythian women, the Amazons undeniably occupy a masculine position; they roam over the outdoor space, wielding weapons and riding on horseback, and know nothing of "women's work."

In relation to the Scythian *neotatoi*, their position is more that of husband than of wife, for it is the husbands who bring a dowry and who leave the paternal *oikos*, and they too who obey.[26] Overall, the story shows from start to finish that the Amazons retain the initiative;

---

24. Cf. above, pp. 165ff.

25. On what qualifies somebody as a warrior and on the difference between a fighter and a warrior, see P. Clastres, *Libre 2* (Paris, 1978), pp. 69ff. Similarly, for Hippocrates (*Airs, Waters, Places* 17), an Amazon may not marry until she has killed three enemies.

26. The same expression is used twice to describe the behavior of the husbands: *epeithonto kai (epoiesan) tauta hoi neeniskoi.*

it could well be entitled "the origins of the Sauromatae or how to ensure a line of descent." But even if the Amazons are more like husbands than like wives, that is not to say that their mates become "wives." The text does not rest on a systematic, mechanical inversion of roles; it functions in a more subtle fashion. The women reject *erga gunaikeia* but these do not then devolve upon the men, as happens in Diodorus Siculus. Herodotus tells us: "Ever since, the women of the Sauromatae have followed their ancient usage: they ride out hunting with their men or without them; they go to war and wear the same dress as the men." So who does perform the "women's work"?

While Herodotus's narrative activates some elements of inversion, it is not organized purely and simply according to that schema: its mainspring is not a generalized inversion. If inversion is a procedure of translation, the translation here is of a more complex nature. If inversion implies a dual relationship, does the presence of more than two figures on stage suffice to account for its inadequacy? In the earlier sequence, the two parties present were the Amazons and the Greeks. [27] The Amazons live up to their title of "killers of men"[28] and also show their deficiencies in the field of technical knowledge: they know nothing of the Athena who guides ships or of the Athena of the horse's bit. [29] They do not know how to navigate (although, of course, they do know how to ride horses). The second scene is played out between the Amazons and the Scythians, who themselves may be divided into "ephebes," adults, and women. The interesting point to note here is how in the course of the text the Scythian society turns into a quasi-Greek society, as if in order to convey the otherness of the Amazons to the Greek spectator, the only thing to do was to present them with Greeks disguised as Scythians. The text thus almost imperceptibly tends to fall back on a dual relationship: Amazons on the one hand and Scythians/Greeks on the other.

27. After the battle of Thermodon "the Greeks sailed away, carrying in three ships as many Amazons as they had been able to take alive; and out at sea the Amazons set upon the crews and slew them. But they knew nothing of ships or how to use rudder or sail or oar; and the men being slain, they were borne at the mercy of the waves and winds."

28. Herodotus gives the Scythian "etymology" of their name but makes no allusion to the Greek "etymology" (*a-mazos*, she who is breastless).

29. J.-P. Vernant and M. Detienne, *Cunning Intellignece in Greek Culture and Society*, (Sussex, 1978), pp. 187–215. There are no connections between the Amazons and Athena, despite the fact that the latter is both a virgin and a warrior.

Comparison and Analogy

Another way for the traveler to tell of "others" is by comparison: it is a way of linking the world recounted with the world in which it is recounted and of passing from the one to the other. It is a net the narrator throws into the waters of otherness. The size of the mesh and the design of the net determine the type and quality of the catch. And hauling in the net is a way of bringing what is "other" into proximity with what is the "same." Comparison thus has a place in the rhetoric of otherness, operating there as a procedure of translation.

Of course, the traveler's tale is not alone in employing this figure, nor is Herodotus the first Greek author to use it. On the contrary, it is, as is well known, a fundamental feature of archaic thought: it is to be found in epic, in particular in the famous Homeric descriptions.[30] It is also used by the Ionian writers, where it is a tool of understanding in the sense that it makes it possible to give a representation of something unknown (an object or a phenomenon).[31] Functioning as a means of translation, in a traveler's tale it establishes resemblances and differences between the world "there" and the world "here"[32] and roughs out some classificatory categories. For the comparison to convey something, the second term must belong to the shared knowledge of those whom the traveler is addressing.[33] For example, when writing of the region of the river Araxes beyond which the Massagetae live, Herodotus explains that many of the islands dotted along its course are "comparable" (*paraplesiai*) in size to Lesbos.[34] Elsewhere, describing the course of the Nile, he remarks that beyond the town of Elephantine its course is winding "like" (*kataper*) that of the Meander.[35] The only interesting question these com-

30. W. Kranz, "Gleichnis und Vergleich in der Fruhgriechischen Philosophie," *Hermès* 73 (1938): 92–132; B. Snell, *The Discovery of the Mind* (trans. New York, 1960), pp. 191–227.

31. Lloyd, *Polarity and Analogy*, pp. 209, 305, 345.

32. I have borrowed this distinction between the world "here" (*par-deçà*) and the world over "there" (*par-delà*) (Brazil) from J. de Léry.

33. A systematic examination of the second terms used in comparisons should in theory tell us something, if not about the public of the *Histories*, at least about the addressee. In particular, they include the Greeks, Cilicia, the Meander (II), Ilium, Teuthrania, Ephesus, Cyrene (the lotus), Attica, and Iaphygia.

34. Hdt. 1.202.

35. Hdt. 2.29.

parisons raise concerning this obvious mechanism is that of whom they reached. To whom would the references to Lesbos and the Meander mean something? Consider, for instance, that abstraction in our Greek history, the typical Athenian: what would all this convey to him?

Next, let us reflect on the classificatory comparisons which, by noting resemblances, in effect also indicate differences. They are to be found mainly in descriptions of customs: sexual *mores*, for example, as when the reader is told that such and such a people have intercourse "like" (*kataper*) animals;[36] or *nomoi* in general, as when the Lydians have "more or less the same" (*paraplesioi*) customs as the Greeks, except that they prostitute their daughters.[37] These comparisons also make it possible to extend knowledge by moving from one group to its closest neighbors: the Giligamae (a group in Libya) have "more or less the same" customs as the other Libyans (whose *nomoi* Herodotus has already described).[38] Finally, in this group of comparisons the Greeks, as such, frequently occupy the position of the second term.[39]

As well as these elementary comparisons of the "*a* is like *b*" type (where *a* and *b* are directly comparable), there are comparisons in which the traveler has to deploy rather more subtlety; these depend on a change of register. When it happens that the first term has no direct equivalent in the world where things are recounted, or that the world where things are recounted does not function directly as a reference, the translation has to be turned into a transposition.

Thus, Herodotus describes the relay team of Persian messengers, which spans the entire length of the royal route all the way to Susa, the residence of the Great King. Then, to make this institution which has no direct equivalent in Greece more comprehensible to his addressee, he adds that this relay team of messengers is like the *lampadephoria* which takes place in Greece: "the first rider delivers his charge to the second, the second to the third and thence it passes on from hand to hand even as in the Greek torch-bearers' race in honour of Hephaestus."[40] Of course, the messenger service and the

36. For example, Hdt. 1.203.
37. Hdt. 1.94.
38. Hdt. 4.169.
39. Hdt 4.169, as well as 1.94; see also 1.35, 2.92, 4.26.
40. Hdt. 8.98.

lampadephoria are really not the same thing at all, but Herodotus reckons that the one can help the reader to form a better picture of the other and that it is worth introducing a comparison, however fleeting, between the two: the torches passed from hand to hand are like the news relayed from one messenger to the next until it reaches the royal palace in Susa. This is one more example in which, thanks to the comparison, the otherness of a mode of behavior, initially placed before us uncompromisingly, is subsequently rendered intelligible. When the Issedones, a people of the northeastern borders of Scythia, lose their fathers, they organize a cannibal banquet in the course of which they eat the father's corpse mixed with the meat of other animals; "as for the head, they strip it bare and cleanse and gild it and keep it for a sacred relic to which they offer yearly solemn sacrifice." We are apparently in an extremely non-Greek context here, but Herodotus's words immediately return us to Greece by noting that the sons are in this way honoring their father "even as" (*kataper*) the Greeks celebrate the anniversary of the dead (*genesia*).[41] These ceremonies and the Greek *genesia* are very different, but from a functional point of view they fulfill the same role: the one is to the society of the Issedones what the other is to Greek society. This form of comparison, which operates by setting one term alongside the other and by transfer, corresponds to the *similitudo per collationem* of the *Rhetorica ad Herrenium*. The *Ad Herrenium* lists four forms of similitude: *similitudo per contrarium, similitudo per negationem, similitudo per brevitatem,* and the fourth kind, *similitudo per collationem,* which we may call the parallel.[42] Each form is assigned a function, that of the fourth being "to set the thing before the eyes [*ante oculos ponere.*]"

To set the thing before the eyes, maybe, but precisely by setting something else there: therein lies the originality of the traveler's tale. As a figure of rhetoric in this type of narrative, the parallel is thus a fiction which enables the reader to see how it was, as if he were there,

---

41. Hdt. 4.26.

42. *Ad Herrenium* 4.46; see M. Charles, "Bibliothèques," *Poétique* 33 (February 1978): 19–20. P. Fontanier, *Les Figures du discours* (Paris, 1968), defines the parallel as follows: "The parallel consists of two descriptions, either consecutive or intertwined, by which a comparison is made between the physical or moral relationship between two objects, in order to show the resemblance or difference between them."

but it does so by presenting to his view something else. Thus while Herodotus is surveying Scythia and constructing its image, he comes across the promontory of the country of the Tauri, which he represents as follows:

The sea to the south and the sea to the east are two of the four boundary lines of Scythia, *even as* (*kataper*) the seas are the boundaries of Attica; and the Tauri, dwelling as they do in a part of Scythia which is like Attica, it is *as though* (*paraplesia, hos ei*) some other people, not Attic, were to inhabit the heights of Sunium from Thoricus to the township of Anaphlystus, did Sunium but jut farther out into the sea. I say this insofar as one may compare small things with great. Such is the situation of Tauris.[43]

So Tauris is to Scythia what Sunium is to Attica. That is the first parallel presented to the reader. The surveyor goes on to specify the conditions under which his comparison is valid: it is valid "insofar as one may compare small things with great."[44] But those scruples are also a way of saying that the difference between the two is purely quantitative, not qualitative at all, just a matter of measurements. Of course, Tauris is bigger than Sunium but that aside, Tauris is exactly like Sunium. The difference is not denied but is contained.

Then the traveler proceeds to deploy a second parallel: "But to those who have not coasted along [*parapeploke*] that part of Attica I can *make it clear* in another way [*allos deloso*]: it is as though [*hos ei*] in Iapygia [Apulia], some other people, not Iapygian, were to dwell on the promontory within a line drawn from the harbour of Brentesium [Brindisi] to Taras [Tarentum]." So in relation to Scythia Tauris is as the heel of the boot of Italy in relation to Apulia. This second parallel draws on other geographical knowledge. Is that other knowledge in fact a different set of shared knowledge, which is limited to the Greeks of Magna Graecia? It is worth noting that the traveler does not say "those who do not live in Attica" but "those who have not coasted along that part of Attica." To whom, then, is this parallel primarily addressed? To the Greeks of Magna Graecia, bearing in mind that those who have made that voyage, either traveling to Greece or from it, could only have traveled by sea? Or to sailors in general? In that case, these comparisons would seem to stem, rather, from the literature of the *Periplous*, those compen-

---

43. Hdt. 4.99.
44. Hdt. 4.99: *lego de hos einai tauta smikra megaloisi sumbalein.*

diums of nautical instructions for the use of travelers. Whatever the case may be, the comparison closes with the (virtually limitless) possibility of devising other parallels, for "of these two countries I speak, but there are many others of a like kind which Tauris resembles." The traveler in this way shows off his own knowledge. "I could show you many other examples," he says and he thereby gives license to his listeners or readers to construct other, even more satisfactory parallels for themselves if they still do not "see" clearly how it is.[45]

The parallel rests on the interplay of four terms, associated in pairs, in accordance with the formula "*a* is to *b* what *c* is to *d*." In other words, the comparison, adopting the form of an analogy, turns itself into what might be termed an analogical vision. For when the narrator, in order to show the relationship between Tauris and Scythia, "places before the eyes" of the addressee the relationship between Sunium and Attica, he conjures up an analogical vision. Or, one might say, he takes over Anaxagoras's expression: *opsis adelon ta phainomena*,[46] from what one sees to what one does not see, from the known to the unknown.

Analogy plays a role of the first importance in the earliest stages of Greek science, where it functions both as a method of invention and as a system of explanation.[47] So it is interesting to see a narrative such as the *Histories* resorting to and adopting to its own particular use this mode of understanding, which is constituted by understanding "through comparison." An extreme example is the parallel Herodotus constructs between the Ister (the Danube) and the Nile.[48] The Ister, which flows through a number of inhabited countries, is known to many people, whereas nobody is in a position to speak of the sources of the Nile since Libya, across which it flows, is an uninhabited desert. So I pass from the known to the unknown, from what is manifest to what is hidden: to "find" the sources of the Nile, I make

45. Another example of a parallel can be found at Hdt. 2.10.

46. H. Diller, "*Opsis adelon ta phainomena*," *Hermès* 67 (1932): 14–42.

47. Lloyd, *Polarity and Analogy*. On the power of analogy, see M. Foucault, *The Order of Things* (London 1974), p. 21: "An old concept, already familiar to Greek science. . . . Its power is immense, for the similitudes of which it treats are not the visible, substantial ones between things themselves; they need only to be the more subtle resemblances of relations."

48. Hdt. 2.33, 34.

a detour by way of the sources of the Ister and I proceed by inference, "as I guess, reasoning as to things unknown from visible signs."[49] The general hypothesis is that the Nile is like the Ister. But if this comparison is to have any heuristic value, I must postulate a symmetry between the north and the south of the inhabited world and, by applying this principle, the comparison can be changed into a real parallel: the Nile is, to the south, what the Ister is to the north; or the Nile is to Libya what the Ister is to Europe. This example represents an extreme case because, in the first place, in order to make the "discovery," the pertinence of the principle of symmetry needs to be assumed; this principle must be applied if the parallel is to operate successfully. Second, and more important, this example is extreme because, unlike Sunium and Attica, the second term in the comparison (the course of the Ister) is not an immediate part of the world in which things are recounted. It is not part of the concrete horizon of the addressee, nor yet—in all probability—a part of the shared knowledge of the Greeks, nor is it guaranteed by the eye of the narrator (saying, "I myself have seen"). Nevertheless, the whole demonstration rests on the narrator's affirmation, which he makes in passing, to the effect that its course belongs to the sphere of what is well known: he knows about it and so, equally, do many others.

The comparison, which is part of the fabric of the world in which things are recounted, enables one to see how things are, either directly (*a* is like *b*) or analogically (*a* is to *b* as *c* is to *d*). As an operator of translation, it filters what is "other" into what is the "same." As a narrative fiction, guaranteed by the eye of the traveler or the knowledge of the narrator, its aim is to instill belief in the addressee. Even if, when the net is hauled in, some differences remain, they can be explained and measured and so can be controlled ("insofar as one may compare small things with great").

The Measure of *Thoma*

Any traveler's tale that claims to be a faithful report must contain a category of *thoma* (marvels, curiosities). The *Histories* are no exception. It has, indeed, often been shown that the ethnographic *logoi* are, for the most part, organized as follows: an introductory passage on the nature of the country in question, an account of its *nomoi*, a

49. Hdt. 2.33: *hos ego sumballomai toisi emphanesi ta me ginoskomena tek-mairomenos*, an expression that echoes the formula of Anaxagoras.

mention of its *thomasia*, and, finally, a report on its political history.[50] The introduction to the chapter on Lydia proves that the *thoma* is truly a *topos* of the ethnographic narrative. It runs as follows: "There are not, in Lydia, many marvellous things for me to tell of, if it be compared with other countries, except for the gold dust which comes down from Tmolos."[51] And that it is indeed such a *topos* is confirmed by the repetition of a similarly structured sentence, this time relating to Scythia[52] and the dearth of marvels that it has to offer the traveler. The fact that the narrator is much exercised over marvels/curiosities is indicated quite clearly in his prologue to the *Histories*, in which he defines his objectives: among other things, he is determined to mention and display *erga megala te kai thomasta*, both those of the Greeks and those of the barbarians. What are these *erga*? There have been many discussions and differing opinions on the subject. Are they "monuments," that is to say, the most remarkable of the monuments constructed by the Greeks and the barbarians? Are they actions, that is to say, "high deeds"? Or, as seems most likely, are they a combination of the marvels of nature, monuments, and high deeds? It does not really matter. All we are concerned with is the word used to describe them, *thomasta*.[53] The narrator is anxious to report them because they are *thomasta* (and *megala* or great ones) and are therefore worth recording, so that, as Herodotus puts it, there is no danger of them ever ceasing to be renowned (*aklea*).

Thus accommodated by the narrative, *thoma* may be reckoned among the procedures used by the rhetoric of otherness. Generally speaking, the impression it conveys is one of trustworthiness, for the narrator cannot fail to produce this rubric, which is expected by his public. To omit it would be, at a stroke, to ruin his credibility. It is as if it were postulated that far away, in these other countries, there were bound to be marvels/curiosities. So when Herodotus describes the *eschatia*, the extremities of the inhabited world, we find an echo of

50. Jacoby, *RE*, Suppl. 2, 331–32.
51. Hdt. 1.93: *thomata ge he Ludie es suggraphen.*
52. Hdt 4.82: "As for marvels, there are none in the land, save that it has rivers by far the greatest and the most numerous in the world."
53. For a study of the meaning of *ergon*, see H. R. Immerwahr, "*Ergon*: History as a Monument," *American Journal of Philology* 81 (1960): 263–64: the article by H. Barth, "Zur Bewertung und Auswahl des Stoffes durch Herodotus (Die Begriffe, *thoma, thomazo, thomasios* und *thomastos*)," *Klio* 50 (1968): 93–110, also provides a contribution to determining the meaning of this expression.

this "theory": "it would seem that the fairest blessings have been granted to the most distant nations of the world, whereas in Greece the seasons have by much the kindliest temperature." Similarly: "the most distant parts of the world, as they enclose and entirely surround all other lands . . . have those things which we deem the best and rarest."[54] Great beauty and extreme rarity are the constituents of *thoma*. In other words, *thoma* can be regarded as translating difference: one of the possible transcriptions of the difference between what is here and what is there, far away.

Of course, *thoma*, as a category in the ethnographic narrative, was not an invention of Herodotus's; it is to be found in epic and also in Hesiod, where the word means not only "a marvel" but also "a miracle as an object of stupefaction." When a marvel stems from the divine and relates to the gods, the word used is *sema; thoma* is used when it relates to mortal men.[55] In the *Histories*, all reference to the divine sphere in this context has disappeared and the structure of *thoma* appears to be twofold: it is qualitatively extraordinary and quantitatively remarkable.

The extremities of the world, where the "fairest" and "rarest" blessings are to be found, possess, in particular, mysterious spices.[56] The Arabs harvest incense by lighting fires to smoke out winged snakes which mount guard over the trees that produce it. Cassia has to be gathered in a lake inhabited by a species of bat from which it is necessary to protect oneself by covering one's whole body with the hides of oxen. "Even more extraordinary" (*thomastoteron*) is the harvesting of cinnamon. Certain birds use it to build their nests, and a subterfuge must be devised to make the nests fall to the ground, for they are inaccessible. As for laudanum, that is "more extraordinary still." This spice, with such a delicious perfume, becomes entangled in the beards of he-goats, a place which stinks abominably. Such admirable products could only be found in the most extraordinary of places.

But are qualitative criteria the only ones that operate? Apparently not, for it is noticeable that the order in which the narrator chooses to present his descriptions moves from the extraordinary to the

54. Hdt. 3.106, 116.

55. G. Nenci, "La concezione del miracoloso nei poemi homerici," *Atti Accad, Scienze, Torino*, 92 (1957–1958): 275–311, and "La concezione del miracoloso in Esiodo," *Critica Storica* 31 (1962): 251–57.

56. Hdt. 3.107–12.

increasingly extraordinary nature of the harvesting of spices. Myrrh, the harvesting of which presents no problems, barely rates a mention. In the last analysis, *thoma* operates as a criterion of classification in which the categories range from the least to the most extraordinary. To all intents and purposes, there is thus a scale and measurement of *thoma* to which the narrator refers. The various types of gathering are recounted to the listener in accordance with the measure of *thoma* contained in each, are in fact recounted solely on account of that said measure of *thoma*. Thus, the rule determining what is qualitatively extraordinary seems, in the narrative, to be what is quantitatively remarkable. As for the scale of *thoma*, that is set up solely by the narrator but always with the addressee in mind: it is constructed according to what for "us" (you and me) is implicitly regarded as extraordinary or as more and more extraordinary. It is thus governed by the ear of the public. It is not hard to see that in some circumstances *thoma* takes on the rhetorical figure of an inversion. For example, the extraordinary character of the gathering of laudanum stems from the fact that it is to be found in the beards of he-goats. That is to say, something that gives off the best of fragrances becomes entangled in something that gives off the worst of smells: it is the attraction of opposites that is so surprising. Immediately after declaring Egypt to be the country that offers the "most marvels," Herodotus produces his account of how different Egypt is, which promptly turns into an inversion; he passes from *thoma* to an inversion, using inversion as a possible transcription of *thoma*.[57]

Thoma may also be a singularity which it does not seem possible to explain, an exception: such is the case of the mules in Elis or, rather, of their absence there. When describing the Scythian climate, Herodotus notes that horses there are able to tolerate the cold, while mules (and donkeys) are not, whereas in other countries quite the reverse obtains: horses cannot tolerate the cold but mules can. He then moves on to the horns of the oxen: if the oxen there have no horns that is because of the cold, the proof for this being that Homer said that in Libya "lambs are born with horns upon their foreheads." He assumes there to be a symmetry and inversion between the cold and the hot, Scythia and Libya. His general conclusion is: "There [*enthauta*], that of which I speak happens because of the cold."

"But I hold it strange [*thomazo*] that in the whole of Elis no mules

---

57. Hdt. 2.35.

can be begotten, albeit neither is the country cold nor is there any manifest cause."[58] If Elis were a cold region one could invoke the Scythian precedent to account for this absence and for this anomaly. However, as Elis does not obey the general rule nor yet the converse of that general rule, all I can do is register my astonishment (*thomazo*). These remarks, which the narrator presents as a "digression" (*prostheke*),[59] show that there is a connection between *thoma* and digression. A digression may be a way of expressing *thoma*, and *thoma* may operate in the narrative to determine the form of a digression.

Thoma in terms of quality, or *thoma* in terms of quantity? The gathering of spices has shown that, overall, the qualitative could be transcribed as quantitative through the implicit application of a scale of *thoma* which also provides a ready-made order in which to introduce the examples. In the *Histories*, however, *thoma* is more frequently described in terms of quantity and measurement. It is assessed not in relation to a whole scale of *thoma* (ranging from the least extraordinary to the most extraordinary) but directly, in terms of numbers and measurements, as if number and measurement constituted the essence of *thoma*. The greater the measurements and numbers, the greater the *thoma*. It is as if the narrator had decided that the implicit, shared scale of *thoma* recognized by himself and his public alike seemed to him to be too vague or unreliable and so he had converted it into the immediately available and more reliable scale of numbers. For example: "The Arabs have two marvellous kinds of sheep, nowhere else found." That is the singularity. This is then expressed in quantitative terms: "One of these has a tail no less than three cubits long . . . The other kind of sheep has a tail a full cubit broad."[60] Similarly, among the few curiosities of Scythia, mention may be made of a footprint that is remarkable for its size: it is two cubits long.[61] And it was Heracles who left this gigantic footprint. Not for a moment does Herodotus question that attribution, particularly since, in the version of the origins of the Scythian people

58. Hdt. 4.30. The text continues: "The Eleans themselves say that it is by reason of a curse that mules cannot be begotten among them."

59. Hdt. 4.30: "But I hold it strange (for it was ever the way of my *logos* to seek after digressions)."

60. Hdt. 3.113.

61. Hdt. 4.82.

told by the Black Sea Greeks,[62] Heracles did indeed pass through Scythia. In general, the Greeks have at their disposal a whole stock of personages available for use in every situation. As operators of intelligibility, they serve to classify phenomena and set them in order. They make it easier to understand the world, operating almost as instruments of thought, even tools of logic. A large footprint equals a track left by Heracles—not at all the modern reaction, which might be that a large footprint means that there must be some wild man or Scythian yeti at large.

To describe *thoma*,[63] Homer and Hesiod use the adjective "great" (*megas*), but the exact size of the *thoma* is not specifically measured. Instead, the adjective *deinos*, terrible, daunting, is to be found in association with *megas*. The "miracle" is thus great or terrible, and great because it is so daunting. In the *Histories*, in contrast, *thoma* is often conveyed by a number. There are many examples,[64] but I will mention only one more: the labyrinth of Egypt which produces "a thousand surprises" for the visitor, a *thoma murion*, that is to say, a surprise the intensity of which can itself be appreciated in terms of measurement. What Herodotus says is:

Were all that Greeks have built and made added together, the whole would be seen to be a matter of less labour and cost than was this labyrinth. . . . This maze surpasses even the pyramids. . . . It has twelve roofed courts. . . . There are also double sets of chambers, three thousand altogether, fifteen hundred above and the same number underground. We ourselves viewed those above ground and speak of what we have seen; of the underground chambers we were only told; the Egyptian wardens would by no means show them. . . . Thus, we can only speak by hearsay of the lower chambers; the upper we saw for ourselves and they are creations greater than human. The outlets of the chambers and the mazy passages hither and thither through the courts were an unending marvel to us as we passed from court to apartment and from apartment to colonnades and from colonnades again to more chambers and then into yet more courts.[65]

So evaluating, measuring, and counting are necessary operations in order to translate *thoma* for the world in which things are

---

62. Hdt. 4.8–10; cf. above, pp. 19ff.
63. Nenci, "Miracoloso in Esiodo," p. 254.
64. Examples of manifest transcriptions of *thoma* into measurable size: Hdt. 1.184, 185, 2.111, 148, 149, 155, 156, 163, 175, 176, 3.113, 4.82, 85, 199.
65. Hdt. 2.148, 199.

recounted. Consider the title sometimes given to Marco Polo's book, *The Million.* No doubt it was a way of indicating the omnipresence of number and of testing its credibility. And in referring to the *erga megala te kai thomasta* the prologue of the *Histories*, was, even then, connecting *thoma* with size. Even if the formula is indeed an echo of Homer and Hesiod, it also indicates that size is now measurable. The case of the labyrinth furthermore makes it clear that *thoma* relates to the eye of the traveling beholder: "I saw it with my own eyes." Those eyes are there to guarantee the *thoma*.

When Hesiod describes Tartarus, he makes it clear that this is a marvel "even for the immortal gods."[66] In the ethnographic narrative, it is the traveler who becomes the measure of *thoma*: it is *thoma* to me, not to the gods, and it is I who am the judge of whether such and such a countryside or such and such a construction is "marvellous to behold" or "extraordinary." "I will now show what seems to me to be the most remarkable thing [*thoma megiston*] in Babylon, writes Herodotus.[67] There is thus a connection between *thoma* and the identity of the speaker: the eye of the traveler operates as a measure of *thoma* and the narrator makes his addressee "see" the *thoma*, precisely by measuring its size. All in all, *thoma* belongs to the techniques of the surveyor.

While *thoma* may serve to model a digression, more generally it produces narration. It prompts the narrator to speak or write. "Concerning Egypt I will now speak at length, because nowhere are there so many marvellous things [*pleista thomasia*] nor in the whole world besides are there to be seen so many works of unspeakable greatness; therefore I shall say all the more about Egypt."[68] The length of the narrative is certainly a consequence of the size of the *thoma*; the greater the *thoma*, the longer my narrative will be. But however long, the narrative cannot exhaust the *thoma*, which is always likely to exceed it; there is always something more, over and above the *verba*, something which remains inexpressible.[69] Thus, Egypt is the country where, more than anywhere else, there are to

---

66. Hesiod *Theogony* 743–44.
67. Hdt. 1.194, 3.12, 4.129.
68. Hdt. 2.35.
69. For example, Hesiod mentions, in connection with Cerberus, the inexpressible nature (*ou ti phateion*) of *thoma*; cf. Nenci, "Miracoloso in Esiodo," p. 255.

be seen "many works of unspeakable greatness [*erga logou mezo*], but one way to capture those things in the *logos* and to explain and account for them is, precisely, to express them in terms of numbers and measurements.

Thoma translates the difference between there and here and, as such, in the last analysis produces an impression of reality. It declares: I am the reality of otherness; the fact is that *there* things, the *erga,* must be *thomasta.* It is on that postulate that their verisimilitude rests. The presence of *thoma* in the narrative creates the effect of trustworthiness, the effect of reality (the former stems from the latter). To that extent and to the extent that it depends on the measuring eye of the witness-traveler, *thoma* is certainly a procedure used to promote the credibility of the traveler's tale.

Translating, Naming, Classifying

A rhetoric of otherness is basically an operation of translation. Its aim is to convey the "other" to the "same" (*tradere*). It is a conveyor of what is different. But what about translation in the strict sense of the term, in the *Histories*? What place does that occupy? Is the narrator concerned to translate, that is to say, "to render what is stated in one language into another, aiming for a semantic and expressive equivalence between the two statements"?[70]

The year 1578 saw the appearance of Jean de Léry's narrative entitled *Histoire d'un voyage fait en la terre de Brésil* (The Story of a Voyage in the Land of Brazil). This text is organized in accordance with a veritable "translation system,"[71] that is to say, through the very fashion in which it proceeds it gradually makes the point that it is not so much things in themselves that differ between "here" and "there," but their appearance. For, all in all, human nature remains the same; only the language is different. But the language is translatable and so the difference may be apprehended. Translation between the Old World and the New both maintains and reduces the distance represented by the ocean. It is thus simultaneously the ever-present mark of the severance between the two and also the constantly renewed sign of their stitching-together. Severance and stitching-together are

70. Definition given in the Robert dictionary.
71. M. de Certeau, *L'Ecriture de l'histoire* (Paris, 1975), p. 233.

two phases in a single movement at work within the text. The setting up of such a system of translation presupposes the possibility of referring to a set of distinctions between being and appearance.

In Léry's book, the concern to translate is made quite explicit, for chapter 20 is a French-Tupi dictionary "or, rather, a crib [*assimil*],"[72] presented in the form of a dialogue between one of the Tupinamba and a Frenchman. If the difference between them is a matter of language, this chapter provides "a code for linguistic transformation."[73] Furthermore, this phrase book completes the picture of Indian life, for it is followed only by the last two chapters of the book, which are devoted to the adventures of the return journey to "here."

Is it possible to make out a system of translation in the *Histories*? Strictly speaking, certainly not. There is no phrase book for Egyptian and Greek or for Persian and Greek, let alone for Scythian and Greek. Marco Polo learned Persian, Mongolian, and a little Chinese. Léry has recourse to the "mediation" of an interpreter, but he had himself learned the Tupi language and it was on the strength of his competence in it that he launched his attack against his old enemy Thévet; the latter had devoted a chapter in his *Cosmographie* to the language of the American Indians but, according to Léry, he merely "jabbered confusedly and without order," for the truth was that he could not speak a word of it. Léry himself frequently uses Tupi words, usually nouns, which he then proceeds to translate and explain. Such a way of proceeding certainly makes for an effect of exoticism but also creates an impression of trustworthiness. Herodotus himself in all likelihood knew no language but Greek.[74] Of course, his travels were not limited to a single country as Léry's were, nor had he lived for sixteen years in a single region, as Marco Polo did. All the same, the fact remains that, generally speaking, the Greeks did tend to speak nothing but Greek. Momigliano writes: "It was not for them to converse with the natives in the natives' languages. . . . There was no tradition for translating foreign books into Greek." And the look that Herodotus cast over other civilizations is likely to have been one

---

72. Ibid., p. 232: the chapter in Léry is entitled "Colloque de l'entrée ou arrivée en la terre du Brésil, entre les gens nommés Toupinamboults . . . en langage sauvage et français."

73. Ibid.

74. P.-E. Legrand, *Hérodote* (Paris, 1955), Introduction, p. 75, and his note to Herodotus, 1.139.

that was cold and sure of itself. "There was no temptation to yield to foreign civilizations. In fact, there was no desire to get to know them intimately by mastering foreign languages."[75]

Herodotus spoke either with Greeks or with people who spoke Greek, or else he acquired his information through the intermediary of interpreters, as he is seen to do when he travels in Egypt. Visiting the pyramid of Cheops, he mentions a particular inscription, adding, "So far as I well remember the interpreter when he read me the writing."[76] But that is the only time this happens. On other occasions when he cites a text or inscription, the problem of a translation does not even arise. Generally speaking, the Greeks in the *Histories* do not appear to have had relations with the Persians other than through the intermediary of interpreters,[77] with the sole exception of Histiaeus of Miletus, the tyrant and puppet of the Great King, who on one occasion does utter at least a few words in the Persian language. But the occasion was a quite exceptional one: on the point of being killed in battle by a Persian solder, Histiaeus identified himself—it was, to put it mildly, an emergency.[78] Book 2 provides some interesting information on the subject of the training of interpreters. Psammetichus, who had come to power thanks to the help of the Ionians and Carians, conceded land to them, and he "put Egyptian boys in their hands to be taught the Greek tongue; these, learning Greek, were the ancestors of the Egyptian interpreters of today."[79] So an interpreter's skills were handed down from father to son, but the main point is that it was the Egyptians who learned to speak Greek, not the Greeks who learned Egyptian.

Although the *Histories* are not organized in accordance with a "translating activity," they do contain a number of translations (about thirty). What type of translations are these and what do they indicate from the point of view of the relations that they establish with "others"? The majority are nouns, in particular proper nouns. On the other hand, there are no direct translations of statements. Translation is thus fundamentally linked with the business of naming

---

75. A. Momigliano, "The Fault of the Greeks," *Daedalus* 104, 2 (1975): 12–15.

76. Hdt. 2.125. It appears that the translation can only be a fantastical one.

77. Hdt. 3.38, 140.

78. Hdt 6.29. On the other hand, in the course of a banquet given for Mardonius in Thebes a Persian addresses the Greek seated next to him in Greek (9.6).

79. Hdt. 2.154.

things. In a narrative concerned to tell of "others," it is a way of naming.

Proper nouns have a meaning, as is shown, for example, by the names of the Great Kings, Darius, Xerxes, and Ataxerxes. Translated into Greek they mean, respectively, "the Repressor," "the Warrior," and "the Great Warrior," and "such the Greeks would rightly [*orthos*] call them in their language."[80] Through the operation of translation, the name is thus perceived both as a proper noun and as a label. To say Darius or Xerxes is like saying Richard the Lionheart or Ivan the Terrible; the translation gives the names more meaning. What at first sight appeared to be simply a classification (one king was called Darius, another Xerxes) is now also understood as a label, to the extent that these names say something about their owners: Xerxes is the third sovereign in the dynasty, following Cyrus and Darius, but he is also "the Warrior."

There is a second, and richer, example of translating-labeling: that of the Amazons. The Scythians called the Amazons *Oiorpata*, a name which, translated into Greek, means "female killers of men," for the Scythian word for man is *oior* and *pata* means to kill.[81] So this translation appears to pass through two stages: in Scythia, the Amazons are called *Oiorpata*, a name which, translated into Greek, means "female killers of men." In other words, although *Oiorpata* may truly be the translation of "Amazons," the two names nevertheless do not have the same "etymology." Through the Scythian "etymology" one indeed obtains the meaning of "female killers of men" but in the popular Greek etymology, which Herodotus does not mention (but which was, in all likelihood, known to his addressee), one obtains *A-mazos*, "breastless."[82] Thus, by playing on both the Greek and the Scythian registers, a simple naming in translation

---

80. Hdt. 6.98.

81. Hdt. 4.110. Legrand, *Hérodote*, 4.110, n. 1. on the basis of remarks made by Benveniste, describes this translation as fantastical. Another example of translation occurs at 4.27: "We . . . call these people by the Scythian name, Arimaspians; for in the Scythian tongue *arima* is 'one,' and *spou* is the 'eye.'"

82. In the shared knowledge of the Greeks, the Scythian "etymology" may also evoke or call to mind what Homer calls them (*Iliad* 6.186): the Amazons are said to be *anti-aneirai*, that is to say, playing on the prefix *anti*, both the "equals" and the "enemies" of males.

helps to construct an image of the Amazons. Thanks to the translation, the name *Oiorpata* becomes, for a Greek, a description that adds to his knowledge about the Amazons.

The last example I shall give is that of Battus, the founder of the colony of Cyrene in Libya: "There was born to him a son of weak and stammering speech, to whom he gave the name Battus [that is, in Greek, the Stammerer], as the Theraeans and the Cyrenaeans say; but *to my thinking* the boy was given some other name and changed it to Battus on his coming to Libya, for the Libyan word for king is *battus*."[83] So the same name Battus designates the person as "the Stammerer" in the Greek register and as "the king" if one adopts the Libyan point of view. What makes it possible to pass from the one to the other is precisely the naming in translation guaranteed by the knowledge of the narrator ("to my thinking").

Apart from these examples,[84] naming in translation takes place in the particular domain of the names of the gods. What are the gods' names? Are they proper nouns, labels, or perhaps even common nouns? What do they mean? The question of names, of *ounamata*, is a vast and complex one, for it leads to the question of divine space and to that of the representation of the divine in the *Histories*. As that is a subject which, as such, is beyond the scope of this work, I will simply attempt to evaluate the activity of translation insofar as it relates to a rhetoric of others—translation regarded as one of the procedures of that rhetoric.

Translations occur both from the Greek into foreign versions (the name of the god given first in Greek, then in the barbarian language) and also from foreign versions into Greek, but the former is more common (eleven examples as opposed to five).

The examples of translation from the foreign version into the Greek all occur in the Egyptian *logos:* such and such a god (then comes the Egyptian name) is, in the Greek language (*kata Hellada*

---

83. Hdt. 4.155. What is amusing about this example is that one and the same person is being named but the same name, Battus, is for a Greek a label and for a Libyan a description (according to Herodotus), and vice versa. See V. Descombes, "Une Supposition très singulière ou comment désigner la porte d'Ali Baba," *Critique* (May 1978): 467–92.

84. To which should be added Hdt. 1.110, 2.30, 143, 3.26, 4.52, 192, 6.119, 8.85, 9.110.

glossan), such and such a god.[85] The Scythian pantheon, on the other hand, is entirely presented in the form of Scythian versions given to Greek names.[86]

The second point worth noting relates to the importance of names. Ever since the narrative of Genesis it has been clear that naming involves a degree of mastery. By naming God's creatures, Adam proclaims his preeminence over them. The practice of secrecy is another method of registering the importance of names: many primitive societies are known to keep the individual names of men secret (that is to say, they are revealed only to certain people and according to a precisely defined ritual). Giving names or knowing names thus implies a measure of power. A name is always more than the mere sound of it.

In the context of Greece, Democritus, who had himself composed an *Onomastikon*, states that the names of the gods are "sacred statues endowed with a voice [*agalmata phoneenta*]."[87] The name of a god is thus his "audible representation" just as his statue is his visible representation. And well before Democritus, the Pythagoreans had also considered that not only the names of the gods but all names were the images (*agalmata, eikones*) of things.[88] Seen from this point of view, names teach of things, and the gods' names teach of the gods: to know the gods is to know their names. Antisthenes, for example, for whom education starts with the study of names, wrote a book entitled *On Education, or Names*.[89] Such themes were to be readopted later, in the *Cratylus*, which also devotes a number of pages to the question of the names of the gods.[90] Socrates amuses himself by undertaking an examination of the correctness of the composition of their names, giving etymologies of the various names based on the functions of the respective gods. Such, broadly speak-

---

85. Hdt. 2.144 (Horus = Apollo), 137 (Boubastis = Artemis), 59 (Isis = Demeter), 144 (Osiris = Dionysus), 153 (Apis = Epaphos).

86. Hdt. 4.59. Other examples of translations from the Greek: 1.131, 2.42, 46, 79, 3.8.

87. Democritus, 68 B 142 (D.-K.).

88. V. Goldschmidt, *Essai sur le Cratyle* (Paris, 1940), p. 27; P. Boyancé, "La Doctrine d'Eutyphron dans le *Cratyle*," *Revue des Etudes Grecques* (1941): 143–75; W. Burkert, "La Genèse des choses et des mots: Le Papyrus de Derveni entre Anaxagore et Cratyle," *Les Etudes Philosophiques* 4 (1970): 443–55.

89. Diogenes Laertius 6.17.

90. *Cratylus* 397c–408d.

ing, is the context for this question of the divine *ounamata* and, in particular, for the controversial affirmation of the Egyptian origin of the names of the gods. Herodotus writes: "Wellnigh all the names of the gods came to Greece from Egypt."[91]

The third question I would take up is this: what is the implication of the fact that it is possible to make such translations, that one can say that Hestia is Tabiti in the Scythian language, or that Osiris is Dionysus in Greek? Linforth concludes that the names of the gods are treated as common nouns.[92] In the last analysis, the gods' names occupy the same position as other nouns in the language, which is conceived as a repertory; like them, they are, thanks to the setting up of tables of equivalence, able to be translated into another language.

But is the distinction drawn between a proper and a common noun really pertinent? Without going into the discussions of logicians and linguists on the subject of what constitutes a proper noun, we may nevertheless note that the *Cratylus*, in which Plato seeks to elaborate a theory about the naming of things in general, passes indiscriminately (or so it seems) from a proper noun to a common one: out of one hundred and thirty-nine examples of naming, forty-nine are derived from proper nouns.[93] It therefore appears that these two naming operations may be assimilated. Lévi-Strauss, for instance, points out that "the more or less 'proper' nature of names is not intrinsically determinable, nor can it be discovered just by comparing them with the other words in the language; it depends on the point at which a society declares its work of classifying to be complete." For an ethnologist, a proper noun, like a landmark in space, is a point of reference within the social group in question and is impossible to define otherwise than as "a means of allotting positions in a system admitting of several dimensions." Through the application of rules of attribution, the proper noun identifies a place

91. Hdt. 2.50. On this question the best article, in my opinion, is still that by I. M. Linforth, "Greek Gods and Foreign Gods in Herodotus," *Univ. of Calif. Publ. in Class. Phil.* 9 (1926): 1–25. See also R. Lattimore, "Herodotus and the Names of Egyptian Gods," *Classical Philology* 35 (1940): 300; and also A. B. Lloyd, *Herodotus, Book II, Commentary* (Leiden, 1976).

92. Linforth, "Greek Gods," p. 11: "[Just] as *hudor* and *aqua* mean the same thing, so that a Greek uses the word *hudor* when writing Greek and a Roman *aqua* when writing Latin, so Zeus and Amon mean the same thing and Herodotus, writing in Greek, naturally uses Zeus."

93. G. Mounin, *Les Problèmes théoriques de la traduction* (Paris, 1963), p. 26.

and "confirms the *named* individual's belonging to a preordained class." Under conditions such as these, "to say that a word is perceived as a proper name is to say that it is assigned to a level beyond which no classification is requisite, not absolutely but within a determinate cultural system."[94] A proper noun classifies, so it always has at least that kind of meaning.

To the extent that they "identify a place," the *ounomata* of the gods seem to fall on the side of proper nouns. They indeed "confirm the named individuals, belonging to a preordained class" (that of the gods); furthermore, it is clear that the gods cannot be given just any name: their names are derived from a paradigmatic whole. So they must be proper nouns. However, translation, the fact that they can be translated from Egyptian into Greek or from Greek into Scythian, seems to classify them on the side of common nouns. Meanwhile, consultation of Herodotus's "dictionary" shows it to be by no means complete. There are plenty of gods' names that are not translated. Thus, while we know that the Libyans pray to Athena, Zeus, Helios, Poseidon, and so forth, we do not know what these deities are called in Libyan. We are given the Greek names but not the native ones.[95] What is the meaning of this absence of translation into the native language? Did the narrator not know the equivalent names, or did he reckon that it was pointless to give the equivalences since naming native pantheons in Greek provided a quite adequate point of reference for his addressee?

But there is also the converse case of an absence of translation from the native language into Greek: the text provides the native name but not its Greek equivalent. This produces a blank space in our table of correspondences between the names of the gods or, rather, three blank spaces, for it happens in respect to three separate deities, Kybebe, Pleisthorus, and Salmoxis. Each of the three is said to be "a native deity [*theos epichorios*]" and the presence of that adjective indicates their nontranslatability. Kybebe is described as "the local goddess of Sardis." Why is it not possible at that point to translate her name as Cybele or as the Mother of the Gods? For two reasons: the Ionians, who had revolted against the King, on their arrival at Sardis burned down her temple (so that place could not be

94. C. Lévi-Strauss, *The Savage Mind* (London, 1974), pp. 180, 187, 215.
95. Even when translation occurs, no series is drawn up except at Hdt. 1.131: Aphrodite Ourania = Mylitta = Alalat = Mitra.

Greek); and the Persians, by way of retaliation, "made this their pretext for burning the temples of Greece" (so that deity must belong to the Persian domain).[96] As for Pleisthorus, he was a god of the Thracian Apsinthians to whom human sacrifices were offered;[97] that probably explains the blank left in the table of correspondences, for there could not possibly be a Greek equivalent for him. In the case of Salmoxis,[98] the uncertainty surrounding his identity (was he a god, a man, or a *daimon?*) and the horrible way a messenger was "dispatched" to him account for the absence of any translation here. Not only is his otherness untranslatable but it is reinforced twofold by the other name by which he is sometimes called: "Salmoxis, or Gebeleizis, as some of them call him." By shifting from Salmoxis to Gebeleizis, which is such a strange-sounding name, we move even further away from the possibility of a translation.[99] In these three cases, the absence of a translation probably does indicate a gap in the table of equivalences. There simply are no words to enter in the Greek column opposite Kybebe, Pleisthorus, and Salmoxis.

All in all, the blank spaces in the "dictionary" confirm that to name what is "other" is to classify it. The examples of Pleisthorus and of Salmoxis-Gebeleizis furthermore show that not to translate is also a way of classifying not only the deities but the native people in question. The otherness of the name is in fact simply a metonymy of the otherness of the people. Not to translate is thus to classify but, clearly, to translate is no less so. This is made quite explicit by the repetition, in descriptions of barbarian pantheons, of the expression "the *only* gods which they revere are . . ."[100] The Massagetae, for instance, recognize "only" the sun, and the Scythians pray to "only" eight deities, but in every case the barbarian pantheons are less numerous than the Greek pantheon of the twelve great gods. In

---

96. Hdt. 5.102.

97. Hdt. 9.119.

98. Hdt. 4.94–96.

99. There remain the cases of Ares and of the *daimon* of the Tauri. Human sacrifices are offered to Ares although he has a Greek name with no Scythian equivalent (*contra* Pleistorus); cf. above, p. 187. The Tauri offer up prisoners to their *daimon*, whom they assimilate to Iphigenia, but Herodotus makes it clear that that is *their* translation.

100. Massagetae (Hdt. 1.126); Arabs (3.8); Persians (1.131); Ethiopians (2.29); Scythians (4.59); Thracians (5.7).

other words, by classifying others I classify myself, and it seems that the translation is always made from the Greek into the native language, that is to say, the pantheon that provides the reference is the Greek one and the narrator always proceeds according to a system of presences and absences.

Should we conclude from this operation of translating names that the difference between these deities is no more than nominal, that all one need do is translate a name in order to discover the identity of its subject and that, in the last analysis, the gods are everywhere the same, even if not everywhere has the same gods? If that were the case, the place of the activity of translation would be assured, for the narrative would work to get under the heterogeneous surface-appearance of languages to reveal the identity of the substances lying beneath. And, over and above the diversity of geographical spaces, the unity of divine space would become apparent. That is what is suggested by the equivalences given for the name of Aphrodite Ourania, taken as a point of reference: Aphrodite Ourania is called Mylitta by the Assyrians, Alilat by the Arabs, Mitra by the Persians.[101] It is also what is suggested by the narrator's remarks about the "native goddess" (*authigenes*) of the Auseans and the Machyles, "whom we call Athena".[102] That "we" refers to the Greeks, distinguishing them from *them*, the Libyans, but all the same (for the one group as for the other) it is a matter of one and the same goddess. It is also what is suggested by the remarks on the subject of Linus, both the song and the personage, celebrated in Greece, Egypt, Phoenicia, Cyprus, and elsewhere. In Greece the name is Linus, in Egyptian it is Manerus, and "each nation has a name of its own for this, but it is the same song that the Greeks sing and call Linus."[103] Here again, over and above the diversity of names, the identity of the personage is the same.

On the other hand, the practices of the Geloni, a people situated to the north of the Scythians, appears to run counter to all this. They pray "in the Greek fashion" (*hellenikos*) to Greek gods (*theoi hellenikoi*).[104] Herodotus points out that the Geloni had Greek ancestors. As for Xerxes, he does not appear to believe in the unity of divine

101. Hdt. 1.131.
102. Hdt. 4.180.
103. Hdt. 2.79.
104. Hdt. 4.108.

space, for before he crosses into Europe over the Hellespont, he suggests praying to the gods "who hold Persia for their allotted realm" (*lelogchasi*).[105] Of course, that is Xerxes speaking. Herodotus does not lend this prayer his own backing.

In this operation, the most important moment is that of the naming, translation being, after all, simply a double naming. For the most part, the translation moves from a Greek term to a foreign one and the narrator never vouchsafes any explanation concerning the organization of the tables of equivalences: the translation is presented as if it went without saying and were well known. He does not justify it, lend it his own backing, nor even explain it. It is an agent of classification, that is to say, it is not intended to bring what is "other" closer to what is the same by listing differences, but is content to deploy the same categories of classification throughout the world. Thus, at the limit, it is not a matter of translation but, rather, of superimposing a grid onto the divine space of "others," a grid by means of which it may be decoded and so constructed. Under circumstances such as these, it is enough to "read" in accordance with the simple system of presences and absences.

Translation has led us to naming, and naming has turned out to be a way of classifying. Now, the one who is doing all this classifying, naming, and translating is the traveler. For the traveler is the one who knows the names: within the geographical space he can pick out the names of places, within the web of events he can pick out the names of the principal actors, and within the divine space he can pick out the names of the gods. He knows how to give *the* name to those listening to him (with all that such a sonorous pronouncement implies in the way of knowledge and power over those listening and also over the thing named); and, in an even more advantageous situation, he can emulate Adam and give *a* name to something that has never had one, no longer has one, or does not yet have one (so far as he knows, at any rate). He is carried away by a great appetite for naming and feels great jubilation as he does so. Herodotus frequently declares that he knows the names; that, as far as a certain point in the world, to the north or to the south, the names of the different peoples are known but beyond it nothing more is: "I know and can tell the names of all the peoples that dwell on the ridge as far as the

105. Hdt. 7.53.

Atlantes in Libya, but no further than that."[106] Elsewhere, he likes to emphasize that he could perfectly well give the names (for he has noted them down) of all the soldiers who took part in such and such a battle. He knows that Battus the stammerer is also Battus the king, he knows that the goddess of the Auseans and the Machlyes is the same one whom *we* call Athena. He is the one who makes it possible to pass from one label to another; he is the *poros* and guarantor of that passage.

One of the methods adopted by the narrative of Marco Polo is to progress from one exotic name to another, each time setting out whatever is remarkable about them. Léry, too, names first the flora, then the fauna, then the *nomoi* of the Tupi.

If it is true that naming is one of the mainsprings in the writing of a traveler's tale,[107] if it is true that pleasure is to be derived from naming, it is also true that translation, naming in translation, affords double the pleasure of naming and that it therefore takes its place as a figure of the rhetoric of otherness.

To Describe: To See and Make Seen

To describe is to see and make seen. It is to say what you have seen, all that you have seen, and nothing but what you have seen. But if you can only say what you have seen, you can only see what can be said:[108] you, the reader or the listener, but also you, the witness who reports.

In Herodotus, description holds an important place: the *Histories* may be regarded as now a juxtaposition, now an interlocking of descriptions and stories, or pictures and narratives. Descriptions juxtaposed: the four first books are, in the main, a description of the different *nomoi* of non-Greek peoples; the next five are a history of the Persian Wars. Descriptions interlocked: chapters 2 to 82 of Book 4 present a description of Scythia and a picture of its *nomoi*, while

---

106. Hdt. 4.185, and cf. 197.

107. See M. De Certeau: "Essentially, J. Verne's explorers are namers; they take part in the genesis of the world by naming. . . .The explorers give meaning to the gaps in the universe," in Jules Verne, *Les Grands Navigateurs du XVIIIᵉ siècle* (Paris, 1977), p. ix.

108. I am here referring to a colloquium held in Urbino (July 1977) on the subject of description and, in particular, to the comments of C. Imbert and P. Hamon.

chapter 1 and, later, chapters 83 to 144 are a narrative of Darius's expedition.

With the figure of Salmoxis[109] and, even more, with the description of the funerals of the kings,[110] we have already confronted the question of description. Before returning to those strange descriptions, I should like to consider another type of description which is very common in traveler's tales: the picture supported by a "seeing." For example, consider the description of the hippopotamus encountered in Egypt:

This is how they look: for their outward form, they are four-footed, with cloven hooves like oxen; their noses are blunt, they are maned like horses, with tusks showing (or, the tusks of a boar) and have a horse's tail and a horse's neigh; their size is that of the biggest oxen. Their hide is so thick that, when it is dried, spear shafts are made of it.[111]

The description of the nature (*phusis*) of a crocodile makes use of the same model. It is a quadruped that lives both on dry land and in the water; it lays eggs not much larger than a goose's but the little crocodile which emerges grows to be as long as seventeen cubits or more. It has the eyes of a pig and teeth that are large and projecting (or tusks like a wild boar). It is the only animal that has no tongue.[112]

There is assumed to be a line of demarcation between the world in which one speaks and the world that is spoken about, between "them" and "us," between "there" and "here." As Léry notes, at the beginning of his chapter "On the Animals, Deer, Large Lizards, Snakes, and Other Monstrous Beasts of America," "with regard to four-footed animals not only in general but without exception, there is not a single one to be found in this land of Brazil in America which is in every way similar to our own."[113] Difference thus reigns supreme. The problem is how to contain it. The "image of what is unlike" will be constructed in opposition to what is to be seen "here" and by virtue of the very fact that it will be an unfamiliar combination of forms that are current "here." Thus, the hippopotamus has features of an ox, a horse, even a boar, yet it is neither ox, horse, nor boar. The

109. Cf. above, pp. 84ff.
110. Cf. above, pp. 131ff.
111. Hdt. 2.71.
112. Hdt. 2.68.
113. Léry, *Histoire d'un voyage*, p. 105.

monster is always a combination of elements which are familiar,[114] and it is even desirable that every single element should be familiar so that the combination of them will be altogether monstrous.

Such a description is authorized by the eye of the witness, whether it be that of the principal narrator or that of a local or delegated narrator: "I have seen" or "he says that he has seen." The eye of the traveler is, moreover, in the position of a link connecting the heterogeneous elements that compose the various animals of "there"; it is he who sets up this combination and guarantees its veracity and so it is he who produces all these monstrosities through his way of selecting and assembling what is visible. Were it not for him, the elements would not hold together.

Having given a long and completely neutral description of the cannibalistic practices of the Tupinambas, using a technical vocabulary, Léry concludes his narrative as follows: "So that, *as I have seen*, is how the American savages cook the flesh of their prisoners of war: they smoke it, which is a way of roasting unknown to us."[115] The description thus establishes the practice of a type of roasting unknown in Europe and is based on an autopsy which authorizes it. It presents itself as a speaking eye, Léry's in this instance, an eye speaking without mediation, directly, and one that is objective or attempts to be so. The eye speaks and tells of what is to be seen.

When Herodotus describes the hippopotamus and the crocodile of Egypt or the hemp of Scythia,[116] and when Léry describes the tapir and the flora of the New World, they bring taxonomy into play; when the one constructs a picture of the Egyptian or Scythian world and the other a picture of the Tupi world, they engineer a spatializa-

---

114. R. Descartes, *Meditations on First Philosophy*, trans. J. Cottingham (Cambridge, England, 1986) I: "For even when painters try to create sirens and satyrs with the most extraordinary bodies, they cannot give them natures which are new in all respects; they simply jumble up the limbs of different animals. Or if perhaps they manage to think up something so new that nothing remotely similar has ever been seen before—something which is therefore completely fictitious and unreal—at least the colours in the composition must be real."

115. Léry, *Histoire d'un voyage*, p. 179.

116. Hdt. 4.74: "They have hemp growing in their country, very like flax save that the hemp is by much the thicker and taller. This grows both of itself and also by their sowing, and of it the Thracians even make garments which are very like linen; nor could any, were he not a past master in hemp, know whether they be hempen or linen; whoever has never yet seen hemp will think the garment to be linen."

tion of knowledge.[117] Hamon has shown that in naturalist texts, description introduced taxonomy into the narrative.[118] Taxonomy appeals not to the logical but to the lexical and metalinguistic skills of the reader. Of course, description cannot be reduced to taxonomy alone, for it is also the means for bringing the latter into play.

Neither Herodotus nor Léry is a naturalist, but it cannot be denied that in the works of both the descriptions do have something to do with taxonomy. A first conclusion may be drawn at this point: to describe is to see and make seen but, if it is concerned with space and with knowledge and if it involves a spatialization of knowledge— in short, a picture—to describe is also to know and to make known (that *make* refers precisely to the introduction of taxonomy).

These descriptions make things seen and known. Their focal point is the eye; it is the eye that organizes them (what is visible), that restricts over-proliferation and controls them (the field of vision), and that authenticates them (witness). It is thus the eye that makes the reader believe that he sees and knows; the eye produces *peitho*, persuasion: I have seen, it is true.[119]

If the eye, established within the description, is the point of view that constitutes it, what of the strange descriptions such as those of the ceremony in honor of Salmoxis, or the funeral rites of the Scythian kings, which appear to exclude the presence of an eye or, rather, if there is an eye it is one that belongs to nobody—just a speaking eye. In Herodotus, no separation is made between saying and seeing. To see and to say, what is seeable and what is sayable, overlap completely or, rather, do not belong to two separate spheres.

117. De Certeau, *L'Ecriture*, p. 235: "Objects are distributed over a *space* organized not in terms of localizations or geographical areas (such indications are extremely rare and always vague) but in terms of a taxonomy of living things (for example, when he is writing about birds, Léry refers to the famous *Histoire de la nature des oyseaux* [Paris, 1555], by P. Belon), a systematic inventory of philosophical 'questions,' etc.; in short, a reasoned 'table' of knowledge."

118. P. Hamon, "L'Appareil descriptif du texte naturaliste," colloquium at Urbino, 1977. The most striking example of a switch to taxonomy is probably that of the porthole of the *Nautilus* in *Twenty Thousand Leagues under the Sea*, in front of which passes a procession of all the fish and animals of the sea noted and classified in encyclopaedias.

119. One could challenge this process of making the reader believe, which is so fundamental for description, by considering, for example, texts that claim to have seen and that are not believed—Ctesias, etc.

The descriptions mentioned above (pictures of the world) called for emphatic indicators as to who is speaking ("I have seen"). Those we are now considering, in contrast, appear to lack such indicators altogether. They are not based on seeing, nor on any saying that, in the end, refers one, whether explicitly or implicitly, to an original seeing. All the same, although such indicators may not be positively present (neither the narrator nor any of his delegates appears to be present), might it not be possible to discern some hint of them?

Let us return to the narrative of the funeral rites of the kings, which begins as follows: "The burial places of the kings are in the land of the Gerrhi, which is where the Borysthenes ceases to be navigable. There [*enthauta*]. . . ."[120] What does this way of putting it imply? That one is speaking Greek, for to locate the tombs by stating them to be situated where the Borysthenes becomes unnavigable is clearly to be speaking Greek and addressing Greeks. It is surely safe to assume that the Scythians would not have used those particular terms, for they are quite irrelevant to their way of life. They are neither sailors nor river boatmen, but a people who depend on wagons and horses; they do not know how to make use of waterways except when these are frozen and can, precisely, be crossed by their wagons.[121] If I speak of the limits of the river's navigability, I am addressing myself to Greeks, among whom it is common practice to travel by boat and for whom, furthermore, a boat is a means of surveying and mapping a country (thus I specify that the river's course is navigable for forty days); in particular, perhaps, I am addressing the Greeks of the cities on the Black Sea, who have an interest in the possibilities of penetrating into the interior of these regions. Finally, I am also addressing other Greek travelers whose information I may complete or correct and, by specifying the spatial configuration of the frontier region, I am operating as a geographer. This limit is also the limit of knowledge; nobody knows what lies beyond. It is a limit of navigability which, as Herodotus constructs his world, becomes the limit of space and the limit of what is tellable: "beyond that, no man can say through what nations it flows."[122]

The "there" (*enthauta*) that immediately follows ("There . . . the

120. Hdt. 4.71.
121. Hdt. 4.28.
122. Hdt. 4.53.

Scythians dig a great four-cornered pit") comprises a measure of ambiguity. It is a "there" that is meaningful in relation to the Scythians (far away, to what is the north for them), but it is also meaningful in relation to the Greeks (far away, to what is the north for *us*). The same applies to the description of the land of the Gerrhi as *eschata*. For the Scythians it is indeed a frontier zone compared to where they normally live, and that is the very reason for their choosing it as the place to bury their kings. But it is also an *eschata* land in relation to me, a Greek, telling (or listening to) this narrative. The land of the Gerrhi, situated at the limit of the known world, is by definition a zone of margins. But from the point of view of a Greek, the whole land of Scythia is no less so.

Actually, the narrator's use of this term *eschata* conveys yet more. The country of the Gerrhi stands in relation to Scythia as *eschata* lands stand in relation to the territory of a city. When the funeral rites for the king take place, we find proof of the fact that it is indeed the Greek schema that implicitly underpins this representation of space. The Scythians turn the *eschata* lands into a center, but for their behavior to have any meaning, that is to say, for the addressee to decode it as a reversal of Greek funerary practices, it is necessary that in the shared knowledge of the Greeks an analogy between the Gerrhus and the *eschata* on the one hand and Scythia and the territory of a city on the other should at least be conceivable.

At the end of this text is another hint as to who is speaking, this time one more definite than that mentioned above: "So, having set horsemen *of this fashion* [*toioutous*] round about the tomb [these are the corpses of the fifty young men who have been stuffed], they ride away."[123] This *toioutous*, which brings the description to a close, enables the narrator both to evaluate the description he has just given and also to distance himself from it: "horsemen of this fashion, . . . well, I need say no more!"

Finally, one last hint appears in the parenthesis on the subject of slavery: "these are native-born Scythians, for only those serve the king whom he bids to do so, and none of the Scythians have servants [*therapontes*] bought by money [*arguronetoi*]." It is quite clear that

---

123. Hdt. 4.72. Furthermore, the *toioutous* balances the *hode* positioned a little before it.

this remark can only be addressed to Greek listeners, Athenians in particular perhaps, if is true that for them a slave was first and foremost a piece of merchandise which could be bought. That brief remark thus indicates the measure of the difference between "them" and "us."

Whereas at the end of the story of Salmoxis the narrator intervenes quite openly, speaking in the first person— "For myself, *I* neither disbelieve nor fully believe . . . but I think"—the same cannot be said of the first part, telling of the deputation to Salmoxis, which is much more mysterious but is quite deliberately left devoid of any explicit indicator as to who is speaking. Nevertheless, as in the case of the funeral rites, it seems to me that the source of the statement is hinted at. Thus, when Herodotus begins his chapter with the words "the Getae [*hoi athanatizontes*], those practitioners of immortality," he is letting his own voice be heard in the narrative, all the more so if we accept, with Linforth, that the expression is a quotation, if not a nickname, which evokes and ridicules the image of the Pythagoreans.[124] Applied as it is to the Getae, the expression provokes surprise and at the same time it classifies them. We may also call to mind the remark made about the *theos*, or heaven, which is a surreptitious importation from the Greek vision of the world and therefore a way of assessing the behavior of the Getae, who are busy shooting arrows at the sky: an action as pointless as it is derisory, truly that of people who do not know what they are doing.

In this way, these strange descriptions, although they lack clear indicators as to who is speaking, nevertheless contain hints. There may not be a particular eye at the focal point, but there are a number of winks which the addressee may seize upon.

These descriptions, whether "with an eye" or "without an eye," are all given in the present tense. Now, that present tense does not connote the actual present, "the time in which one is," that is to say, "the time in which one is speaking":[125] there is no simultaneity between the story and the narrative, between the funeral rites of the kings and Herodotus telling of them or writing about them.

---

124. Cf. above, and Linforth, "Greek Gods."

125. E. Benveniste, *Problems in General Linguistics*, vol. 1 (Coral Gables, 1971), p. 227.

This present tense, which instead connotes a temporal indeterminacy, is reserved for particular types of narrative (riddles, proverbs, scientific experiments, summaries of plots).[126] Grévisse calls it the "gnomic present."[127] Here, it tells of the Scythian *nomoi* relating to the royal funeral rites. According to Weinrich, the present is the most common of "commenting tenses" (and he distinguishes between two main categories of tenses, commenting ones and narrative ones).[128]

These descriptions in the "gnomic" present are, furthermore, intercalated between moments of action. Thus, the description of the Scythian *nomoi* is intercalated between Darius's decision to take revenge on the Scythians and the preparations he makes for doing so. The impact of the present tense is therefore also determined by the references to the "narrative time" of the action. When the description begins, there is a switch to the present tense; then, at the end of the description, a return to the aorist and the narrative proper.

Alongside the present tense, we find pronouns used as descriptive operators: the description is introduced by *tode, toionde, tonde ton tropon, hode*, "this," "thus," "in this way," "this is how"; in short, for the most part by what are known as demonstrative first-person pronouns. We should therefore ponder their relationship to the discourse as a whole: are they not a discreet form of indicator as to the source of the statement?[129] But perhaps that is not quite the right way to pose the question, for it is noticeable that these first-person pronouns which introduce a description are generally followed by second-person pronouns which bring it to a conclusion: *houtos, toioutos, houto*, "that," "that is how." So what we have here is a method of oral composition, namely, ring composition (this is how they bury their kings . . . that is how they bury their kings). These indicators nevertheless provide a way for the narrator to intervene in the text, albeit at a different level: by drawing attention to the construction of the text and the fashion in which it is divided up, he is organizing his narrative from within. In connection with an operation such as this, in which the narrator himself is at work on his

126. G. Genette, *Figures III* (Paris, 1972), p. 228.
127. M Grévisse, *Le Bon Usage*, § 115.
128. H. Weinrich, *Le Temps* (trans. Paris, 1973), p. 39.
129. On deictics, see the remarks of Benveniste, *Problems*, pp. 217–22.

narrative material, we may adopt the terminology of Genette and speak of the presence of "stage directions."[130]

At nightfall, on the terraces of the royal palace, Marco Polo and Kublai Khan talk together, and the emperor has the towns in his empire described to him through the intermediary of this foreign ambassador. On one particular evening, Kublai Khan presses for descriptions of one town after another until Marco Polo's vast repertoire is quite exhausted:

"Sire, now I have told you of all the cities I know."
"There remains one about which you never speak."
Marco Polo inclined his head.
"Venice," said the Khan.
Marco smiled. "And what else did you think I was telling you about?"[131]

This dialogue squarely poses the fundamental question: in the last analysis, what does a traveler talk about? About what is "the same" or about what is "other"? The traveler's procedure comes down to constructing an image of what is other that will be a "telling" one for the audience from the world of the same. Now, seen from the point of view of the traveler's tale, descriptions are among the procedures which allow the narrator to produce and convey an impression of otherness. That is their main effect, and it is to the extent to which they aim to produce it that they form part and parcel of the traveler's "project."

One way of producing this impression of otherness is to describe practices which are abominable (to us) in an altogether neutral fashion, even using technical vocabulary, as if they were the simplest and most common practices in the world. When Herodotus describes the ritual of Salmoxis or the macabre ring of stuffed horsemen, he does so in neutral terms just as, when Léry describes the cannibalistic behavior of the Tupinambas, he gives a detailed account of all the operations and notes that this is a method of roasting that is quite unknown to us. This way of indicating the otherness of savages or barbarians may be used both in descriptions organized around one eye in particular, with emphatic indicators as to who is speaking, and, equally, in descriptions where such indicators are

130. Genette, *Figures III*, p. 262.
131. I. Calvino, *Le città invisibili* (Turin, 1972), p. 94.

present only in the form of hints; but is the overall effect produced in the two cases exactly the same?

A description of the first type involves an explicit introduction of taxonomy (the description of the hippopotamus or the tapir); the impression of otherness made on the addressee is a deliberate and calculated effect. Again, it may construct an impression of otherness but do so by instructing one how to read it. For example, when Herodotus describes the sacrificial customs of the Scythians he notes at one point that the Scythians strangle the victim, "lighting no fire, nor consecrating the first fruits nor pouring any libation."[132] The string of negatives points to a difference and conveys the meaning, even the measure of it: that (in part) is the extent of the otherness of Scythian sacrifice. To put it another way, this description is like a picture with its legend, for it is presented accompanied by directions as to how to "read" it.

In contrast, the second type of description, which cannot be referred to an explicit point of view, does not make the differences explicit nor does it provide instructions as to how it should be read. If the first type of description is like a picture with a legend, the second is like a picture without one or like a picture whose legend (that is, the hints as to the source of the statement) is disseminated within it. Of course, it is quite possible to slip imperceptibly from one form to the other, the only indication of the shift being the presence or absence of a number of rhetorical figures. Thus, the second type of description does not make use of comparison (*a* there is like *b* here) or analogy (*a* is to *b* there what *c* is to *d* here) or negation; it does, on the other hand, resort to inversion.

Considering that it provides neither the meaning nor the measure of the differences, it could be said that it creates a more powerful impression of otherness than the first type of description and that this is indeed precisely the effect it is intended to make on the addressee. Consider the great macabre scene of the Scythian funeral rites. It is a picture without a legend, or perhaps a *fable* to the extent

132. Hdt. 4.60. It might be objected that this description is not organized around an authorizing eye. However, to the extent that it conveys a negation, there is at least an indirect implication of a reference-eye, which gives a measure of the differences.

that it is simply proffered, leaving the addressee to provide a legend or calculate what it means.

The absence of indicators as to who is speaking or the deletion of such indicators is thus one technique the narrator employs to increase the impression of otherness made by his narrative: he seems to be presenting the otherness in its "crude" or "wild" state. Meanwhile, the hints that appear here or there in the description, pointing to the source of the statement, are addressed to the implicit knowledge of the addressee, and they orient his reception of it.

To describe is to see and make seen, but the swift realization that description introduces taxonomy into the narrative leads one to add that to describe is also to know and make known or even to allow knowledge to be seen.[133]

But within a particular narrative, description also has another function. The knowledge that it allows to be seen is not simply juxtaposed alongside the telling of events; it has an effect within the narrative as a whole. For example, the description of the ceremonies in honor of Salmoxis makes known why it is that of all the Thracians the Getae are the only ones to stand up to Darius (because they have Salmoxis); there is, then, no radical opposition between narrating and describing.

Studying description as a procedure used in the rhetoric of otherness leads one to the question of belief. How is the credibility of the discourse, which depends on an interplay between the eye and the ear, produced?

The Excluded Middle

By way of conclusion to these notes on Herodotus's rhetoric of otherness, let us consider one more feature of the narrative that tells of "what is other": it is what might be called the rule of the excluded middle. Or, rather, it is not so much a rule obeyed by the narrator or procedures he deliberately adopts, as a rhythm, a beat which runs through the narrative. It appears that, in the end, in its effort to translate the "other" the narrative proves unable to cope with more than two terms at a time.

133. In both senses of the expression: the narrator shows that he knows and is therefore to be believed, and the description makes the addressee see the scene.

Take the Greeks, the Persians, and the Scythians: they fight, the Persians against the Scythians and the Greeks against the Persians. In Greece, the Persians behave as "Persians," that is to say as people who do not know how to fight, as anti-hoplites.[134] But in Scythia, faced with Scythians, their only thought is of pitched battle according to all the rules of Greek "traditional strategy." They therefore conduct themselves in the manner of hoplites and in this sequence are portrayed as "Greeks." Why do they take on a different aspect when they move from one space to another?

How is it possible to convey the otherness of Persian practices to the Greek addressee when what the narrator is, for the moment, interested in is the Scythians' way of fighting and when his purpose is to show that the Scythians live as they fight and fight as they live? It seems that, incapable of coping with a twofold otherness and translating it, the narrative operates by making a shift. To make the Scythian otherness more appreciable, all it need do is turn the Persians into "Greeks." There are no longer three terms, the Greeks and their way of fighting, the Persians and their way of fighting, and the Scythians and their way of fighting; there are only two, the Scythians and the "Persians/Greeks."

In a similar fashion, the story of the Amazons starts off with a triangular arrangement, with the Greeks, the Scythians, and the Amazons all on stage.[135] But imperceptibly, in order to bring out the otherness of the Amazons, the narrative changes the Scythians into "Greeks." We find the Scythians reasoning like Greeks (one does not make war against women) and it seems that for them, too, the polarity between war and marriage is meaningful. Furthermore, schemata relating to the *ephebeia* may also be at work: the Amazon way of life is "suited" to ephebes. When the matter of marriage between the Amazons and the young Scythians arises, the model to which the narrative implicitly refers is the Greek one. Finally, except for living in wagons, the Scythian women are regarded by the Amazons as Greek women, given as they are to "women's work" (*erga gunaikeia*).

The rhetoric of otherness thus tends to be dual and, as might be expected in this narrative, *alter* truly does mean the other one (of two).

134. Cf. above, pp. 46ff. 135. Cf. above, pp. 209ff.

Seven

The Eye and the Ear

So the traveler's tale translates what is other, and the rhetoric of otherness is the means by which the translation is effected: it is what makes the addressee believe that the translation is a faithful one.[1] Overall, it produces the effect of belief. But how does it create that effect? How does it make it credible? Through the use of certain rhetorical figures, through the implementation of the procedures which we have identified as belonging to it, through their manipulation each time the narrator intervenes in his narration. Description, for example, certainly consists in making seen and making known; but from the point of view of the transcription of otherness, what is important is the presence or absence of strong indicators as to who is speaking: depending on whether or not the description is organized around an initial "I have seen," the impression of strangeness it makes on the listeners will vary.

Fundamentally, the two poles between which this rhetoric is contained and deployed are the eye and the ear—the eye of the traveler, the ear of the public (but also the ear of the traveler and the eye of the public)—but the path linking the eye and the ear is not a linear one. On the contrary, there exists a whole network of corridors, stairs, and bridges, which break off to resume further on, sometimes on a different level. And the ways through this edifice or

1. In connection with the whole of this chapter, the reader may refer to F. Haible, "Herodot und die Wahrheit: Wahrheitsbegriff, Kritik und Argumentation bei Herodot," diss. Tübingen, 1963.

scaffolding correspond to all the different forms of utterance as they are combined by the narrator.

I Have Seen, I Have Heard

The eye or, rather, autopsy: by this I mean the eye used as an indicator as to who is speaking, the "I have seen" as an intervention in his narrative on the part of the narrator, as a way of providing proof. I will limit myself to a brief resumé of the context for Herodotus's autopsy. As Benveniste has pointed out, *histor*, at a very ancient date, meant "witness," "a witness in that he *knows*, but first and foremost in that he has seen." In Homer, when oaths are sworn, appeal is made to the gods that they should know, that is to say, that they should see and stand as witnesses to the oath: "Let Zeus . . . the Earth, the Sun know [*histo*]" (*Il.* 19.258ff.). In this respect, Greek resembles other Indo-European languages, and "the correct meaning of the root *wid* is illuminated by the rule set out in the *Satapatha Brahmana:* "If, now, two men are in dispute [in litigation], one saying, 'I saw for myself' and the other saying 'I heard for myself,' the one who says 'I saw for myself' is the one whom we must believe."[2]

Second, autopsy refers us in two different directions, at the intersection of which Herodotus's work is positioned: on the one hand to epic, on the other to the Ionian thinkers of the sixth century B.C. Homer distinguishes between witnessing by seeing and other types of witnessing, in particular by hearing, and the expression "to see with one's eyes," that is to say, "to see with one's own eyes," carries more persuasion than simply "to see," especially when it is a matter of some astonishing or marvelous (*thaumasion*) phenomenon.[3] To say that one has seen it with one's own eyes is both to "prove" the marvel, and the truth: "I have seen it, it is true and it is true that it is a marvel."

From the philosophers of Ionia down to Aristotle, including the

---

2. E. Benveniste, *Vocabulaire des institutions indo-européennes* (Paris, 1969), vol. 2, p. 173. In Latin, in contrast, if the gods' names are taken in the swearing of an oath, they are called on to "hear" (*audi*): "For the Roman, who attaches such importance to the utterance of solemn formulae, seeing is less important than hearing." On the *histor* as *Richter*, see P. Hohti, *Arctos* 10 (1976): 37–48.

3. G. Nenci, "Il motivo dell'autopsia nella storiografia greca," *Studi Classici e Orientali* 3 (1953): 14–46.

doctors and the historians, sight was considered an instrument of knowledge. That remark is not intended to reduce all these types of discourses to a single common denominator, but simply to indicate what is indisputably "a constant epistemological assumption."[4] Xenophanes says that in order to know it is necessary to have seen,[5] and in the first lines of *Metaphysics*, Aristotle writes: "We prefer sight, generally speaking, to all the other senses. The reason for this is that, of all the senses, sight best helps us to know things, and reveals many distinctions."[6] And Heraclitus concludes that "the eyes are more trustworthy [*akribesteroi martures*] witnesses than the ears."[7]

That this is a constant assumption is borne out by the fact that Lucian attributes that observation of Heraclitus's to Herodotus.[8] And it is true that a formula very close to it does appear in the *Histories*, not pronounced by the author himself as he reflects on the historian's profession, but in the course of a story he tells. Candaules, the king of Lydia, seeks to convince Gyges, his close friend, of the beauty of his wife. Soon after his marriage "Candaules, being doomed to ill-fortune, spoke thus to Gyges: 'I think Gyges, that you do not believe what I tell you of the beauty of my wife; men trust their ears less than their eyes [*ota gar eonta apistotera opthalmon*];

4. A. Rivier, "Remarques sur les fragments 34 et 35 de Xénophane," *Etudes de littérature grecque* (Geneva, 1975), p. 344.

5. Ibid.; the earlier bibliography is to be found in the notes.

6. Aristotle *Metaphysics* 980a25.

7. Heraclitus, 22 B 101a (D.-K.). We may also note the following remark attributed to Thales (Stobaeus *Florilegium* 3.12.14 Wachsm.): when asked how much distance separated the truth from lies, he answered "as much as that between the eye and the ear"—a manifestly ambiguous formulation, since that distance is both minimal and huge. Nenci ("Il motivo," p. 27), who comments on that remark, also includes in this collection of texts to do with autopsy the opening lines of the *Thesmophoriazusae* (5–18), where Aristophanes caricatures such discussions on the eye and the ear: "But there is no need for you to hear what you will soon be seeing with your own eyes." "What's that? Say it again: there is no need for me to hear . . . ?" "No, what you are going to see." "And there is no need either for me to see . . . ?" "No, what you are going to hear." "What advice you give me! But you do speak cleverly: you say that I should neither hear nor see?" "The two things are indeed naturally distinct."

8. Noted by G. Schepens, "Ephore sur la valeur de l'autopsie," *Ancient History* (1971): 166. This article provides a bibliography on the problem of autopsy and a discussion of Nenci's point of view on the indifference toward autopsy shown by historians after Thucydides.

do you, then, contrive so as to see her naked.'"9 As well as this apologist for "seeing is believing," the narrator himself on several occasions makes use of autopsy to support his narrative: "I have seen with my own eyes as far as the city of Elephantine, and beyond that I learned by question [*historeon*] and hearsay."10 The eye of the traveler thus marks out the geographical space, dividing it into more or less well known zones (ranging from "what I have seen with my own eyes" through "what others have seen" to "what no one has seen") and similarly, within the space of his narrative, the eye of the narrator or, as the case may be, that of one of his delegates divides up different zones according to the greater or lesser degree of their credibility to the addressee.

At the very start of his book, Marco Polo affirms the eminent worthiness of autopsy, which is the guarantor of what he says: "In this way, our book will recount to you [all the greatest marvels and diversities of Greater Armenia] clearly and in orderly fashion, just as Sire Marco Polo, the wise and noble Venetian from Venice, describes them, for he has seen them with his own eyes."11 As well as calling on autopsy, the statement is remarkable by reason of the equation it assumes between the orderliness of vision and the orderliness of exposition. The book "will recount to you clearly and in orderly fashion just as" Marco Polo has seen it to be; between seeing and saying (not to mention writing) is no distance at all. They are all controlled by the same "order."

In similar fashion, Léry declares that to tackle an undertaking such as his successfully, what is needed are "good feet and a good eye," for it is a matter of "seeing and visiting." And, as he states in his preface, his narrative is simply the sum total of the "notable things observed by me in my travels." That statement likewise presupposes an equation, not exactly between the visible and the sayable, but between what is observable and what is notable: I have observed what was notable and I have noted what was observable. The veracity of the statements is founded on autopsy. In addition, autopsy accounts for why the author writes as he does. It justifies the repeated presence of strong indicators as to who is speaking: "If anyone should deem it wrong that, when I speak hereafter of how

9. Herodotus, 1.8.
10. Hdt. 2.29; cf. also 2.99, 156, 4.16.
11. Marco Polo, *La Description du Monde*, ed. L. Hambis (Paris, 1955), p. 1.

savages behave (as if *I were trying to seem important*), I so frequently
use the following way of talking: 'I saw, I happened to be there, that
happened to me, and so on,' I would reply that, quite apart from the
fact that these are matters that I know about, furthermore, you might
say, it is a way of speaking of knowledge, that is to say, of things seen
and experienced."[12] Do not take these signs as marks of vanity, for
they are really the marks of a scientific approach—all the more
reason for you to believe me. Lescarbot, at the end of the sixteenth
century, showed that he fully recognized the value of autopsy when
he set out the reasons for his voyage to Canada: "Being anxious, not
so much simply to travel, but to recognize the world with my own
eyes."[13] Generally speaking, what moves these travelers is "curiosity," which means "the power of wide-open eyes and acceptance of
the diversity of the world"; thus, traveler's "discover strange things in
just the same way as they would calmly draw up an inventory"; they
"are not amazed, but note things down."[14] The eye writes; at least, so
the narrative would have us believe.

This connection between vision and persuasion became a juridical
principle in the Indian text mentioned above: the one who has seen
is to be believed. The traveler's tale turns the connection into a
principle of writing and a persuasive argument aimed at the addressee. The "I have seen" is, as it were, an operator of belief. Just
before the battle of Salamis, Aristides, noticing that the Persians
have surrounded the Greeks during the night, comes to warn
Themistocles and asks him to alert the council of allies. The latter
(despite knowing full well what is going on, since it was he himself
who suggested this maneuver to the Persians) tells him: it is better
that it should be you, who have seen what the Persians are up to with
your own eyes, who takes this piece of news to the allied generals, for
they will be more inclined to believe you.[15] In another example,
vision and persuasion are interestingly and more subtly associated,
for here we find an analogical autopsy. The Carthaginians *say* that

12. J. de Léry, *Histoire d'un voyage fait en la terre de Brésil*, ed. M. Contat
(Lausanne), p. 24.
13. M. Lescarbot, cited by A. Dupront, "Espace et humanisme," *Bibliothèque
d'Humanisme et Renaissance*, vol. 8 (Paris, 1946), p. 95.
14. Ibid., pp. 25ff., where Dupront analyzes curiosity.
15. Hdt. 8.80.

there is a lake in Libya where girls extract flakes of gold from the mud, using birds' feathers coated with pitch. At this point the narrator makes an intervention: "Is it true? I do not know, I am writing what is said. But anything is possible." I myself, "I have seen," at Zakynthos (that is, in Greece) a lake from which pitch is extracted by means of branches. In this case the pitch is what is extracted, in the other it is what is used as a tool of extraction. Nevertheless, the conclusion is that this story conforms [*oikota*] to the truth; "conforms" does not mean that it is necessarily true, simply that it is "in conformity" with the truth, that it "resembles" the truth founded on autopsy, that structurally there is no break between what the Carthaginians say and what the narrator has seen.[16]

This pride of place given to autopsy in any form of inquiry (*historie*) produces a number of consequences for history in the strict sense of the term. If one applies this methodological principle to the letter, the only history possible is contemporary history. Such is, indeed, Thucydides' position: for him, the only history that it is possible to produce is the history of the present. He set himself to that task at the start of the Peloponnesian War and relied on *opsis* to complete it successfully. The only events he regards as certain are those at which he himself was present and "those which his contemporaries observed or could have observed themselves, when the report that they give of them stands up to examination. . . . Experience upon which historical knowledge [*saphos eidenai*] is founded is not reduced solely to the sense of sight, but it is organised on the basis of the evidence that the latter procures."[17] Thus, nothing assured can be said of past events and there can be no question of putting one's trust in the poets who have sung of them or the logographers who have recounted them: "Serious Greek historical writing was about contemporary history," writes M. I. Finley,[18] who then cites the following passage by Collingwood, which is perhaps "too simple . . . but not simply false": "The Greek historian cannot,

16. Hdt. 4.195; on the stronger meaning of *oikotes*, see Rivier, "Remarques," p. 352.

17. Rivier, "Remarques," p. 345; cf. F. Jacoby, *Atthis: The Local Chronicles of Ancient Athens* (Oxford, 1969), p. 216 and p. 389 n. 3. The passages in which Thucydides makes his position clear are 1.1; 1.21; 1.22.2; 1.73.2.

18. M. I. Finley, *The Use and Abuse of History* (Oxford, 1975), p. 31.

like Gibbon, begin by wishing to write a great historical work and go on to ask himself what he should write about. . . . Instead of the historian choosing the subject, the subject chooses the historian; I mean that history is written only because memorable things have happened which call for a chronicler among the contemporaries of the people who have seen them. One might almost say that in ancient Greece there were no historians in the sense in which there were artists and philosophers; there were no people who devoted their lives to the study of history; the historian was only the autobiographer of his generation and autobiography is not a profession."[19]

Thucydides, for whom the only history possible is contemporary history, was, paradoxically enough, to be promoted to the very topmost rank of the historians of antiquity (in the nineteenth century) by men for whom history could only be written about the past.[20] Thucydides, the historian of the present, became a model for the positivist historians, people for whom history meant history of the past. "The history of a period is only born when that period is quite dead; the domain of history is the past."[21] Writing history meant consulting archives and unfolding long chains of events, all in the past.

But having been thus exorcised, the current event is today making a comeback. It is different now, a product of the mass media, and the question of contemporary history is thus posed anew. Now, does not the return of the current event also imply the return of the eye? "The symbolic beginning of contemporary history," wrote the French historian P. Nora, "might well be Goethe's words at Valmy, 'And you will be able to say, I was there!'"; in other words, autopsy. To which one might oppose Fabrice del Dongo's uncertainty, after the battle of Waterloo, "his greatest concern being to know whether he really had been present at the battle." But the point is that the current event which is making a comeback is staged and, as it is set up to be seen, it constructs its own field of visibility. "It is never without its reporter-spectator and its spectator-reporter; it is seen as it happens and this 'voyeurism' gives the current event its own specificity in relation to

19. R. G. Collingwood, *The Idea of History* (Oxford, 1946), p. 26.
20. A. Momigliano, *Studies in Historiography* (London, 1966), p. 218.
21. J. Thiénot, *Recueil de rapports sur les progrès des lettres et des sciences en France*, Rapports sur les etudes historiques (Paris, 1867), p. 356.

history and its already historical smell."[22] Autopsy it may be, but autopsy of a different kind, constructed autopsy.

The first form of history, the one Hegel calls "original history,"[23] is organized around an "I have seen" and, from the point of view of what is said, that "I have seen" lends credibility to the statement insofar as I say what I have seen. Through my discourse I render visible what is invisible (for you).[24] In contrast, in the second type of history, which we may as well call positivist, indicators as to who is speaking are deleted and frowned upon. The long chain of events is unrolled in the silence of the archives, stretching from the links that are causes to those that are consequences. Although indicators as to the source of the statement are absent, there are still hints—in the form of footnotes, for example, footnotes that signal "I have read," that is to say, "I too have read." We have both read; I am credible, and you can recognize me as your peer.[25] With the return of the current event, the situation changes. For if "I have seen" the event, *you* have seen it too. Under these circumstances, to be a historian is no longer to say what I have seen, for what would be the point? It is more a matter of pondering what is visible and the conditions of visibility. What is it that is visible? Not *what* have I seen, but *what is it* that I have seen?

J.-L. Borges observes: "A Chinese writer has remarked that by very reason of its anomalies, a unicorn would pass unnoticed. The eyes see what they are accustomed to see. Tacitus did not notice the Crucifixion, although he noted it down in his book" (*Enquêtes*, p. 249–50). In other words, the visible is not something given, which is immutable; it ought to be possible to write a history of the eye and what is visible. That has been superbly demonstrated by *The Birth of the Clinic*, on the topic of the medicine of the second half of the eighteenth century. As the subtitle of this work indicates, what

22. Nora, "Le Retour," p. 218, to which we may add the following remarks by J.-L. Borges, *Enquêtes* (Paris, 1957), p. 249: "Since that day (Valmy), historical days have abounded and one of the tasks facing governments (particularly in Italy, Germany, and Russia) has been to fabricate or simulate them, relying heavily upon preliminary propaganda and persistent publicity. Such days, reflecting the influence of Cecil B. de Mille, have less to do with history than with journalism. I have sometimes suspected that history, real history, is more modest and that its essential dates may sometimes remain secret for many years."
23. G. W. F. Hegel, "Introduction," *Philosophy of History*, (New York, 1956).
24. K. Pomian, "Entre l'invisible et le visible," *Libre 3* (1978): p. 23.
25. M. de Certeau, *L'Écriture de l'histoire* (Paris, 1975), pp. 72–73.

Foucault wanted to write was "an archaeology of medical perception." It would, equally, be interesting to write an archaeology of
historical perception, but probably impossible to do so where
ancient Greece is concerned.

In the work of a naturalist such as Aldrovandi, Buffon was amazed
to find, alongside correct remarks (that is to say, remarks suited to
natural history) a whole "hodgepodge of writing," a jumble of
quotations, fables, mythology. "There is no description here, only
legend," he said. Foucault explains this as follows: "Aldrovandi was
neither a better nor a worse observer than Buffon; he was neither
more credulous than he nor less attached to the faithfulness of the
observing eye or to the rationality of things. His observation was
simply not linked to things in accordance with the same system or by
the same arrangement of the *episteme*."[26]

That poses the problem squarely. What was the situation in
Greece in the sixth and fifth centuries B.C.? I do not know and so will
limit myself here to two remarks concerning the visible and the
invisible and the division between the two. For the visible and the
invisible to be divided into two clearly distinguishable domains, it is
necessary that "the opposition between *being* and *appearing* should
have developed its first consequences and that the *phanera* or
phainomena, interpreted as appearances, should have found a basis
in the sphere of *aphane* or *adela*, that is, of invisible things."[27] That
was happening during the fifth century, as a consequence of the
inquiries of the Eleatics. But until then there had been no *phenomena;* beings and things had manifested nothing but themselves.

The word *opsis* means "sight" (subjective and objective), presence
but also dreams.[28] Herodotus uses the word in the latter sense at
least twenty-one times.[29] A dream is thus a part of what is visible, and
for the one who dreams it counts as autopsy. It causes one to believe

26. M. Foucault, *The Order of Things* (London, 1974), p. 39.

27. Rivier, "Remarques," p. 364.

28. Like our word *vision;* the point is, precisely, that to have had a vision is not to
have seen. *Opsis* also means the vision of the initiate in a mystery religion, the
epoptie.

29. Hdt. 1.34, 38 (Croesus), 107, 108 (Astyages), 209 (Cyrus), 2.139 (the Ethio-
pian), 141 (Sethos), 3.30, 65 (Cambyses), 124 (the daughter of Polycrates), 149
(Otanes), 4.172 (Nasamons), 5.56 (Hipparchus), 6.107 (Hippias), 118 (Datis), 131
(Agaristes), 7.12, 15, 18, 19 (Xerxes), 8.54 (Xerxes).

and to take action (more often than not, precisely the action that should not be taken). When Xerxes is on the point of deciding to abandon his project of an expedition to Greece, the same dream returns to him night after night and persuades him against it.[30] So in the world of the *Histories,* the "invisible" seems to encroach on the visible; a dream is visible, or at any rate it is on the side of the visible. However, the question is rather more complicated than that, for dreams are not equally distributed among the different peoples. The fact is that dreams come only to barbarians (in particular to the Great Kings) and to tyrants. The pair constituted by the visible and the invisible thus operates differently depending on which side of the Aegean Sea is involved.[31] On the Asiatic side the invisible is seen, on the Greek side it is said. In Greece, that of course means the oracle, that is to say, words which fill the role played in Asia by the dream (within the context of the *Histories,* at any rate).

More fundamentally, what is at stake when one ponders the conditions of visibility is the question of what is visible and what is sayable. I see, I say; I say what I see; I see what I can say, I say what I can see. The relationship between the two is implicitly posed as an equation. Marco Polo "recounts clearly and in an orderly fashion," just as he has seen, while Léry closely associates that which can be noted with that which can be observed. There is no separation between the way you see and the way you say. In the last analysis the problem concerns the structures of language and of what is visible: Is "the framework of reality drawn by the model of language"[32] the same for Herodotus as for the doctors of the eighteenth century?

After *opsis* comes *akoe*: not "I have seen" but "I have heard"; it is a second way for the narrator to intervene in his narrative, another kind of indicator as to the source of the statement. The "I have heard" takes over from the "I have seen" when the latter is not, or is no longer, possible. As the story of Gyges reminds us, from the point of view of credibility the ear rates lower than the eye. It follows that a narrative attached to an "I have heard" will be less credible or less

30. Hdt. 7.12–18.
31. The only Greek personage in the *Histories* (Hdt. 6.131) to have a dream, apart from the tyrants, is Agariste, the granddaughter of Megacles. While pregnant, she dreamed that she gave birth to a lion; shortly afterward, she brought Pericles into the world.
32. M. Foucault, *The Birth of the Clinic* (London, 1973), p. 74.

persuasive than another, set in proximity to it, which is organized around an "I have seen." This indicator as to the source of the statement is less strong. The narrator commits himself less fully, stands back somewhat from his narrative, and the listener is allowed more latitude to qualify his belief; he is held on a looser rein.

In a positive sense, *akoe* means "I have found out" (*punthanomai*), "I have made inquiries" (*historeo*)[33] among people who "say," having seen for themselves or having heard from others who have seen, or who say that they have seen, and so forth. *Akoe* takes not one form only but several, and therefore operates on a number of different levels. First level: "I have not seen" but "I have [myself] heard" (*autekoos*). On his visit to the labyrinth in Egypt, Herodotus draws a clear distinction between what he has seen (the upper chambers) and what he has not been permitted to see (the lower chambers) and about which he speaks from hearsay.[34] Similarly, concerning everything beyond the city of Elephantine, he has made inquiries, he has asked questions, he has listened (*akoe historeon*).[35] Ctesias of Cnidus, the historian of the fourth century B.C., adopts the same method, but does so in order to criticize Herodotus and convict him of lying. Ctesias, too, states that he himself has seen what he writes, and anything he has not seen, he has himself heard (*autekoon*) at first hand.[36]

There are further levels: *akoe* is no longer firsthand and the string of mediators may stretch out further and further into the distance. When Herodotus wants to speak of what lies "above" Scythia, he explicitly states that nobody knows exactly (*oide atrekeos*). "I can learn from none who claims to know as an eye witness. For even Aristeas [a poet] . . . did not claim to have gone beyond the Issedones . . . ; but he spoke of what lay northward, by hearsay [*akoe*], saying that the Issedones had so told him. But as far as we have been able to reach by hearsay of exact reports [*atrekeos*] of the farthest land, all shall be set forth."[37] Similarly, nobody knows for certain (*sapheos*) about the deserts of Libya from which the Nile flows. All the same, I have heard things from the Cyrenaeans, who

33. Jacoby, *Atthis*, pp. 216ff.
34. Hdt. 2.148.
35. Hdt. 2.29.
36. Jacoby, *FGrHist*, 688 T 8 (Ctesias).
37. Hdt. 4.16; 3.115: "nor have I been able to learn from one who has seen it that there is a sea beyond Europe, to the north."

themselves heard them from the king of the Ammonians, who himself had heard them from the Nasamons, who themselves were repeating what they had heard some "young fools," who had ventured into those parts, claim that they had seen.[38] The distance between the *opsis* and the *akoe* may thus vary considerably, the extreme example being this last one in which no fewer than four successive mediators are needed before we come to the "I have seen" on which the report is founded, and this last eye is only that of some "young fools" (*hubristes*).

Akoe also has a role to play when it is a matter not of advancing to the limits of the earth but of going back in time, but in this case the "I have heard" refers back to an original speaker, usually described as "knowing" (*logios*). In Egypt, these speakers are the priests.[39] "Thus far all I have said is the outcome of my own sight [*opsis*], judgement [*gnome*] and enquiry [*historie*]. Henceforth, I will record what the Egyptians say [that is to say, the priests, about Egypt's past], according to that which I have heard."[40]

Finally, there is the last and lowest level of *akoe*, the one grammars refer to as the impersonal passive: "*legetai*, it is said that," "there is an account which says." This is a kind of floating narrative. It is not known when, how, by whom, or for whom it was produced. It is an utterance without either an utterer or an addressee, or so it would appear. There is no strong indicator as to the source of the statement, but that is not to say either that the narrator credits it totally or that he altogether disbelieves it. The source of the statement may manifest itself more subtly, through *hints*,[41] and may thus discreetly qualify the "it is said."[42] These reported statements are like so many

38. Hdt. 2.32.

39. Hdt. 2.3. Among the priests, those of Heliopolis are said to be the most knowledgeable (*logiotatoi*) of the Egyptians. Among the Egyptians, those who live "in the region where seed is sown" are by far the wisest (*logiotatoi*) as regards the past (2.77). Concerning the ancient causes for the hostility between Greeks and barbarians, the Persian wise men (*logioi*) say . . . (1.1).

40. Hdt. 2.99; or again, on the subject of the past of the Carians (1.171), "so far as I can learn by hearsay [*akoe*]."

41. For hints of the source of an utterance, see, for example, the story of Salmoxis, above, pp. 104ff.

42. It would practically be a matter of studying each case; a list of them is to be found in Jacoby, *RE*, p. 399. For a study of the use of *legetai* in Thucydides (to some extent different from that in Herodotus) see H. D. Westlake, "*Legetae* in Thucydides," *Mnémosyne* 4 (1977): 345–62.

citations, cited by nobody and from nobody, and their authority
varies from one context to another.

This distinction between *opsis* and *akoe* is also made in the
introduction to Marco Polo's book: "No doubt there are some things
here which he did not see; but he was told of them by men worthy of
trust and of being cited. That is why we shall present things seen as
seen and things heard as heard, so that our book may be sincere and
true, without lies, and so that what it says may not be taxed for being
fable."[43] The adoption of such a methodological position carries a
certain weight as a guarantee of credibility. By making this distinction, I reinforce the credibility and veracity of the "I have seen" and
at the same time also the credibility and veracity of the "I have
heard," which is presented not as the absolute truth but as a faithful
report of a particular account. What I am recounting may be
incredible but it is no "fable," and I am no liar.

The juridical sense of *histor* (the one we should believe is the one
who has seen, not the one who has heard) is a clear expression of the
ear's inferiority to the eye. For Thucydides, historical knowledge is
founded above all on *opsis* (either I have myself seen or I have
questioned somebody who has seen, and both cases rate as *opsis*).
Akoe has no great value as truth and there is therefore no way of
knowing the past with any certainty.[44] Is that also Herodotus's view?
The story of Gyges seems to suggest so. Nevertheless, alongside the
phrase "I know through having seen" we find "I know through having
heard." In both cases the narrator produces knowledge (*oida*), but in
the first it is founded on *opsis*, while in the second it depends on
akoe. "I know that . . . because I heard it from the people of
Delphi," or "I know that . . . because I heard it at Dodona."[45] If
there is a connection between seeing and knowing for Herodotus,
there is in principle no break between knowing and hearing,[46] even

43. Marco Polo, *La description du Monde*, p. 1.

44. Thucydides 1.20.1, 1.73.2.

45. Hdt. 1.20, 2.52; the expression *autopteo eidenai* is to be found at 4.16.

46. Jacoby, *Atthis*, p. 391 n. 16: "The use of the etymological connection between
oida and *idein* may appear justified in regard to Thucydides, because of that
historian's use of *opsis* and *akoe*, but the application to Herodotus is misleading. The
latter does not base his 'knowledge' on *opsis* in particular . . . because for him *akoe*,
opsis, and even *gnome* are sources of 'knowledge of equal reliability, that is, when he
trusts the narratives of his authorities.'"

if there are different levels of *akoe*, that is to say, a presence whose proximity to the ear of the narrator may vary considerably.

Between the Written and the Oral

By virtue of the principle that the ear may be used when the eye cannot be, the "I have heard" may be as valuable as the "I have seen," with a value that is not absolute but relative, that is to say, relative to me. You have no reason to believe me less when I say "I have heard" than when I say "I have seen." What is the meaning of that "I have heard"? That I am not claiming to have seen what I have only heard (Marco Polo), so I am not a liar; that I am faithfully reporting what I have heard, so I am not a braggart. As to the content of my words, you are not obliged to believe it, but, then, no more am I. This is a point to which we shall be returning.

What is the presupposition suggested by the close connection between seeing and hearing in the production of knowledge and by the fact that Herodotus may equally well say either "I know because I have seen" or "I know because I have heard"? A world in which it goes without saying that the word counts as knowledge, in which the word knows. That means a world in which oral discourse is not devalued in relation to written discourse—a world of orality, or still largely so.

That was still the situation in Greece in the fifth century B.C. It was not a world of writing, hardly even a world of the written word. Of course, writing had been known for a long time. The Syro-Phoenician alphabet made its appearance in the first half of the eighth century B.C., but oral culture remained very much alive, was indeed preponderant. It was still shaping the mental structures and shared knowledge of the Greeks of the period. "Greece never experienced a revolution of writing, and the written text did not take over from an oral tradition which had suddenly collapsed."[47] To assess the slow advance of writing, we may refer, at least by way of analogy, to the conclusions of Furet and Osouf in their inquiry relating to France:

Between the seventeenth century and the 1914–18 War, the French made

---

47. M. Detienne, *Annuaire* Ecole pratique des hautes études, fifth section, vol. 85, p. 286 and vol. 89, pp. 387–96. See E. A. Havelock, *Preface to Plato* (Oxford, 1963), and, D. Lanza, *Lingua e discorso nell'Atene delle professioni* (Turin, 1979), pp. 52–87.

their entry into written culture. But this long, submerged history is not the story of a radical substitution of written for oral culture. For writing had pre-existed this collective acculturation; the oral tradition, meanwhile, has survived right into the middle of the twentieth century. Probably the most useful concept in seeking to understand the point at issue is that of restricted literacy, as defined by the English anthropologist, Jack Goody. What happened in France between Louis XIV and Jules Ferry is not, properly speaking, the spread of literacy among the French people; rather, it is a transition from restricted literacy to mass literacy.[48]

The concept of restricted literacy also applies to Greece, and there too an "interference" between the written and the oral took place.

Herodotus and his *Histories* bear witness to that interference.[49] The historian Diyllos reports that Herodotus received a prize of ten talents from the Athenians. Eusebius in his *Chronicle* (at the entry for 445–444 B.C.) also mentions this prize, and he knows what occasioned it: Herodotus had given a public reading of his work. Lucian likewise mentions a recitation at Olympia which was such a success that the nine books were forthwith given the names of the nine Muses.[50] Olympia is also the setting for the anecdote according to which Thucydides, as a child, heard Herodotus recounting the *Histories*, and was so moved that he burst into tears.[51] Also falling into this tradition of a Herodotus who was half-Sophist, half-rhap-

48. F. Furet and J. Ozuof, *Reading and Writing* (Cambridge, 1982), p. 305. The conclusion of this work gives an acute analysis of the conditions necessary for passing over from orality to writing and also of all that such a passage signifies. On pp. 311–12, the authors examine the relations between writing and history, suggesting that writing makes it possible to establish the "pastness of the past." They go on to say: "Even when much in this history has come down from the oral tradition or mythology, it is obliged, merely because it is written down, to rationalise the passage of time. Herodotus paved the way for Thucydides." To be sure. Yet Thucydides, precisely, deduces from the efforts of Herodotus that it is impossible to write the history of the past.

49. L. Canfora also considers the sources of testimony, "Il ciclo storico," *Belfagor* 26 (1971): 658–60, and "Storici e società Ateniese," *Istituto Lombardo* (Rend. Lett.) 107 (1973): 1158; A. Momigliano, "The Historians of the Classical World and Their Audiences," *Annali della Scuola Normale Superiore di Pisa* 8, 1 (1978): 59–75.

50. Lucian *Herodotus or Aetion* 1, where Herodotus is represented as an *agonistes* coming on to recite his *Histories* (*agonisten Olumpion pareichen heauton aidon tas historias*).

51. *Suda*, s.v., *Thukudides*.

sode, both a reciter and a lecturer, is the proverb about standing in
"Herodotus's shade."[52] Finally, Aristophanes, who allowed himself a
number of allusions to Herodotus, suggests that the *Histories*, or at
least some passages from them, had certainly become part of the
domain of the well known—in Athens, at any rate. The most famous
of his nods and winks comes in the *Acharnians*, where Diceopolis
recalls the causes of the Peloponnesian War: "But then some young
men who had got drunk while playing *kottaboi* went off to Megara
and carried off the courtesan Simaitha. The Megareans, being
affronted and as angry as fighting cocks, then abducted two courte-
sans from Aspasia, by way of reprisals: and that is why the war broke
out, setting all the Greeks to fighting one another, and all because of
three whores!"[53] It is a transparent allusion to the prologue of the
Histories and the succession of abductions (Io, Europa, Medea,
Helen) which, according to the Persian scholars, were the cause of
the hostility between the Greeks and the barbarians.

As well as these indirect sources of evidence, the work itself, in
some of its aspects, stems from the world of orality. In the first place,
there are all the indications which, in the composition procedures of
archaic literature as analyzed by Van Groningen,[54] suggest that a
listener rather than a reader is being addressed; the technique of
ring composition provides the most obvious example. Also, the text
seems, at certain moments, to be registering the echo of a dialogue
or discussion held with the audience. One case in point is the famous
Persian debate on different types of constitutions. After the as-

52. E. Leutsch and F. G. Schneidewin, *Corpus Paroemiographorum graecorum*, vol. 1, p. 400: "[said of] those who do not fulfill what they had said they would
do. The story goes that Herodotus, the logographer, being anxious to present his
history on the occasion of the Olympic games, put it off day after day, saying that he
would do so when there was some shade in the sanctuary of Zeus. The spot lies in the
full sun. The gathering was over before he realised that he had still not presented his
work."

53. *Acharnians* 523–29. R. Drews, *The Greek Accounts of Eastern History*
(Cambridge, Mass., 1973), p. 90, observes that Aristophanes laughs *with* Herodotus,
not at him. A list of Aristophanes' allusions to the *Histories* may be found in K.
Riemann, "Das Herodoteische Geschichtswerk in der Antike," diss. Munich, 1967,
pp. 9–10.

54. B. P. Van Groningen, *La Composition littéraire archaïque* (Amsterdam,
1958), a work it is worth consulting even if it deliberately leaves the *Histories* out of
its analysis. H. Immerwahr, *Form and Thought in Herodotus* (Cleveland, 1966), pp.
46–79.

sassination of the usurper Smerdis, the conspirators apparently met together to deliberate on the best form of government to set up (monarchy, aristocracy, or *isonomia*) and the narrator says, quite explicitly: "words were uttered which to some Greeks seem incredible; but there is no doubt that they were spoken."[55] Three books further on, when writing about the events that took place in Ionia, he returns to the subject: "I here set down something for the wonder of those Greeks who will not believe Otanes to have declared his opinion, among the Seven, that democracy was best for Persia."[56]

Herodotou Halicarnesseos histories apodexis is how the *Histories* begin: "What Herodotus of Halicarnassus has learnt by enquiry is here set forth." Now, the term *apodexis* belongs to the world of orality; it refers one to epic and "surely implies oral publication."[57] So Herodotus is a rhapsode and the prologue to the *Histories* sets out both to invoke the epic tradition and to rival it. The *Iliad* and the *Odyssey* are certainly present, but the intention is at the same time to mark out a distinction from that tradition: here, it is not the goddess who sings of "which of the gods it was that made the son of Atreus and the divine Achilles quarrel," but Herodotus of Halicarnassus who tells "the reason why the Greeks and barbarians warred against each other"; it is not the Muse singing of "the man who saw the cities of many peoples and learned their ways," but Herodotus, who "goes forward with his history and speaks of small and great cities alike."[58]

However, this same prologue also incorporates a feature that does not belong to the world of orality. Alongside the name of the author, his city is mentioned: Herodotus of Halicarnassus (or of Thurii). Such a feature, quite unknown in epic poetry, really makes no sense unless what is communicated is intended to cross the frontiers of the city, thus overflowing from the face-to-face world it shapes.[59] One might say that there is a link between the writing of this work, the mention

55. Hdt. 3.80.

56. Hdt. 6.43.

57. Havelock, *Preface to Plato*, p. 54 n.8. The term *apodeixis* is to be found in Thucydides, in particular at 1.97, to refer to the account he has just given of the development of the Athenian empire (*kai tes arches apodeixin echei tes ton athenaion en hoioi tropoi kateste*).

58. Hdt. 1.1, 6; *Iliad* 1.8; *Odyssey* 1.3.

59. A remark made by Van Groningen, *Composition*, p. 65. He also observes that such beginnings resemble the beginning of a letter.

of the author's name, and the general development of cities, for the rhapsode traveled from city to city, moving from one competition to the next, and did not reserve his composition solely for his native city. In a similar fashion, Hecataeus begins his *Genealogies* as follows: "Hecataeus of Miletus . . . recounts this; I write what I regard as being in conformity with the truth [*hode mutheitai tade grapho hos moi dokei alethea einai*]." What is so surprising, of course, is this combination of *mutheitai* (he says, he recounts), from the world of orality, and *grapho* (I write), which clearly belongs to the world of writing. It is by writing and by virtue of the very fact that he is writing that he will establish that which, in the many narratives (*logoi*) of the Greeks, "looks like the truth [*dokei moi*]." Finally, Thucydides starts off with his famous "Thucydides of Athens has written [*sunegrapse*]"; and his work as a whole is called a *sung-graphe*, that is to say, a syn-graphy or writing-put-together. At the very outset, this author takes up his position in the world of writing.

Whether it belongs to the world of orality, the world of writing, or the world between the oral and the written, what, in the last analysis, is writing in the *Histories*, and to what does the act of writing amount? Writing was introduced in Greece by the Phoenicians who came there with Cadmus ("as I think"). The Greeks, "having been taught the letters by the Phoenicians, used them with some few changes of form and in so doing gave to these characters . . . the name of *phonikeia*."[60] The word *graphein* means "to write," but also "to paint," "to represent," "to draw," "to survey."[61] What was writing used for? Oracles were set down in writing,[62] written inscriptions were carved on monuments or to commemorate such and such an event,[63] letters were written, and if one was Egyptian, one kept books, made lists, kept archives. But the letter was used above all in the barbarian world, not in the Greek one, although there are some exceptions. For instance, the pharaoh Amasis and Polycrates of Samos exchanged letters,[64] but Polycrates was a tyrant and tyrants were people who fell between Greece and Asia. A similar case is that of Histiaeus, the tyrant of Miletus. When

60. Hdt. 5.58.
61. For example, Hdt. 2.46, 3.136, 4.36.
62. Hdt. 1.47, 7.142, 8.135.
63. Hdt. 1.93, 2.106, 125, 4.87, 7.30, 228.
64. Hdt. 3.40, 42.

he wishes to order Aristagoras to launch the Ionian revolt against the Persians, he sends him a letter that he writes on the head of a loyal slave, after having it shaved and waiting for the hair to grow again.[65] Finally, Demaratus resorts to a secret letter to warn the Lacedaemonians of Xerxes' plans, but of course Demaratus, an exiled king of Sparta, had taken refuge in the court of the Great King.[66] So the letter was a means of transmitting intelligence or instructions, a secret means of communication, and, all in all, a way of exercising power. Darius sent instructions by letter to Megabazus, who had remained in Europe after the Scythian expedition.[67] A letter most emphatically conveyed the royal will, but it might also be used as an instrument of vengeance, to kill its addressee, as, for example, in the story of Oroites, a satrap of whom Darius desired to be rid. An envoy from Darius arrived in Sardis, bringing a number of royal letters. On being ushered into the presence of the satrap, he handed the letters to the royal scribe, to be read. Seeing that the guards showed the greatest respect for these letters, he handed over one that ran, "King Darius forbids you to be Oroites' guard," at which the guards promptly laid down their spears. He then handed over the last letter: "King Darius charges you to kill Oroites." The guards immediately drew their scimitars and killed him.[68] A letter could thus be tortuous, secret, and linked with the exercise of power; it could also be an instrument of betrayal and a means of seizing power. Harpagus invited Cyrus to revolt against Astyages and the rule of the Medes, by smuggling to him a letter hidden in the stomach of a hare that had been slit open and then carefully sewn up again. To make sure of the Persians' support in this undertaking, Cyrus, in his turn, wrote a letter, a false one, in which he said that Astyages had appointed him, Cyrus, to be governor of Persia. On hearing this, the Persians obeyed him.[69]

Cunning is certainly not absent from the Greek world, but this

65. Hdt. 5.35.
66. Hdt. 7.239.
67. Hdt. 5.14.
68. Hdt. 3.128.
69. Hdt. 1.123–25. We may also cite the example of Deiokes (1.100). Having been chosen as king of the Medes, he has a palace built for him from which, without being seen, he wields his power: he administers justice by having a written account of the lawsuits brought to him.

cunning use of writing in the form of a missive was not current practice. For example, when Themistocles, himself a master of cunning, secretly warned the Persians that the Greeks were planning to retreat from Salamis (with the express purpose of preventing them from doing so), he used a messenger, not a secret letter.[70] Writing was linked with power, was a form of power, and seems to have been first and foremost an affair for the royal scribe: it was he who both wrote and read the letters.[71] About learning how to write in the Greek world, the *Histories* provide no more than two hints: in Chios, the roof of a school collapsed on the children who were learning their letters there;[72] and the mother of Scyles, king of the Scythians, was a woman from Istria (a colony of Miletus) and it was she herself who had taught him the "Greek language and letters,"[73] so she must have known how to read and write, or at least how to read.

Thus writing is certainly present in the *Histories*, but what is interesting in this connection is Herodotus's attitude toward the written word. On seeing an inscription which he reads or has translated to him, does the traveler feel more confident as a result of what his eye has seen? Does the written word confer an "extra knowledge" or, at any rate, a surer knowledge than an oral narrative? Not necessarily. Herodotus has seen a number of inscriptions, and he cites some of them: inscriptions on the monument dedicated to the father of Croesus stating that the latter contributed to its erection, on the statues set up by Sesostris during his campaigning, on the pyramid at Cheops which (according to the interpreter) stated how much it cost to employ the workmen.[74] But in all these cases, the inscription comes as an extra: in the course of the description of the

70. Hdt. 8.75. When he wants to persuade the Ionians to defect he does not send letters either to the Ionians or to the Persians, to warn them to beware of the Ionians, but instead sets up inscriptions close to the springs of drinking water (8.22), where they will be seen by both the Ionians and the Persians.

71. Hdt. 7.100, 8.90, 3.128. Polycrates also has a scribe (3.123).

72. Hdt. 6.27. Cf. H.-I. Marrou, *Histoire de l'éducation dans l'antiquité*, 6th ed. (Paris, 1965), p. 83. On the question of reading aloud and silent reading, cf. the study by B. Knox, "Silent Reading in Antiquity," *Greek, Roman and Byzantine Studies* 9 (1968): 421–35.

73. Hdt. 4.78.

74. Hdt. 1.93, 2.106, 125. A total of twenty-four inscriptions are to be found, eleven of which are in "foreign languages." See H. Volkmann, "Die Inschriften im Geschichtswerk des Herodot," *Convivium* (1954): 41–63.

monument it is mentioned, but it is not there simply for its own sake. Furthermore, an inscription may lie: on a golden vase in Delphi it is written that it is an offering from the Lacedaemonians, but that is false, since it was Croesus who presented it. I even know who engraved the inscription, but I will not tell.[75] Writing may lie. At all events, Herodotus is not particularly concerned to track down inscriptions. He is no epigraphist traveling about carrying the tools of his trade. The inscription is not an archive.

In Egypt, on the other hand, he encounters people who use books. The Egyptians are people of very ancient knowledge, the most ancient—or almost the most ancient—of all men, or who have existed ever since there have been men.[76] They record things in writing. They know, for example, the age of the gods and how much time elapsed between the youngest god and the pharaoh Amasis, and Herodotus refers to this calculation in order to underline the inanity of what the Greeks say about the genealogy of Heracles. Of all these figures "the Egyptians claim to have certain knowledge, seeing that they had always reckoned the years and chronicled them in writing."[77] Similarly, it is from a book (*ek bublou*) that the priests provide their visitor with a list of the kings of Egypt;[78] they number three hundred and thirty-one in all. Finally, to write is also to be able to foresee: "They have made themselves more omens than all other nations together; when an ominous thing happens, they take note of the outcome and write it down [*graphomenoi*]; and if something of a like kind happens again they think it will have a like result."[79] Thus, the Egyptians are men with memories: they know very well, thanks to written texts, that they were not born yesterday and are the most learned (*logiotatoi*) of all men when it comes to remembering things,[80] in contrast to the peoples of the Black Sea, among whom not a single "learned man" (*logion*) is to be found and who, like the Scythians, claim to be the youngest of men.[81]

75. Hdt. 1.50.

76. Hdt. 2.15.

77. Hdt. 2.145: *atrekeos phasi epistasthai, aiei te logizomenoi kai aiei apographomenoi ta etea.* Egypt is the land of the papyrus, (2.92); unlike the Greeks, the Egyptians write from right to left (2.36).

78. Hdt. 2.100.

79. Hdt. 2.82.

80. Hdt. 2.77.

81. Hdt. 4.46.

There is thus a connection between writing and knowledge; all the same, the one who knows how to write is not necessarily always right. Thus, the scribe of the treasury of Athena at Saïs claims to have exact knowledge (*atrekeos*) about the sources of the Nile, but in Herodotus's view he is nothing but a simpleton; *paizei*, like a child, he does not know what he is talking about. This is an interesting inversion of a situation that was later to become classic, in which the traveler, a man of writing, understands what is true in the discourse of the native. Here, in contrast, is a man of writing who does not know what he is talking about and a traveler, who is not altogether a man of writing, who can sort out how much of what his informant tells him is true.[82] "This, then, he showed, as I think," namely, that the sources of the Nile are not, in an absolute sense, impossible to sound, but on account of "the eddies and upward flow of the water" they cannot be sounded.

Above all, it is enough for the priests to *say*. That does not mean that all that they say is bound to be true or that I believe all that they say, but let us not forget that I, for my part, can say, "I know because I have seen" or "I know because I have heard"; and that they, in order to tell me of their distant past, read books and keep records. Very well, perhaps they are bound to do so. However, for me, composing my own *logos*, there is no need to look at those books or to consult those records. What would be the point? To reproach Herodotus for not having done so would be to fail to see that there was no reason for him to do so nor could he have done so, since the very notion of *archive* did not exist.

J.-P. Faye writes:

In its attempt to reconstitute the entire history of Egypt from Min to Cambyses, the very first of narratives by historians or historicizers produced a double and paradoxical result. Book 2 of the *Histories* indeed brings us the most ancient names in human history. . . . But at the same time Book 2 of this, the first history, is also the first collection of popular tales. . . . The story of Pherus, the tale of the master robber of the treasures of Rhampsinitus, and that of the revenge of Nitocris all belong to the worldwide inventory of popular tales, with the same claims to do so and in the same sense as do the collections of popular tales produced by G. Maspero. It is ironical that when the first *historeon* 'sought to know' at first hand by making inquiries on the spot, in the sanctuary of Ptah at Memphis,

82. Hdt. 2.28.

at Saïs, Boubastis, or Bouto, the oral narrative that he received by way of reply was a pack of fictions. That is all the more ironical, to our eyes, since archives and documents did already exist at this date in—precisely—the Egyptian sanctuaries, and are now at the disposal of historians. That the very first historicizer venturing on a narrative should have discovered fictions is not a fortuitous accident. It was indeed part and parcel of the fundamental process. The 'sources' of Herodotus are fictitious despite all his good intentions, as a historian, to go about 'acquiring information,' since fiction belongs to the process of primitive narration in the making. [83]

Ironical perhaps, but only to us as we contemplate the process of historiography. We know that there is no such thing as an archive as such, independent of the historicizer, and that archives only came into existence when people decided to regard them as such; we also know that the selection of new archives goes hand in hand with the formulation of new questions. In the first place, the existence of archives presupposes men of writing, and to use archives, to work from archives, presupposes in one way or another prizing what is written as being more *true*, more *authentic*, more *sure* than what is oral (it being nevertheless accepted that the written word, too, can lie). Herodotus, situated as he was between the written and the oral, listened to people who used books, but the idea of going "to consult the archives" of the sanctuaries of Saïs or Bouto for himself would never even have occurred to him: "I know because I have heard." Finally, his remarks about the connection between the knowledge of Egyptian history and the presence of the Ionians provides further proof of the "nonexistence" of archives and even of the assumed superiority of the oral over the written. "It comes of our intercourse with these settlers in Egypt (who were the first men of alien speech

---

83. J.-P. Faye, *Théorie du récit* (Paris, 1972), pp. 111–12. A. Momigliano notes, on the subject of archives, *Studies in Historiography*, p. 135: "The pre-eminence of personal observation and oral evidence lasted until historians decided to go to the record office. Familiarity with the record office, as we all know, is a recently acquired habit for the historian, hardly older than a century." See also his "Historiography on Written Tradition and Historiography on Oral Tradition," ibid., pp. 211–20; and E. Posner, *Archives in the Ancient World* (Cambridge, Mass., 1972). To see the books might suggest reading them, and therefore learning the language. But why learn a foreign language if *saying* (under certain conditions, *historeon*) is just as good as *seeing*? Paradoxically, it was perhaps partly because the world of Herodotus was not a world of writing that he felt no need to learn any foreign languages.

[*alloglossoi*] to settle in that country) that we Greeks have exact knowledge [*epistametha atrekeos*] of the history of Egypt from that time onward."[84]

I Say, I Write

If that is Herodotus's attitude toward what is written and if there are no archives in the strict sense of the term, what is the situation so far as Herodotus as a speaker, or as a writer, is concerned? Similarly, just as we have posed the question of "I have seen" and "I have heard" regarded as indicators as to who is speaking and as punctuation marks in the narrative, let us examine the matter of "I say" and "I write," these too being regarded as marking the narrator's interventions into his narrative. From the point of view of the addressee and the credibility that the narrator hopes to convey, does the one carry more weight than the other? Does "I write" (supposedly) carry more conviction than "I say"?

Let us first consider the matter from the negative angle of "I do not say" or "I do not write." On several occasions, when tackling religious matters, Herodotus makes it clear that he knows certain things and is familiar with certain explanations but will not, prefers not, or does not judge it seemly to tell them.[85] This "not saying" carries a positive message to the addressee and is a way of winning his trust: I know more than I am willing to say. In parallel fashion, he sometimes uses the formula "I do know but will not write." Telling of the doctrine of metemsomatosis, which was first propounded by the Egyptians and which certain Greeks later claimed as their own, he concludes: "I know their names but will not write them."[86] Similarly, on the way Polycrates died, he states that "it is not fit to be reported [*ouk axios apegesios*]."[87] It is an expression balanced by one that is written down: concerning the ways of hunting the crocodile, he *writes* "only of that one way which I think most worthy of being reported [*axiotate apegesios*]."[88] As negative indicators of the source

84. Hdt. 2.154.
85. For Example, Hdt. 2.46, 47, 65.
86. Hdt. 2.123.
87. Hdt. 3.125.
88. Hdt. 2.70.

of the statement, "I do not say" and "I do not write" (although, of course, in both cases I know) thus seem to carry equal weight. Both are equally intended to elicit the belief of the addressee.

Now let us look at it from a positive angle. Herodotus reckons that "it is his business to tell that which is told to me [*opheilo legein ta legomena*]" and adds that this principal holds good not only for the moment at which he makes the remark but for all the rest of his *logos* as well, [89] and so for the *Histories* as a whole. Similarly, he knows of two accounts of the way Cambyses crossed the Arabian desert in order to attack Egypt: the first, and the more persuasive (*pithanoteros*), he records, and the second, less persuasive, he also records, for "it must be said," since, after all, it is told (*dei . . . epei ge de legetai, rethenai*).[90] The narrator offers himself as mouthpiece, making himself a herald to relay all these *logoi* which, here and there, sometimes anonymously, sometimes not, are pronounced and then repeated: he is "the sonorous echo of his age."

He offers his own hand and pen to write down all those accounts: "I write what is said [*ta de legetai grapho*]."[91] He notes in his account of the Egyptians: "It is my business throughout this *logos* to *write* what *I have heard said* [*akoei grapho*] by each group of people."[92] And again, "In what I *write*, I follow what is said by the Greeks [*kata ta legomena hup' Hellenon ego grapho*].[93] In this instance, the narrator presents himself to the public simply as the scribe who notes down the accounts by whose rumors he is surrounded: he does no more than transcribe them and, later, repeat them. They say, it is said, it says, I write: there is no distance at all between saying and writing. Whether I act as herald or as scribe—and I am each in turn—it appears that from the point of view of the impression of credibility which I aim to produce, for the addressee of my *logos* it makes no great difference. Regarded as positive indicators of the source of the statement, "I say" and "I write," the narrator's mouth and his hand, appear to carry equal weight. In either case, my *logos* is valid because it is faithful to whatever was originally said, authenticating it and authenticated by it. Always it is a case of writing down something said, never of transcribing something written.

89. Hdt. 7.152.
90. Hdt. 3.9.
91. Hdt. 4.195.
92. Hdt. 2.123.
93. Hdt. 6.53.

However, in one case writing does appear to carry more weight (although very little more) and seems to commit the narrator more (although very little more) than simply saying: It is when his function is to make a record. On three occasions when it is a matter of naming, of recording names or not recording them, we find "write" rather than "say." I know the names of the Greeks who claim to have invented the doctrine of metemsomatosis, but I will not record them (or write them down). On the occasion of the Ionian revolt, he says, "Which of the Ionians did acquit themselves ill or well (during a naval battle against the Phoenicians) . . . I could not with any accuracy write down."[94] And again, on the subject of Ephialtes, the traitor at Thermopylae: "the man who guided them by the path round the mountain was Ephialtes, and I here *write down* that he was the guilty one [*touton aition grapho*]."[95] The narrator sets up, as it were, within his *logos* a stele of infamy to match the inscriptions engraved in honor of the heroes who fell with Leonidas, defending the pass. More generally, the historian's interventions in his narration are connected with his fundamental purpose, which is to see to it that the deeds of man "may not be blotted out . . . by time." His intention is whenever possible to report and establish who won the prize for valor in a particular battle,[96] and by doing so he elaborates a new memorial for the Greeks. Knowing how to name and naming thus call for an "I write" rather than an "I say" and—one might be tempted to assume—rather than simply "saying." However, at no point is there any explicit affirmation that writing has the value of *ktema es aiei*, as in Thucydides. "I write," to be sure, but this affirmation, which is destined to be spoken, is not presented as valid for all time.

Thucydides, for his part, certainly seems to stand fully and firmly on the side of writing: "Thucydides of Athens has set down the war in writing [*sunegrapse*]." A comparison between the two opening passages shows that the Herodotean exposition (*apodexis*) is replaced, in Thucydides, by writing (*sungraphie*). As for the *ktema es aiei*, that can only be understood fully in the context of writing.[97] What Thucydides in effect is saying is that his work obeys rules other than those which govern oral composition; under no circumstances

94. Hdt. 6.14.
95. Hdt. 7.214.
96. For example, Hdt. 7.227, 8.11, 9.71.
97. Havelock, *Preface to Plato*, p. 54 n. 8.

does he want anything to do with "a prize essay to be heard for the moment."[98] The spoken word is transitory, necessarily a thing of the moment, bound to obey the ear of the public. But writing avoids such pitfalls and can pass beyond such limitations.

But even while rejecting orality he cannot entirely escape it, since the normal fate of a work is to be read aloud, spoken before a public: it is destined "to be heard" (*es akroasin*). There is thus a danger that between the rules of composition observed and the mode of communication employed some distortion may take place and the public may be disappointed: "It may well be that the absence of the fabulous from my narrative will seem less pleasing to the ear."[99]

Ktema and writing express on the one hand a desire to escape from the world of orality, on the other the impossibility of doing so entirely. But the case of Thucydides is even more complex. For him, *opsis* is more prized than *akoe;* but *opsis* does not constitute a rejection of orality. On the contrary, when he does not state "I have seen for myself," he declares, "I make enquiries from someone who has seen and I criticize what he says," and in both cases that same word *opsis* may be used. *Opsis* is thus steeped in orality,[100] and it is because this oral verification is necessary that history is first and foremost "vision" and that producing history must, strictly speaking, mean producing contemporary or immediate history. Consequently, Thucydides by and large criticizes the logographers, Herodotus in particular, for having both abused and misused orality. They abused it in the sense that they spoke *for* the ear of the public, and they misused it in that they believed that no difficulties stood in the way of their speaking of events and people of the past. There is a good way of using orality and a bad way, and their way was doubly bad. Thus, albeit no doubt differently from Herodotus, Thucydides too is positioned between the written and the spoken.

In the *Histories*, the dividing line between the world that is recounted and the world in which things are recounted is not represented by writing. It is not writing which immediately makes the difference between "them" and "us," peoples with writing and those without. In Léry, in contrast, writing does occupy that position and presents itself as the truth of a discourse which, because it does not know what it is talking about, can only be classed as fable. In their

98. Thucydides 22.4.
99. Thudydides 22.4; 1.97 on the use of *apodeixis*.
100. Thucydides 22.2.

songs the Tupi say that "when the waters overflowed so much that they covered the whole earth, all the men in the world were drowned, except their own grandfathers, who took refuge on the highest treetops in their country." At this point the narrator makes an intervention: this is the closest thing they have to the Holy Scriptures. "The fact is that it is quite likely that they may have heard something about the world flood handed on from father to son; and as is customary with men, who have always corrupted the truth and turned it into lies, and furthermore being without writing of any kind so that it is difficult for them to retain anything in its pure state, they—just as poets do—added on this fable that their grandfathers had taken refuge in the trees."[101] Admittedly, when the Egyptians speak of the distant past and the genealogies of the gods, on the basis of what is written in their books, Herodotus is inclined to back them against the Greeks; thus he dismisses the Greeks' version of the story of Heracles as *muthos*.[102] However, when he intervenes in his own name, when the position he adopts in the discourse is that of one who knows the basic truth about what others say, he never does so in the name of writing. The Scythians, for example, say that in the north of their country one cannot see a thing or even move about, on account of all the feathers which cover the earth and fill the air. Of course, they do not know what they are talking about and are in fact using a metaphor without realizing it, for what they call feathers are really snowflakes.[103]

Léry produced an unequivocal lecture on writing: "On account of which I declare that, for whoever would say more, a fine subject is here to be found both for praising and exalting the art of writing and for showing to what extent the nations that live in these three parts of the world, Europe, Asia, and Africa, have good cause for praising God more than the savages of the fourth part known as America; for whereas they can communicate nothing except orally, we in contrast have the advantage that, without moving from a place, through the means of writing and the letters we send, we can declare our secrets to whomsoever we like, even should they be as far distant as the ends

101. Léry, *Histoire d'un voyage*, p. 198.

102. Hdt. 2.45.

103. Hdt. 2.7, 31. G. Dumézil, *Romans de Scythie et d'alentour* (Paris, 1978), p. 339, 351, shows, by referring to an Abkhaz tradition, that the feathers must have some "special, mythical significance" and that they belong to the account of the origins of the Scythian people.

of the earth. Therefore, as well as the sciences which we can learn from books, of which the savages are equally destitute, this invention of writing which we have and which they totally lack should also be reckoned among the singular gifts which men over here have received from God."[104] Words, no sooner spoken than obliterated, do not carry far, whereas writing can be preserved intact and carries to the ends of the earth. Whether it is prized as "a singular gift" or depreciated as "treachery,"[105] for ethnology, lecturing on writing was to play something of the role of a primal scene. But Herodotus avoids that way of operating; from that point of view, he is not the father of ethnology. When all is said and done, Léry's writing "invents" the savage, whereas Herodotus's narrative "invents" the barbarian; a barbarian is not a savage since, unlike the savage, the barbarian knows how to write. The Persian knows how to write and has produced writing, even in the form of the mutilation of human bodies, a writing of power, and he is the barbarian par excellence. The Egyptian also knows how to write, yet he too is a barbarian.[106] So although savagery and writing may stand in opposition to each other, barbarianism and writing fit very well together.

For ethnology, writing is ultimately the yardstick by which to measure the truth of the speech of the savage, but at the same time something about that speech always eludes it. De Certeau has demonstrated that fact admirably in connection with Tupi speech, which seems to be "the gem missing from the casket of jewels which is the narrative."[107] Now, that speech, elusive to the extent that it is itself lost, is what in some indefinable sense makes the writer write; it is what produces the ethnological text. That is not the case with Herodotus, for whom the speech of "others" is not at once the *subject* of his discourse and also the deep stimulus which prompts it: that is not what makes him write.

Writing amasses and preserves, and the ethnologist is the first or, on the contrary, the last to witness a particular ceremony or to hear a

---

104. Léry, *Histoire d'un voyage*, p. 188. De Certeau, *L'Ecriture*, pp. 222–26, analyzes this text.

105. C. Lévi-Strauss, *Tristes Tropiques* (Paris, 1955), "Leçon d'écriture."

106. For example, Hdt. 2.50: "Wellnigh all the names of the gods came to Greece from Egypt. For I am assured by enquiry that they have come from the *Barbarians*, and I believe that they came chiefly from *Egypt*."

107. De Certeau, *L'Ecriture*, p. 221.

certain song (for in this domain you could well say that the first are also the last). But before it preserves, writing kills, as is meticulously demonstrated by Victor Segalen. Writing, in the form of the Scriptures, destroyed the orality of the Tahitians, who were forced to become people without memories so that whichever of them could, by some extraordinary chance, still remember the sayings of the bygone days would be nothing better than a pagan, that is to say, an ignorant savage, for he was ignorant of the Christian doctrine. That is the point at which to begin preserving or, rather, embalming, for as the young Tahitian discovered, what writing collects are dead words.[108] But that is not the way the *Histories* function, either.

The *Histories* do not lecture on writing, and Herodotus is a man between the oral and the written. However, he too aims to preserve and the *Histories* are set down in writing. It is as if, in his prologue, he thought he was competing with epic, whereas in reality he was doing something else. He had not the words to express what he was actually doing; he wanted to be rhapsode but could only be a rhapsode in prose. He set out to be a new Homer but instead became Herodotus. Fundamentally, he set out to do something quite different, and in writing the *Histories* he produced a new memorial, very different from the memories of epic.[109]

The Interplay of Utterances from Different Sources

We have considered the four indicators as to the source of a statement, "I have seen," "I have heard," "I say," "I write," from the point of view of their impact on the addressee (although they do not all operate at the same level in the narrative). Now we must tackle the question of other narrators alongside the principal narrator and correspondingly, if need be, that of other addressees alongside the primary addressee. To put it another way, who, at which point, is speaking to whom? And with what effects on the narrative?

There is a primary narrator who is omnipresent and who alone speaks. He makes his interventions in the first-person singular ("I know," "I have seen," "it seems to me") but may also use the first-

108. V. Segalen, *Les Immémoriaux* (Paris, 1956).
109. On this new memorial, which both resembles and yet is profoundly different from epic, see a number of comments by Drews, *Greek Accounts*.

person plural: "we have ourselves measured," "we have ourselves seen," "so far as we know," "to our knowledge." These latter expressions punctuate statements: beyond the land of the Neuri, to the north, there extends, "so far as we know," a desert empty of men; Polycrates is the first of the Greeks, "to our knowledge," who had the idea of ruling the seas.[110] Just once, at the very beginning of his work, he even signs himself in the third person, using his own name ("Herodotus recounts"), but already by the fifth paragraph, "I" is introduced to bring the prologue to a close.

Except in the passages of direct speech, the second person ("you," singular or plural) is not attested and the addressee thus remains in the shadows. In contrast, in his *Description of the World*, Marco Polo, who to refer to himself uses not only the first-person singular and plural but also the third-person singular (Marco Polo, he), accommodates his addressee squarely within the text, making abundant use of the second person ("you should know," "and I tell you that," "we wish you to know that"). Nevertheless, the addressee is not absent from the scene in the *Histories*. He appears there in the third-person plural (the Greeks) and the first-person plural (we, us). "We" means the world *in which* things are recounted as opposed to the world that is recounted; "we" as opposed to "them." For example, "What *we* call cinnamon is a word the Phoenicians have taught us"; "the name that *we* give the Arimaspians is Scythian"; "I have no knowledge of the existence of the Tin Islands, but I know that tin and amber come to *us* from the most distant parts"; "the most distant parts of the world have those things which *we* deem best and rarest"; "in Libya, the Auseans honour after the manner of their ancestors that native goddess whom *we* call Athena."[111] The "we" is so malleable that it can shrink to "I" or, on the contrary, expand to include the Greeks as a whole. Between the former extreme concentration and the latter extreme expansion, a number of subgroups may be accommodated, depending on the audience in question: it is always possible for the "I" to include itself within a "we." The addressee may

110. Cases where we = I: Hdt. 2.127, 131, 3.122, 4.16, 20, 46. Sometimes it is hard to tell the exact extension of "we": is it simply co-extensive with "I," or is its significance wider, covering the whole group of those who know, to which "I" belong? Cf. below, pp. 367ff.

111. Hdt. 3.111, 427, 115, 116, 4.180.

be sensed to be present in the form of the third person, through the comparisons or parallels that are introduced. Tauris, for example, is evoked in terms designed to reach first and foremost the Athenians and the Greeks of Apulia.[112] Sometimes it is made explicit that it is the Greeks who are the collective addressee. When Herodotus reports the Persian debate on the best regime to set up following the assassination of the usurper Smerdis, he insists that, incredible though such suggestions may seem to "some Greeks," they nevertheless were made.[113]

The third person, finally, means all the rest—all those who speak and of whom I speak, all those whom I make to speak, but also all the narrations which speak themselves (*legetai*), apparently without the mouth of any narrator or the ear of any recipient.[114] This covers a multitude of secondary narrators who are called on to speak for a moment but who then, having said their say, disappear. (Even where direct speech is used they do not speak in their own name.) Take the origin of the Scythians: the first (collective) narrator to make an intervention is the Scythians (the Scythians say that); next, it is the Black Sea Greeks who, in their turn, say that; then it is the Greeks and barbarians who say that; and last of all it is Aristeas, the poet, who says that.[115] That makes a total of four different narratives superposed upon one another and produced by four different narrators (collective or individual) vis-à-vis which, at the moment when they are produced, the position of the primary narrator is that of recipient of the narrative. He may even be a secondary recipient, for these versions may not be produced specially for him but primarily be addressed to another recipient. For instance, when the Black Sea Greeks are trying to understand about Salmoxis, they resort to Pythagoras and proceed by means of a dialectic between what is near

112. Hdt. 4.99.
113. Hdt. 3.80, 6.43.
114. On the subject of the Romans, Condorcet noted: "An 'it is said,' or 'it is reported,' placed at the beginning of a sentence, seems to them enough to shield them from being ridiculed as childishly credulous. This indifference is chiefly attributable to the misfortune of their ignorance of the art of printing. It was an indifference which corrupted the art of history as practiced by them and which stood in the way of their making any progress in the understanding of nature": *Esquisse d'un tableau historique des progrès de l'esprit humain* (Paris, 1970), p. 88.
115. Cf. above, pp. 19f.

and what is far away;[116] it is reasonable to suppose, then, that that particular schema is in the first instance intended for the Black Sea Greeks themselves.

At all events, the important point is that the principal narrator is alone mobile. He may at one time or another occupy any of the positions in the discourse. From being the narrator, he can turn himself into the recipient of the narrative and then, when he feels so inclined, switch back to being the narrator. The various narratives are like strata each with its own particular level (rather like Braudel's schema of long cycles)[117] and each of these strata is (if necessary) related to the others by the principal narrator, who intervenes to introduce indicators as to who is speaking. As he links them together, he cuts some short and extends others, in a word, classifies them from the point of view of their credibility. Of course, even the order in which the successive versions are presented is no indifferent matter and itself constitutes an implicit form of indicator (to the extent that this comes "before" the actual lexical expression).[118]

The Scythians tell of their origins. Suddenly, the principal narrator intervenes to slip in an observation concerning the birth of the first Scythian, whose parents are said to be Zeus and a daughter of the river Borysthenes: "for my part, I do not believe the tale, but it is told [*emoi ou pista legontes*]." The story then resumes. Then follows what is said by the Black Sea Greeks, which is not interrupted by any intervention on the part of the primary narrator. Next comes what is said by Greeks and barbarians alike, which is immediately described as the version to which "I myself do especially incline." That is followed, finally, by the version given by Aristeas. Thus through the interplay of the primary narrator's interventions, the third version is presented as being the most credible, the first is definitely rejected, while the second and the fourth are indirectly discounted.

As indicators of the source of the utterance, "I have seen" and "I have heard" affect not only the relation of the locutor to his utterance

---

116. Cf. above, pp. 84f.

117. F. Braudel, *Ecrits sur l'histoire* (Paris, 1969), p. 13.

118. What is meant by *modalities* is whatever affects the relationship between the locutor and his utterance. They include the characteristics that give propositions the property of truthfulness (*alethic* modalities), the property of understanding or knowledge (*epistemic* modalities), and, finally, the property of moral obligation (*deontic* modalities).

but also its reception by the addressee. They are thus already given a modal value, either an "alethic" or an "epistemic" one. "I say" and "I write" operate slightly differently. What I say is what is said and what I write is also what is said. My *logos* simply reproduces original sayings which it authenticates and which authenticate it: these sayings are, I assure you, what has been said, so you (the addressee) can believe me; on the other hand, I am only saying what is said and so, since I am not attempting to make you believe it is true, you can believe me. This fidelity to what was originally said is presented as a duty: if I write or say what is said, that is because it is what I should do. "For my part, it is my business [*opheilo*] to tell that which is told me. . . . Let that saying hold good for the whole of my history."[119]

There is a corollary to this duty: "I say" and "I write," but anyone is at liberty to believe or disbelieve what is said. And in the first place, I myself am free to believe or not to believe, or to believe one version in preference to another, to the extent that "in my opinion" [*dokei moi*][120] it is more "credible" (*pithanos*): though "it is my business to tell that which is told me, to believe it *is none at all of my business*" I am neither over-credulous nor a liar, so you can believe me. I am free but, equally, so is the addressee: "These Egyptian stories are for the use of whoever believes such tales; for myself, it is my rule throughout this history that I write down whatever is told me [*akoei grapho*], as I have heard it."[121] So you are free to believe or not to believe, to

119. Hdt. 7.152; cf. 3.9.

120. Of course, account should also be taken of the use of modalities that qualify the "I" (it seems to me, I think that . . .) and that refine the relations between the locutor and his utterance still further within the major indicators as to the source of the utterance which I have mentioned. I may also suspend, or pretend (?) to suspend, belief; cf. above on the existence of Salmoxis, p. 109: the Getae *believe* he is a divine being, the Black Sea Greeks *say* that he was Pythagoras's slave and tell the story of an underground dwelling. As for myself, neither do I not believe (*apisteo*) in the underground dwelling nor do I altogether believe in it (*pisteuo ti lien*), but it seems (*dokeo*) that Salmoxis lived many years before Pythagoras. As to whether he was a man or a divine being of the land of the Getae, let us leave all that (*chaireto*).

121. Hdt. 2.123, 5.45 (on the subject of the difference between the Sybarites and the people of Croton: "These, then, are the evidences brought by each party; we may take whichever side seems to deserve most credence"; 3.122 (on the death of Polycrates): "These are the two reasons alleged for Polycrates' death; believe which you will"; 2.146 (on Heracles): "with regard to these two allegations [those of the Greeks and those of the Egyptians], a man may follow whatsoever story he deems most credible; but I here declare my own opinion."

believe what I believe or to believe something else. Since I am not trying to get you to believe it, all in all you have all the more reason to believe me.

This superposition of layers of narrative and the interplay of utterances from different sources are fundamental to the narrative's ability to persuade the addressee to believe it. The primary narrator, who is omnipresent, thus shows that he *knows* (sometimes more than he will say; the death of Cyrus, for example, is the subject of a number of *logoi* that he knows of, but he records only the one that, in his view, is the most credible).[122] He thereby shows that he is doing his duty (it is my business to say) and at the same time is neither over-credulous nor a liar—in short, he demonstrates his own credibility.

Finally, the narrative's ability to inspire belief poses the question of the desire to believe, in other words the audience's reception. In the case of the *Histories* it is extremely difficult to obtain a clear appreciation of that reception, and I will limit myself here to one generalization and a single example. The narrator's ability to elicit belief depends on the public's desire to believe and equally, of course, on its refusal to believe. On the subject of the Persian debate, Herodotus twice refers to "the Greeks who will not believe" that such a debate can have taken place in Persia. Why does he make those interventions, and what is their effect? In the first place, when I speak of these matters I know what I am talking about. Second, I am well aware that some Greeks do not believe this. If I persist in saying so notwithstanding, it is because I have "good reason" to do so, which is all the more reason for you to believe me. The refusal to believe is thus recuperated and in the end serves to reinforce the narrative's ability to elicit belief.

Kublai Khan asked Marco Polo whether, when he returned to Venice, he would tell his fellow countrymen the same stories as he was telling to him. Marco Polo replied: "For my part, I talk and talk, but whoever listens to me takes in only the words that he expects. The description of the world to which you pay such gracious attention is one thing, the one that will make the rounds of the brawlers and gondoliers on the *fondamenta* in front of my house on the day of my return is another, and the one I might dictate in my old age is something else again. What governs a narrative is not the *voice* but the *ear*."[123]

---

122. Hdt. 1.213.
123. I. Calvino, *Le città invisibili*, (Turin, 1972), p. 143.

Muthos and Pleasure or *Philomuthia*

A narrative never wells up from a single, original, source; it is always entangled with some other narrative. The ground covered by the traveler's tale or narrative is also covered by other narratives: before the wake left by the discoverers of the Pacific was converted into writing, it was already overlapping a trail left by the written narratives of their predecessors. When Christopher Columbus set sail he took Marco Polo's book with him.

In the hands of the narrator, the earlier narrative becomes a tool in the game of persuasion. For one way of eliciting belief for one's own account is to point out all that is "incredible," "lying," or "mythical" in the narrative of another. Herodotus is certainly mindful of that and frequently punctuates one or another *logos* with *emoi ou pista*, "for my part, I do not believe it." I do not believe the Chaldeans when they say that the god comes to the temple and, in the bed set up there, lies with the woman of his choice. I do not believe the Egyptians when they say that the phoenix carries away its father's corpse. I do not believe the Phoenicians when they say that they had the sun on their right side when sailing around Libya.[124] Conversely, there is the category of what is credible (*pithanos*), with its various gradations constituted by the comparative (the more credible of two narratives) and the superlative (the most credible narrative of all).[125] Where Herodotus makes use of the "credible," Thucydides was to use the category of verisimilitude (*eikos*).

When the Greeks speak of Heracles coming to Egypt, they are speaking in a "thoughtless fashion" (*anepiskeptos*) and recounting a *muthos*.[126] Of course, the Egyptians did not try to sacrifice him; after all, they are a people who may only sacrifice one or two animals, and even those only according to an extremely strict ritual. The Greek *logos* contradicts the Egyptian *nomoi*. What Hecataeus says about the Ocean is rated as *muthos* in an even more positive fashion: "As he

---

124. Hdt. 1.182, 2.73, 4.42, to which may be added 2.121, 5.86, 7.294, 8.119. Another expression Herodotus uses is *mataios logos* (a vain account) (2.2, 118, 3.56). The example of 2.118 is particularly interesting, because it concerns the Trojan War: "when I asked the priests whether the Greek accounts of the Trojan War were vain or not, they gave me the following answer." So on this point of fundamental importance, Herodotus does judge it to be useful, or at any rate interesting, to tap the knowledge of the Egyptian priests.

125. Hdt. 1.214, 2.123, 3.3, 9, 4.95.

126. Hdt. 2.45.

extended his *muthos* to what is invisible, there is no proof for it [*es aphanes ton muthon aneneikas ouk echei elegchon*]. For I know of no river Ocean; and I suppose that Homer or some older poet invented this name and brought it into poetry."[127] So *muthos*, situated beyond what is visible, eludes proof, and to refer to it is to allude to the work of a poet. Furthermore, each time Hecataeus is mentioned by name, he is called a *logopoios:* Hecataeus, "who makes up *logoi*," just like Aesop, the writer of fables. And Aesop, who is once mentioned in passing, is indeed referred to as Aesop, the *logopoios*.[128] The repetition of this expression is surely not fortuitous. To single out an element of *muthos* in another's *logos* is thus a way of distancing it from my own narrative: *muthos* is what, in another's narrative, I pick out as being other than a narrative (*es aphanes*).

Also, the traveler writes partly to denounce the "lying" narratives of other travelers. Thus Léry resolves to write his *Voyage* in particular because he has read Thévet's *Cosmographie* which, he says, is "stuffed with lies." This Franciscan friar who goes "looking for nonsense in the kingdom of the moon" is, to crown it all, a "paid liar": "What angers me even more is that not only does the one of whom I speak, being puffed up with the title of cosmographer to the king, receive such badly earned money and wages, but—what is worse— by these means nonsense unworthy to be written even in a simple letter is protected and authorized by the king's name." If he is a cosmographer, that means that he has lied "cosmographically, that is to say, to the whole world . . . so that, to hear him hold forth to all and sundry, you would think he had not only seen, heard, and personally observed all the customs and ways of behaving of this multitude of different savage peoples living in this quarter of the world, but also that he had surveyed every region of the West Indies," whereas the truth is that he only stayed there a few days and

127. Hdt. 2.23. On Ocean, cf. 4.8 and 36. It might, after all, be considered quite normal to speak of *muthos* where Hecataeus is concerned, since he himself starts off his *Histories-Genealogies* as follows: "Hecataeus of Miletus *mutheitai*, recounts." In his case it is reasonable to associate *muthos*, an inquiry into the *logoi* of the Greeks, and writing; whereas, in the case of Herodotus, *muthos* is immediately associated with *aphanes*, the invisible, and a lack of proof.

128. Hdt. 2.134, 143, 5.36, 125. See K. von Fritz, "Die Sogenannten *log-ographen, logopoioi* und *logioi*," *Die Griechische Geschichtsschreibung* (Berlin, 1967), vol. 2, pp. 337–47; J. Svenbro, *La Parole et le marbre* (Lund, 1976) pp. 208–11, points out that Herodotus is the first witness for a critical use of the poetic *poiein*.

without moving from one spot, on the little island of Villegagnon.[129] Lies or *muthos* thus have a double function. They produce narratives and allow narratives to proliferate: I write to denounce the narrative of another. So they cause people to write. And they cause people to believe, since to call someone else's narrative a fiction is a way for the narrator to validate his own narrative as a trustworthy piece of work. He wants to make you believe that he has seen, but I know that is not true, for I myself really have seen, so I am the one you should believe.

Herodotus persistently called Hecataeus a *logopoios*, but he was himself soon to suffer the same treatment. He was to be represented as a "teller of *logoi*," a liar, a "*muthos*-teller," or a "mythologist." What happened was that his credibility collapsed; people no longer believed his text. The first to make the break and to distance himself by consigning Herodotus's narrative to the side of *muthos* was the man who carried on from where he left off, the one who took over history at the point where he had left it, namely, Thucydides. The image of the son murdering his father rises up unbidden. So perhaps the *Archaeology* commits murder too, on top of everything else!

At the beginning of the fourth century B.C., Ctesias of Cnidus reaffirmed such a dissociation, but in quite a different manner. Ctesias, who was a doctor at the Persian court of king Ataxerxes, wrote *Persika*, in which he began by "taking the opposite view from Herodotus on just about everything," condemning him as a liar on many counts and labeling him a *logopoios*. As a result, Herodotus's credibility was ruined and denounced as a mere attempt to seem such, while high claims were made for Ctesias's own credibility: *he* had really seen (autopsy) or, failing that, had heard what he set down in writing (*suggrapsai*).[130] Needless to say, what follows is generally accepted to be a heap of the most arrant lies.

But the damage was done, and for a long time Herodotus was to be represented as a liar, a well-known figure with an almost inevitable label.[131] At the end of the first century A.D., Flavius Josephus

129. These quotations from Léry are taken from the work's preface.

130. Jacoby, *FGrHist*, 688 T 8.

131. On Herodotus in historiography, apart from A. Hauvette, *Hérodote, histo-rien des guerres médiques* (Paris, 1894), who devotes the first part of his book to this question, and W. Schmid, *Geschichte der griechischen Literatur*, vol. 2 (Munich, 1934), pp. 665ff., see K. Riemann, "Das Herodoteische Geschichtswerk in der

assessed the situation and, listing the successive critics who form the links in the chain of Greek historiography, pointed out that the only point of unanimity between them lay in their attacks on Herodotus.[132] Entire books were devoted to attacking him. Manethon wrote an *Against Herodotus*, denouncing his lies about Egypt. Later, the rhetors joined in with *On the Thefts of Herodotus* by Valerius Pollio, *On the Lies of Herodotus* by Aelius Harpocration, and an *Against Herodotus* by Libanius, not forgetting the most famous work, and the only one extant, Plutarch's treatise *On the Malice of Herodotus*. At just about the same time as Josephus was assessing the record of Greek historiography, Plutarch was writing his pamphlet, which was presented as a defense of ancestors, first and foremost his own, the Boeotians, who were particularly ill-used, but also the ancestors of all the cities that Herodotus had slandered. His postulate is a simple one. Herodotus is a liar, so much is indisputable; furthermore, he is a malicious liar; the fact is that there is no greater pleasure than that of maligning people, almost without appearing to do so. That is exactly what is meant by malice (*kakoetheia*). The demonstration that he produces to confound the liar is equally simple: he calls on the tradition relating to the Persian Wars and notably upon all its most jingoistic elements, by virtue of his deep-seated conviction that "everything is splendid in the history of the Greeks' victorious struggle against the Persians and that our ancestors left nothing but glorious examples behind them. (Whatever appears to cast a shadow over the shining picture of that brilliant period is open to question and should be effaced.)"

However, any defense of the tradition ought to take in more than

---

Antike," diss. Munich, 1965, and (briefer) J. Evans, "Father of History or Father of Lies: The Reputation of Herodotus," *Classical Quarterly* 64 (1968): 11–17. Finally, A. Momigliano, "The Place of Herodotus in the History of Historiography," *Studies in Historiography* (London, 1966), and his "Erodoto e la storiografia moderna: Alcuni problemi presentati ad un convegno di umanisti," *Aevum* 31 (1957): 74–84.

132. Flavius Josephus, *Against Apion* 1.3: on the contradictions between the Greek historians, "there is no need to tell the readers, who know more about it than I do, how much Hellanicus differs from Acusilaus on the genealogies, the corrections that Acusilaus makes to Hesiod, how on almost every point the mistakes of Hellanicus are picked out by Ephorus, as those of Ephorus are by Timaeus, those of Timaeus by his successors, and those of Herodotus by all and sundry."

just the Persian Wars, for nothing escaped Herodotus's malice. As
early as in his prologue, for example, he has a go at Io, whom "all the
Greeks suppose to have received divine honours at the hands of the
barbarians." According to Herodotus, however, she became pregnant by the captain of a Phoenician ship. Naturally, he pretends to
make this lying narrative come from the lips of the Phoenicians
themselves. The Trojan War, too, "the greatest and noblest exploit of
Greece," is presented as no more than an "act of folly" undertaken
"for the sake of a worthless woman," if it is true that those women
"would not have been carried off unless they themselves had wanted
it."[133] Plutarch omits to say that it was "the Persian scholars" who
made that remark about the abduction, not Herodotus himself, but
in all likelihood he would have added, if need be, that Herodotus was
simply pretending that the calumny came from them. Even more
serious, he "acquits" Busiris, the Egyptian pharoah, of the practice of
human sacrifice and of the murder of foreigners but meanwhile
accuses Menelaus of committing such crimes during his stay in
Egypt.[134] Finally, everything he says about the influence of Egyptian
religion on Greek religion is truly scandalous. "He uses worthless
stories to overthrow the most solemn and sacred truths of the Greek
religion."[135] He says things that a priest of Delphi, even a philosopher, could not accept, particularly as he shows no respect for
anyone, not even for the Pythia. The fact is that he treats people as
Aesop treats the animals in his fables, making them say things that
he himself has "fabricated" (*plasmata*); and Plutarch at one point
notes that, not content with making the Scythians, Persians, and
Egyptians pronounce his own words, Herodotus even has no compunction in using the Pythia in the same fashion.[136]

All in all, "many books" would be necessary "to describe all
his . . . lies and fabrications."[137] When Plutarch calls him a *philobar-
baros,* we should understand that as meaning not someone with a
weakness for barbarians, but a traitor to Greece. Besides, is he even

---

133. Plutarch *On the Malice of Herodotus* 856 E.

134. Plut. *On the Malice* 857A–B. In fact (2.45), Herodotus does not mention
Busiris.

135. Plut. *On the Malice* 857E.

136. Plut. *On the Malice* 871D. (It is a question of whether the prize for valor at
Salamis was awarded to the men of Aegina or to the Athenians.)

137. Plut. *On the Malice* 854F

truly Greek? Although "some regard him as a citizen of Thuril, his attachment is really to the Halicarnassians, those Dorians who took their harem with them on the expedition against Greece."[138]

That treatise of Plutarch's certainly marked an important stage in the construction and diffusion of the image of the liar, an image which from the Middle Ages was handed on to the Renaissance and to modern times. When from the Renaissance onward, attempts were made to defend Herodotus, it was primarily a matter of demolishing Plutarch's accusations. That is partly explained by the fact that between 1450 and 1700, Plutarch was one of the Greek authors most frequently published. There were, for example, sixty-two editions of the *Parallel Lives* as compared to forty-four editions of the *Histories*.[139] Nevertheless, for J. L. Vivès at the beginning of the sixteenth century, Herodotus incontestably remained the "father of lies": *Herodotus quam verius* **mendaciorum patrem** *dixeris quam quomodo illum vocant nonnulli*, **parentem historiae**."[140]

One more picture taken from this gallery of portraits of the liar comes from Abbé J.-B. Bonnaud, who in 1786 published a work entitled *Hérodote, historien du peuple hébreu sans le savoir*. It was introduced as a "letter in reply to a young philosopher's manuscript criticizing the work entitled *Histoire véritable des temps fabuleux*, by M. Guérin du Rocher, priest."[141] On the basis of Herodotus alone,

138. Plut. *On the Malice* 868.

139. The treatise *On the Malice* is not a part of the *Lives*. Nevertheless, Plutarch was one of the best known of authors. Flavius Josephus was the most frequently published Greek author of this period (sixty-three editions of the *Antiquities*, sixty-eight of the *History of the Jewish Wars*). But there were a total of two hundred and eighty-two editions of Sallust, the foremost of the Latin authors; cf. P. Burke, "The Popularity of Ancient Historians," *History and Theory* 5 (1966): 136.

140. J. L. Vivès, *De disciplinis libri XII* (Lugduni Batavorum, 1636), p. 155 (De causis corruptarum artium, liber II), p. 627 (De tradendis disciplinis, liber V). Vivès returns to the subject of Herodotus as the father of history which, following Cicero, he explains on stylistic grounds: *Herodotus pater nominatus historiae, quod primus ad rerum narrationem, elegantiam, et nitorem orationis adjunxit. Habet fabulosa permulta, sed operis titulo excusatur, inscripsit enim musas: quo significavit quaedam dici licentius.*

141. Abbé Bonnaud, *Hérodote, historien du peuple hébreu sans le savoir* (The Hague, 1786); Guérin du Rocher, *Histoire véritable des temps fabuleux* (Paris, 1776). Both men, who had played roles in the Catholic opposition to the French Revolution, died on 2 September 1792, when a group of refractory priests were massacred in the Carmes prison in Paris.

Abbé Bonnaud set out to defend and justify the "most fortunate discovery" of his master, Guérin du Rocher, namely, that Herodotus's history of Egypt is quite simply a "clumsy distortion" of the history of the Hebrew people.

By writing his *Histoire véritable des temps fabuleux*, the Jesuit Guérin intended to strike a blow against the incredulity of the age. Opposing those who claimed to confuse the history of the Bible with "the fables of antiquity," he tried to make those very fables testify in favor of the Scriptures, by demonstrating that they themselves were simply a "travesty" of those very Scriptures. The procedure was in fact an old one initiated by the Church Fathers who wrote about the Greeks' "travesties," "distortions," and "plagiarisms" of the history of the Bible. We now find the same theme taken up, following others, by these two priests who were so concerned to "reveal" the truth of those fabulous times.[142] Since, of all profane history, Egyptian history was reputed to be the most ancient, it was quite natural to tackle it first, and since Herodotus was the most ancient historian to have told of it, it was inevitable that they should have concentrated chiefly on him.[143] The origin of the travesty was to be sought in language itself and, above all, in the difficulties encountered in passing from one language to another. The "distortions" stem from incorrect translation or erroneous interpretations of proper names. It is as if, once a language escaped from those who normally used it, it engendered fables. Recourse to etymology therefore provides the scholar with a sure method of bringing the truth to light, a fact of which Abbé Guérin is well aware. Thus beneath Thebes, the Egyptian town, we should in fact discern Noah's Ark, which in Hebrew is called *Thbe;* and beneath Menes, the first Egyptian sovereign, we should discern Noah, for Noah is pronounced *nê* or *mnêe* in Hebrew and Noah is certainly "in a sense, the first man to reign after the Flood."[144]

As for Herodotus himself, Abbé Bonnaud can only conclude that the father of history is indeed the father of lies even if, writing "on the

142. F. E. Manuel, *The Eighteenth Century Confronts the Gods* (Cambridge, Mass., 1959), pp. 112–15.

143. Guérin, *Histoire*, pp. xxix, 91: the history of Egypt is a "distorted translation" of sacred history from Noah down to the end of the captivity of the Jews in Babylon.

144. Ibid., p. 126.

basis of incomplete extracts from the Bible . . . provided for him by
the priests of Memphis," he lied without realizing it. The "vanity" of
profane history is thus clearly revealed, for it is history which does
not know what it is saying, which in effect says something other than
what it believes it says; in comparison with the Scriptures, the only
truth about it is precisely that it is nothing but fable.

The *historical truth*, elaborated in all moral certainty and based on the
testimony of men, thus turns out, so far as the ancient secular annals are
concerned, to have been for more than two thousand years no more than a
shadow of the truth of our divine Scriptures. Thus, the first masterpiece of
the human mind in the historical genre becomes a remarkable monument
to the illusion of testimony provided by men and also to the vanity of all
secular literature.

Sic transit secular history, which dries up at its "source" and itself
becomes a part of mythology. Once that illusion is dissipated, all that
remain, forever indestructible, are the Scriptures and sacred history,
and these provide the truth for all other discourse.[145]

For Abbé Bonnaud, secular history belongs to mythology and
Herodotus, who lies without knowing it, is not a historian but a
mythologist, a teller of *muthoi*. Whether he really lies without
knowing it or whether he pretends to lie, he was quite indepen-
dently from and well before the apologist's stand taken by Abbé
Bonnaud, often represented as a "mythologist," that is to say, some
kind of liar. Aristotle describes him as *ho muthologos*, and six
centuries later Aulus Gellius was to refer to him as *homo fabula-
tor*.[146] When Hecataeus of Abdera reviews the sources of knowledge
on Egypt, he is at pains to make it known that he will simply omit the
stories fabricated by Herodotus and one or two others "who deliberately choose to produce paradoxes [*to paradoxologein*] and to
fabricate *muthoi* [*muthous plattein*] rather than tell the truth." He,
in contrast, will base what he says on "the archives written by the
priests." That is a way of both criticizing Herodotus for having
deliberately ignored that source and also disparaging *muthos* in the

---

145. Abbé Bonnaud, *Hérodote*, pp. 3, 276 (ed. Liège, 1790).
146. Aristotle *GA* 3.5.56b6 (on the absence of any detectable copulation between fish, everybody repeats what was said by Herodotus, *ho muthologos*); Aulus
Gellius *Attic Nights* 3.10.

name of the truth of what is written.[147] In similar fashion, Strabo denounces the tendency toward *philomuthia* among ancient authors, Herodotus in particular; they are inclined to tell stories.[148] Of course, this *philomuthia* is particularly prevalent concerning border areas and in connection with the distant past.[149]

When Hesiod speaks of "long-headed" men or "Pygmies," it is not through "ignorance" but as the result of a deliberate choice; he has opted for the "mythical form" (*muthou schema*).

But no more should one charge Homer with ignorance when he tells these mythical stories of his, one of which is of these very Pygmies; nor Alcman when he tells about "web-footed men"; nor Aeschylus when he speaks of "dog-headed men" or of "men with eyes in their breasts" or of "one-eyed men"; since at all events we do not pay much attention to prose writers either when they compose stories on many subjects in the guise of history [*historias schema*] even if they do not expressly acknowledge that they are dealing in myths [*muthographia*]. For it is self-evident that they are weaving in myths intentionally, not through ignorance of the facts but through an intentional invention of the impossible, to gratify the taste for the marvellous and the entertaining. But they give the impression of doing this through ignorance, because by preference and with an air of plausibility they tell such tales about the unfamiliar and the unknown [*pithanos mutheousi*]. Theopompus expressly acknowledges the practice when he says that he intends to narrate myths [*muthoi*] too in his History—a better way than that of Herodotus, Ctesias, Hellanicus and the authors of the Histories of India.[150]

The result is that in the end "it is easier to believe" Hesiod, Homer, and the tragic poets than Ctesias, Herodotus, Hellanicus, and the rest of them,[151] since the former deliberately chose "the mythical form," whereas the latter, who chose "the historical form," slipped into the "mythical" while pretending to remain within the "historical."

147. In Diodorus, 5.69.7.
148. Strabo 11.6.2.
149. For example, Strabo 12.3.21: "some call the Scythians beyond the Borysthenes river 'Alazones' and also 'Callipidae' and other names—names which Hellanicus, Herodotus and Eudoxus have foisted on us (*katephluaresan hemon*)."
150. Strabo 1.2.35.
151. Strabo 11.6.3.

What is the mainspring for this *philomuthia*? The answer is pleasure. Here again, the one to put his finger on the point was Thucydides: when they spoke of Greece's past, the logographers were seeking pleasure more than the truth and allowed themselves to be guided by the pleasure of the ear.[152] Thucydides distances himself from the words of the logographers, calling them *muthoi* and denouncing them as words of pleasure:

> It may well be that the absence of the fabulous from my narrative will seem less pleasing to the ear; but whoever shall wish to have a clear *view* both of the events which have happened and of those which will some day, in all human probability, happen again in the same or a similar way—for these to adjudge my history *profitable* will be enough for me. And, indeed, it has been composed not as a prize essay to be heard for the moment but as a possession for all time.[153]

He thus sets up an opposition between *muthos*, the ear, the present moment, and pleasure, on the one hand and the truth, writing, a possession forever, and what is useful, on the other. And he is determined to make that dichotomy clear in his work. Subsequently, the principle of pleasure mentioned by Thucydides was consistently reaffirmed by all those who called Herodotus a "mythologist" or a "liar"—not only Hecataeus and Strabo, as we have seen above, but also modern writers such as Niebuhr.

Seen from that point of view,[154] the mythical is whatever one decides to call such, and nothing can be *muthos* except in relation to some other type of discourse, which can only be deployed once that fundamental division has been made. Once that has happened, I can consider *muthos* as an object of derision and use it to set off my own discourse to better advantage, or I can treat it as a scientific object and submit it to an investigation. The criterion for designating a story as mythical is that it no longer elicits belief. After Thucydides,

152. Thucydides 1.21.
153. Thucydides 1.22.4.
154. For a wider view on mythology, see M. Detienne, "La Mythologie scandaleuse," *Traverses*, 12 September 1978, pp. 3–20. To pass from *muthos* as "other" than historiographical discourse to myth as primitive speech is an easy step: myth consists of words which do not know what they are saying but which at the same time delight. That is what makes the "mythologist" write: perhaps "to forget" that it is impossible to believe it.

people no longer believed some of the stories recounted by Herodotus, who accordingly became a "mythologist," that is to say, credulous or a liar. He believed when he should not have (unconscious liar); he pretended to believe when he should not have (liar, pure and simple). The organizing principle of this mythical discourse is pleasure—pleasure for the listeners and also for the narrator, who allows himself to be carried away by it and anticipates the pleasure of his listeners. Words of pleasure and pleasure in words: *muthos* thus appears as the "other" in relation to historiographical discourse.

Even as Herodotus is stigmatized for seeking after pleasure or abandoning himself to it, both of which ruin his credibility, his style is praised: he is the master of the Ionian dialect. And just as there is a pleasure in his style, which is recognized, there is a danger in his text, which is denounced, by Plutarch for example. For Plutarch, what Herodotus writes is all the more dangerous because, like the presents the Persians give to the Ethiopians, it is "deceptive": "His style, which is apparently so simple and effortless, slipping easily from one subject to another" has fooled many a reader.[155] Cicero, who relished this pleasure, speaks of Herodotus's style "which flows like a quiet river [*quasi sedatus amnis fluit*]."[156] And Lucian would be content if he could imitate not all the qualities of Herodotus's style—for that would manifestly be impossible—but even just one of them, such as the "beauty of his diction," "the order of the words or his mastery of Ionian."[157] In the conclusion to his treatise, Plutarch, again, recognizes that Herodotus "is an artist, that his history makes good reading, that there is charm, skill and grace in his narrative," and he goes on to cite the *Odyssey*: Alcinoos tells Odysseus that he sings "as a bard tells a tale, with knowledge," and Plutarch takes over the expression to apply it to Herodotus, except that he denies him

155. Plut. *On the Malice* 863E (Hdt. 3.20–22) and 854F. As we know, for Aristotle it was the model of the *lexis eiromene*, i.e., of the "close-knit," "consecutive" style in which one says one thing which leads to another which leads to yet another. One translates, with a "coordinated style." Aristotle himself did not find this ancient style, no longer much used in his own day, attractive (*Rhetorica* 3.9.1409a27).

156. Cicero (*Oratore* 39, *De oratore* 2.55) mentions the pleasure afforded by his eloquence, *tanta est eloquentia magno opere delectat*. These texts are collected in Reimann, "Das Herodoteische Geschichtswerk."

157. Lucian *Herodotus or Aetion* 1.

"knowledge," recognizing only the musicality and polish of his style;[158] he is just like a bard, except that he does not sing of the truth.

The comparison with Homer is assuredly not fortuitous. To pass from mythologist to poet is an easy step, for the mythologist is, after all, simply a poet in disguise. Herodotus himself, in his prologue, has epic in mind and hopes to rival it; he even echoes the opening lines of the *Iliad* and the *Odyssey*. As Lucian attests, each of the nine books of the *Histories* was called after one of the Muses.[159] Dionysius of Halicarnassus regarded him as an imitator of Homer: "Herodotus, the great imitator of Homer, was at pains to introduce the greatest variety into his History. As we read it, everything, right down to the last syllable, enchants us and we would like it to be longer."[160] That idea was to continue to gain a wide currency, for in the eighteenth century Abbé Geinoz was to pick it up and give it a new lease of life by setting up a parallel between the *Iliad* and the *Odyssey* on the one hand and Herodotus's *Histories* on the other. In his view, such a theory "was bound to be of great interest to all who love literature; it could even be of some use to those who undertake to write history."[161] More generally, Strabo was of the opinion that the first logographers (Cadmus, Pherecydes, and Hecataeus) endeavored to imitate the poetic form, "abandoning the use of metre but in other respects preserving the qualities of poetry."[162] Thus, they were all rhapsodes or bards, but in prose.

A Renewed Belief

When the fifteenth century rediscovered Herodotus, it did so with pleasure. Lorenzo Valla's translation had a great impact even before it was published (1474). But as they read Herodotus, the scholars of the

158. Plut. *On the Malice* 874 B: *graphikos aner, kai edus ho logos, kai charis epesti kai deinotes kai ora tois diegemasi muthon d'hos hot' aoidos, epistamenos men ou liguros te kai glaphuros ehoreuken.*

159. Lucian *Herodotus or Aetion* 1.

160. Dionysus *Letter to Cn. Pompey.*

161. Abbé Geinoz's defense of *Hérodote contre les accusations de Plutarch, Mem. Acad. Inscript.* 19 (1753): 115–45; 21 (1754): 120–44; 23 (1756): 101–14.

162. Strabo 1.2.6.

quattrocento were also reading his critics, Plutarch in particular. The pleasure of discovery soon became tinged with a certain mistrust, as can be seen from the preface written by Giovanni Pontano for an edition of Herodotus in Valla's translation, which was never published.[163] This mistrust reached a climax at the point where all belief in Herodotus was undermined, as we find expressed in the judgment recorded by J. L. Vivès cited above: more like the father of lies than the father of history.

In the sixteenth century the situation changed. Herodotus's defenders, timid at first, became bolder with time, sometimes launching veritable counterattacks such as the famous *Apologio pro Herodoto* by Henri Estienne (1566). No, Herodotus is not a liar. Estienne leads off with that image of the liar, an image known to everyone, one even proverbial.[164] Similarly, in another work, published in the vernacular, with the title *Introduction au traité de la conformité des merveilles anciennes avec les modernes, ou Traité préparatif à l'Apologie pour Hérodote*, he starts off with the well-known affirmation according to which "Herodotus does nothing but tell lies." Why are the stories that he tells considered "suspect"? "Because they have no verisimilitude," people answer.

Now, let us consider, gentle reader, whether they speak categorically when they infer that these stories are not true because they do not seem true.

But that is by no means all. The fact is that I flatly deny what they hold to be generally admitted and proven, namely, that they lack verisimilitude. And if it were so, on what grounds do they base their judgment? On two: in the first place, the excessive wickedness manifest in some of the actions described by Herodotus and the excessive stupidity in some of the others are more than they can credit. Second, seeing that much of what we read there bears no relation at all to the customs and ways of doing things of today and has nothing in common with the latter, they reckon the ancient stories

163. G. Pontano, *Opera*, vol. 3 (Venice, 1516), p. 298: *et Musis aliquanto etiam liberius, ut scitis, loqui concessum est;* cf. Momigliano, "Erodoto," p. 81.

164. Recent edition, *Henrici Stephani: Apologia pro Herodoto*, ed. J. Kramer (Meisenheim am Glan, 1980). The full title of the *Defense* is "H. Stephani Apologia pro Herodoto sive Herodoti historia fabulositatis accusata" (preface to his edition of Herodotus in the Valla translation). The *Apologia* and the *Epître au lecteur* of the *Traité* list a number of examples from the *Histories* which no longer elicit belief and endeavor to show that their lack of verisimilitude need not prevent them from being true.

to be as far from the truth as what they read is far from what they are used to seeing and hearing.[165]

Estienne proceeds to show the inanity of those two reasons, by using a comparison. So far as stupidity and wickedness go, as much if not more has been committed since then, both in the past, not only elsewhere but in France too, their own country, and in their own day. As for *mores*, Estienne finds it "strange that they should be found so strange as to be incredible, for if we consider the differences between our own and those of neighboring peoples, we shall find them hardly any the less strange in their own places." So the point can be made without even going to the lengths of invoking the countries of primitive people. Thus the conclusion to the *Apologia* is absolutely clear and firm: contemporary accounts confirm those of the past. Contemporary autopsy is invoked to guarantee and renew belief in the stories told by Herodotus.

Carrying the argument a step further, the contemporary *thoma* can even function as a criterion of belief in the narratives of the ancient writers, as can be seen from Léry's text (the first edition of which appeared in 1578):

And indeed I am not ashamed to confess here that since I have been in this country of America . . . without approving the fables which may be read in the books of a number of authors [first and foremost among them, his enemy Thévet, the Franciscan] who, trusting what they were told, or for some other reason, wrote down things which were entirely false, I have nevertheless retracted my earlier opinion of Pliny and a few others who described foreign countries, *because I have seen* things just as bizarre and marvelous as some mentioned by them which have been held to be incredible.[166]

Thanks to autopsy, there is even a switch in positions: Thévet the cosmographer takes the place of the liar, and Pliny, who previously occupied it, now takes that of the trustworthy author. The expansion

---

165. *Apologie ou L'introduction au Traité de la Conformité* (Paris, 1879), vol. 1, p. 11.

166. Léry, *Histoire d'un voyage*, p. 28. Estienne, *Traité*, vol. 1, p. 31: "Those especially who today write stories about barbarian countries tell us of a number of marvels with which those of Herodotus do not even come close to comparing: I mean marvels of nature as much as marvels concerning both the behavior and appearance of men."

of the world and the narratives that told of it made this renewal of belief possible.

On the subject of Herodotus's credibility, the most important texts, after Thucydides' *Archaeology* and Plutarch's treatise, are Estienne's two works. Strictly speaking, only the first, the *Apologia*, is really concerned with Herodotus. In the *Traité préparatoire*, he is used simply as a pretext and starting point.[167] Estienne's main concern is to attack the papists and show that contemporary marvels by far outstrip those of antiquity: so far as wickedness, cruelty, and lust go, the men of the church need fear no rivals. His book, which was published in Geneva, was publicly burned and was subsequently reprinted many times during the sixteenth century. Herodotus was thus enlisted in a contemporary battle; defending him was simply a way of attacking the church.

From then on, Herodotus was no longer the master of error and falsehood—that is, up until the moment when Abbé Bonnaud embarked on his radical enterprise and with a single stroke of his pen scored through the whole of secular history, relegating it all to the position of mythology. Nevertheless, there was still a burden for Herodotus to shoulder. Herodotus's burden was his old rival, Ctesias. More often than not, the editions of the *Histories* in the sixteenth, seventeenth, and even eighteenth centuries included fragments of Ctesias, and very often these volumes would close with Estienne's *Apologia*. Whether through an irony of fate or the "malice" of a publisher, a single volume would thus bring together the author who defended Herodotus against the charge of lying, the one who—a confirmed liar himself—denounced him as a liar, and Herodotus himself, the father of history and of lies. In the silence and stagnation of many a library, the three of them must surely be regaling each other with a host of whispered liar's tales.

167. G. Atkinson, *Les Nouveaux Horizons de la Renaissance française* (Paris, 1935), pp. 424–25.

Eight

The *Histories* as Representation

As we embark on this last chapter, let us return for a moment to Scythia. We started off by making our way step by step through the Scythian *logos*, posing the question of the "place" occupied by these nomads within the area over which the *Histories* range. Imaginary Scythians, Scythians in Herodotus's mirror: a discourse on "the other." From there we moved on to a generalization, sketching in a rhetoric of otherness with its figures and procedures. Rhetoric means the art of persuasion: how can belief be elicited? Precisely by the narrator putting to use these figures and procedures. But there is a limit to instilling belief, a limit which negates it as such by the failure to instill belief any longer: that is the "worm i' the bud," the instilling of doubt which knows no limit to its development until it has completely rotted the fruit or cracked the edifice from top to bottom. The narrator is nothing but a liar and the narrative nothing but a fiction. That would be so, after all, if the indicators as to who is speaking that punctuate the text are merely fictions, if the "I have seen," "I have heard," or "I say," "I write" what is said are no more than tricks on the part of the narrator, literary procedures designed to elicit belief in order to deceive the public. If one allowed that spiral of a fiction to uncoil, it would soon engulf everything and the *Histories* would be in danger of becoming as elusive and enigmatic as a story by J. L. Borges. Indeed, they come close to that in the study by D. Fehling who, after examination, concludes that Herodotus's sources were merely fictitious.[1] It is only in order to create an impression of trustworthiness that he apportions his account to the various sources he cites. So it is not a matter of *historie* at all, simply of a number of literary techniques, or of a faked *historie*, and the work is a total fiction (*Gesamtfiktion*).

To note the point at which credibility rebounds against itself, to be converted into exhausted credibility, is also to realize that the traveler's tale is pervaded by otherness just as much as historical discourse is. Both proceed by setting at a distance something "other" which they label *muthos* precisely in order to distinguish themselves from it and thereby render themselves the more credible. Otherness is thus not simply a question of others for, in the process of being produced, historiography elaborates a discourse that is "other" than its own: a leftover, a mistake, a fiction.

How to elicit belief; but also, to follow the theme right through, elicit belief in what, and why? There are two ways to formulate that double question: "elicit belief in what, and why?" or "the *Histories* as representation." Beyond it, on the horizon, there lurks yet another, still more general question but one that it would be pointless to pose in an abstract form: the question of the status of the historical text and the function of the *histor*.

It might be objected that I am presuming to consider the status of the *Histories* or—as I put it—the *Histories* as representation, when I have only incidentally mentioned the Persian Wars which are, after all, their main subject. If Herodotus is a historian, he is first and foremost "the historian of the Persian Wars."[2] It is quite true that it is upon that Herodotus that historiography has chiefly concentrated. The Herodotus who reports facts and narrates military and political events is the one whom scholars cite and use as a source, showing no hesitation about correcting his "mistakes" or his "exaggerations" (particularly in the case of battles and the sizes of the forces involved) and being fully prepared to question *his* sources.

1. D. Fehling, *Die Quellenangaben bei Herodot* (Berlin, 1971).

2. A. Hauvette's work, *Hérodote, historien des guerres médiques* (Paris, 1894), was submitted in the 1891 competition held by the Académie des Inscriptions et Belles-Lettres, as an essay on the following: "Study the tradition of the Persian Wars; determine the elements from which it is composed, examining the narrative of Herodotus and the information supplied by other writers."

It is true that I have spoken hardly at all of that Herodotus. I have concentrated upon the other one, the surveyor of the *oikoumene* and the rhapsode of otherness, the one whom Greek scholars sometimes find it difficult to cope with, seeking either to discount him or to make excuses for him—another Herodotus, but also Herodotus's "other self," his shadow. If we set the interminable debates between the partisans and the adversaries of the work's unity in this perspective, I think it becomes easier to understand them. One point of view has it that the first *logoi* (the Lydian, Babylonian, Egyptian *logoi*) were composed earlier and separately and were only later tacked onto the rest of the work; the other, on the contrary, claims that Herodotus had an overall plan right from the start. Sometimes the discussion takes a different form: Herodotus started off as a geographer and ethnographer and only later became a historian (Jacoby's view). History then appears as a fruit of maturity and one which—naturally—could ripen only in Athens. The birth of history in Greece thus becomes a part of Herodotus's own biography and that makes it possible both to praise him as the father of history and simultaneously, on occasion, to call him a pre-historian or even a non-historian (when he is *still* an ethnographer or *only* a geographer).[3] But throughout all these pages of discussion, fundamentally the purpose is to explain or reject or, alternatively, to exorcise that part of the *Histories* which is marked off as "other," the place of fables, the liar's lair.

The fact still remains that I have indeed spoken little of the Persian Wars except insofar as they relate to the Scythian War, where they play the role of model of intelligibility,[4] and it is quite true that it is not my intention to speak of them as themselves. To do so, it would be necessary to see how, step by step, in order to recount them and in the process of recounting them, Herodotus constructs a new memorial: a collection of memories different from those elaborated and transmitted by epic poetry.

What I would question are the grounds for making a separation between one Herodotus, who is the historian of the Persian Wars, and another or, rather, Herodotus's other self. It is perfectly possible to see the "ethnographic" part and the "historical" part with the same eye and to read both with the same voice, for they are situated at the

3. Jacoby, *RE*, 352–60.
4. Cf. above, pp. 34ff.

same distance. To separate one from the other, making one come before the other or hiding one behind the other, is after all to fall victim to Thucydides, for whom history means the history of a great contemporary war and for whom to produce history is to recount a major conflict. I also believe (and in this respect I must of course be counted among the supporters of the unity of Herodotus's work) that his way of setting about his task is the same throughout: when Herodotus makes his inquiry into the Persian Wars, he elaborates for the Greeks a representation of their recent past and, similarly, when he makes his inquiry into the margins of the world and foreign peoples, he constructs a representation of the world. In the two cases, the discourse produces analogous effects.

To pose the question we have put: "to elicit belief in what, and why?" is also to formulate the question of the status, function, and reception of the work and perhaps also that of its public. Momigliano, considering the matter of the ancient historians and their audiences, begins by pointing out that of all the literary genres, history occupied a special place precisely in that it had no place of its own: the other genres "were written for a given situation and had an intrinsically ceremonial character," whereas the historians "neither became a profession nor had a ceremonial task, nor did they have a clearly defined type of knowledge to discover or to transmit."[5] And he mentions an inquiry (then taking place) to arrive at "a few precise conclusions on the position of the historian in the Greek and Roman societies." The question is thus far from being resolved, as is confessed even by the scholar who is the foremost contemporary expert on ancient historiography.

For some, of course, the question *is* immediately resolved—or, rather, misunderstood. For example: who is Herodotus? "A curious traveler? An adventurous merchant? One of the first historians? No, a geographer, an agent collecting information, in the service of Athenian imperialism."[6] If the context of this quotation were overlooked, the implication of the author's purported way of proceeding would certainly appear to be that the text is a reflection of society and the struggles that shape it. At any rate, imperialism makes it possible to lose no time in "moving outside" the text, to discover the real

5. A. Momigliano, "The Historians of the Classical World and Their Audiences: Some Suggestions," *Annali de la Scuola Normale Superiore di Pisa* 8, 1 (1978): 59–60.
6. Y. Lacoste, "Attention Géographes," *Hérodote*, vol. 1 (Paris, 1976), p. 5.

struggles taking place. That is the function of the text, and all the rest
is merely literature.

"Moving outside" the text is also what Momigliano suggests, albeit
doing so in a very different fashion. Since Herodotus's and Thucydides' works themselves tell us hardly anything about the relationships between the texts, their authors, and their public,[7] we must
collect all the evidence—mainly, but not exclusively, literary—
written around them, on the subject of the historians and their
works, so as to learn more, indirectly, about their position in society.

But before "moving outside," whether deliberately or without
realizing it, we may suppose that there is still plenty to be done *in*
and *with* the text itself. That is a hypothesis which, in the case of
ancient history, may well prove to be a necessity: not only is there
more to be *done* with the text but it must be done, for it is almost
impossible to move outside it. Consider the Homeric poems: in their
case, how is it possible to bring context and intertextuality into play?
The only chance of understanding anything about the world of
Odysseus is to pay serious attention to the text and nothing but the
text.[8] It is only then that the next question arises: how should we pay
serious attention to it? That is to say, how should it be read? Of
course, the *Iliad* and the *Odyssey* represent an extreme case. The
context for the *Histories* does not elude us entirely nor is it completely impossible to resort to intertextuality where they are concerned. Nevertheless, I do not think there is anything to be lost by
pursuing our interrogation of the text itself. However, not to "move
outside" the text, or not to do so over-hastily, does not necessarily
mean "immuring oneself inside" it, in cloistered seclusion with all
doors and windows shut; nor is it my purpose to set up a "cult" of the
text, which would simply be "a barely modernized form of the old
cult of the heroes."[9] But we must pay serious attention to the text

7. Momigliano, "Historians."

8. M. I. Finley, *The World of Odysseus* (Harmondsworth, 1962).

9. J.-P. Faye, *Théorie du récit* (Paris, 1972), p. 130: "Stepping beyond these two
symmetrical reefs—to wit, the naively mechanistic conception of 'economic deter-
minism' mistakenly attributed to Marx, and the cult of the 'text,' a barely modernized version of the old cult of 'heroes'—another method, capable of advancing on
two fronts, both the *sociology* of languages and the semantics of *history*, would set
out to decipher the materiality of the meaning just at the point where, as Pasternak
puts it, that meaning comes to fill the entire century."

(whether historical or not), examining the procedures used in it. All in all, it seems to me that it is thus that ancient history might make its own theoretical contribution to history in general and, in particular, to an investigation into what should be understood by the terms *document* and *source*.

The question of the status and function of the *Histories*, and therefore of their meaning, remains to a large extent unanswered. Herodotus was born in Halicarnassus, lived for some time in exile, traveled, passed through Athens, went to live in Thurii, composed his *Histories*, and died. So neither the biographical context nor the social, political, and cultural ones elude us entirely; nonetheless, they remain relatively vague. Although we may to some degree glimpse a play of intertextuality, it is no easy matter to determine its pertinence with any precision.[10] As for the place of the *Histories* in the long term, it is connected with the familiar image of the liar: that is an indication of the mistrust that they elicited but also of the place that they occupied, since it became customary to repeat and recall the lies told by their author, every time they were mentioned.

To take into account only the avowed intentions and declared purpose of the narrator clearly will not do. For, despite the fact that as early as the prologue, Herodotus declares his intention of rivaling Homer and epic poetry, in reality what he does is something quite different: where the poet invoked the Muse, claiming to be no more than its mouthpiece, Herodotus introduces *historie*, inquiry.[11] And by the end of the nine books, he has replaced the epic memories with a new type of memorial for the city. No doubt the inventory of the Persian army in Book 7 does "resemble" the catalogue of ships in Book 2 of the *Iliad*,[12] but the one is dictated by the Muse whereas the other is presented simply as the transcription of an inventory. So let us, at least for the time being, substitute the question of narrator and addressee for that of author and public and replace the question of the function of the work by that of its effects; and let us play the card of intratextuality for all it is worth.

As an example of how to pay serious attention to the text while in no way making it the object of a cult—quite the contrary—let us consider the undertaking of J.-P. Faye, who tries to "seize upon the

10. T. Todorov, *Symbolisme et interprétation* (Paris, 1978), pp. 60–61.
11. J. Svenbro, *La Parole et le marbre* (Lund, 1976).
12. Herodotus 7.60ff.; *Iliad* 2.484ff.

point at which the narrative structures—whether or not fictitious—
engender a particular process and through their *transformations*
produce an effect on *another* level: the level of action, with all its 'real
interests.'"[13] But of course the combined transformations of the
discourse *do not in themselves* constitute action.

It was not a combination of the accounts of Saint-Just and Tallien, together
with all the speeches that followed that effected the arrest of Robespierre,
but the hands of the officers of the law. . . . However, a field of language was
constituted and it resulted in certain decisions becoming *acceptable*. What
we must investigate is how those fields of language are constituted—and we
must do so by means of precisely what it is that illuminates them and
explores them in the immediate instance: namely, the narrative function of
the discourse.[14]

Consider the speech delivered by Barnave on 15 July 1791, in defense
of the king, who had taken to flight, and of the constitutional
monarchy. First and foremost, it is a narrative of the history that had
been unfolding since the night of 4 August 1789; but it also makes the
point that "it is not metaphysical ideas which sweep the masses along
in the path of revolutions, but, rather, their real interests." That is a
way of repeating that the level of narrative and ideology (in the sense
of the utterance of ideas) does not constitute action, and also a way of
emphasizing that Barnave's own discourse

is no more than the surface, or appearance, of what has happened at a
deeper or more "real" level. At the same time, though, it encapsulates the
latter, it contains it, for it discloses and utters it. And, more important, it
produces an effect on the very level that it has just disclosed; for by revealing
to the National Assembly the interests of the majority of its members, it
undeniably leads the latter to vote in favor of promulgating a decree
prepared on the basis of the report produced by the committees. The
promulgation of the Constitution, the election of the Legislative Assembly,
a whole year of live history and all the effects that stemmed from it: such was
the tally of what narrative produced in this instance.[15]

Despite the schematic nature (accentuated by my own presenta-

13. The expression is borrowed from Barnave (speech of 15 July 1791). But the
point is that by saying that, he *produces* an effect on that very level (he reveals to the
Assembly what its own real interests are).

14. Faye, *Théorie du récit*, p. 112.

15. Ibid., p. 107.

tion of it) of this analysis of the narrative process, it is clear that the point Faye is making is an important one. It is equally clear that revolutionary speeches provide a splendid field of experimentation for anybody posing the question of the *Wirkung* of a narrative. But perhaps the revolution is too peculiar an area, one in which power and words interact more directly with each other and where the power of the word becomes the word of power. The Revolution was the moment when

power was in the hands of those who spoke for the people. Therefore, not only did that power reside in the word, for the word, being public, was the means of unmasking forces that hoped to remain hidden and were thus nefarious; but also power was always at stake in the conflict between words, for power could only be appropriated through them, and so they had to compete for the conquest of that evanescent yet primordial entity, the people's will. The Revolution replaced the conflict of interests for power with a competition of discourses for the appropriation of legitimacy.[16]

Now, while Barnave may indeed have produced "a year of live history" by his narrative, he was also deeply committed in that competition of speeches: effectiveness and commitment went hand in hand. It thus seems to me that the conclusions of these analyses, which first and foremost take account of the discourse of the revolutionaries themselves (rather than that of the historians of the Revolution, or which do not compare the two) are not ones from which it is possible to generalize.[17]

Let us return to the *Histories*. What effects does the work

---

16. F. Furet, *Interpreting the French Revolution* (Cambridge, 1981), p. 49.

17. Faye certainly does consider (*Théorie du récit*, p. 111) history and its "fundamental process" from the simple or primitive narrative down to the "historicizing account" (that is to say, the account of the historian): "At the two ends of the chain and enclosing the superposed and adjacent or entangled levels of history in action are, on the one hand, the web of simple or immediate narrative, which articulate and produce the fundamental sequence of events and, on the other, the historicizing account which reduces to one all the different versions of a particular fact" and "which erases beneath the true account the continuing and active play of the primitive narrative." But he is more concerned to study the first end of the chain (Barnave) than the second, or, rather, he refers to it, taking Herodotus as an example—Herodotus, whose account to a large extent does not fit into this definition of the "true" account as one that erases the primitive narrative. Faye (quite justifiably, in my opinion) makes the "classical age" of history begin with Thucydides.

produce, on whom, and on what? In the first place, it affects the addressee. It is for him that the narrator calculates its effect; in other words, it is on him that the work is intended to have effect. Effect on what? Not on the level of action. Herodotus does not directly make things happen; he does not cause the war or the peace or the extension of democracy. We have just seen the extent to which over-hasty attempts to move outside the text may turn out to be false ones. They may stem from a false entry into the text, occasioned by an obsession not to leave reality, or *terra firma*, or to return to it without delay. But, I would suggest, he does produce effects on the "imaginary" in the sense of the faculty of representation.[18] What are these effects? Of course, the text purveys knowledge; it explicitly provides new information. But concentrating solely on the effect produced by knowledge leads to taking no account of the way the text is organized into a narrative, to ignoring it as a narrative, concentrating solely on the discursive content (which the commentator proceeds to divide up in an arbitrary fashion according to his own implicit criteria, such as verisimilitude, rationality, superstition). The effect that I have in mind is produced at the level of the structure of the narrative or, rather, at the level of whatever it is that provides the structure of the narrative—whatever makes it possible for the narrator to construct it, but also whatever makes it possible for the addressee to "read" it, to calculate the meaning of the statements or even of the implicit codes that organize it.

Take the Scythian *logos:* what provides its structure and, so to speak, generates it is the question of nomadism. What is a nomad, to someone who lives in a city? To take another example: the grid by which to read the passage on Scythian sacrifice, which appears to be sacrifice in no more than name, is implicitly provided by the civic sacrifice of the ox.[19] The word *Scythian* is certainly no new signifier,

---

18. Effect: we may also think of the metaphor of the billiard ball to which a certain effect is imparted so that, as it hits another ball, the original ball itself propels the second in the calculated direction. *The imaginary (imaginaire)*: a word historians are increasingly prone to use. We pass from a history of mentalities to a history of the imaginary. This latter word, which has the advantage of being even more vague (and so potentially more vast) than the former, makes it possible to construct completely new historical subjects . . . at least up to the point where too much indeterminacy becomes counterproductive.

19. Cf. above, pp. 173ff.

forged by Herodotus; on the contrary, it drags along with it, as if in a trawling net, a whole body of shared knowledge in which, precisely, *Scythian* means people of the north but also nomad, and the two meanings are simultaneously present without it being possible to determine which comes first and which second; in this body of shared knowledge, the Scythian thus symbolizes the nomad.[20] Merely by proffering that word, the narrator thus introduces the question of nomadism into his narrative. But having introduced it, he is not content simply to leave it there, inert. He proceeds to work on it, turning the symbolic meaning of the word into the very code of the *logos*. If in the shared knowledge of the fifth century B.C, the Scythian represents the nomad, it is clear that that is exactly what the Scythian *logos* will set out to say, but it does so by attempting to make this symbolic equivalence of Scythian-nomad explicit and to deploy it in space. Let us recall the sequence. First stage: the ethnographic inventory in which the Scythians are *not only* nomads. Second stage: that of Darius's war; here they are *only* nomads. Finally, they can be *nothing but nomads* (an effect of the symbolic pressure of the word but also a way of explaining the equivalence; nomadism, before being a way of life, is a strategy). Such is the effect produced by the Scythian *logos* on the imaginary representation of the addressee. Let us call it the symbolic effect, and thereby distinguish it from the simple effect of *knowledge*, to make the point that it does not need to be formulated explicitly and emphasize that it plays a structuring role: it makes it possible to see the Scythians.

But what about the *Histories* as a whole? Is it possible to make out an overall effect, or a series of effects, running through the entire work?

Let us begin by making a digression and a change in image, using the metaphor of a watercolorist. Imagine a painter in a field, at work. In the foreground is his table and attached to it is a squared frame through which he looks at what he is sketching. In a *Treatise on Perspective* this device is described as follows: "Some artists make use of a frame containing a mesh of equidistant threads through which they divide up the natural scene into squares. . . . Albert Dürer must be credited with the invention of this method of operation. The mesh of threads could quite well be replaced by a

20. Todorov, *Symbolisme et interprétation,* p. 11.

pane of glass on which squares are drawn."[21] The grid is invisible in the finished painting, so the viewer never sees it. Yet it was through it that the painter saw and it is that grid which, implicitly, allows the viewer to see what the artist saw, or which makes him believe he does, because it is what provides the structure for what he sees. He is all the more unconscious of the fact since it was probably thus that he learned to see. A way of verifying the picture would be to make the grid appear on the painting or reappear there.

Setting the whole question of perspective aside, is this not exactly what happens in the *Histories?* Except that here the grid and the painting merge together. But, just as the watercolorist's frame divides up his sketch into squares, similarly one or several grids exist for the *Histories*. And *grid* may be understood in two ways: first, the grid that structures the narrative entitled the *Histories* (the *Histories* are in the position of the painting and it is a matter of working back from the painting to try to reveal the grid that governs it). Second, the *Histories* themselves may be considered as a grid, that is to say, as "that through which" the narrator sees and makes it possible for the addressee to see the world, others, the past of Greece, and so forth. But now a further question arises, to wit: did the *Histories* also function as a grid, so to speak, beyond themselves or, to return to our watercolorist, were there other watercolorists who in later years used the *Histories* as a grid to see what they wished to draw?

The metaphor of the watercolorist must clearly be qualified in the case of the *Histories*, since the grid is formed not by threads or lines, but by language. And since, whatever Montaigne may say, there is no dictionary "purely for one's own use," that language is permeated by the shared knowledge of the Greeks. It manipulates and works on that shared knowledge which, at the same time, makes the language itself possible: the language corrects the shared knowledge, completes it, in some cases even helps to transform it. Through the code by which it is organized, the Scythian *logos* thus adopts and elucidates the symbolic meaning given to the word *Scythian* in the shared knowledge of the Greeks of the fifth century B.C.

At this point the question of a movement in the opposite direction arises: not from the shared knowledge of the Greeks toward the text, but in the opposite direction, from the work toward the shared knowledge. For, seen logically, there is no reason why the code that

21. G. Tubeuf, *Traité de perspective* (Paris, 1898), p. 208.

organizes Herodotus's Scythian *logos* should not, in return, enrich the shared knowledge of the Greeks (Scythians-nomads via strategy). The movement here would be from the (symbolic) constitution of the work to the work as a (symbolic) institution, that is to say, as the grid through which, even without realizing it, one sees. The question posed is certainly that of "moving outside" the text, but it is a movement outward that takes place through and in the language and on the level of the imaginary. It is not a matter of arguing in terms of influences here or of producing a history of ideas—especially not one constructed on "air-cushions"[22]—by maintaining that it is simply the way things are. But neither is there any point in using words such as *imaginary* or *grid* as if they could produce miracles and as if, just by manipulating them, one could settle the problem once and for all or, rather, spirit it away.

My aim is simply to determine exactly what, in relation to the *Histories*, should be understood by "the effect of the narrative," and my decision to remain at the level of the text is therefore a very deliberate one. I agree that the full extent of the processes involved is more complex and will limit myself to showing that by returning, yet again, to the Scythians. The Scythian *logos* "enriches" the symbolic meaning of the word *Scythian*, but it will be noted that to comprehend the symbolic equivalence of Scythians-nomads, reference is made to the Persian Wars (the Scythians defend liberty, and the Persian Wars function as a model of intelligibility for Darius's expedition to Scythia) and to Periclean strategy (through the metaphor of insularity, at the least). Despite the fact that the Scythians may well remain nomads after Herodotus, it is not certain that once that context has receded into the distance, Herodotus's narrative continues to "enrich" the shared knowledge of the Greeks. (I use the word *context* to cover the sequence of events itself and its imaginary and symbolic significance.) To judge from Ephorus's Scythians, one might indeed be tempted to infer that it does not. For Ephorus the important thing was not to come to terms with nomadism but to establish the fact that alongside the primitive and cannibalistic Scythians, other Scythians also existed, others who were vegetarian

---

22. An expression I have borrowed from M. Vovelle: "Philippe Ariès makes the evolution of attitudes to death move along on air-cushions by virtue of the dynamism peculiar to a 'collective unconscious,' which is not further defined" (*Dictionnaire de la nouvelle histoire* [Paris, 1978], p. 343). For a critical study of the notion of influence, see, for example, M. Foucault, *L'Archéologie du savoir* (Paris, 1969), p. 32.

and just, whom he likened to Homer's Abioi;[23] he thus gives particular meaning to Homer's remark and discerns a continuity between the just Abioi and the good Scythians.

Such a reading could probably also be applied to each of the other *logoi*, taken one by one, but it would be a lengthy and perhaps over-fastidious task, and possibly one of only limited usefulness. But it seems to me that in the Scythian *logos*, taken on its own, we may detect an element which holds good for the *Histories* as a whole.

The question of nomadism raises another: that of power and the impossibility of conceiving of a nomad power. The text concurrently affirms, on the one hand, that nomadism (that is to say, its representation) excludes any structure of power, that the nomad space is an undifferentiated one in which all points are of equal value, and, on the other, that the Scythians have kings who are positioned at the center of both the social and the geographical space. The representations of nomadism and royal power appear to be mutually exclusive and yet Herodotus's narrative accommodates them together and even elaborates a compromise between the two propositions, which is expressed in spatial terms: the kings are indeed positioned "at the center," but not until they are dead and buried on the margins of Scythia.[24] But why cannot the narrative do without the kings?

Because the Scythians are "made for war," but fundamentally also because they are barbarians. That was the hypothesis I formulated above: the barbarian is royal. Now, it seems to me that the question of power, barbarian—hence, royal—power, set in opposition to the world of the city runs right through the *Histories*, constituting an important element in its organization. Just as the watercolorist's grid cuts up and organizes the space of his painting, so the question of power provides the structure (at least in part) for the space of the *Histories:* there is a code of power.

A Representation of Power?

Posing the question of power is not a way of reintroducing the (interminable) debate about Herodotus's own position. Was he, who was fortunate enough to have known Athens, a partisan of democ-

---

23. *FGrHist*, 70 F 42 Jacoby, (Ephorus): he is the first historian (fourth century B.C.) to write a universal history.

24. Cf. above, pp. 141ff.

racy? Perhaps; but he does sometimes criticize such a regime. So did he perhaps favor oligarchy? No. Or did he perhaps, as a compromise solution, support a moderate democracy? And then, was he really hostile to tyranny? Some say yes, some say no—and so on.[25]

By the end of his voyage, Jean de Léry had "invented" the savage who did not know how to write but who caused the one who discovered and observed him to write. Herodotus, for his part, "after having visited the towns of men, great and small alike," did not return with the savage, for he does not "lecture on writing." If he invents anybody, it is the barbarian, who knows, if need be, how to use writing as a form of power. But what does "inventing" the barbarian mean, given that the barbarian, from the very first words of the prologue, is already present? Herodotus wishes to ensure that "the great and marvellous deeds done by Greeks and barbarians may not lack renown." So there are Greeks on the one hand and barbarians on the other, and that is all there is to be said on the matter. This is the realm of what is well known; it is part of the shared knowledge and, as Thucydides was to point out, the two terms form a pair. In Homer, there are no barbarians but, then, there are no Greeks either; subsequently, to affirm some to be Greeks went hand in hand with declaring the others to be barbarians. Without Greeks there can be no barbarians and so, to that extent, Herodotus is not the "inventor" of the barbarian.

It might be supposed that it was with the Persian Wars that the two terms were constituted as a pair and passed into the shared knowledge of the Greeks and that barbarian came to mean, first and foremost, Persian. Or, you could say, Persian is the symbolic meaning of barbarian: a barbarian means a Persian. This symbolic equivalence indisputably does play a role in the *Histories,* even if there are many barbarians who are not Persians; but I believe that the narrative develops and enriches that equivalence by means of a process which may be set out schematically as follows. Persian and barbarian are symbolic equivalents; now, the Persians obey a king; they are the subjects of the one whom the Greeks call the Great

---

25. As an example of that type of judgment, we may consider that of K. H. Waters: Herodotus "has no hierarchy of constitution; the traditional hate of tyranny is shown to be a mirage, the admiration for democracy, qualified" ("Herodotus and Politics," *Greece and Rome* [1972]: 150). Or K. Wust, "Politisches Denken bei Herodot," diss. Munich, 1935.

King. So barbarians know a royal power. To be more precise, there is a link between barbarianism and royalty: among barbarians, the normal mode for the exercise of power tends to be royalty. And reciprocally, royalty is likely to have something barbarian about it; or, every barbarian king—perhaps even every king—is likely to some extent to resemble the Great King, the one who is also *ho barbaros*, the barbarian par excellence.

The *Histories* testify to the fact that barbarians are royal, or at least that most of them are. As we have seen, even the Scythians are no exception, despite the difficulties of combining royal power and nomadism. In the barbarian world, royalty appears to be unavoidable, as can be seen from the following observation concerning the Egyptians: "After the reign of the priest Hephaestus, the Egyptians were made free. But they *could never* live without a king, so they divided Egypt into twelve portions and set up twelve kings."[26] The same goes for the peoples of Asia who fought against the dominion of the Assyrians and "shook off" the yoke of "servitude" (*doulosune*) and "made themselves free." For a while they all remained "autonomous," but in no time at all they gave themselves a new tyrant, in the person of Deiokes, whose deepest desire it was to become just that.[27] To that extent, the peoples of Asia are incapable, not of seeking liberty, but of living with it.

Furthermore, all barbarian power, without further specification of its exact nature or the manner in which it is exercised, simply because it *is* power, tends to appear as royalty. Thus at the assembly of the peoples of the north, on the occasion of Darius invading Scythia, we find a gathering of the kings of the Tauri, the Agathyrsae, the Neuri, the Black-cloaks, the Geloni, the Budini, the Sauromatae, and even the Man-eaters, of whom it is notwithstanding said, a little further on, that they observe neither justice nor law.[28] It is as if in the barbarian world an assembly was bound to consist solely of kings.

To verify the proposition that kings are barbarian, that is to say, that they have something in common with the Great King, we need to investigate the nature of his power. But if such an investigation is to prove illuminating, we are bound to introduce another figure: the

, 106. To the south, the Libyans have kings (4.159); the Indians, to .tly do not, but some of them are subjects of the Great King.)out the Celts, to the west.

tyrant. He is very much present in the *Histories* and, as I see it, the King and the tyrant are two of a kind. Each provides a mirror image for the other. The image of tyrannical power is thus fashioned in relation to royal power, and the image of royal power is constituted in relation to tyrannical power. At the intersection of these two images the representation of despotic power is constructed.

An objection may be made to this image of a double mirror in which the king and the tyrant reflect each other: what about that famous Persian debate?[29] The claim is that the barbarian is royal, yet Herodotus brings on stage Persians who quite clearly envisage a regime of a different type for their country. How can we suggest that royalty and tyranny reflect one another when the monarchical regime favored by Darius is notable for its originality and excellence?

Having assassinated the usurper, the conspirators gather together to discuss the regime to set up in his place. Otanes favors *isonomia*, Megabyzus is for an oligarchy, and Darius, of course, wishes to restore the monarchy. Of the three propositions, that of Otanes (we are told by the text) is greeted with incredulity by certain Greeks. In other words, they cannot believe that a barbarian could possibly think in terms of popular power. But Herodotus insists on the veracity of these speeches (they truly were made) and by way of proof he refers to the conduct of Mardonius after the conquest of Ionia. Once Persian dominion was restored, he deposed the tyrants and replaced them with democratic regimes.[30] But what does that prove? That a Persian is indeed capable of having some conception of democracy, since he can even take it upon himself to promote such a regime. However, it so happens that to establish democracy is also a way of ridding himself of tyrants whose recent Ionian revolt revealed them to be untrustworthy; above all, even if he finds democracy conceivable, even applicable, it is only conceivable in Greek cities and applicable to them alone. So, on the whole, this proof put forward by Herodotus in fact shows that Otanes is "speaking Greek."

The truth is that for Herodotus every monarchy is tyrannical. Monarchy necessarily means tyranny, and the portrait that he draws

29. Hdt. 3.80–82. The bibliography on this text is extremely abundant. See, most recently, the article by F. Lasserre, "Hérodote et Protagoras: Le Débat sur les constitutions," *Museum Helveticum* 33 (1976): 65–84, with bibliographical references.

30. Hdt. 6.43. We may note that Herodotus uses the verb *demokratesthai*, so for him the *isonomia* of Otanes = democracy.

of the monarch is none other than that of the tyrant.[31] The tyrant is himself defined as the reverse of the isonomic regime. He gives no account of his actions, puts people to death without judgment, does not respect the customs of the ancestors, violates women, surrounds himself with the worst people while getting rid of the best, and so forth. This is the original portrait of the tyrant, the one repeated by tradition right down to Aristotle. For Megabyzus, who is the next to speak, the same is true: monarchy-tyranny, and he summarizes all this part of Otanes' speech as follows: "I agree to all that Otanes says against the rule of *tyranny*."[32] He thus understands Otanes to be speaking of tyranny and, like him, reckons that the mainspring of that regime is *hubris*. They are both "speaking Greek" and do so from "inside" the city; what they say only makes sense in relation to the political model of the city.

The next to speak is Darius and—perforce—it is he who has the last word, for, as everybody knows, it was he who subsequently ascended the throne. In his view, what Megabyzus has said on the subject of "power for the crowd" was well said, but not what he said about oligarchy; as for Otanes' words about monarchy-tyranny, he quite simply did not hear them. If Otanes and Megabyzus were "speaking Greek," Darius speaks both Greek and Persian. He "speaks Greek" when he explains that oligarchy and power for the people give rise to an internal struggle for power (*stasis*) which, sooner or later, leads to monarchy; so one might just as well skip those preliminary stages. However, a Greek might also describe such an inevitable degeneration as the introduction of tyranny—a Greek might, but not Darius. For him, monarchy means power for a single individual, and it is the best regime precisely because it is the power of a single individual (so one can understand how it was that he was deaf to Otanes' words). It hardly matters how it is established or who establishes it. But he also "speaks Persian" in the way he refers to a past that belongs to the Persians and to Persian customs. Whereas, for Otanes, monarchy is something opposed to the ancestral customs, for Darius it is in conformity with them. The

31. Otanes starts by using the words *mounarchos* and *mounarchie*, next, uses *turannos*, and then reverts to *mounarchos*.

32. When Otanes speaks of monarchy, he also means tyranny, but when he refers to *isonomia* he means "power to the crowd" (*plethos*), which according to him is a tyranny even worse than real tyranny, for one is then faced with an ignorant *hubris*. On the latter point, Darius's "understanding" is the same.

contradiction between the two arguments disappears once one realizes that two different worlds are involved here. All in all, Darius does not refute Otanes' thesis (monarchy-tyranny) by proving that monarchy is different from tyranny. His entire gist shows that for him the question simply does not arise: monarchy is the best regime, because it is monarchy. Period.[33]

Thus the Persian debate does not ruin the hypothesis of the double mirror between the King and the tyrant. But it might be objected that we are distorting Herodotus's text and that, besides, at that point there was as yet no theory of tyranny. Thus, according to K. H. Waters, Herodotus

shows no revulsion for a tyrant nor any ideological antipathy to the institution: nor does he seek to use the rise and fall . . . of tyrants as illustrations of any moral scheme, nor even of any divine control of human affairs; they, like all other men, have their successes and their failures, their happiness and their misery; it is simply the inexorable march of events which is to be seen in their stories.[34]

The same applies to the Great Kings. Waters's position is based on a simple conviction: Herodotus is the father of history; that means that he is first and foremost interested in events and his narrative recognizes no law other than that of facts. Reality is always too diverse to be reduced to any theory. As for the question of representation of power, it simply does not arise. If such an assumption must be regarded as thoroughly simplistic, the consequences are no less so.

As for tyranny, the *Histories* present a number of explicit declarations on the subject. Having ejected the Pisistratids of Athens, the Lacedaemonians decide to restore them to the throne. Why? Not out

---

33. When Otanes says that the "best man" (*aristos*), being invested with monarchical power, cannot do otherwise than become a tyrant, Darius replies, or, rather, does not reply: "Nothing could prove preferable to government invested in a single individual if he is the best one."

34. K. H. Waters, *Herodotus on Tyrants and Despots: A Study in Objectivity* (Wiesbaden, 1971), p. 41 (with a bibliography for this subject). Waters refers, precisely, to the Persian debate to show that there is consistency in the use of the vocabulary of power (*contra* see A. Ferrill, "Herodotus on Tyranny," *Historia* 27 (1978): 385–99). Waters also remarks: "The detailed study of his treatment of tyrants and of his handling of the king of Persia, only proved a completely objective stance, a concern with *facts* and their rational causal relations, becoming a true historian" (p. 100).

of a sudden love for tyranny, but because they realize that without a tyrant the Athenians may well become as powerful as themselves (*isoroppoi*) and may thus eventually threaten their own preeminence in mainland Greece. To this end, they gather their allies together and propose an expedition aimed at reinstating Hippias. The Corinthian Socles then delivers a speech, speaking as one who is a specialist in such matters; in Corinth they know what tyranny is, for they have lived through the Cypselid rule as well as under the notorious Periander. But before embarking on the story of the Cypselids, he begins with a short preamble in which he explains that a tyrant means disorder in the universe and tyranny spells confusion, and that to establish a tyranny is literally to turn the *kosmos* upside down. "Indeed, the heavens shall be beneath the earth and the earth aloft above the heavens, and men will live in the sea and fishes where men lived before, now that you, Lacedaemonians, are destroying the rule of equals [*isokratias*] and making ready to bring back tyranny into the cities—tyranny, a thing as unrighteous and bloodthirsty as anything on this earth."[35] Yes, but, one might point out, that is Socles the Corinthian speaking, not Herodotus. And that is no doubt true, but all the same, just by recounting the tyranny of the Cypselids, Socles wins over his allies, and the effect of his speech is that in the end the expedition does not take place.

The Lacedaemonians reckon that the disappearance of tyranny would entail an increase in the power of Athens. Here again one might object that that is the opinion of the Lacedaemonians, not of the narrator. But this would be wrong, for the narrator himself explains the phenomenon in terms of a general rule:

it is not proved by one but by many instances that equality of speech [*isegorie*] is a good thing; seeing that while they were under despotic rulers, the Athenians were no better in war than any of their neighbours, but once they got rid of tyrants they were far and away the first of all. This then shows that while they were oppressed they willed to be cravens, as men working for a master [*despotes*], but when they were freed each one was zealous to achieve for himself.[36]

The tyrant is thus a *despotes* for whom one would be foolish to work, and he is a factor of disorder in the *kosmos*.

---

35. Hdt. 5.92, 93.
36. Hdt. 5.78.

Let me now return to my hypothesis of the double mirror. At the level of the narrative, it is noticeable that the Great King plays the role of guarantor and supporter, defender and refuge for tyrants and also for ex-tyrants who, for one reason or another, have lost their positions. Histiaeus, the tyrant of Miletus, expresses the point bluntly when Darius is in Scythia. The Scythians try to persuade the Ionians, who are guarding the bridge over the Ister, to destroy it, but Histiaeus points out to his colleagues that to destroy the bridge would be to saw off the branch on which they are sitting. If Darius disappears, their own tyranny disappears with him.[37] Polycrates, the tyrant of Samos, makes an agreement with Cambyses: he offers a fleet to help Cambyses invade Egypt but, to man its ships, he chooses those citizens of whom he wishes to be rid and is at pains to tell the king not to send them back to him.[38] When Hippias, the son of Pisistratus, is ejected from Athens, he quite naturally takes refuge in Asia and from there does all that he can to make Athens "subject to him and subject to Darius"; and it is he, a little later, who acts as guide to the barbarians at Marathon.[39] Herodotus also mentions members of the Pisistratid family, installed at the court of Susa, who encourage Xerxes to invade Greece and who, furthermore, follow in the train of his army.[40]

But it is not only tyrants and ex-tyrants that the King receives. Sometimes he also takes in ex-kings: when Demaratus, the king of Sparta, is dethroned, he takes to flight and eventually, after a number of stops, ends up in Susa. There, when he reaches Darius, his flight is at last at an end, for Darius "receives him royally and gives him lands and cities." Only here does he find security and continue to be recognized as what in Greece he no longer is, a king[41]—which also means a vassal to the Great King.[42]

37. Hdt. 4.137.
38. Hdt. 3.44.
39. Hdt. 5.96, 6.107.
40. Hdt. 7.6, 8.52.
41. Hdt. 6.70. The role he played as "interpreter" for Xerxes is well known. Xerxes, being completely baffled by the behavior of the Greeks, several times requests a "translation" from Demaratus. Xerxes listens carefully to what he has to say but does not believe a word of it (7.101, 209, 234).
42. This collection of information on the relations between kings and tyrants might also include the narrative of their childhoods; for example, there is a similarity between the childhood of Cyrus (Hdt. 1.107f.) and that of Cypselus (5.92); cf. M. Delcourt, *Oedipe ou la légende du conquérant* (Paris, 1944).

Despotic Power

As Otanes remarked, the mainspring of monarchy-tyranny is *hubris* and the personality of a tyrant is all-craving, feeding on itself but unable ever to find satisfaction. Furthermore, the *despotes* is prey to desire (*eros*), both sexual desire and desire for power, illegitimate love and love of power. Throughout the *Histories*, the word *eros* is applied only to kings and tyrants; they alone experience this excessive desire.[43] As one character observes, tyranny indeed has many "lovers" (*erastai*).[44] Deiokes, who is to cause the Medes to revert to servitude, "desires" to become a tyrant.[45] Pausanias, the regent of Sparta, was reputed to have sought to marry the daughter of a cousin of Darius, for he was filled with a "desire" to become tyrant of Greece.[46] For the kings, for whom *eros* cannot be desire for power, it becomes desire for what is forbidden: Cambyses "desires" his sister, Mykerinos; the pharaoh is reputed to "desire" his own daughter; Xerxes "desires" the wife of his son.[47] Ariston, king of Sparta, "desires" a woman who, while not absolutely forbidden, is nevertheless the wife of his best friend; besides, he already has two wives, so she will make the third and, to obtain her, he resorts to a trick.[48] Candaules, king of Lydia, for his part, "desires" his own wife. Although this is not in itself illegitimate, the text states that his love is "excessive" and that evil is bound to befall him.[49] For a Greek, this kind of desire was not supposed to preside over the relations between husband and wife.

If despotic power has *hubris* as its mainspring and *eros* as its vocation, it should be added that transgression and repetition are its law, that it operates in secret, manifests itself through physical marks and mutilation, and is doomed to ultimate failure.

Among those who, quite literally, transgress and who generation

---

43. S. Benardete, *Herodotean Inquiries* (The Hague, 1969), p. 137.

44. Hdt. 3.53.

45. Hdt. 1.96.

46. Hdt. 5.32.

47. Hdt. 3.31, 2.108, 9.108.

48. Hdt. 6.62: he makes his friend swear that they will give each other whatever "object" each may choose from among the other's possessions. Once again, we find a Spartan king included in this company of kings and tyrants.

49. Hdt. 1.8. He praises her extravagantly and, believing her to be the most beautiful woman in the world, he wants Gyges, his intimate friend, to see her naked.

after generation repeat that transgression are, first and foremost, the Great Kings. To transgress means, through *hubris*, to step outside one's own space and enter a foreign one, and the material sign of such transgression is the construction of a bridge over a river or, worse still, over a stretch of sea. Cyrus, the founder of the dynasty, the first in the line, goes too far: he throws a bridge over the Araxes in order to attack the Massagetae in the north, and as a result he dies.[50] Darius crosses the Bosphorus and the Ister. He invades Europe and attacks the nomads; and he is defeated.[51] Xerxes succeeds in linking the two shores of the Hellespont only at the second attempt; his first bridge is destroyed by storms as soon as it is constructed.[52] This spatial transgression is also a transgression of divine space and aggression against the gods. Aggression is certainly what it is for, as Themistocles tells the Athenians, "the gods and the heroes deemed Asia and Europe too great a realm for one man to rule, and that a wicked man and an impious one."[53] It is also aggression against the gods, for sometimes we are made aware of a link between the divine world and the political space. Thus, the fact that the Athenians burned down the temple of the "local" (*epichorios*) goddess Kybebe (Cybele) at Sardis is used by the Persians as justification for their burning of the Greek sanctuaries in Greece.[54] Similarly, when about to cross the bridge, Xerxes urges the Persians to pray to the gods who were allotted the land of Persia (*Persida gen lelogchasi*);[55] so there appears to be a divine *moira* that corresponds to the allotment of territory.

A *despotes* is bound to violate the *nomoi*—the social, religious, and sexual rules. Candaules, for example, by asking Gyges to spy on his wife when she is naked is asking him to perform an action that breaks the rules (*anomos*),[56] for among barbarians it was considered wrong to be seen naked. Cambyses is probably the *nomoi*-violator par excellence. When on military campaign in Egypt, he contrives to

50. Hdt. 1.205. As for Cambyses, his project is to cross the desert, which is a kind of sea, in order to attack the long-lived Ethiopians (3.25).

51. Cf. above, pp. 46ff.

52. Hdt. 7.34. The list of these intrepid builders of pontoon bridges might also include Croesus (1.75) who, by crossing the Halys—the frontier with the Medes—destroys a "great empire," which turns out to be his own.

53. Hdt. 8.109.

54. Hdt. 5.102.

55. Hdt. 7.53.

56. Hdt. 1.8.

respect neither the Egyptian nor the Persian *nomoi*.[57] It is not that he takes against the Egyptian *nomoi* and tries to impose Persian customs in their stead; no, he turns them all upside down, crazily. The gallery of tyrants also includes figures from the past such as Pisistratus and Periander. Pisistratus marries the daughter of the Alcmeonid, Megacles, but as he does not wish to have a child, his relations with her are *ou kata nomon*, not in accordance with the *nomos* of marriage, which is for the procreation of legitimate children.[58] As for Periander, not content with killing his wife, he then has sexual relations with her dead body.[59] Periander, among the archaic tyrants, represents what Cambyses does among the kings: transgression by excess.

Finally, the *despotes* exercises his power over people's bodies, marking them as he will, in the first place with the whip. Kings wield the whip: the Persian army marches to the lash of the whip, and in the kings' view nothing can be achieved without it. As will be remembered, Xerxes goes so far as to have the Hellespont whipped.[60] Cambyses has the priests of Apis whipped.[61] Only one Greek, on one occasion, uses a whip, and he is Cleomenes, the king of Sparta.[62] The whip is the weapon the master holds over the body of the slave, as the narrative clearly shows through the story of the Scythian slaves. While their men are away, the Scythian women sleep with their slaves. When the Scythians return (twenty-eight years later), they find a whole generation of young men who oppose them. They start off by fighting these slaves' sons but then decide to replace the weapons with the whip. At the sight of this, the young men immediately stop fighting and take to flight.[63] The whip, the symbol of mastery, forces them to acknowledge themselves to be slaves, for whom the only weapon now is flight.

The king cuts, mutilates, and marks the bodies of his subjects.

57. Hdt. 3.16, 27, 30, 37.
58. Hdt. 1.61.
59. Hdt. 5.92.
60. The whip is mentioned at Hdt. 3.130, 7.22, 35, 54, 56, 223, 8.109 (Hellespont). While still officially the child of the cowherd, Cyrus is chosen as king by the children with whom he plays. He immediately whips the son of a noble Mede who pays no attention to his orders. This typically "royal" behavior causes Astyages to recognize him.
61. Hdt. 3.16, 29.
62. Hdt. 6.81.
63. Hdt. 4.3—a Scythian story, perhaps, but in the Greek manner.

When the funeral rites of the king take place, all those in the long caravan of Scythians mutilate themselves, and the outrages they inflict upon themselves declare them to belong to him, marking them out as Scythians and subjects.[64] Battus's wife Pheretime, to avenge the assassination of her son Arkesilas by the people of Barke, in Cyrenaica, uses a Persian army to capture the town and proceeds to impale the men all round the walls and to cut off the women's breasts, which she also uses to decorate the town walls.[65] Periander exerts his power over the bodies of future citizens: he sends three hundred young men from the first families of Corinth off to Sardis, where they are turned into eunuchs. In assuming such an exorbitant power over reproduction, his intention is to control the civic body itself.[66] As for the Great King, he cuts off noses, ears, heads;[67] it is a current mode of exercising power but one reserved for the sovereign alone. When Zopyrus, one of the most important Persians, sets out to make the Babylonians besieged by Darius believe that he is a deserter, he cuts off his own nose and ears, shaves his head, and flagellates his body. When Darius sees him he is filled with indignation and asks him who had the audacity to mutilate a man of his high rank. Zopyrus replies, "There is no man save yourself who has the power to bring such a one as me to this plight."[68] It will also be remembered what treatment Xerxes meted out to the corpse of Leonidas, and Pausanias's reply to a man of Aegina who suggested that he should do the same to the corpse of Mardonius: such behavior befits barbarians but not Greeks.[69] Finally, the king brands his subjects, as a master might his slaves or as the city brands its public slaves with its civic emblem. When the Thebans surrender to the Persians, they are branded with the royal insignia. It is said that

---

64. Hdt. 4.71–73; cf. above, pp. 141ff.

65. Hdt. 4.202. After acts of vengeance so excessive, especially on the part of a Greek woman, Pheretime comes to a bad end: while still alive, she is internally devoured by worms. Other examples of impaling: 3.132, 159 (Darius), 4.43, 9.78 (Xerxes).

66. Hdt. 3.48. P. Schmitt-Pantel, "Histoire de tyran ou comment la cité construit ses marges," *Les Marginaux et les exclus dans l'histoire* (Paris, 1979), pp. 217–31. On a merchant of eunuchs and the disadvantages to the practice of this "most impious" profession, see Hdt. 8.105–6.

67. Hdt. 3.69, 79, 7.35, 238; 8.90 (118), 9.172.

68. Hdt. 3.154–55. Cf. also 3.118, where a Persian claims this royal prerogative for himself and pays the price for doing so.

69. Hdt. 9.78–79.

Xerxes, not content to have the Hellespont lashed, also had it branded with a hot iron.[70]

The marking of the body, always shaming, is the sign of slavery.[71] All in all, despotic power manifests itself as the power of master over slave. Does that mean that the representation of the relationship between master and slave is the model for despotic power, the model that makes it possible to conceive it? Or should we simply say that each of the two representations refers to the other? The power of the master of slaves is a symbol of despotic power while, equally, despotic power is a symbol of the power of a master of slaves. Looking no further than the vocabulary used, in the *Histories* the same word, *despotes*, applies to the master of slaves, to the tyrant, to the King, to the gods, and also, on occasion, to the law.[72]

To Xerxes' mind, the Greeks, who are not driven by the whip, have no chance of showing any bravery at all against the Persians who, under the lash of the whip, are in contrast obliged to appear braver than they really are. What these men who are not people of the whip need is a *despotes*. To this Demaratus replies: not at all, they have a *despotes*, but their master is the *nomos*, the law. And what he particularly has in mind is the *nomos* of war: the Spartan must not flee from the battlefield but must stay in his place in the ranks (*menein*).[73] *Nomos* instead of a king, then—one kind of despotic power in place of another? Not at all, for to establish *nomos* is to eject the tyrant. The law does not mutilate, it is the negation of transgression, and it is what replaces *hubris* with moderation.[74]

---

70. Hdt. 7.233, 7.35.

71. Except for the Thracians, for whom to be marked (*stizein*) is a sign of nobility (*eugenes*), an absence of markings being, on the contrary, a sign of low birth (Hdt. 5.6).

72. For example, Hdt. 6.83 (the rebellious slaves of Argos and their masters), 5.78 (Athens liberated from tyrants), 4.127 (when Darius demands to be recognized as *despotes*, the king of Scythia replies that, so far as *despotes* are concerned, he recognizes none but Zeus and Hestia); similarly, the Massagetae recognize the sun as *despotes* (1.212); it appears that it is only barbarians who have such relationships with their gods, which is yet another indication that in their world all power can only be conceived on the model of that of the King; finally, 7.104 (the liberty of law is a surer constraint on the Spartans than fear is for the subjects of the King).

73. Hdt. 7.104.

74. Hdt. 3.80, 142; J.-P. Vernant, *Myth and Thought among the Greeks* (London, 1983), pp. 190–212.

King-subject, master-slave: from the point of view of power, the two pairs overlap. The king is like a master of slaves, and the master is like a king. And to this first way of conceiving of the *despotes* we may perhaps add another: are not the destinies of these personages sometimes likened to those of the tragic heroes? Attention has been drawn to all the "little tragedies" incorporated in the great narrative of the *Histories*.[75] Croesus, Candaules, Polycrates of Samos, Cleomenes of Sparta, Cyrus, Cambyses, Xerxes—are they not all tragic heroes?

The role played by tragedy in the birth of history has already been noted in a general fashion. With Phrynicus's *The Capture of Miletus* and *The Phoenician Women* and Aeschylus's *Persae* (472 B.C.), the Persian Wars became an acceptable subject: "The *peripeteia* of Persia could be ranked with the fate of the Seven who marched against Thebes, or the career of the house of Atreus. The Greeks had come to the realization that an event of their own time was just as appropriate a literary theme as the events of the distant past."[76] Tragedy is not at the origin of history. It is just that such tragedies created a field of acceptability in which it became possible to recount the wars between the Greeks and the barbarians to one's contemporaries; the principal actors in the drama could thus be tragic heroes.

But tragedy is an invention of the city, for its own use—even the invention of one city in particular (Athens) at a precise moment (the end of the sixth century and the beginning of the fifth). Now, in the *Histories*, tragedy is external to the city and the tragic heroes are, precisely, the despots, while the city, for its part, "functions as an anti-tragic machine."[77] We are thus presented with the following paradox: it is in the world where tragedy in effect exists that it does not take place, whereas it is present in the world where it does not exist. Although connected with the city, within the space of the *Histories* tragedy nevertheless only functions in the world outside the *polis*, setting on stage heroes who know nothing of the city or reject it and its values.

But the paradox is no more than apparent. The tragic hero is a

75. K. H. Waters, *Herodotus on Tyrants*, pp. 86ff., together with the bibliography. Waters, of course, is hostile to such a view: Herodotus is producing history, not literature—"*vivant res, pereant tragoediae* might have been his motto" (p. 100).

76. R. Drews, *The Greek Accounts of Eastern History*, p. 35.

77. P. Vidal-Naquet, *Sophocle, Tragédies* (Paris, 1973), preface, p. 17.

being who is prey to *hubris*,[78] so tragedy can only unfold in a world where *hubris* has a place. Now, the city, precisely, insists on denying and rejecting the action of *hubris* and instead favors moderation, whereas despotic power is the locus par excellence of *hubris*, which, as Otanes shows, is indeed its mainspring. Since they are moved by *hubris*, the representatives of despotic power are bound to behave in a tragic fashion and for them, as for Xerxes in the *Persae*, "immoderation, as it grows, produces the fruit of fatal error and the harvest that is reaped is nothing but tears."[79] They are indeed people who, in Herodotus's words, "are doomed to ill-fortune."[80]

Miltiades is one of these: he is bound to come to a bad end and yet he is an Athenian and even a strategus at the battle of Marathon. But he is also the tyrant of the Chersonese and plans to lead an expedition against Paros in his own name and for his own purposes.[81] He thus passes from the "anti-tragic" world of the city to the world of despotism and *hubris*. He moves from the one to the other and finally dies, after having committed a major transgression: he enters the precinct of Demeter Thesmophoros, a place forbidden to men. Leaping over the wall of the sanctuary, he dislocates his thigh; gangrene sets in, and he dies, exactly as Cambyses does.[82]

The tragic schemas thus serve as a model of intelligibility for despotic power, in the *Histories:* they make it possible to include it in the narrative, to give an account of how it functions, and to explain why it fails; they provide a way for the narrator to make the addressee believe that he has a hold on this other world so far away from him in space or in time. But the *Histories* are neither a tragedy nor a combination of tragedies. For real tragedy, what is needed is the presence of both the world of heroes and the world of the city, and it is the clash between them that produces the tragic situation.[83] Now,

78. L. Gernet, *Recherches sur le développement de la pensée juridique et morale en Grèce* (Paris, 1917); A. Atkins, *Moral Values and Political Behavior in Ancient Greece* (London, 1972).

79. Aeschylus *Persae* 821–22.

80. Hdt. 1.8 (Candaules), 2.61 (Apries), 3.40, 43, 124, 125 (Polycrates), 4.79 (Scyles), 205 (Pheretime, *apethane kakos*); 6.84 (Cleomenes, *apethane kakos*), 135 (Miltiades); 9.109 (the house of Masistes), 3.65 (Cambyses: it is not within the power of human nature to deflect what is bound to happen).

81. Hdt. 6.132–36; see Vidal-Naquet, *Sophocle*, p. 18.

82. Hdt. 3.66.

83. J.-P. Vernant and P. Vidal-Naquet, *Tragedy and Myth in Ancient Greece* (Brighton, 1981).

the *Histories* separate the world of the city from that of the heroes or, rather, those who take that role, to wit, the despots. Consequently, these heroes of the *Histories* who might be called tragic to the extent that they are moved by the *hubris* inherent to their power, these heroes who one by one are summoned on stage by the narrator, ought really simply to be called Herodotean heroes. And rather than call the despotic world tragic, we ought really to say that it is a place that accommodates the tragic.

The law of despotic power is transgression. But two men live in a veritable excess of transgression and carry its repetition to the extremes of madness and death. These two companions in madness are Cambyses, the Great King, and Cleomenes, the king of Sparta. Both of them are mad: some say mad from birth, others that they became so with time.[84] Both transgress the sacred laws. Cleomenes suborns the Pythia, fells the trees at Eleusis, burns down the sanctuary of the hero Argos, wants to sacrifice in person to Hera despite his being a foreigner, and has a priest whipped.[85] Cambyses may go even further in his transgressions, for he heaps derision '(*katagelan*) upon the Egyptian *nomoi*, and his entire behavior runs contrary to Egyptian and Persian customs alike: he has a dead body whipped and burned; he kills the bull Apis; he mocks the temple statues and has them burned.[86] In his madness he no longer even knows who he is; he is not Egyptian and is no longer Persian. The transgressions of these kings are also sexual: Cleomenes is accused of repeatedly going with (*phoitan*) the wife of his host;[87] Cambyses seems to delight in accumulating every kind of perversion—he marries his sister, then kills her when she becomes pregnant and proceeds to marry another, younger sister.[88] Both kings die as a result of their madness. Cambyses injures his thigh at the very spot where he struck at Apis, although once he realizes he is dying he recovers his sense. Gangrene overcomes him and he dies.[89] Cleomenes not only no longer knows who he is (he flings his scepter in the faces of the Spartans) but treats himself as though he were

84. Hdt. 3.33, 5.42. It would be possible to write "parallel lives" of these two companions in transgression.
85. Hdt. 6.75.
86. Hdt. 3.16, 27ff., 37.
87. Hdt. 5.70.
88. Hdt. 3.31–33.
89. Hdt. 3.64.

another person: when he is chained up he hacks himself to pieces with a knife.[90]

For an understanding of despotic power, we may thus refer to master-slave relationships and the tragic model. But its heroes, the despots, are Herodotean heroes in the same sense that the Cesare Borgia of *The Prince* is a Macchiavellian hero for Claude Lefort.[91]

In this gallery of despots, in the company of the Great Kings, the barbarian kings, and the tyrants, we find kings of Sparta, and it is one of them, Cleomenes, who occupies this special position alongside Cambyses. His presence there comes as no surprise, for we have already noted an explicit similarity between the Spartan kings and the barbarian princes in respect to their funeral ceremonies.[92] This tendency of theirs to barbarianism is at the same time a sign of the problem that they must have posed to other Greeks, to the point where, to account for this institution, a detour by way of Asia seemed necessary. It is a detour which must be made in any study of the representation of power in the *Histories* and the code by which that representation is organized.

It is also a sign of the fact that there was always a danger that a king, simply because he was a king, might swing over to despotic or barbarian power. The major difference between the city and other political systems (and Sparta is a city, albeit one with kings) is truly that of power, and one of the effects of the *Histories* is to translate that difference.

Looking backward, this portrait of the *despotes* as a depository of every kind of perversion, all existing within him potentially if not in fact, provides the archaic tyrannies with a face. There is henceforth a typical image for them, one that makes meaningful all the stories

90. Hdt. 6.75.

91. C. Lefort, *Le Travail de l'oeuvre: Machiavel* (Paris, 1972), p. 68: "The Caesar Borgia of *The Prince* is a Machiavellian hero who provides food for thought on the function of the prince and whose characteristics are only *significant* because they are *distinguishable* from those of other Machiavellian figures—Giovompagolo Baglioni and Francesco Sforza, for example." But he is also a Machiavellian hero in another sense, not because he is different from other figures within the work itself but because he is different from "the historical Caesar Borgia": the differences and distortions are "a precious indication of the symbolic constitution of the work." Similarly, if Herodotus's Cambyses is mad, it is by no means proven that the "historical Cambyses" was.

92. Cf. above, pp. 151ff.

told about tyrants. For Herodotus, for example, Periander is a transgressor, rather like Cambyses and Cleomenes and not a bit like one of the Seven Sages.[93] But it seems reasonable to suppose that those stories also contributed toward the formation of the portrait. Looking forward, the portrait was to be adopted, in tragedy but elsewhere too, and in particular in the fourth century B.C. by Plato and Aristotle.[94] It is not my intention to produce a historiographical study of the tyrant, nor do I wish to make out that there was any reference to Herodotus or even any influence of Herodotus's involved. Besides, as is well known, influence is a handy word for indicating a link while concealing a lack of knowledge. I would simply like to suggest that it is at this point, in connection with power being recognized as a fundamental element in the symbolic constitution of the *Histories,* that we may perhaps seize on a transition from the constitution of the *Histories* (the grid for them) to the *Histories* as an institution (used as a grid). From now on, in the shared knowledge of the Greeks, the king is a despot and the tyrant is a despot, that is to say, that imaginary figure produced by the reflections of the double mirror (king-tyrant) who is moved by *hubris* and who behaves as a master among his slaves.

Thus for Plato the Persian regime is defined by an excess of *servitude* and an excess of *despotism.*[95] According to Aristotle, certain barbarian monarchies could be defined as hereditary tyrannies in conformity with the laws. But once the theory of slavery was further developed, he continued, since the barbarians were "more servile in their nature than the Greeks, and the Asiatics than the Europeans, they endure despotic rule without any resentment."[96] Or take one more example, also constructed in accordance with the double mirror: most of the measures that made it possible to preserve a tyranny were introduced by Periander, but "many similar methods may also be adopted from the Persian power":[97] the tyrant and the king.

93. It is Nicholas of Damascus, in Jacoby, *FGrHist,* F 58, who alludes to a Periander being numbered among the Seven Sages, but he himself denies the truth of it.

94. See, in particular, Euripides *The Suppliant Women* 452ff.; Plato *Republic* 565d ff., 615c ff.; Aristotle *Politics* book 5.

95. Plato *Laws* 694a ff.

96. Aristotle *Politics* 1285a20.

97. Aristotle *Politics* 1313a14.

Herodotus, Rhapsode and Surveyor

*I desire, I insist that everything around me
be henceforth measured, proven, certified,
mathematical, rational. The island must be
surveyed, the horizontal projection of all the
land must be reproduced in miniature, and all
this information must be recorded in a register. I should like each plant to be labeled, each
bird to be ringed, each mammal branded. I
shall not rest until this opaque, impenetrable
island, so full of muted fermentations and evil
currents, is transformed into an abstract construction that is transparent and intelligible
all the way to the bone.*

M. Tournier, *Vendredi ou les limbes du Pacifique*

Thus in answer to the question "elicit belief in what?" we may
reply, "The *Histories* elicit the belief that the difference between
Greeks and barbarians is one of power." It is on the code of power that
the narrative is based, and this imaginary figure of the despot, at
once a king and a tyrant, is one of the symbolic effects produced by
the text.

To this we may add a second effect, of an equally all-pervading
nature. For the addressee, the *Histories* unfold as a representation of
the inhabited world. And even today, on closing the ninth book the
modern reader forms a picture of the world from what he has read:
not just a map like that of Anaximander or Hecataeus, but a map in
movement. Here again we should not content ourselves with specific items of information (such and such a people lives here, such and
such a river flows in this direction). The important thing is to
concentrate on the major organizing procedures: the surveying, the
classifying, the listing and ordering; and to see how the *Histories* are
constructed through the interplay of these operations; if, despite its
inadequacy, we may once again have recourse to the metaphor of the
grid, let us say that the combination of surveying, classifying, listing,
and ordering forms one of the grids of the *Histories*, one that cannot
fail to produce an effect on the addressee. Thus once again the
question posed is that of the *Histories* considered as a grid and their
effect outside themselves.

The Surveyor

Herodotus is not unaware of the joys of surveying. He enjoys giving the measurements of a building, a road, a river, a sea, or a country and, even more, he enjoys making it clear that it was he himself who obtained those measurements. It is "I" or "we" who took the measurements of, for example, the pyramids of Cheops,[98] or the total dimensions of the Black Sea: "Its length is eleven thousand one hundred stades and its breadth, at the place where it is widest, three thousand three hundred." But here the measurements are the result, not of his own surveying operation, but of his own calculations. I have measured in the following way (*moi memetreatai*): knowing that a ship takes x days to cross and also knowing that a ship covers y stades a day (and he distinguishes between the distance covered during the day and that covered during the night, which is slightly less), it is possible to deduce the total length and breadth.[99]

Surveying also means converting native measurements into stades. It involves knowing that the Persian measurement, the parasang, is the equivalent of 30 stades, that the Egyptian *schoinos* is the equivalent of 60,[100] and that the royal road from the sea to Susa is thus 13,500 stades long and the Egyptian seaboard measures 3,600. In other words, it involves introducing the stade as a common measurement for all regions and, more fundamentally, since the earth is "one,"[101] it emphasizes that the stade can account for each and every space, that each and every space is, in principle, measurable in stades.

Of course, although surveying takes place primarily in space, it is also practiced in time. When, following Hecataeus, Herodotus visits the temple of Thebes and is shown the series of statues of the high priests, he converts their number into years: 341 statues equals 341 generations—of men, so to speak, passing on each time from father to son—and if one calculates three generations to a century, one arrives at 11,340 years,[102] quite without the need for divine interven-

---

98. Hdt. 2.127. On the technical aspect of these measurements (the length of a stade, etc.), see the table in F. Oertel, *Herodotus ägyptischer logos: Mit einem metrologischen Beitrag und Anhang* (Bonn, 1970).

99. Hdt. 4.85. Other examples of measurements: 1.93, 2.31, 149, 5.52.

100. Hdt. 2.6, 5.53.

101. Hdt. 4.45.

102. Hdt. 2.142, 143.

tion. Hecataeus, who goes back no more than sixteen generations before finding a divine ancestor, is made to look very naive. The distinctive feature of this chronological surveying is that it is carried out visually; the eye of the traveler, passing from one statue to the next, measures the time that has elapsed.

The joys of surveying are also the sign of a certain power. What better way of making people believe that one knows a building or a country, especially if it is far away, than showing oneself capable of giving its measurements? It is an operation of translation, an easy way of bringing what is other down to what is the same. In the traveler's tale, metrology certainly has the function of inspiring trust. The following anecdote neatly illustrates the nature of the power that accompanies the knowledge of measurements. When Croesus, wishing to test the veracity of the Greek oracles, questions the Pythia, her reply begins: "I know the number of the grains of sand and I measure the spaces of the ocean";[103] in other words, I am the oracle who knows the most, since I know the numbers of things regarded as innumerable and the dimensions of things that men consider to be limitless. Thus, to know the dimensions of the Black Sea, not through inspiration but through calculation, is to demonstrate exceptional, almost superhuman, knowledge. Such knowledge carries a certain power with it, since mastery over space begins with the knowledge of dimensions and distances: if I know the time it takes to pass from A to B, this knowledge in itself provides me with a hold upon B.

When this knowledge is transmitted, it may take the form of nautical instructions and a guide for travelers; it is then known as the *periplous*. This genre, by definition, is partial to measurements: the distance from A to B is so many stades or so many days', or nights', sail. But the principal characteristic of the *periplous* is its circularity, its repetition. It gives an account of a circumnavigation and takes the form of a belt passing right around the Mediterranean: starting from the pillars of Heracles, it passes from the west eastward until it returns to its point of departure, along the coast of Africa. Its raison d'être is repetition, since anybody, having learned from it, should be able to repeat the journey in the same stages and making the same stopovers. The *periplous*, a circuit closed upon itself and repeatable,

103. Hdt. 1.47.

like a vector, is an oriented and ordered journey. It proceeds by passing from one toponym to another, advancing not step by step but in leaps from one point to another, from one name to another name. It is concerned to identify and locate: to identify the various points (places, towns, or peoples) and locate them in relation to one another, linking them concretely by specifying how long it takes to travel between them, but also connecting them linguistically through the interplay, within the discourse, of everything by means of which place is indicated (the use of prepositions and prefixes, the order of words, and so on).[104] The *periplous* is thus the discourse of a journey (a discourse presented as a transcription, purporting to be a faithful imitation of the journey), but it is also a journey of discourse (the language "creates" the journey).

The *Histories*, too, interconnect the discourse and the journey: "I will go forward with my history, and speak of small and great cities alike. For many states that were once great have now become small and those that were great in my time were small formerly."[105] But this journey, which is at once spatial and temporal, is adjusted to the scale of the entire inhabited world. The *periplous* jumps from name to name and from toponym to toponym without any concern for what may lie beyond, but Herodotus delights in surveying distant lands and marking out boundaries. He measures not only Egypt but also the Black Sea and Scythia, and Libya too. Neither is the *periplous* concerned with what lies *between*. The space between two toponyms is at best seen as a distance or as the time taken to complete the journey; otherwise it is left as a blank. But Herodotus makes use of this "in-between area" where, quite often, different *nomoi* apply. The measure of the profound difference between the two types of discourse may be appreciated from the different statuses the two accord to the digression. In the *periplous*, a digression is truly a step to one side, a loop, a momentary interruption in the journey; if, for example, while following a coastline, the narrator moves away from it just long enough to mention the outlying islands, he then returns immediately to pick up the main thread of the discourse. In the *Histories*, in contrast, digression is the general rule in the journey and also a rule of the discourse. That is a less exaggerated statement

104. For example, Hecataeus in Jacoby, *FGrHist*, 1 F 49, 113a, 166, 207, 299.
105. Hdt. 1.5.

than it might seem. Consider the following declaration made by the narrator: "it was ever the way of my *logos* to seek after digressions [*prostekas edizeto*]."[106] They were not thrust on him nor did he simply stumble upon them; on the contrary, the purpose of his travels is to seek them out. We have already noted the connection between *thoma* and digression: a *thoma* constitutes the main thread of the digression, and a digression is the form adopted to tell of a *thoma*.[107] However, that is only one of the forms taken by a digression; there are many others. For example, chapters 2 to 82 of Book 4 are one vast digression inserted into the narrative of Darius's expedition. Its subject is Scythia, its inhabitants and its *nomoi*, and it ends as follows: "Having so described this, I will now return to the story which I began to relate [*anabesomai es ton . . . logon*]," I will "reembark" on my *logos*.[108] This example is a gloss from the narrator on his own narrative, "for the service of those with weak or inattentive ears."[109] By signposting the bifurcations in his text and producing what Genette calls his "stage directions,"[110] the "I" of the narrator intervenes in the capacity of organizer of the digressions which he introduces and interrupts at will; and in the many-faceted aspect (also deliberately engineered) of his work,[111] in which the various narratives are juxtaposed or even overlap or intersect, it is he who makes it clear to the addressee which is the main "channel" and which the subsidiary one.

The Rhapsode

But the surveyor also turns himself into a rhapsode, a rhapsode in the primary sense of the term. He is the one who sews the different

106. Hdt. 4.30. On the digression, see Jacoby, *RE*, 379–92; P.-E. Legrand, *Hérodote*, Introduction, pp. 234–35; J. Cobet, *Herodots Exkurse und die Frage der Einheit seines Werkes, Historia* 17 (1971).

107. Examples of digressions: Hdt. 2.35, 3.60, 4.30.

108. Hdt. 4.82. Other examples: 1.40 (*aneimi es ton logon*), 7.137 (*epaneimi*), 239 (*aneimi*).

109. Montaigne, *Essais*, is keen to avoid precisely such glosses (the subject matter should suffice on its own); see M. Charles, "Bibliothèques," *Poétique* 33 (February 1978): 15.

110. G. Genette, *Figures III* (Paris, 1972), p. 262.

111. Dionysus of Halicarnassus *To Pompey* 3, *poikilen eboulethe poiesai ten graphen.*

spaces together; he is the linking agent whose task it is to connect one space to another, continuously, as far as the limits of the inhabited world. He knows, thanks to the voyages of the Phoenicians and of Scylax of Caryanda, that Asia and Libya are surrounded by water, for Scylax landed at the very spot where the Phoenicians set sail.[112] He knows that to the east, India is the last inhabited land and that beyond extends a desert about which it is impossible for anyone to speak.[113] On the other hand, he does not know, nor does anybody else, whether there exists a northern sea beyond Europe.[114] Nor does he, any more than anybody else, know what really lies at the limit of Europe to the west. Is there a sea there or not?[115]

But within these imposed or supposed limits he knows, for example, all the different zones by which Libya is successively divided: the coast occupied by nomads, then the region of wild animals, then the sandy hills, and finally a desert devoid of any trace of life.[116] Similarly, he knows the different peoples who, from the seaboard inland, occupy the whole expanse of Scythia: starting from Olbia, for example, first there are the Callipidae; above them, the Alazones; above them, the Scythians, who till the land; and, finally, the Neuri, beyond whom "the land is uninhabited so far as we know."[117] On either side of this area the narrator installs other columns of peoples, stretching from the coast across to the impassable deserts or mountains.

It is important to enumerate everything, omitting nothing, until there is no more to be said and the words become lost in the deserts or rebound from the mountain faces. "Of what lies north of the bald men no-one can speak with exact knowledge, for mountains high and impassable bar the way and no man crosses them"; as for what the bald men themselves say, that is marginal talk which has no real validity.[118] While this listing may seem a heavy duty for the narrator to discharge, it is also a way for him to show off his knowledge and thereby elicit the belief of his addressee: for the narrator is the one

112. Hdt. 4.44.
113. Hdt. 4.40.
114. Hdt. 4.45.
115. Hdt. 3.115.
116. Hdt. 4.181, 185.
117. Hdt. 4.17.
118. Hdt. 4.25.

who knows these expanses and who also knows the names: here are those of "all the Libyans whom we can name,"[119] or "as far as the Atlantes" (a Libyan people living in the sandy region) "I know and can tell the names of all the peoples [*echo ta ounomara . . . karalexia*] but no farther than that."[120] This is another sense in which he is a rhapsode: like the singer of the epic, he has a taste for catalogues. And, making due allowance for proportions, he might himself have devised the following project of Jules Verne's: "No more of those great gaps on the maps of central Africa, no more blank spaces tinted with pale colors and crossed by dotted lines, no more of those vague designations that are the despair of map-makers."[121]

His intention is to establish the boundaries of a country, the list of the peoples who inhabit it, and the dimensions of the territory. That is how he proceeds in the case of Egypt, converting the Egyptian measurements and making calculations on the spot. It measures 3,600 stades along the seaboard and 7,920 stades from the sea to Elephantine. It is composed, first, of a plain that stretches as far as Heliopolis (that is, a distance almost equal to that from the altar of the twelve gods at Athens to the temple of Olympian Zeus at Pisa [in Greece]); then the country becomes narrower for the distance of a four-day's journey by ship, at the narrowest point measuring no more than 200 stades in breadth ("it seems to me," adds the traveler); it then widens again.[122] Further on, the narrator does the same for Scythia. But although in both cases we find surveying and measurements, it is my belief that we are not dealing with the same kind of space in the two cases, for we have imperceptibly moved from a concrete space to an abstract one, from the space of a journey to a space of knowledge.

In the case of Scythia, Herodotus's intention is to "indicate," "make known," "reveal" (*semainein*) the measurements.[123] Having stated that it is surrounded on two sides by the sea, like Attica, having fixed the position of Tauris, which corresponds to Sunium's

119. Hdt. 4.197.

120. Hdt. 4.185.

121. J. Verne, *Robur le conquérant;* this is exactly the project which a geographer could carry out if he had the *Albatross* at his disposal.

122. Hdt. 2.6–9. A. B. Lloyd, *Herodotus, Book II, Commentary* (Leiden, 1976), pp. 41–59, analyzes the difficulties raised by these measurements.

123. Hdt. 4.99–101.

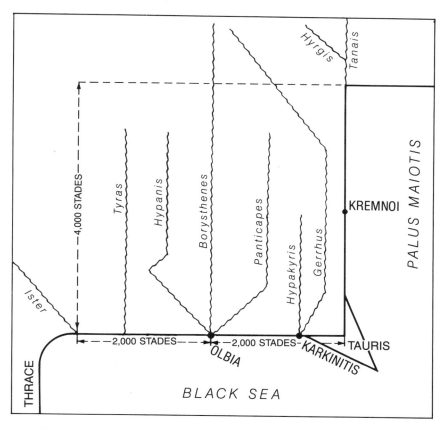

2. "Scythia, being a square . . ."

position in relation to Attica, and having mentioned the peoples who bound it "above" (to the north), he goes on as follows: "Scythia, then, being a four-sided country [*hos eouses tetragonou*] whereof two sides are seaboard, the frontiers running inland and those that are by the sea make it a square." In other words, a twenty days' march, which—if I reckon a day's march to be two hundred stades—means four thousand stades. The geometrization of the space is beyond argument and the main lines of his reasoning run as follows: if Scythia is like (*hos*) a square, its sides are equal in length; if the length of the seaboard is indeed equal to that of the interior, Scythia is a square. The equality of the sides is thus implicitly used both to prove that it is a square and also as a consequence of the initial proposition, to wit, it is *like* a square. We move from "like a square" to "these are what its [concrete] dimensions are" simply by means of a surveyor's ploy.

The fact that measurement is indeed given a double status is indicated by an "error" of calculation: from west to east Scythia measures a twenty days' march, ten days from the Ister to the Borysthenes and ten from the Borysthenes to the Palus Maeotis. But in chapters 18–19 we are told that to cover the distance from the Borysthenes, in the middle of Scythia, to the Gerrhus, which is inside the eastern frontier, a seventeen days' march is needed. Under these circumstances it seems that less than half of the total length is almost equal to the total length. But that is impossible. One can correct the manuscript; or one can maintain (as some scholars indeed have) that Herodotus used two different sources and that in chapter 101 he had forgotten what he had reported earlier. The "error" is thus made out to be a defect in the rhapsody; an overlooked inconsistency, a lacuna. It has even been suggested that in chapter 101 he was using a map.[124] Perhaps he was.

But the interesting thing is that in his narrative he makes no distinction between the concrete space of the journey and the abstract space of geometry. On the contrary, he gives one to believe that one and the same space is involved. How does he do that? Precisely in his capacity as a surveyor. In the traveler's tale, the surveying functions for the addressee as a criterion of trustworthiness: I have taken the measurements of the land over which I have traveled, I have a hold upon the spaces about which I am telling you,

124. Legrand, *Heródote*, note on book 4, p. 40.

so you can believe me. By applying the tactics of surveying to an abstract space, I am treating that space as a concrete one, with my addressee in mind. I make him believe that I am surveying Scythia, whereas I am really moving along the sides of a geometrical figure. Strictly speaking, then, there is no error of calculation, since two different kinds of space are involved; but through his use of surveying, the narrator mystifies the addressee by superposing one space on top of another, meanwhile making it appear that he is doing nothing of the kind.

The case of Libya also provides evidence of this process of the geometrization of space, particularly of far-distant areas. In Libya, the sandy zone is bounded by a succession of salt hills, each separated from the next by a distance equal to a ten days' march, stretching from Egypt to beyond the pillars of Heracles.[125] Now, of all the countries mentioned in the *Histories*, Libya is the inaccessible region par excellence.[126] But more generally, the clearest indication—not for any particular region, but for the *oikoumene* as a whole—of the presence of this space of shared knowledge is the use of the principle of symmetry: in relation to an imaginary line that counts as an equator, the Nile and the Ister are, as will be remembered, symmetrical and represent the two "tropics"; on the basis of the course of the Ister, I can even show what course is followed by the Nile and also where it rises.[127] Here again one kind of space is superposed on another, for as he produces his arguments concerning the space which is geometrically ordered, he lets it be believed that he is exploring concrete space; to be more precise, he has it believed that there are not two spaces but only one, one that is geometrical through and through.

Of course, this abstract, geometrical space is also culturally oriented. There is in fact a significance to these columns of peoples which the rhapsode delights in setting out. As one moves away from the equator one passes, by and large, from the more civilized to the more barbarian, or at least from the less barbarian to the more savage, before eventually reaching the immense deserts where there is no longer anything, where the space vanishes into the distance and words fade away.

125. Hdt. 4.181, 185.
126. Hdt. 3.25, 26, 4.150, 179.
127. Hdt. 2.33–34.

The Order of the Discourse

Within this space, already culturally oriented, directions are also indicated, directions for which the principal points of reference are provided by the visible movements of the sun and by the winds.[128] The sunrise and sunset indicate the east and the west, while the position of the midday sun marks the south. As for the north, the Great Bear points toward it but more often it is indicated by the north wind, that is to say, Boreas. The sun is more often used to mark out the west and the east, while the winds tend to be used to orient north and south. Herodotus mentions six winds altogether: first, Boreas,[129] then its opposite, Notos, the south wind; Zephyr, the west wind, is infrequently mentioned; Apeliotes is an east wind; Euros indicates the southeast; finally, Lips, the southwest wind, is mentioned only once.[130] To these directions should be added the particularly noticeable point represented by the summer and winter rising and setting of the sun—what we should call the tropics. Herodotus speaks of the winter rising of the sun but, more important, the respective courses of those two remarkable rivers, the Ister and the Nile, are for him probably a materialization of those imaginary lines, with the Ister marking the summer tropic and the Nile the winter one.[131]

That is the way the space is organized. The interesting thing is that this space, which purports to be simply "space," is in reality a Greek space of shared knowledge. It is quite clear that such a construction is only coherent if one assumes Greece to be "in the middle," to be—as the Hippocratic formula has it—"halfway between the two sunrises" (that of the summer and that of the winter);[132] in short, on the "equator." It is equally clear that to use the names of the winds to indicate directions which are universally valid is to transform a

128. A. Rehm, "Griechische Windrosen," *Sizungberichte der Bayerischen Akademie* 3 (1916): 1–104. The question has been further considered by K. Nielsen, "Les Noms grecs et latins des vents," *Classica e Medievalia* 7 (1945): 1–113.

129. For Herodotus, Boreas is the north wind or a wind of the northern sector, not a wind of the northeast, as in the Hippocratic treatise *Peri hebdomadon;* cf. 2.26—supposing Boreas and Notos to be reversed—3.102, 4.99.

130. Hdt. 2.25.

131. Hdt. 2.26.

132. Hippocratic Corpus *Airs, Waters, Places* 12 (relating to the Greek territories of Asia Minor).

relative point of reference (the Aegean Sea) into an absolute one. To say that Notos represents the south is like saying that the stade is the measure of the whole of space. Furthermore, to function, this space of shared knowledge must constantly include the observer or whoever uses it. It is valid for the movements of the sun and also for the winds; for instance, when we come across "in the direction of Boreas [*pros Boreen*]," we immediately translate "to the north," but the expression precisely means in the direction of Boreas, that is to say, in the direction *from which* Boreas blows, which, furthermore, means that it presupposes an observer who, as he turns to "face the north," is aware of the direction. In the last analysis, the abstract space wins out over experience. When the Phoenicians, having completed the *periplous* around Libya, claim to have had the sun on their right (moving from east to west, they passed into the southern hemisphere), what they say can only be "incredible":[133] since their assertion contradicts his representation of space, Herodotus is bound to reject it.

To orient himself, the surveyor makes use of these cardinal points which the narrator has only to mention in order to orient his addressee in the narrative. But fundamentally there is yet another kind of space, as it were in reserve or to be considered as a last resort in relation to the other two: the space of language. Obviously, the minute I wish to tell of a space I have recourse to words and—more generally—to language, which inevitably plays its part as a means of expressing this space: it produces a description of it. But its role does not end there. A mode of expression it most certainly is, but it appears, at the same time, to function as a model of this space. It is as if there were a correspondence between the articulations of the language and the way the space is divided up, between the order of the words and the ordering of the peoples and places; as if, as it made the space be seen, it simultaneously made it exist.

Let us return once more to the country of Scythia, which Herodotus describes twice. The first time he does so, he is traveling through it as an ethnographer; the second time, he constructs it as a geometrician.[134] In both instances, what to a large extent organizes the description is the use made of prepositions and their cases, of

133. Hdt. 4.42.
134. Hdt. 4.17–25, 99–101.

prefixes and adverbs, of all the elements in language that make it possible to indicate contiguity, proximity, or separation, all those elements which make it possible to indicate directions. For example: "above" (*huper*) the Callipidae are the Alazones; "above" them, the Scythians, who till the land; "above" (*katuperthe*) them, the Neuri; then you cross (*diabainein*) a river—and so it goes on from one people to the next, until the space is exhausted and all the peoples are listed. All this, too, is the work of the rhapsode, and all the possibilities offered by language are used to get all these different "sections" of the space to stick together or—to be more precise—to make us believe that they stick together. For, as can clearly be seen, we pass imperceptibly from the expression of space and movement in language to the space of language itself, language as a representation of concrete space, that is to say, as an imitation. Implicitly, my discourse assumes that the structure of concrete space corresponds to the divisions that exist in language; and we are back with the question of the homology between what can be seen and what can be said.[135] If saying and seeing are no distance apart, at the limit it is enough to say to elicit the belief that one has seen.

But the description of Scythia does more than simply deploy the space of language by containing it within an apparatus designed to appear trustworthy ("we are going to report all the precise information that we have been able to gather through *akoe*, stretching as far afield as possible"); it also calls on the space of shared knowledge. As well as using prepositions and prefixes, it has recourse to the cardinal determinations (in the direction of Boreas, of the setting sun, of the dawn, of the midday sun, of the east wind). The two systems are set to work concurrently: we pass from one to the other as we move from one sentence to the next or even within a single sentence. Sometimes the two systems are used together: the Black-cloaks live above (*katuperthe*) the Royal Scythians and "in the direction of Boreas."[136] Juxtaposing these different spaces within the discourse is one of the means available to the narrator to make the addressee believe that no more than one space is involved. The continuity of the discourse

135. For example, at 4.17–25, Herodotus uses *apo* (3 times), *huper* (3), *katuperthe* (8), *para* (1), *epi* (7), *ana* (1), *meta* (2), *mechri* (3), *ek* (1), *es* (1), *emprosthe* (1), *peren* (1), *sunechees* (1). To which should be added the composite verbs such as *huperoikein*, *diexelthein*, *diabainein*, for a total of 36 spatial determinations of this type.

136. Hdt. 4.20.

masks the fact that there is a discontinuity between the space of language and the space of shared knowledge, even if the latter is unable to do without the former. However, the two systems do not play equal roles in the fabrication of this mixture of spaces (which purports to be nothing of the kind), for the specifications fixed by language are far more numerous than those provided by the space of shared knowledge: thirty-six versus fourteen, to be precise. And in the case of the second description, in which Scythia is represented as a square, the inequality is even greater: forty-eight purely linguistic specifications versus a mere five cardinal determinations; that is to say, a relationship of virtually ten to one in favor of the space of language. At this point the rhapsode changes from drawing up an inventory of space by means of surveying and measurement and turns to inventing it by means of language, with the cardinal determinations lending weight to the description by producing an "effect of reality."

If the space of shared knowledge positions the observer within itself (for the expression "in the direction of Boreas" presupposes the presence of an observer), the same applies to the space of language. First, the description explicitly presupposes a subject journeying through the territory and for whom the territory unfolds. For example, for whoever crosses such and such a river (*diabanti*), for whoever passes through such and such a region (*diexelthonti*), for whoever turns to the side (*apoklinonti*), there is. . . .[137] This linguistic subject is the person for whom and before whom the space unfolds; at the same time, he is a mobile point of reference within the space his progress marks out. The description presupposes the presence of this observer in a second fashion also. If it is hardly surprising for us to find the expression "above" used to indicate that one people lives further to the north than another, it is more astonishing to find that same expression used to indicate a progression southward: for example, "above" the nomad Libyans, as one penetrates inland (*es mesogaian*), one comes to the Libya of wild animals; "above" that is the Libya of the sandy ridge with its series of hillocks, each one positioned a ten days' march from the last; and still further "above" is the desert.[138] The strangeness of the expression

137. Hdt. 4.19, 21, 22, 23.
138. Hdt. 4.181, 185.

disappears as soon as we realize that it is used by someone who is positioned, for example, at Cyrene or who is at any rate facing the interior of the country. Under these circumstances, the various zones of Libya are indeed "above" me, whether I am a traveler, an observer, or just someone using the language. Whether I speak of the "north" or the "south" and whether my starting point be the Black Sea shore or the coast of the Mediterranean, *katuperthe* does indeed mean "above." But that can only be true successively, not simultaneously. Using such an operator, I cannot simultaneously construct a representation both of the space of the north and also of that of the south. I can construct first one, then the other; but I cannot represent them both at once, since the same word means in one case "in the direction of Boreas" and in the other "in the direction of Notos." All in all, the mark of the limitations of such a representation of the world is that the subject cannot dissociate himself from it: one way or another, he is included in the picture he constructs, since the space of language and the space of shared knowledge both position him within them.

The space of language is like a grid that can be applied to concrete space. Out of a jumble of dispersed, unapprehendable pieces, it constructs a puzzle in which the pieces fit together. But this stage—of the Greek expressions of place and movement—is only the first. Next, we come to the stage of sentences which form utterances (concrete manifestations of language), the sum total of which eventually constitutes Herodotus's discourse on space, in which the concrete space, the space of language, and the space of shared knowledge intersect and are combined; so there is also a space of discourse where, now, the narrator-rhapsode is positioned.

The narrator is thus a surveyor and, in a number of senses, a rhapsode, but he is also a bard, in that the inventory of the *oikoumene* cannot fail to be an invention of the world, if only by reason of the use of the space of language, for correlations exist between "the order of the discourse" and the order of the world. Herodotus considered that Hesiod and Homer, four hundred years before him, had established a theogony for the Greeks: "they gave the gods their several names and honours and arts and indicated their outward forms."[139] As they produced an inventory, they at the

139. Hdt. 2.53.

same time invented a pantheon; they set the divine world in order. Might not Herodotus be considered to have done the same for the human world? As he produced his inventory of distant peoples and border territories, did he not invent the *oikoumene* and set the human world in order? The space of the narrative purports to be a representation of the world and he, the rhapsode, is the one who *eidea semainei*, who indicates the forms, who makes things seen, who reveals;[140] he is the one who knows.

Clearly, although we have distinguished among all these different kinds of space in our brief analysis, they are never isolated from one another; on the contrary, they can only exist and function in combination with one another. But even when thus organized within and by the discourse, they remain, so to speak, empty frames. They need to be filled and brought to life. That is the task of the narrative, which makes agents, travelers, or soldiers pass through them. They are occupied by peoples who themselves may move from one spot to another. Within this framework, actions are taken, meetings occur, and battles are fought. In short, we must add yet another kind of space to all the rest: the space of the narrative. Thus, the space of Scythia, which is the product of the intersection of these various kinds of space, is something else as well: it is the space of nomadism, that is to say, a space that offers no hold. And it is the narrative that establishes that particular characteristic of the country of Scythia, by describing the funeral rites of the Scythian kings, or, better still, by recounting Darius's war.[141] The space of the narrative is thus more than simply the product of all the other kinds of space which we have just described.

So much for the *Histories* themselves: the space of the discourse purports to give a faithful copy of concrete space (the discourse imitates the world), and the text is valid as a representation of the world. But what of the situation outside and beyond them? Would

---

140. On *semainein*, designating knowledge of a specific nature, see in particular Hdt. 2.53, 4.179, 5.54, 8.41. We may also recall Heraclitus's expression describing the lord of Delphi, "who neither tells nor conceals, but who signifies (*semainei*)," fr. 93; the more so given that, as we have seen above, p. 341, there is an at least metaphorical connection between the knowledge of the surveyor and that of the Pythia.

141. Cf. above, pp. 34ff.

not travelers and other surveyors tend to see the world through Herodotus's spectacles? And were not the *Histories* to become the mirror in which they would see the world, even as they believed they were describing it?

As in the case of power, the question posed is that of a transition from the work as constituted (the grid used in the work) to the work as an institution (the work used as a grid); to put it another way, it is the question of the *Histories* as a device to make things seen. We must therefore evaluate the effect of the *Histories* on the Greeks' imaginary representation of the world. What I mean by *effect* is not the impact of knowledge, but whatever (possibly imperceptibly) models the representation of the world that one elaborates for oneself. Let me repeat that I am not suggesting that this is all that is necessary to construct a representation of the world, for, were that the case, the representation would be supported, as it were, by nothing but air (an "air-cushion") and would then be transmitted or transformed down the years still supported by nothing but air. I am simply trying to put my finger on what can here be defined as the effect of the text (for were we to content ourselves with merely replacing the word *influence* by *effect*, our achievement would be meager indeed).[142]

I will concentrate on two effects. The first, at hardly any distance from Herodotus, is really more of a pointer. Thucydides, who was so keen to make a profound break with his predecessor, has no quarrel with him on this point and is not concerned to elaborate a different representation of the world. No doubt his subject did not demand that he should do so (no more, for that matter, than a narrative of the Persian Wars did), but was he not thereby recognizing that there was no call to return to the matter, that it had been settled once and for all? What happened beyond the frontiers of the Greek world was of no interest to Thucydides, and an ethnographic enterprise would have been wasted effort since, for him, "the ancient Greek world lived in a fashion similar to the existing barbarian one."[143] What Thucydides does is operate a rotation: he expresses in temporal terms what ethnography expresses in spatial ones, for he identifies with a point in time what ethnography sets out in space. By means of this projection back through time, which establishes the Greeks'

142. For an interesting way of posing the problem in the field of literary history, see H. R. Jauss, *Pour une esthétique de la réception* (trans. Paris, 1978).

143. Thucydides 1.6.6.

superiority over the barbarians (since the barbarians of today live as the Greeks did in the past), he suppresses all interest in ethnography; what would be the point of recording the spatial diversity of *nomoi* if, at the end of it all, one would only find what the Greeks of the olden days already knew? Nor does it cross his mind that a digression by way of the barbarians might be worthwhile in order to gain a better understanding of the Greeks of past times. For decidedly, if the past is not really knowable, neither is it in itself at all interesting.

The second example, which is rather more distant from Herodotus, introduces Nearchus, an admiral and companion to Alexander, who wrote a book which is known to us only indirectly, through Arrian and Strabo. This work, the title of which is uncertain, recounted his voyage by sea from India to Arabia, and it included a description of India.[144] Now, Nearchus, who had been to India, saw the country, or at least made his reader see it, through Herodotus's spectacles. In his book, which was probably written in the Ionian dialect, he refers not only to the chapters of the *Histories* that are directly devoted to the Indians, but also to Book 2 (which is entirely devoted to Egypt). He sees India as Herodotus saw Egypt and no doubt aims to do for India what Herodotus had done for Egypt. Thus, what implicitly informs his vision is Herodotus's representation of the world. To speak of India means naming the rivers that cross it, the first and foremost of which is the Indus. Now, how can one speak of the Indus without comparing it to the Nile and the Ister, the two rivers which, as we know, occupy such a privileged position in the geography of Herodotus?[145] More precisely still, speaking of India meant resorting to analogy: India is to the Indus what Egypt is to the Nile, namely, to use Herodotus's expression, "a gift of the river."[146] If Egypt explains India, so equally must India explain

---

144. Jacoby, *FGrHist*, 133 F 128; L. Pearson, *The Lost Histories of Alexander the Great* (London, 1960), pp. 112–49. More generally, O. Murray, "Herodotus and Hellenistic Culture," *Classical Quarterly* 22 (1973): 200–213.

145. Hdt. 2.5: Nearchus in Jacoby, *FGrHist*, 133 F 17; Arrian *Anabasis* 5.6.6–8. Arrian *India* 2.5–6: "The western part of India is bounded by the river Indus right down to the ocean where the river runs out by two mouths not joined together as the five mouths of the Ister, but like those of the Nile, by which the Egyptian delta is formed; thus also the Indian delta is formed by the river Indus, not less than the Egyptian"; see also 3.9. The Indus is larger than the Nile and the Ister put together.

146. Hdt. 2.5.

Egypt, and Nearchus is determined to produce a new explanation
for the summer flooding of the Nile. In India, it rains in the summer
and the rivers break their banks; so the same must be true of Egypt,
for "probably the mountains of Ethiopia receive rain in summer, and
from them the Nile is swollen and overflows its banks onto the land of
Egypt."[147] What goes for India goes for Egypt, and so a satisfying
resolution is found for the question that so sorely perplexed Herodotus: why does the Nile behave "the other way round" (*empalin*) from
other rivers?[148]

There are two other examples of such marginal notes to Herodotus. Nearchus recounts that during the voyage, they saw the sun to
the north: "Where they were making for the high seas and steering a
southerly course, their shadows appeared to fall southerly too."[149]
The proposition is inadmissible, since throughout his voyage Nearchus in fact remained this side of the equator and even to the north of
the Tropic of Cancer. However, it at least becomes comprehensible
once we set it alongside Herodotus's opinion of the *periplous* of the
Phoenicians: he does not believe that when they sailed round Libya
the sun was to the right of them (that is to say, in the north).[150] So
Nearchus is using Herodotus's text to validate his own narrative: he
experienced what Herodotus, who had never been there, reckoned
to be incredible. So what he is saying must be true; by affirming what
Herodotus refused to believe, he makes any addressee who is
familiar with Herodotus believe in Nearchus's own narrative.

The ploy of referring back to Herodotus may operate differently, as
in the case of the Giant Ants. According to Herodotus, there exist in
India ants which are smaller than a dog but larger than a fox and
which are gold-diggers without knowing it, for as they hollow out
their lair, they dig up sand and gold.[151] What does Nearchus have to
say? "About ants also, Nearchus says that he himself saw no ant . . . ;
he saw, however, several of their skins brought into the Macedonian
camp."[152] He thus identifies the disposable signified ant with a

147. Arrian *India* 6.5–8.
148. Hdt. 2.19–28.
149. Arrian *India* 25.5.
150. Hdt. 4.42.
151. Hdt. 3.102.
152. Arrian *India* 15.4.

signifier, to wit the skins; he sees, or at any rate has the reader see, these skins as being those of the "ants." No doubt, at that particular juncture, no traveler visiting India could sidestep the question of these ants. Had he done so, the trustworthiness of his enterprise would have been jeopardized.

So Nearchus cites Herodotus, and the *Histories* are the pattern in accordance with which his own text is organized. These two examples, that of Thucydides in opposition and close in time, the other more distant but positive, suffice to show how much of an institution the Herodotean representation of the world became. Despite his evident desire to break away, Thucydides makes no break in this particular respect; and Nearchus travels with Herodotus in his pocket. The spectacles and the mirror are certainly used: the spectacles are donned and the mirror is looked into by whoever, having returned from a long voyage, wishes to "translate" his experience of distant lands and other spaces. They are spectacles that he cannot avoid donning and it is a mirror into which he cannot avoid looking, even if he ends up by smashing the lot.

A Herodotean representation of the world, then? Yes, but does it not involve a number of retrospective illusions and a certain abuse of language? Since he is the only author of his time who has come down to us in such a complete text, is there not a tendency to exaggerate his importance? And after all, one might object that what I have just called the Herodotean representation of the world may well have been something that was widely shared, among intellectuals at least; no doubt it would be said, for example, that it was a representation which owed a great deal to Ionian science.

But perhaps it is not simply by chance that the only author to be transmitted to us so fully is precisely Herodotus. Besides, I am not claiming that Herodotus was the first to construct a representation of the world nor that he was the inventor of such a thing. However, I do believe that the *Histories* offer a representation of the world, one which is organized around a spatial code (a spatial code constituted by the interplay of the various spaces analyzed above, ranging from concrete space to the space of the narrative). It is not a code intended for the discursive mode, and it remains largely implicit. It is, as it were, the framework or the grid for this representation of the world, and I believe that it is at this level and in this manner that the text exerts an effect on the processes of imaginary representation of the addressee and makes an impact that reaches far beyond it. That, for what it is worth, is what I have tried to convey using the metaphor of Herodotus's spectacles.

In what do the *Histories* elicit belief and what kind of a representation are they? To put that more precisely, the text as a whole, from beginning to end, constructs a representation of power and a representation of the world. It no doubt contains other representations too, but those two and the codes that organize them (the code of power and the spatial code) seem to me to produce greater effects than the others. If I have made such a clear distinction between the two, that is for convenience' sake, for there is obviously interference between space and power: no representation of the world would be complete without a representation of power and no representation of power would be worth much without a representation of the world.

These pages on representation are really prompted by the metaphor of the watercolorist who sees and makes things seen through his artist's device, and they have been developed around that metaphor: the grid for the *Histories* and the *Histories* used as a grid; the *Histories* as a machine for making things seen and Herodotus as a master of seeing. I am well aware that to speak of a grid does not resolve all the problems, nor am I forgetting that it is no more than a metaphor. However, it has the advantage, first, of making the reader see what is being said and, second, of posing another question—and not an easy one: that of the effect of the text. What is it in the text that creates an effect? How far-reaching is it? How does it do it? Meanwhile we avoid starting down the dangerous slope of talk of "influences," as well as of hasty "movements outside" the text such as we mentioned above. It is a question that I can do little more than raise in the present work.

Why Elicit Belief?: The Effect of the Text

There remains one final question, the question of why: how to elicit belief, elicit belief in what, and *why* elicit belief? By and large it includes the question of the place of the *Histories* and of their function, in the first instance in the world of the Greece of the fifth century B.C. It also includes the question of the status of the *histor*.

One immediate answer (which I will do no more than mention) is that offered by Diyllus, Lucian, Plutarch, Eusebius, and a number of others, hence by an indirect and mainly late tradition: Herodotus delivered lectures. Did he really recite or read passages of the *Histories* in Athens, Corinth, Thebes, and Olympia? And was he really paid for doing so?[153] If so, since history did not exist and being a historian was not a profession, he would have occupied a position halfway between the sophist, who sold knowledge, and the rhapsode, who sold stories: a rhapsode in prose, you might say.[154]

The second approach is a negative one, a process of elimination and comparison with other figures mentioned in the course of the present work, whether or not they belong to the *Histories* themselves. Not "what are his aims in producing his narrative," but "what aims does he not have, what positions does he not fill?"

When, at the time of the Ionian revolt, Aristagoras the tyrant of Miletus comes to ask for Sparta's aid, he brings with him a "bronze tablet in which the map of all the earth was engraved, and all the seas and all the rivers."[155] Having stressed the weaknesses of the Persians (who do not know how to fight) and also their wealth, *he makes his audience see* on the map that the operation is an easy one since, all the way from the cities of Ionia to Susa, the capital of the King, all the peoples "border on one another." The map is there to make Cleomenes, his interlocutor, believe that the concrete space really does correspond to the space of language, that is to say, to his enumeration of the series of peoples who succeed one another without a silence, without a hiatus from one to the next: the Ionians border (*echontai*) on the Lydians, the Lydians border on the eastern Phrygians, the Phrygians border on the Cappadocians, the Cappadocians are bordered (*prosouroi*) by the Cilicians, and so on, all the way to Susa. Aristagoras pretends he believes this map to be a realistic representation, as if Anaximander, like those cartographers described by Borges,[156] had produced a map "which had the format of the Empire and which coincided with it on every point." The success of this trick depends on Cleomenes not knowing how to "read" a map and

153. See, most recently, Momigliano, "Historians," p. 62.

154. The sophists are well known, and studies have been made of the rhapsodes of the classical period, for example, N. J. Richardson, "Homeric Professors in the Age of the Sophists," *Proc. Cambr. Philol. Soc.* (1975): 65–81; R. Sealey, "From Phemios to Ion," *Revue des Etudes Grecques* 70 (1957): 312–51, but the question of the position of Herodotus in relation to these two groups has not been tackled.

155. Hdt. 5.49–50.

156. J.-L. Borges, *Histoire de l'infamie, histoire de l'éternité* (Paris, 1975), pp. 129–30.

believing what he sees, that is to say, the words he hears. The proposed autopsy is nothing but an illusion since, in reality, it is no more than an *akoe*. But in the end Cleomenes refuses to go along with this and instead of asking, for instance, for further details about the scale of the map, he abruptly poses an unexpected question: how many days' march would it take? Aristagoras is taken by surprise although "till now he had been cunning and fooled the Spartan right well; but here he made a false step," and he replies that it would take three months. At this Cleomenes sends him packing.

There can thus be no doubt that Aristagoras regards geography as useful, if not for "waging war," at least for getting war to be waged; not because it supplies the general staff[157] with information but, on the contrary, because it mystifies it. He is an experienced and determined user of the performative lie, but turns out to be a clumsy one. Whatever would Anaximander have thought of his work being used in such a way?

Does Herodotus himself get war to be waged? Is the knowledge of barbarians and distant peoples contained in the *Histories* used by some Aristagoras or other, either in good or bad faith, in the waging of war or in getting war to be waged? I think not, in the fifth century B.C. and at the beginning of the fourth. Nevertheless, we may well pose the question of the role played by Herodotus's text in the planning of Philip's expeditions and in the preparations made for the conquests of Alexander.[158]

Nor is Herodotus's position comparable to that of his predecessor Hecataeus of Miletus, who was one of those who supported (*stasioteon*) Aristagoras. When, in the course of a meeting, the decision of whether to revolt has to be made, he uses his knowledge to try to persuade the conspirators not to revolt:

All the rest spoke their minds to the same effect, favouring revolt, save only Hecataeus the *logopoios*; he advised them that they would be best guided not to make war on the king of Persia, *enumerating* [*katalegon*] all the nations subject to Darius and the forces at his disposal. But when they would not be persuaded by him, he counselled them that their next best plan was to make themselves masters of the seas.[159]

---

157. Y. Lacoste, *La Géographie, ça sert, d'abord, à faire la guerre* (Paris, 1976).

158. O. Murray, "Herodotus and Hellenistic Culture," *Classical Quarterly* 22 (1972): 206 n. 1.

He too is one who knows the names. In similar fashion, when the revolt is unsuccessful, he again offers his advice to Aristagoras, who again ignores it.[160] True, Hecataeus does speak on the strength of what he knows (albeit without the slightest effect, as Herodotus underlines at every opportunity), but the reason why he can do so is above all that he is a citizen of Miletus and one who belongs to an aristocratic family. Herodotus, on the other hand, is an exile: once exiled from Halicarnassus, he is a foreigner everywhere, whether it be Samos or Egypt, the Black Sea region or Athens. As a foreigner, or at the best a metic—at least, that is, until his arrival in Thurii[161]— he is excluded from politics and there is no way for his knowledge to be directly converted into power. His words are not directly political.

He is a traveler, but not in the manner of Marco Polo, who, before he came to dictating his memories in the dungeons of Genoa, had been the seeing eye of the Khan in the distant provinces of the latter's empire. As he performed his missions, he learned to see what the Khan wished to know: "Like a wise man and one who knows all the whims of his lord, he took great care to learn and hear everything that he knew would please the Great Khan. He carried out his task well, thanks be to God, and knew how to tell of many new and strange things. As for the Great Khan, the behavior of Messire Marco Polo pleased him so much that he became extremely fond of him."[162] But Herodotus was not directly the eye of anybody; he was not entrusted with a mission nor was he the cosmographer of a prince.

No more was he the historiographer of a prince. To put it more generally, he held no contract with any power which afforded him authorization or which needed him to write its history.[163] For example, his position was in no way comparable to that of William the

159. Hdt. 5.36. See G. Nenci, "Le fonti de Erodoto sull' insurrezione ionica," *Accademia Nazionale dei Lincei* (Rendiconti) 5 (1950): 106–18.

160. Hdt. 5.124.

161. Momigliano, "Historians," p. 61. For the indirect tradition, Herodotus comes from Thurii, not Halicarnassus: this "hesitation" over his identity is not insignificant.

162. Marco Polo, *La Description du Monde*, p. 14, ed. L. Hambis.

163. See the analyses by L. Marin, *Le Récit est un piège* (Paris, 1978), and "Pouvoir du récit et récit du pouvoir," *Actes de la Recherche en Sciences Sociales* 25 (January 1979): 23–43.

Breton, chaplain to Philip Augustus, who was the first to turn the battle of Bouvines into an "event."[164] Despite what has sometimes been suggested, Herodotus was not Pericles' liege-man, defending his imperialistic policies in the name of the city's glorious past, nor— if one distinguishes between the two, as Jacoby does—was he the herald of Athens at the point when the Peloponnesian War was about to break out.[165] He was neither a cosmographer nor a historiographer nor advisor to a prince or a city. Even if one judges by Plutarch's reading of the *Histories*, his "malice" spared no one, were they individuals, families, or cities (including Athens and the Alcmeonids) and his pro-barbarianism made him a traitor to the Greeks.[166]

I have mentioned a number of negative ways of describing him, a number of places he does not occupy; they amount to so many reasons why he does not elicit belief. All in all, the difficulty in this matter stems from the fact that the father of history is not a historian. And even if it is true that one's place "allows" a certain type of production and "excludes others,"[167] in his case we cannot set up a direct relationship between his text and some such position. Not that we would attempt to do so in order to reduce the text to that position, but in order to attempt, by setting the two side by side, to seize on one of the laws organizing his discourse. But just because Herodotus the author does not appear to fill any particular spatial or official position, that is no reason not to continue our inquiry.

So far, the question of why (why elicit belief?) has prompted two kinds of reply, both unsatisfactory, the one because it draws on an external and decidedly late tradition, the other because it does no more than express the question in a negative fashion (why does he not elicit belief?). But there remains a possible third approach, one which our preceding discussion has already suggested: to stake everything on the text itself. It is my conviction that the results of the preceding chapters have revealed the elements of an answer to this question of why. It is not a matter of what Herodotus explicitly says about himself and his function since, except in the prologue, he says

---

164. G. Duby, *Le Dimanche de Bouvines* (Paris, 1973), pp. 14–18.

165. H. Strasburger, "Herodot und das perikleiche Athen," in *Hérodote*, ed. Marg (Darmstadt, 1965), pp. 574–608. And C. Fornara, *Herodotus: An Interpretative Essay* (Oxford, 1971), pp. 37–58.

166. Cf. above, pp. 152f.

167. M. de Certeau, *L'Ecriture de l'histoire* (Paris, 1975), p. 15.

nothing at all (and, of course, his very silence has significance). Rather, it is a matter of the effect of the text on its addressees, an effect it is possible to evaluate in particular on the basis of the functions the narrator assumes in the text and through the entire interplay of the indicators as to the source of utterances. So, instead of establishing a relationship between a place and a text or reducing the text to that place, we should try to define the position of the narrator within the narrative; and that may point to a position beyond the text and at the same time "exclude others"; in other words, it may mark out a place for him.

The prologue echoes Homer, and the epic model clearly plays a role of importance in Herodotus's enterprise. But while the epic is what he aims to rival, it is also important for him to dissociate himself from it; the narrator may be a rhapsode or even a bard, but he is a rhapsode in prose. And in the two different texts the task of eliciting belief proceeds along different lines. In one case it is the Muse[168] who stands as the ultimate guarantor; in the other, the narrator. "I know because I have seen" means autopsy, and "I know because I have heard" means inquiry (*historie*). In epic, it is the Muse who speaks through the mouth of the poet. In the *Histories*, it is the narrator who says "I say," "I write." Here, unlike in epic, he is the only person who speaks. The *histor* sees and hears, says and writes, and the narrator exists purely within and through the deployment of these various indicators as to who is speaking, indicators that are the mainspring of the text's power to elicit belief from the addressee.

The narrator, the only person to speak, is the one who knows. Just as Homer and Hesiod set the divine world in order and "depicted" the images of the gods, Herodotus sets the various peoples in their places, distributes roles, and fixes frontiers; he makes what can be seen, what can be surveyed, and what can be said coincide; he constructs a representation of the world that reflects both knowledge and power (*dunamis*). For the narrator, knowledge and power, whether he affirms them or whether he claims them, stem from the very production of this representation; but there are also knowledge and power for the addressee or addressees, depending on how they "read" this representation. On the part of the narrator, the word that best sums up this knowledge and power is *semainein*. Through all his

---

168. Svenbro, *La Parole*.

interventions, direct or indirect, in the narrative, the narrator aims to *semainein,* to make seen and make known. For *semainein* is to make seen and make known to people who have not seen it for themselves, just as the lookout on the promontory comes to warn others of the movements of the enemy fleet;[169] so we are back with autopsy. But it also means to make seen and make known to people who do not possess this particular type of knowledge: superhuman knowledge of an oracular kind, for example, like that of Triton;[170] exceptional knowledge, such as that invoked by Croesus in giving advice to Cyrus;[171] or, indeed, the knowledge of the *histor,* of the one who has made his inquiry and who knows the mistakes made by his predecessors,[172] knows the name of the man who initially provoked hostilities between the Greeks and the barbarians[173]—knows the length of the seaboard of Scythia and the exact measurements of the royal road stretching to Susa all the way from the sea.[174] The science of the surveyor and the knowledge of the Pythia are metaphorically related insofar as the Pythia, in her reply to the envoys of Croesus, describes herself as the one who knows the number of the grains of sand and the measurements of the seas. *Semainein* certainly means that the narrator is both a rhapsode and a surveyor.

As well as being the only person who speaks, the narrator is the translator of what is different; he is the one who takes the listener from here to there, the *poros* between the world in which one recounts and the world that is recounted. To elicit belief in the world that is recounted, inside the world in which one recounts, he cannot do otherwise than deploy and maneuver a whole rhetoric of otherness the figures and procedures of which, in the last analysis, depend on the polarity of two terms, "them" and "us," the "others" (however different from one another they may be) and the "Greeks." This brings into play comparison and analogy, but also *thoma* (I am reality for these "others"), translation, and inversion too, inversion which represents the limit since they are *nothing but* our opposite.

The full import of this polarity (them/us) is such that its expression

169. Hdt. 7.92, 219.
170. Hdt. 4.179.
171. Hdt. 1.89.
172. Hdt. 2.20.
173. Hdt. 1.5.
174. Hdt. 5.54.

is not confined to these rhetorical figures alone, for it is what, in the last analysis, justifies reading the Scythian *logos* according to the principle of systematic differentiation. The only way to understand anything about the Scythian *nomoi* is to adopt the hypothesis that they are informed by the Greek *nomoi*. Setting those *nomoi* along-side their "absent model" reveals differences which, at a second reading, it may be possible to define, by discovering the law by which they are organized. Such was the case with the kings' funeral rites and with the Scythian sacrificial practices culminating in that bizarre image of the self-cooking ox, and also with the warrior practices organized around the figure of Ares.

We are presented with "them," and "they" certainly differ among themselves: the Persians are clearly different from the Egyptians, who, for their part, are quite distinct from the Scythians, and so on. We even find differences in the ways of life followed by different peoples who are all nomadic. Nevertheless, the narrative is im-plicitly based on the principle of the excluded middle,[175] as can be seen in the case of the Scythians and the Amazons. The otherness of the Scythians is certainly apprehended in relation to the Greeks who, as the second term implicitly present in the knowledge shared by the addressee, play their part as a term of reference. But as soon as the Amazons make their appearance, the mechanism imperceptibly changes and the Scythians turn into quasi-Greeks. So the narrative seems to be incapable of coming to terms with the otherness of the Amazons, at one remove, in relation to Scythian otherness, which has itself already been grasped through its relation to the Greek world; and it seems that, to make this second otherness comprehen-sible to the addressee, all the narrative could do was reestablish a binary structure: "them" (the Amazons)/"us," "them"/the Scythians, who are almost "us."

We have already come across this polar organization in connection with Darius's Persians in Scythia. In Scythia, the Persians behave as quasi-hoplites, whereas in Greece they behave as barbarians, people who do not know how to fight.[176] This behavior is all the more surprising considering that the logic of the narrative turns the Scythians into some kind of Athenian defenders of liberty. Quasi-

175. Cf. above, pp. 259ff.
176. Cf. above, pp. 45ff.

hoplites opposed to quasi-Athenians, then? How, indeed, could one give an account of the otherness of Scythian strategy, being simultaneously faced with the otherness of the Persians' way of fighting? For both are conceived in relation to the Greek model (*aporia*/absence of *taxis*). So how could they be conceived in relation to each other? How could *aporia* and an absence of *taxis* come to grips with one another? How could these things be made to be seen and believed? The narrative eliminates the term which, of the two, incorporates the least otherness—in this instance the Persians, who thus become quasi-hoplites. We are then left with *aporia* (now promoted to the rank of a veritable strategy) set in opposition to the phalanx, a situation which makes its otherness all the more apparent.

In the last analysis, to tell of "others" is clearly a way of speaking of "us," since the narrative is unable to escape from the them/us polarity which constitutes its indestructible framework. One of the effects—at any rate an indirect effect—of the text is to help to focus on this "us."[177]

To speak of "others" is indeed to make seen a representation of the world, fixing its limits and listing the peoples who inhabit it, but it also presupposes a central position for the Greeks. For confirmation, we have only to think again of the geography of the *Histories*, of the courses of the Nile and the Ister and of the way the principle of symmetry is applied. It also means that this representation is constructed on the basis of a Greek space of shared knowledge which, implicitly, invariably positions a (Greek) observer inside it.

To speak of others is to make it known that, over and above the variety of *nomoi*, the most profound difference between "them" and "us" is political, a difference of power: *isonomia* stands in opposition to monarchy-tyranny; "others" are royal. To be more precise, it means constructing a representation that is centered on an element that raises a question for "us," or even calls "us" into question. Such is the case with the Scythian *logos*. Scythian practices, and the figures and procedures in the narrative that convey them, in the last analysis revolve around the following fundamental question: how is it possible to be a nomad? What is this being who is so strange—even scandalous—to "us," people with a city way of life? And if nomadism is not reduced to non-being by the narrator of the *Histories*, that is

---

177. The word occurs at least 160 times in the first four books.

because, thanks to the metaphor of insularity, it can be translated in terms of strategy, into "our" strategy.

The text may function ethnocentrically around "them and "us," "them" in relation to "us," the world that is recounted translated into the world in which one recounts, but one of its distinctive features is that it is neither deliberately nor systematically Hellenocentric. "We" are not what the future holds for "them"; unlike Thucydides, Herodotus does not believe that the barbarians of his day live as the Greeks of bygone days did.[178] Nor, where they are concerned, is he in a position to deliver a lecture on writing. What he writes is not presented as if it were the truth behind barbarian discourse, the latter being accordingly reduced to the level of fables. Conversely, these "others" are not the truth for "us": they do not represent a model of some other kind of life lived in accordance with nature, which "we" should do well to imitate. Herodotus's Anacharsis is neither at school in Greece nor a martyr to Hellenism but, then, neither does he represent the Cynics, despising city life with all its soft ways; he is not held up as a model on which the Greeks should school themselves.[179] Rather, like his compatriot Scyles, he is one who transgresses, believing it possible to cross frontiers with impunity; to put it another way, he "forgets" that frontiers exist between "them" and "us." All in all, then, there are "them" and there are "us," and Herodotus appears neither as a zealot of culture nor as an advocate of nature.

The "others," "they," are present in the narrative in the form of the third person, that is to say, the non-personal form.[180] There is nothing surprising about that: introduced by the narrator into his narrative, as they are, as what the utterance is about but never as the subject who utters it, they are produced for "us" (me + you). But what *is* surprising is that, more often than not, the first-person plural, *we*, is replaced by the third-person plural: not *we*, but *the Greeks*, which is again a non-personal form: the "others" and the Greeks, the barbarians and the Greeks, *them* and *they*.[181]

---

178. Thucydides 1.6.6.

179. Diogenes Laertius *Lives of the Philosophers*, 1.101.

180. E. Benveniste, *Problems in General Linguistics* (Coral Gables, 1971), p. 199.

181. According to Powell, *Hellen* and *Hellenes* occur at least 539 times; even if they should not all be placed on the same level, the total figure is significant.

To whom does the label *Greeks* apply? The narrator speaks of the *Greeks* when he reports events which happened in Greece in bygone days: the Greeks did this or did that, thought this or thought that. *Greeks* may also mean *certain* Greeks, who live in one or another region (the Greeks of the Black Sea, for example), or who hold one or another opinion that Herodotus considers to be mistaken or stupid.[182] In short, to speak of the Greeks is a way for the narrator to keep his distance. If "we" is "I + you," "you" being "an indistinct global entity of other people,"[183] to speak of "the Greeks" is a way of emphasizing that the narrator is the sole person who delivers the utterance, the only subject who knows and speaks.

He is the master of seeing, the master of knowing, the master of believing, through his use of all the figures and procedures of a rhetoric of otherness set in motion by the deployment of all the indicators as to the source of the utterance. It is he who names, who lists, who classifies, who counts, who measures, who surveys, who sets things in order, who marks out limits, who distributes praise and blame, who knows more than he lets on, who remembers: he knows. He makes things seen, he makes known, he makes us believe.

182. For example, Hdt. 2.2, 10, 45.
183. Benveniste, *Problems*, p. 203.

Conclusion

The History of a Division

The Scythians are "others"; Herodotus is a traveler and teller of traveler's tales; Herodotus is an ethnographer or ethnologist; Herodotus is a surveyor of otherness and a rhapsode of the *oikoumene:* that comes as no news, since this is the Herodotus whom we have accompanied all the way through these pages. But the question that is now bound to arise is the following: Does this Herodotus represent an "other" Herodotus? Is he really profoundly different from the Herodotus who is "the historian of the Persian Wars"? If we proceed a step further: is he really Herodotus's other half, his shadow?

That question cannot be answered with a simple yes or no, for to answer with any precision would involve considering the entire historiography of Herodotus and tracing the history of the successive interpretations of the work. Nevertheless, if we follow the tradition of the liar, as I have sketched it out, it becomes apparent that the image of the liar is neither immediately nor inevitably superposed on that of the ethnographer or the Herodotus of "others." He is not a liar because, or only when, he speaks of non-Greeks. Indeed, for Thucydides, the *muthodes*, a fabrication of the logographers, applies not only to what is said about barbarians but just as much to the narrative of wars, even recent ones—indeed, perhaps even more to the latter, to the extent that they stem almost exclusively from *akoe.* Ctesias, for obvious reasons, sets out to denounce the lies that are the most "malicious" and most serious; in other words, those that, most of all, concern the Greeks themselves.

371

Estienne, in his *Apologia*, or in his *Traité*, does not mention the Persian Wars directly, being above all interested in the Herodotus of "others." In Herodotus's defense, Estienne appeals to analogous examples taken from a number of other Greek and Latin authors, and he makes use of comparison. The lack of verisimilitude of such and such a custom reported in bygone days by Herodotus is dispelled as soon as one casts a similar eye over customs currently observed in Italy, Germany, Flanders, or Spain. Similarly, the lack of verisimilitude of what is reported, at certain points, on the score of the Persians is whittled away when this is placed alongside what is known of the Turks and of Tamburlaine.[1] Finally, if he is held to be a liar by Abbé Bonnaud, that is by reason of an issue of principle which has absolutely nothing to do with him, even if he is the first historian—the issue being that secular history is bound to be a pack of lies or mythological.

If we now turn to the historian of the Persian Wars or, rather, the way modern scholars have constructed that figure, it appears that, all the way down to the end of the eighteenth century, his narrative of events was not seriously disputed.[2] In the nineteenth century, with its research on sources, the situation was to change and suspicion was to gain the upper hand. By dint of tracing the sources, of all types, on which he drew, the nineteenth-century scholars ended by burying the text of the *Histories*, claiming that Herodotus lived by borrowing, if not plagiarizing. In 1894, Hauvette summed up the situation as follows:

All the scholars so far mentioned—Niebuhr, Nitzch, Wecklein, and Delbrück—agree that Herodotus derived his history of the Persian Wars from an oral tradition or from one that was almost exclusively oral. . . . But they reject the idea that Herodotus reproduced a ready-made history in his

1. *L'Introduction au Traité*, p. 11. On page 25, Estienne makes use of two contemporary *thaumasta:* one is the story of the popess Jeanne, the other one is the story of Martin Guerre (recently studied by N. Z. Davis, *The Return of Martin Guerre* (Cambridge, Mass., 1983).

2. A. Hauvette, *Hérodote, historien des guerres médiques* (Paris, 1894), pp. 114–15. The primary preoccupations of scholars were quite different. It was a matter of bringing the Greek texts on Eastern dynasties in line with the chronological information provided by the Scriptures: for example, Scaliger, Petau, and Président Bouhier.

book. . . . Over the last ten years in particular, quite the opposite theory, suggested as early as the beginning of this century by Creuzer and subsequently supported by a number of other scholars, has predominated. . . . It maintains, with varying degrees of qualification, that the historian, without acknowledgment, put together a large number of earlier works which he literally plagiarized from his predecessors. This theory was originally applied generally to the whole of Herodotus's work, but it has recently become limited to the part of the work concerned with the Persian Wars.[3]

The most perspicacious of the promoters of this idea are Sayce, Diels, Panofsky, and Trautwein.[4] According to them, Herodotus invents oral traditions which never existed or conceals written sources which most certainly did exist. The *Quellenforschung* thus produces a new avatar of the liar.

Not long after this, in 1909 and 1913, Jacoby revived the subject, treating it from a profoundly different point of view.[5] For him, the predominant question was that of the birth of history: when and how did the Greeks become historians, and what is Herodotus's place in this evolution? What interested him was not the image of the liar but that of the father of history, not Herodotus's lies but his paternity. His conclusions are well known: Herodotus, who started out as an ethnographer and a geographer, only became a *historian* after his stay in Athens. The work manifests an "epistemological break" between the time before, when he is not yet a historian, and the time after, when he truly is one. The Herodotus of "others," of the first books, belongs to the earlier period. It is a way of preserving him even while setting him at a distance; but at all events he is still an "other" Herodotus.

Once that framework was fixed, commentators and historians took

3. Hauvette, *Hérodote*, pp. 158–59.

4. A. H. Sayce, *The Ancient Empires of the East, Herodotos, I–III* (London, 1883); H. Diels, "Herodot und Hekataios," *Hermès* 22 (1887): 411ff.; H. Panofsky, "Quaestionum de historiae herodotae fontibus pars prima," diss. Berlin, 1885; P. Trautwein, "Die Memoiren des Dikaios, eine Quelle des herodoteischen Geschichtswerkes," *Hermès* 25 (1890): 527–66.

5. F. Jacoby, "Uber die Entwicklung der griechischen Historiographie und den Plan einer neuen Sammlung der griechischen Historikerfragmente," *Klio* 9 (1909): 80–123; Jacoby, *RE*, in particular 352–60: "Er hat nicht für Perikles geschrieben, sondern für sein neues grosses Vaterland, für Athen."

up their positions in relation to it, sometimes accepting it, sometimes modifying it, sometimes rejecting it.[6] Thus von Fritz, who
supported a theory of such an evolution, refined it by detecting an
earlier (epistemological) "break" during the travels in Egypt, a break
he even dates precisely to the visit to the labyrinth: "The turning
point is probably marked by his visit to the Fayoum where the so-
called Lake of Moiris and the labyrinth made an overwhelming
impression on his mind. From this moment he seems to have
developed a very keen interest in Egyptian customs and religion."[7]
All the same, this widening of his interests still did not really amount
to history, for "even at the end of his journey he seems not yet to have
been aware of the necessity of a chronological order. He had not yet
found out that this was an indispensable foundation of true historiography."[8] The historian can already be glimpsed beneath the
traveler, and the frontier of otherness recedes. But all in all the
Entwicklungstheorie (evolutionary theory) still splits him in two.

Disregarding the question of Greek historiography and also that
of whether Herodotus was the father of history or the father of lies,
some authors have concentrated their attention on the *Histories*
themselves and have, in contrast, concluded that the work is a unity,[9]
which they read as forming a "single *logos.*"[10] Herodotus's duality
disappears, and the ethnographical *logoi* are no longer treated as the
digressions of a pre-historian.

Broadly speaking, that is how the question of the liar and the
Herodotus of "others," the historian and the ethnologist, has been
posed. But in view of the points made in the present work, how
should we pose it now? To put it another way, what axes should we
adopt in order to formulate what, for us, is really a retrospective
question?

In the first place, our study of the narrative constraints has shown

6. R. Drews, *The Greek Accounts of Eastern History*, pp. 36–39.

7. K. von Fritz, "Herodotus and Greek Historiography," *Transactions of the
American Philological Association* 67 (1936): 337. So historians find no less cause for
"amazement" than philosophers.

8. Von Fritz, "Herodotus," p. 338. The article opens as follows: "Herodotus is
called the father of history. Yet whereas the work of Thucydides corresponds rather
exactly to our conception of historiography, the work of Herodotus does not."

9. In particular, M. Pohlenz, J. L. Myres, and H. Immerwahr.

10. H. Immerwahr, *Form and Thought in Herodotus* (Cleveland, 1966), p. 79.

that splitting Herodotus in two will not do. Darius's war in Scythia refers the reader to Xerxes' Greek expedition; the latter is necessary to the intelligibility of the former, which, generally speaking, is a repetition of it.[11]

Furthermore, throughout the *Histories*, it is always a matter of "them," the "others," and "us," the Greeks, though the setting varies from one book to another. Even if, in the *logoi* about "others," the "*we*" is often present no more than implicitly, it nevertheless slips into the narrative imperceptibly, perpetually haunting it. And these *logoi* are also an indirect way of focusing on the "we." The history of the Persian Wars, for its part, places the "we" on stage altogether explicitly, in the struggle against "them," and, as it does so it constructs for "us" a representation of the recent past and elaborates a new collection of memories centered on the *Hellenikon*.[12] The "we" is thus constantly present in the narrative, at least implicitly in some cases, explicitly in others.

The way the *logoi* devoted to "others" do probably differ from those dealing with the Persian Wars is in the position of the addressee; he probably knew more about the Persian Wars than he did about the "others." In the case of the Persian Wars, the world that is recounted is in the world in which one recounts. But, as we have seen, what counts about the way the text elicits belief is not so much the quantity of new information it presents as how it is treated by the narrator (who not only says what is said but says it in a particular fashion and says what is most "notable").

Let us formulate our retrospective question as follows: if the process of eliciting belief operates through the narrator's interventions in his narrative, how does Herodotus intervene in his account of the Persian Wars? Is he more or, on the contrary, less present, and is he present in a different way from that in the *logoi* about "others"? By way of reply, let us take three soundings.

11. Cf. above, pp. 34ff.; and H. F. Bornitz, *Herodot-Studien* (Berlin, 1968), pp. 111–36.

12. Herodotus 1.4, 58, 60, 7.139, 145, 8.12, 144 (according to the famous definition Herodotus ascribes to the Athenians: "the kinship of all Greeks in blood [*homaimon*] and speech [*homoglosson*], and the shrines of gods and the sacrifices that we have in common [*theon idrumata te koina kai thuslai*], and the likeness of our way of life [*ethea te homotropa*]." G. Nenci, "Significato etico-politico ed economico-sociale delle guerre persiane," in *La Grecia nell'eta di Pericle* (Milan, 1979), pp. 12–16.

The first concerns *thoma* and the *erga thomasta*. How are these treated in the narrative of the wars, if it is true that the *thoma* is a rubric for the traveler's tale and that marvels require the seeing and measuring eye of the traveler, and if it is also the case that the aim of the *Histories* is precisely to ensure that the *erga megala te kai thomasta* should never cease to be recounted (*aklea*)? In the narrative of the wars, the remarkable or admirable *ergon* is no longer a river, a site, or a monument, but first and foremost an exploit. However, once that difference has been noted, we find, surprisingly enough, that the *ergon thomasta* is apprehended, constructed, and, eventually, recounted by means of the same procedures as in the *logoi* about "others." The two Spartans, Sperthias and Boulis, behave in a way "worthy of admiration" (*axie thomatos*) just as a Babylonian dike is, by reason of its height and breadth, "worthy of admiration."[13] We remember that the labyrinth of Egypt provokes a *thoma* "beyond words" (*logou mezo*); in similar fashion, the action of the diviner Hegesistratus, who unhesitatingly cuts off his own shackled foot in order to free himself, also provokes a *thoma, mezon logou*.[14] Again, when describing the collecting of spices, the narrator classifies the methods used according to an implicit scale of *thoma*, ranging from the least "extraordinary" to the most "extraordinary." Now, in the narrative of the wars, we also find *thoma* classified as a series of gradations, characterized in particular by the use of superlatives.[15] Finally, just as the eye of the traveler is the guarantor of a *thoma*, similarly the narrator is, in many cases, the reference for the *thoma* (*thoma moi*, it is a *thoma* to me),[16] even if in one case the eye seizes on it, looks all around it, gauges it, and measures it, whereas in the other case the intervention of the "I" instead emphasizes the astonishing or incomprehensible aspect of the reported phenomenon, the fact that it is impossible to establish a hold on it. In both cases it is "I" who am the judge.[17]

13. Hdt. 1.185, 7.135.
14. Hdt. 2.148, 9.37.
15. Hdt. 7.204, 8.135.
16. Hdt. 6.117, 121, 7.99, 153, 8.135, 9.65.
17. H. Immerwahr, "*Ergon:* History as a Monument in Herodotus and Thucydides," *American Journal of Philology* 81 (1960): 266, notes: "The conception of fame underlying both monuments and deeds is exactly the same"; p. 268: "The vocabulary of words associated with *ergon* and *mnemosynon* shows that Herodotus looks at a deed as if it were a monument."

Now we come to our second sounding. It concerns that which is notable or, as Herodotus puts it, "that which is worthy of being reported" (*axios apegesios*). The author uses this same instrument to make his own selection from all the welter of things that are tellable or writable, both in the world of "others" and in our own. Of all the methods of hunting the crocodile, he "writes" the one that seems to him to be "the most worthy of being reported" (*axiotate apegesios*). Similarly, of all the events that took place in Athens between the end of the tyranny and the Ionian revolt, he "tells of those most worthy of being reported" (*axiochrea apegesios*).[18] The recurrence of this expression seems to indicate that the narrator's approach does not change whether it be a matter of distant customs or of past events, and that his inclination is to treat them all in the same fashion.

Finally, from beginning to end in the narrative he is the one who makes things seen and makes things known, *semainein:* I know who first acted unjustly toward the Greeks and I shall make it known (*semainein*). Having done so, "I shall carry on with the rest of my *logos*," that is to say, I shall myself cover this ground that my discourse represents and at the same time I shall act as a guide to it.

There thus appears to be no detectable difference between the positions occupied by the narrator in his narrative, now as the rhapsode of otherness, now as the historian of the wars. He seems to pass from what is "other" to what is "the same," meanwhile himself remaining the same. It therefore seems likely that the Herodotus of "others" is not an "other" Herodotus; or that the "other" Herodotus, who assuredly does exist, is a product of the interpretations that have been given of Herodotus; he belongs to and is conveyed by the historiography of Herodotus.

To make the above suggestions is not to claim that, passing beyond that diachronic perspective, I am in a position to rediscover the text, that is to say, the real Herodotus; such a claim would be both foolish and mistaken.[19] Quite simply, what makes this approach—or re-

18. Hdt. 2.70, 5.65; the expression recurs at 3.125, in the context of the manner of Polycrates' death, which is not "fit to be told." See H. Drexler, *Herodot-Studien* (Hildesheim 1972), who, after studying these expressions, nevertheless concludes that Herodotus was no historian (p. 185).

19. See also the critical study devoted to this "philology which remained more or less idealistic" by R. Jauss, *Pour une esthétique de la réception* (trans. Paris, 1978), pp. 58–63.

turn—to Herodotus possible is the fact that a shift has taken place in the historical field, a shift the most obvious indications of which are the decline of the history of events and political history (or, at any rate, a certain kind of political history), the rise of historical anthropology or ethnohistory (of which Herodotus may even become the father), and the recent inquiries into the imaginary representations of various societies. It is this which, in the field of ancient history, makes it possible no longer to be obliged to see the *Histories* through *The Peloponnesian War* or to regard Herodotus as not only (inevitably) the first historian but also Thucydides' predecessor; and it also makes it possible to read the Scythian *logos* as a discourse on the imaginary Scythians.

However, the fact remains that the judgments passed on him— those we have mentioned above, and others as well—show that Herodotus occasions a certain unease, perhaps because of the uncertainty surrounding the place he occupies. Who is he? Where does he fit in? A rhapsode? A sophist? A historian? But that is no profession. So efforts are made to dispel the uncertainty and to spirit away the unease. No doubt he does claim to tell *logoi*, but in reality his *logoi* are probably *muthoi:* hence, Herodotus the naïf. Alternatively, he presents as *logoi* stories which in reality are *muthoi*, that is to say, *pseudea*, lies: hence we come back to Herodotus the liar. After all, if he is a liar, that is reassuring; at least we know what we are up against. And meanwhile, the interpreter at a stroke demonstrates his own perspicacity. We are offered either a writer who makes inquiries, flanked by his mythologist double; or a teller of *muthoi*, alongside his other self, the historian.

In historical discourse, the prestige of "this happened" produces the surest effect of reality,[20] but in the case of the *Histories* that effect of reality is undermined by doubt: so it is no longer a matter of the prestige of "this happened" shoring up the discourse, but instead a case of the unease of "that did not happen" or "it did not happen like that" undermining it. Did the Scythian War even take place? Was this the course it took? And, pushing yet further, we come to the question of reality. In the practice of the historian, there are two kinds of reality:

20. R. Barthes, "Le Discours de l'histoire." *Social Science Information* 6, 4 (1967): 71.

Reality in the sense of what is *known* (what the historian studies, understands or "resuscitates" of a past society) and reality insofar as it is *implied* by the scientific operation (the present society to which are referred the historian's inquiry, his procedures, his modes of comprehension and, finally, the use of his judgment). On the one hand, reality is the *result* of analysis, while on the other it is its *postulate*.[21]

But in the case of Herodotus, reality appears to be distinguishable neither at the beginning nor at the end, neither as a postulate (because of the uncertainty of the place he occupies) nor as a result (because of the unease occasioned by these *logoi / muthoi*).

More generally, the tactic used to spirit away this unease has been to make him the father of history. It was one way of assigning him a position, but also a way of setting him apart. Furthermore, if he is installed out there on the threshold of history, an old, blackened idol to be ritually saluted, the very mention of his name may have apotropaic effects: it assures the addressee that my own text is not telling lies.

In the last analysis, his position may be summed up in the following paradox: even though he is the father of history, he is not really a historian. It appears that paternity necessarily involves an element of incompleteness. Cicero, in the text that, for us, is the first to ascribe this title of *father* to him, begins by reminding the reader of the difference between history and poetry: one aims for the truth, the other for pleasure (*delectatio*). But Cicero is then immediately obliged to make an exception of Herodotus who, in a sense, antedates this classification since he is both on the side of history and on that of pleasure. If the distinction between history and poetry truly is as I have just suggested, *quamquam et apud Herodotum, patrem historiae . . . sunt innumerabiles fabulae*,[22] Herodotus blurs the categories, eludes the genre laws, and contravenes the professional rules.

When Vivès declared that it would be closer to the mark to call Herodotus the father of lies than the father of history, that was just a wisecrack. But the fact that historiography associates those two images is probably not mere chance: why do they recur, one or the other or both together, so constantly? To see him as the father of

21. M. de Certeau, *L'Ecriture de l'histoire* (Paris, 1975), pp. 46–47.
22. Cicero *Laws* 1.1.5.

history and, unfortunately, also as the liar, a shameful double who dogs his steps, is surely too simplistic. No, he is both the father and the liar, for it is precisely to the extent that he occupies that special position of the father and thus in part eludes the laws of the genre which he is credited with having fathered that he can also be the liar. Seen in this fashion, Herodotus together with the successive interpretations of his work thus constitute a distorting mirror before which to pose a question as old as Herodotus himself, one that today arises once again for us and concerns us: the question of history and fiction.

For the stranglehold of fiction does not stop there. If Herodotus himself defines as *muthos* what, in his own text, he sets at a distance, and if he is promptly described as a mythologist by his successors, it seems, conversely, that in the Hellenistic period he was used by authors of romances to confer an impression of reality on *their* texts. Such is the case of the *Ephesiaca* by the writer known as Xenophon of Ephesus. It has been shown that the author did not know the town of Ephesus (where the action takes place) at first hand and that he had borrowed a number of topographical details, as well as the names of some of his characters, from Herodotus.[23] The liar comes to the aid of fiction to lend it credibility.

Father and liar, history and fiction. More concretely, what does it mean to produce history with a text such as that of the *Histories* if it is true that, according to a formula attributed to Fustel de Coulanges, "history comes from texts"?[24] It is a question that could also be formulated as follows: how should the text be read? And that is a question to which the present work has attempted to provide an answer.

23. B. Lavagnini, *Studi sul romanzo greco* (Florence, 1950), pp. 145–56. More generally, B. E. Perry, *The Ancient Romances* (Berkeley and Los Angeles, 1967), pp. 167–70, points out that in the *Suda*, the authors of romances are described as *historikoi* and that titles such as *Ephesiaca* or *Babylonica* reveal nothing about the contents of the books: "We see that ethnographical titles were conventional in the titling of Greek romances, that the authors professed to be writing history (of a kind), and were classified as historians by ancient scholars who had no more exact term for romance as a literary form."

24. Cited by H.-I. Marrou, *De la connaissance historique* (Paris, 1975), p. 77, who adopts it from Febvre, who emphasizes its restrictive character. For Marrou, "if history is not produced solely from texts, it is produced mainly from texts, for there can be no substitute for their accuracy."

But, in a wider sense, such a reading forces one to ponder the nature of a document:[25] what is a *document*, when it has been used over and over again in the course of twenty-five centuries of historiography? What, indeed, is a historical text? How is it to be recognized? What (particular) effect does it produce?

25. See J. Le Goff and P. Toubert, "Une Histoire totale du moyen âge est-elle possible?" *Actes du 100e Congrès National des Sociétés Savantes* (Paris, 1977), pp. 38–40. In the *Dictionnaire de la nouvelle histoire* (Paris, 1978), p. 238, Le Goff reckons that one task that has yet to be tackled is to elaborate a new concept of a document.

Index

Compositor: Harrington-Young Typography
Text: 11/13 Caledonia
Display: Caledonia
Printer: Braun-Brumfield
Binder: Braun-Brumfield

DATE DUE